Lecture Notes in Computer Science　13821

Services Science

Subline of Lectures Notes in Computer Science

More information about this series at https://link.springer.com/bookseries/558

Javier Troya · Raffaela Mirandola ·
Elena Navarro · Andrea Delgado ·
Sergio Segura · Guadalupe Ortiz ·
Cesare Pautasso · Christian Zirpins ·
Pablo Fernández · Antonio Ruiz-Cortés
Editors

Service-Oriented Computing – ICSOC 2022 Workshops

ASOCA, AI-PA, FMCIoT, WESOACS 2022
Sevilla, Spain, November 29 – December 2, 2022
Proceedings

 Springer

Editors
Javier Troya (iD)
University of Malaga
Málaga, Spain

Raffaela Mirandola (iD)
Politecnico di Milano
Milano, Italy

Elena Navarro (iD)
University of Castilla-La Mancha
Albacete, Spain

Andrea Delgado (iD)
University of the Republic
Montevideo, Uruguay

Sergio Segura (iD)
University of Seville
Sevilla, Spain

Guadalupe Ortiz (iD)
University of Cádiz
Cádiz, Spain

Cesare Pautasso (iD)
Faculty of Informatics
Universita della Svizzera Italiana
Lugano, Switzerland

Christian Zirpins (iD)
Karlsuhe Institute of Technology
Karlsruhe, Germany

Antonio Ruiz-Cortés (iD)
ISA
Universidad de Sevilla
Sevilla, Spain

Pablo Fernández (iD)
University of Seville
Seville, Spain

ISSN 0302-9743   ISSN 1611-3349   (electronic)
Lecture Notes in Computer Science
ISBN 978-3-031-26506-8   ISBN 978-3-031-26507-5   (eBook)
https://doi.org/10.1007/978-3-031-26507-5

This Springer imprint is published by the registered company Springer Nature Switzerland AG
The registered company address is: Gewerbestrasse 11, 6330 Cham, Switzerland

Preface

This volume presents the proceedings of the scientific satellite events that were held in conjunction with the 20th International Conference on Service-Oriented Computing (ICSOC 2022), held during November 29th – December 2nd, 2022 in Sevilla, Spain. The satellite events provide an engaging space for specialist groups to meet, generating focused discussions on specific sub-areas within service-oriented computing, which contributes to ICSOC community building. These events significantly enrich the main conference by both expanding the scope of research topics and attracting participants from a wider community.

As is customary at ICSOC, this year these satellite events were organized around two main tracks, a workshop track and a demonstration track, along with a Ph.D. symposium.

The ICSOC 2022 workshop track consisted of the following four workshops covering a wide range of topics that fall into the general area of service computing:

- 6th Workshop on Adaptive Service-Oriented and Cloud Applications (ASOCA 2022)
- 3rd International Workshop on AI-enabled Process Automation (AI-PA 2022)
- 3rd International Workshop on Architectures for Future Mobile Computing and Internet of Things (FMCIoT 2022)
- 18th International Workshop on Engineering Service-Oriented Applications and Cloud Services (WESOACS 2022)

This year in the workshop track, the themes of Internet of Things and artificial intelligence along with its applications in service computing were particularly noticeable. Workshops were selected based on the submission of a detailed description to the Conference Workshops Co-chairs. After a review of all the submissions, four workshops were selected by the Workshops Co-chairs, in consultation with the General Co-chairs. All submitted papers to the workshops went through a heavy review process where each paper was reviewed by at least three members of the Program Committee of the workshop to which it was submitted. The Conference Workshops Co-chairs checked the assignments and the reviews before the final decisions were made. A total of 36 papers were submitted to the workshops and 23 were accepted, giving an acceptance rate of around 60%. The workshops were held on November 29th, 2022, and included keynote talks from prominent speakers from industry and academia.

The Ph.D. Symposium received 9 valid submissions. Each submission was reviewed by three members of the Program Committee and after a thorough review process 6 submissions were accepted to constitute the program of the Ph.D. symposium. Authors of accepted papers were invited to present their work in front of a panel of experts, giving Ph.D. students an opportunity to showcase their research and providing them with feedback from both senior researchers and fellow Ph.D. students. In addition to the presentations of participants, the students as well as the general ICSOC audience had the opportunity to attend two well-attended coaching sessions on Ph.D. Journey mastery and Academic Career mastery by Prof. Schahram Dustdar (TU Wien, Austria) and Prof. Martin Gaedke (Chemnitz University of Technology, Germany).

The demonstration track offers a highly interactive way to share practical research work in service-oriented computing and related areas. ICSOC 2022 Demo track received 19 submissions, of which 11 were accepted for publication and presentation. Demo authors had the chance to engage the audience's interest in Demo Minute Madness, a single-slide, one-minute presentation per demo. Afterwards, during an hour-long coffee break, all demos were successfully run in parallel and fruitful discussions between the authors and the other conference participants took place.

Finally, this volume also contains the summary of three tutorials that were given during the conference.

November 2022

Raffaela Mirandola
Elena Navarro
Andrea Delgado
Sergio Segura
Guadalupe Ortiz
Cesare Pautasso
Christian Zirpins
Pablo Fernández
Antonio Ruiz Cortés

Contents

Ph.D. Symposium

Demonstrations Track

Tutorials

AI-PA: AI-enabled Process Automation

Introduction to the 3rd International Workshop on AI-enabled Process Automation (AI-PA 2022)

The 3rd International Workshop on AI-enabled Process Automation (AI-PA) was held as one of the workshops of the 20th International Conference on Service-Oriented Computing (ICSOC 2022). The AI-PA workshop aims at providing a forum for researchers and professionals interested in Artificial Intelligence (AI)-enabled Business Processes and Services; and in understanding, envisioning and discussing the opportunities and challenges of intelligent Process Automation, Process Data Analytics and providing Cognitive Assistants for knowledge workers. Recognizing the broad scope of the potential areas of interest, the workshop is organized into FOUR themes, as follows:

– Theme 1: Artificial Intelligence (AI), Services and Processes.
– Theme 2: BigData, Services and Processes.
– Theme 3: Smart Entities, Services and Processes.
– Theme 4: AI in Industry.

   The papers selected for presentation and publication in this volume showcase fresh ideas from exciting and emerging topics in service-oriented computing and case studies in Artificial Intelligence (AI)-enabled Business Processes and Services.

   We have selected 7 high-quality papers from AI-PA 2022 submissions keeping the acceptance rate at around 43%. Each paper was reviewed by a team comprising a senior Program Committee member and at least two regular Program Committee members who engaged in a discussion phase after the initial reviews were prepared. The AI-PA 2022 workshop paid the Workshop Registration Fees for all accepted papers, and offered $500.00 for the best paper award, thanks to the AI-PA Workshop Sponsors:

– SystemEthix (https://www.systemethix.com.au/)
– IBM Australia (https://www.ibm.com/au-en)
– Centre for Applied Artificial Intelligence at Macquarie University (https://www.mq. edu.au/research/research-centres-groups-and-facilities/centres/centre-for-applied-art ificial-intelligence)

   We are grateful for the support of our authors, sponsors, program committees, and the ICSOC Organizing Committee. We very much hope you enjoy reading the papers in this volume.   AI-PA 2022 Workshop Organizers

November 2022

BEDSpell: Spelling Error Correction Using BERT-Based Masked Language Model and Edit Distance

Fatemeh Tohidian[1]($\boxtimes$), Amin Kashiri[1], and Fariba Lotfi[1,2]

[1] Sharif University of Technology, Tehran, Iran
{fatemeh.tohidian,amin.kashiri,f.lotfi}@sharif.edu
[2] Macquarie University, Sydney, Australia

Abstract. The spelling correction problem, the task of automatically correcting misspellings in a text, is critical in natural language processing (NLP). Although it can be considered a standalone task, in most cases, it is an integral component of various NLP tasks as a preprocessing step since a dataset with typos can lead to erroneous results. Many previous automatic spelling correctors use a dictionary, independently search the word in a predefined list of words, and recommend the most similar one without considering the context. Even though these models' output may be a correctly spelled word, it could be semantically incorrect. Therefore, some correctors consider the context when correcting typos based on language models. However, only employing the language model is insufficient, and the corrected word should be similar to the misspelled word. In our approach, we select a candidate for the typo based on masked language model output, character-level similarities, and edit distance. Exploiting the combination of the masked language model, character-level similarities, and edit distance assists us in recommending similar context-related candidates. We have used recall (correction rate) as our evaluation metric, and the results demonstrate a considerable improvement compared with previous studies.

Keywords: Spelling correction · Natural language processing · Preprocessing · Dictionary · Masked language model · Edit distance

1 Introduction

A vast amount of textual data is generated each second, which is noisy and contains different spelling errors. Spelling error correction is an essential and challenging task, requiring a deep knowledge of human language to attain acceptable results. For many reasons, spelling error correction is vital in natural language processing (NLP). First, it is used directly in different software to help people write better articles, books, and comments. Second, since the majority of NLP

F. Tohidian and A. Kashiri—These authors contributed equally to this work.

J. Troya et al. (Eds.): ICSOC 2022 Workshops, LNCS 13821, pp. 3–14, 2023.
https://doi.org/10.1007/978-3-031-26507-5_1

tasks depend on the correct spelling of the input words, error correction enhances their performance by correcting the misspelled words. Accordingly, we can enjoy a higher performance on tasks such as Named Entity Recognition (NER), Part-of-speech (POS) Tagging, and Dependency Parsing. It stands at the core of this domain and is used significantly in pre-processing steps of most NLP pipelines. Spell correction is an important section of web search engines and chatbots. Spell correction can come in handy not only as a preprocessing step but also as a post-process step in tasks like Optical character recognition (OCR).

There are various spelling errors, such as non-words errors and real-word errors. *Non-word errors* are errors that are not actual English words. For instance, in "They talked simultaneously", "simultaneously" is a non-word error because it is not in English words. On the other hand, in "He is a god boy.", "god" is the misspelled form of the word "good", which is an actual word in English. So "god" is considered a *real-word error*. Our work is capable of correcting non-word errors; however, it is not limited to these errors and can also correct real-word errors.

Many methods have been proposed to tackle the problem of spelling error correction. We elaborate on these methods in Sect. 2. Bidirectional Encoder Representations from Transformers (BERT) [9] is a transformer-based architecture that was originally trained on masked language modeling (MLM) and next-sentence prediction. Hu et al. [8] leveraged BERT to correct spelling errors, but they did not effectively combine the word's character-level information with BERT's contextual-level information. They employed BERT for MLM to find candidates for the misspelled word and then selected the best candidate based on edit distance. We investigate these methods in more detail in Sect. 3. As the state-of-the-art approach, this naive method using BERT achieved good results; However, to address the mentioned issue and further boost the model's performance, we propose BEDSpell, a spelling corrector that combines contextual and character-level information, which yields more satisfactory results. The contributions of our work include the following items:

- We introduce α-sorting to combine BERT's contextual information with edit-distance information effectively.
- We added a pure character-level classifier to the original classifier of BERT for MLM to tune classification performance for spell correction.
- Ultimately, the results of our proposed method indicate more than 5% improvement compared with previous approaches.

It is worth mentioning that we achieved this performance only by tuning two hyperparameters, and no further training is required.

This paper is structured as follows. First, in Sect. 2, the related work on spelling error correction has been studied. Then, we discuss our proposed methodology in Sect. 3. Next, we have demonstrated our experiments, including the dataset, the evaluation measures, the results, and our analysis of the results in Sect. 4. Finally, we conclude this research in Sect. 5.

2 Related Work

We can divide spell correctors into three categories based on Hlccccdek et al. [2] classification for spelling correction methods. In the first category, a typo can be corrected with the help of a set of expert rules. The second category of correctors gets help from a language model to select a suitable candidate related to the context. Finally, the third category employs data to learn error patterns. Our proposed approach fits in the second category due to utilizing the BERT [8] as our backbone model.

2.1 Rule Based Methodes

Fahda et al. [3] presents a spelling and grammar checker in Indonesian. The method consists of two main modules: the rule matcher and the spelling checker. The first module uses 38 rules to detect, correct, and explain various writing errors. The second module checks every word using a pre-defined dictionary and edit distance measure to recommend suitable candidates. However, they used language models such as Hidden Markov Model and the trigram language model.

2.2 Language Model Based Methods

The earliest works in the second group use simpler language models. Carlson & Fette [6] used Google Web 1T 5-gram dataset[1]. The data collection gives the number of occurrences of a continuous sequence of tokens in a collection of web pages. Besides this rich n-gram language model, they use memory-based learning techniques. Bassil & Alwani [7] used data statistics from the mentioned Google n-gram dataset. Their method also includes an error detector that detects misspellings. After detecting typos, a candidate spelling generator uses a character 2-gram model to generate correction suggestions.

In a similar method to ours, Hu et al. [8] used a pre-trained BERT [9] model for language modeling to correct spelling errors. In one experiment, they filtered top-N detections, sorted them based on simple edit distance with the misspelled word, and picked the first candidate as the corrected word. In another experiment, they generated all the words with K edit distance and chose the one with the highest score. They concluded that BERT is capable of misspelling correction. We will explore more technical details in the Methodology section.

2.3 Machine Learning Methods

In another work, Zhang et al. [10] proposed a neural architecture for error detection and correction. Their architecture consists of a detection and correction network connected with the soft-masking technique. The detection network initially creates an embedding for each character in the input sentence. Next, it takes the

---

[1] https://catalog.ldc.upenn.edu/LDC2006T13.

sequence of embeddings as input and outputs the probabilities of errors for the sequence of characters. For the correction part, a BERT model takes the sequence of soft-masked embeddings as input and outputs the probabilities of error corrections.

On the other hand, Yunus et al. [4] introduced a spell correction method using supervised machine learning algorithms, which is not context-sensitive and fits in the third group. The main point of this method is the structure of input data, not the algorithm. They generated wrong words with the help of swapping or adding letters and keyboard character mapping. Then, they introduced three types of wrong words against a correct word to be fed into algorithms. First, in the Word Based Tokenization method, the whole incorrect word is identified as the wrong word. Second, in Character Based Tokenization method, the complete word is divided into characters, and all these characters are fed as a wrong word against a correct word. Finally, the Advance Character Based Tokenization method adds character positions to make this more unique among the wrong words of a correct word.

In a general end-to-end approach to sequence learning, Sutskever et al. [10] use a multi-layered Long Short-Term Memory (LSTM) [11] and a deep LSTM. They used the first one to map the input sequence to a vector with a fixed dimension and the second to decode the target sequence from the vector.

3   Methodology

In this section, we briefly describe how BERT was originally used for spelling correction as in [8]. Then, we explain the shortcomings of this method. Finally, we present our novel ideas of how to improve this model.

3.1   BERT for Masked Language Modeling

BERT can be used for Masked language modeling (MLM) with the following structure: A BERT for MLM takes sentences with a "[MASK]" token and returns probability scores for possible words that the masked word can be. These scores are based on the context of the sentence. A higher score suggests that that word is more contextually suitable for the sentence. For instance, the model takes the sentence "Whoever is happy will make others [MASK] too" as its input and returns a list like $[(happy, 0.81), (happier, 0.04), (smile, 0.01), (laugh, 0.003), \cdots]$.

We can efficiently use BERT for MLM in spelling correction. We first mask the misspelled word. In previous methods using the BERT architecture, the predictions (logits) for this masked token, which is the misspelled word, were sorted, and then the top-K predictions were returned. They sorted the returned predictions list by edit distance with the actual misspelled word to integrate character information. [8], proposed to select the first element in the sorted list as the corrected word. We used $K = 500$ in our work.

Table 1 illustrates a correction using this method. The input sentence is "He is a god boy", and "god" is our misspelled word. The input to the BERT for MLM is "He is a [MASK] boy". Initial top-K predictions are shown in the first column of Table 1 with their edit distances. The second pair of columns are created by sorting the first pair by edit distance with the incorrect word. The final candidate for the correct form of the word "god" is "good", as it is illustrated in Table 1.

Table 1. Using BERT for MLM for spell correction

Initial top-K predictions		Sorted top-K predictions	
Prediction	Edit distance	Prediction	Edit distance
Little	6	Good	1
Bad	2	Bad	2
Good	1	Kind	3
Tall	4	Tall	4
Lovely	5	Lovely	5
Kind	3	Little	6

3.2   BEDSpell Classifier

Using BERT for the MLM ignores the misspelled word until the top-K predictions are sorted with edit distance. Two possible scenarios exist when a traditional BERT-based model fails to find the correct form of the misspelled word. In the first scenario, the score of the correct word is not high enough to be in the top-K list of BERT recommendations. Unfortunately, using edit distance after selecting top-K candidates does not assist in correcting these errors. Second, the correct word might exist in the BERT output list; However, there might be another word with a lower edit distance. In this case, the high BERT score will not help the word to climb up the final list.

To solve these issues, we provide character-level information to the classifier in addition to the BERT embedding, using BEDSpell Classifier. Second, we attempt to improve our proposed model by addressing the words with higher scores and lower edit distances. We use a formula described in Subsect. 3.3 to sort the model predictions instead of sorting by edit distance.

Character-Level Classifier. As mentioned in the previous paragraphs, earlier methods did not use misspelled words to improve BERT predictions. In many cases, the correct word is not in the top-K candidates. If this happens, using edit distance at the second stage is ineffective. Since the BERT model for MLM returns the most related candidates only based on their contextual information, we need to increase the scores of words with a low edit distance.

We used chars2vec[2], an open-source word embedding extractor, to extract the embeddings of all words in the BERT's vocabulary. For each misspelled word, we can calculate the distance between its embedding and all other words in the

---

[2] https://github.com/IntuitionEngineeringTeam/chars2vec.

vocabulary. The negative of the distance vector acts as logits for classification. If we apply softmax to this vector, we get probabilities for each word in the vocabulary. Character-Level Classifier (CLC) handles this process. Note that these probabilities are based only on character-level information and have no contextual meaning.

Integration with BERT for MLM Classifier. To integrate CLC with the previous BERT for MLM Classifier, we used the simple strategy of weighted summation of logits. First, the output of the BERT backbone is passed to the BERT Classifier. Next, the misspelled word embedding is passed to CLC. Outputs of these two classifiers are then added together to produce the final logits. We use a hyperparameter named β to control the effect of each classifier. We multiply CLC's logits by β before adding to BERT for MLM's logits. Finally, applying softmax to this layer provides final probabilities. This final classifier is named BEDSpell Classifier and is proposed and used in lieu of the simple network used by previous BERT networks (Fig. 1).

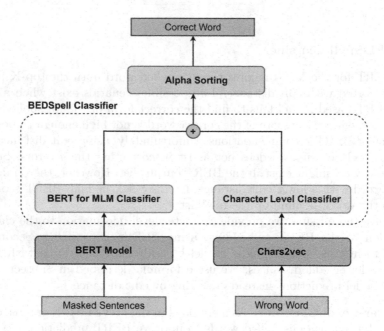

Fig. 1. The architecture of BEDSpell. The input sentence is passed to the BERT model to extract the masked token's embeddings. Misspelled token's embedding is extracted by the Char2vec model. Using these embeddings, BEDSpell Classifier computes final probabilities for the correct word. Finally, the correct word is returned using α-sorting.

3.3 α-Sorting

After getting the candidate list (using BEDSpell Classifier), it is time to select the best candidate. We propose that simply sorting by edit distance, as in earlier methods, is not the best possible approach to follow. A better replacement would be a better measurement that combines contextual score (using the BEDSpell Classifier output) with character-level similarity to the misspelled word (Using edit distance). The new measure should have a direct relation with the BERT score and an inverse relation with edit distance. After examining a lot of different formulas, we decided to use the following simple one:

$$f(s, e) = (\frac{1}{e+1})^\alpha s \qquad (1)$$

where s is the BERT for MLM Classifier score, and e is the Levenshtein edit distance [12] between the wrong word and the candidate. α is a hyperparameter of the model, which We will discuss more in the evaluation section.

The intuition behind this formula is that we should increase the final score if it has a high BERT score and decreases it if the edit distance is high. The previous method of sorting only by edit distance is the limitation of this formula when $\alpha \rightarrow \infty$. We posit that this approach is unnecessarily strict, and our formula can increase the model's recall by a simple hyperparameter.

4 Experiments

In this section, we discuss our experiments and results. We introduce the dataset on which we evaluated our model in Sect. 4.1. Then, we discuss the evaluation measures used for the spelling correction task in detail in Sect. 4.2. Next, in Sect. 4.3, the results of our proposed model have been demonstrated. Finally, in Sect. 4.4, our analysis of the achieved results is further argued.

4.1 Dataset

We have used the Neuspell dataset [1]. In the Neuspell project, they used a generated dataset for the training section, but they used a combined dataset for evaluation. We used the non-generated combined dataset. The datasets for the task of Grammatical Error Correction (GEC) in the BEA-2019 shared task1, the Write & Improve (W&I) dataset and the LOCNESS dataset are a collection of texts in English (mainly essays) written by language learners. The First Certificate in English (FCE) dataset consists of essays in English. These essays came from a language assessment exam for non-native learners. Finally, the Lang-8 dataset consists of English texts from the Lang-8 online language learning website. They combine data from these four sources. We divide the combined dataset test split (We do not need any training data) into two parts: validation and test. We used the validation dataset to tune our hyperparameter (α and β). We reported the final results on the test dataset.

We limited every sentence to only one misspelled word. We converted sentences with more than one misspelled word to multiple sentences with only one incorrect word. BEDSpell can handle sentences with more than one incorrect word, but we have limited this scenario to compare our results with previous works (Table 2).

Table 2. Dataset statistics.

Dataset	Total sentences	Total tokens	Misspelled tokens	Error rate
Validation	10,000	211,890	10,000	4.72%
Test	10,000	201,392	10,000	4.97%

4.2   Evaluation Measure

Hládek et al. [2] stated that there are various evaluation approaches for the spelling correction task. Since our purpose is to introduce a model for automatic correction and not a model to recommend a list of suitable candidates for a misspelled word, we consider the problem a classification task. The following table contains the definitions of confusion matrix elements (Table 3).

Table 3. Classification terms in spell correction methodology.

Outcome	Description
True Positive	Misspelled words corrected by the model
True Negative	Correct words left unchanged by the model
False Positive	Correct words incorrectly changed by the model
False Negative	Misspelled words left unchanged by the model

Rather than tackling the task of "detecting" spelling errors, we focus on spelling "correction" in this paper. In this case, we assume the misspelled words are already known, and the objective is to correct them. We use recall as a metric for evaluating our model's performance. In the literature, correction rate and recall are used interchangeably for the same concept. Note that without addressing detection, using metrics like precision and f1 is meaningless. In our future works, we plan to add a detection system to the correction module and use these evaluation metrics. However, a detection system can be completely independent of the correction model and is out of the scope of this article.

$$\text{recall} = \frac{\text{true positive}}{\text{true positive} + \text{false negative}} \qquad (2)$$

Equivalently, recall demonstrates what fraction of misspelled words are corrected by the model (correction rate).

$$\text{recall} = \frac{\text{count of misspelled words corrected by the model}}{\text{count of misspelled words}} \qquad (3)$$

4.3   Results

We evaluate our model on the test dataset with different α and β. Using $\beta = 0$ is equal to not using CLC (recall that β is the weight of CLC logits). However, using $\alpha = 0$ is different from not using α-sorting. The results are in Table 4. Tuning these two hyperparameters are not independent, as it is shown in the table.

Table 4. Final results.

Model	α	β	Recall
Simple BERT [8]	–	0	0.7579
BERT + α-sorting	14	0	0.7732
BERT + CLC	–	0.7	0.7797
BEDSpell (Ours)	9	1.45	0.8124

Hyper-parameter Tuning. In Fig. 2 and Fig. 3, you can see the effect of our two hyperparameters. When $\beta = 0$, we can see the effect of α-sorting by using different α in Fig. 2. In this scenario, recall is maximized with $\alpha = 14$. However, the best α changes when using CLC in addition to α-sorting ($\alpha = 9$). Similarly, Fig. 3 depicts model performance when using different βs and a fixed α. Again using different α changes the best β. It is noticeable that these two hyperparameters are not independent, and tuning them together yields different results than tuning them separately. For instance, when using CLC, results are maximized using $\beta = .7$, but when we add α-sorting, it is maximized with $\beta = 1.45$.

Improvement. Using only α-sorting, we improved the model's performance by 1.5%. Improvement by using CLC without α-sorting was more than 2.1%. Finally, using two approaches together, we were able to reach 81.24% recall, which is a 5.45% improvement compared with previous methods using BERT.

4.4   Discussion

As our results demonstrate, using the alpha parameter boosts the effect of the BERT score. A lower alpha will make the model select words with higher edit distance and higher relevancy to the context. On the contrary, adding scores of the CLC increases the effect of character-level similarity. It will increase the

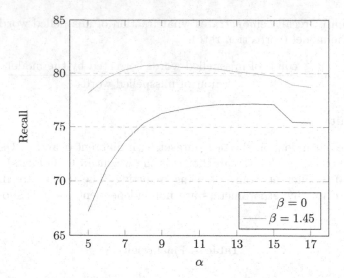

Fig. 2. α-sorting performance for different α values with/without CNC.

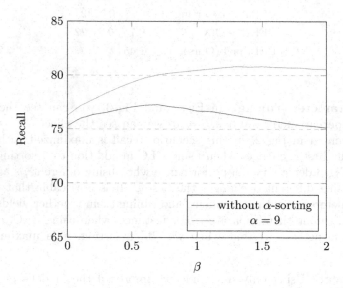

Fig. 3. CNC performance for different β values with/without α-sorting.

probability of selecting a word with a lower edit distance. Therefore, using the output of the CLC, our model will have a top-K candidate list of words closer to the spelling of the target word. On the other hand, using the α-sorting method to choose the best candidate helps us select the more relevant words to the context.

A higher β reduces the need for a higher α. This effect can be inferred from Fig. 3. Increasing β integrates some character-level information, and words with lower edit distances get a higher score. Consequently, we can decrease α in the next step to decrease the effect of edit distance because some character-level information was already included.

In Table 5, we demonstrate the differences between our proposed method and the simple BERT when evaluated on test data. Simple BERT corrects 176 misspelled words that BEDSpell is unable to fix them. All of these 176 words exist in the top-K predictions of BEDSpell. Hence, using CLC does not cause these mistakes. On the other hand, there are 733 misspelled words corrected by BEDSpell that simple BERT cannot fix. From these words, 291 words were in top-K predictions of simple BERT. BEDSpell corrects these words with the help of α-sorting and CLC. The other 442 corrections are not in the top-K predictions of simple BERT. They have reached the top-K predictions of BEDSpell with the additional help of CNC. Therefore, at least 4% of the words that are not in the top-K predictions of simple BERT were able to reach the top-K predictions of BEDSpell, without any correct word leaving the top-K predictions.

Table 5. Models comparison.

Model	BERT	BEDSpell
Total corrections	7,579	8,136
Corrected only by this model	176	733
Model mistakes corrected by the other model while the correct words appear in the top-K predictions list	291	176

5   Conclusion

Spelling error correction is fundamental as a standalone task and pre-processing step in natural language processing. In addition to its challenges, real-word spelling errors further complicate the spelling correction task. In this work, We attempt to use character-level information in two stages, contrasting with the previous methods. First, we improve BERT's initial predictions by integrating a pure character-level classifier (CLC). Moreover, we sort the predictions by combining character-level criteria (edit distance) with BERT's prediction scores. This change increased our performance dramatically compared with the previous studies, as mentioned in Sect. 4.3. Our method needs no training to enjoy its improvement, and the results demonstrate that using more sophisticated methods to integrate character-level and contextual information can lead to significantly higher performance. This improvement is due to the different nature of ordinary MLM, which does not consider the input characters of the masked word. We can enhance MLM predictions by targeting spelling correction rather than simple language modeling. Our proposed architecture and sorting formula are two examples used to demonstrate the potential of using and improving BERT-based spelling correctors. In future work, we intend to improve our spelling error correction model and propose deeper contextual and character-level information integration.

References

1. Jayanthi, S.M., Pruthi, D., Neubig, G.: NeuSpell: a neural spelling correction toolkit. arXiv preprint arXiv:2010.11085 (2020)
2. Hládek, D., Staš, J., Pleva, M.: Survey of automatic spelling correction. Electronics **9**(10), 1670 (2020)
3. Fahda, A., Purwarianti, A.: A statistical and rule-based spelling and grammar checker for Indonesian text. In: 2017 International Conference on Data and Software Engineering (ICoDSE), pp. 1–6. IEEE (2017)
4. Yunus, A., Masum, M.: A context free spell correction method using supervised machine learning algorithms. Int. J. Comput. Appl. **975**, 8887 (2020)
5. Huang, G., Chen, J., Sun, Z.: A correction method of word spelling mistake for English text. In: Journal of Physics: Conference Series, vol. 1693, no. 1, p. 012118. IOP Publishing (2020)
6. Carlson, A., Fette, I.: Memory-based context-sensitive spelling correction at web scale. In: Sixth International Conference on Machine Learning and Applications (ICMLA 2007), pp. 166–171. IEEE (2007)
7. Bassil, Y., Alwani, M.: Context-sensitive spelling correction using google web 1t 5-gram information. arXiv preprint arXiv:1204.5852 (2012)
8. Hu, Y., Jing, X., Ko, Y., Rayz, J.T.: Misspelling correction with pre-trained contextual language model. In: 2020 IEEE 19th International Conference on Cognitive Informatics & Cognitive Computing (ICCI* CC), pp. 144–149. IEEE (2020)
9. Devlin, J., Chang, M.W., Lee, K., Toutanova, K.: BERT: pre-training of deep bidirectional transformers for language understanding. arXiv preprint arXiv:1810.04805 (2018)
10. Zhang, S., Huang, H., Liu, J., Li, H.: Spelling error correction with soft-masked BERT. In: ACL (2020)
11. Hochreiter, S., Schmidhuber, J.: Long short-term memory. Neural Comput. **9**(8), 1735–1780 (1997)
12. Levenshtein, V.I.: Binary codes capable of correcting deletions, insertions, and reversals. In: Soviet Physics Doklady, vol. 10, no. 8, pp. 707–710 (1966)

Image Data Augmentation and Convolutional Feature Map Visualizations in Computer Vision Applications

Fariba Lotfi[1,2]([✉]), Fatemeh Tohidian[1], Mansour Jamzad[1], and Hamid Beigy[1]

[1] Sharif University of Technology, Tehran, Iran
{f.lotfi,fatemeh.tohidian,jamzad,beigy}@sharif.edu
[2] Macquarie University, Sydney, Australia

Abstract. Deep neural networks (DNNs) perform exceptionally well in many vision tasks, including image classification, annotation, and object recognition. However, these networks are like a black box, and high-quality training datasets are required for deep learning models to achieve high performance. Due to the high cost of collecting a vast number of data samples, data augmentation techniques have been employed in many vision applications. Data augmentation aims to increase the dataset size without collecting new data while introducing variability. One of the means of augmenting the image data is by employing image transformations such as flipping, clipping, or rotation. Activation maps, also known as feature maps, illustrate how the filters are applied to the input image. The objective of visualizing a feature map for an input image is to comprehend what input features are captured in the feature maps. In this paper, we apply various transformations on images and investigate their effect on the multiple convolutional layers (at low, middle, and high levels) by employing intermediate feature map visualizations. We use the famous deep learning-based pre-trained network, VGG-16. Finally, we compare the visualization results of the image transformations at multiple levels and analyze their differences to evaluate the validity of these networks.

Keywords: Deep neural networks · Data augmentation · Image transformations · Activation maps · Feature maps · Convolutional layers · Visualizations

1 Introduction

There has been tremendous advancement in deep learning models, and many factors have contributed to this advancement, such as deep network architectures, powerful computational capabilities, and access to big data. With the success of convolutional neural networks (CNNs), deep neural networks have gained a lot of interest and optimism. They have successfully been applied to

J. Troya et al. (Eds.): ICSOC 2022 Workshops, LNCS 13821, pp. 15–26, 2023.
https://doi.org/10.1007/978-3-031-26507-5_2

myriad computer vision tasks such as image annotation [3, 4], object detection [6], and multi-label image classification [5]. These networks have parameterized and sparsely connected kernels that preserve the spatial properties of images. By convolutionally transforming images, much lower-dimensional and more valuable representations are created than traditional hand-crafted features. However, a vast number of samples is necessary to obtain satisfactory robustness and generalization for CNNs, and a limited number of samples may lead to an overfitted model. Consequently, the easiest solution to expand the dataset size is to collect more samples to train the model, which is expensive and time-consuming. On the other hand, data augmentation is used when additional samples cannot be easily collected or generated from the existing samples.

Deep learning can benefit from image augmentation, a powerful technique for working with image data. By modifying the current image data, these techniques produce more samples for the training process, boost the performance of the neural networks, and make them more robust to changes. In addition, image augmentation strategies can produce variations of images that will enhance their generalization capabilities to new unseen images. These augmentation techniques are used in feature engineering for image samples. In image classification, there have been many approaches for image augmentation, such as flipping, noise injection, and applying kernel filters.

On the other hand, the general perception of neural networks is that they are opaque or like a "Black Box". Consequently, they rarely have a concrete sense of how specific decisions or predictions were made. To this end, we can visualize the optimized weights coming into the hidden layer nodes. In this way, we can see the way a neural network breaks down the task and makes a decision about the image samples. Therefore, visualizing the intermediate feature representations across different convolutional layers in various blocks enables us to understand the classification process and these opaque networks. These methods are not restricted to image data and can be applied to videos as well. As an example, there are some cool Nvidia videos showing real-time convolutional neuron activations on autonomous cars[1].

Our work is meant to augment the data by applying several image transformations to the original samples in the dataset and storing them as new samples. The intermediate feature maps are visualized and stored for further analysis. In this paper, we investigate the effects of basic image augmentations on CNN feature map visualizations and examine the effectiveness of various augmentation approaches in image classification tasks. We found that in some transformations, although a bit of the information is lost, it may not affect the decision process of the deep neural network. Some other variations applied to the image can be observed in the feature maps of the convolutional layers, making the network more robust to variations. Moreover, we realized that some color spaces, such as RGB, have more information than others based on the visualized convolutional layers. Therefore, it is necessary to discover the best color space for the intended dataset. Finally, transformations such as sharpening make the details of the objects more visible. In summary, our paper makes the following contributions:

---

[1] http://www.youtube.com/watch?v=URmxzxYlmtg&t=16m51s.

- We randomly select some images from the corel5K [9], a famous dataset in the image annotation task. Then, we apply different image augmentation techniques and investigate the results of each image transformation based on various pre-trained models.
- We extract the low, middle, and high-level layers from some widely-used pre-trained models and visualize the output of each one of these submodels, called feature maps.
- Finally, we investigate the results of different activation map visualizations from several image transformations and some pre-trained models.

The remainder of this paper is structured as follows. First, related work is studied in Sect. 2. Then, the proposed methodology is further discussed in Sect. 3. Next, the experiments, including the dataset information, the results, and the discussion, are brought in Sect. 4. Finally, we conclude this research in Sect. 5.

2 Related Work

In this section, we first shortly mention the famous pre-trained deep neural network, VGG-16 [2], in image analysis. Then, we discuss state-of-the-art studies in the field of convolutional filter visualization.

Pre-trained Deep Neural Network (VGG-16). The VGG-16 [2] is a 16-layer convolutional neural network. From the ImageNet database[2], a pre-trained version of the network can be loaded. Images can be classified into 1000 categories using the pre-trained network. Some of these categories correspond to images of keyboards, mice, pencils, and animals.

Convolutional Layer Visualization. Yosinski et al. [1] have developed two tools to understand and interpret how neural networks work. In the first tool, convolutional networks are visualized on each layer, allowing us to build valuable intuitions about how they work. The second one enables visualizing features at each layer of a DNN by utilizing several new regularized optimization methods in image space. Zeiler and Fergus [7] investigated two issues of proposed neural networks for image classification. These issues include not being able to understand why these networks perform so well or how they could be enhanced. The authors introduce a new visualization method that provides insight into the function of intermediate feature layers and the operation of the classifier.

Yu et al. [10] analyze the internal work mechanism of CNN by visualizing the internal representations developed by the various layers. By visualizing representation spaces constructed from these layers, CNN can sort patterns gradually from low to high levels. From the visualizations of the reconstructed images, it is clear that CNN can extract discriminant information gradually. Moreover, compared to CNNs with different depths, deeper CNNs are better at extracting discriminant data, enhancing prediction accuracy.

---

[2] https://www.image-net.org/.

Mahendran and Vedaldi [12] examined some shallow and deep landmark representations in a series of complementary visualization strategies. They studied in particular three visualizations in the following:

- In "inversion", the purpose is to reconstruct an image from its representation.
- In "activation maximization", they look for patterns that maximally stimulate a representation component.
- In "caricaturization", the visual patterns a representation catches in an image are overstated.

As a regularized energy minimization framework, they ascertain the generality and efficacy of this technique. In another study, through visualizing patches in the representation spaces constituted by various layers and visualizing visual information held per layer, Yu et al. [11] aim to comprehend the internal work mechanism of CNNs. The CNNs with different depths are also compared, and the advantages of deeper architectures are discussed in their study.

3   The Proposed Methodology

Our main objective is to analyze the effects of image transformations as a data augmentation technique on deep neural networks. In Sect. 3.1, first, we study the most common image transformations in image classification-related tasks such as image annotation and object recognition. Then, we further explore these transformations and examine their impacts on intermediate layers in deep networks in Sect. 3.2. The overall block diagram of our visualization process is represented in Fig. 1.

3.1   Basic Image Transformations

Data augmentation techniques are critical when limited data samples are available for a model's training process. The items in the following are used as the basic image augmentation algorithms, which are represented in Fig. 2.

Geometric Transformations: A geometric transformation involves transforming the image by modifying its geometry without changing its actual pixels. The pixel values will remain intact regardless of how many operations are applied.

Color Space Transformations. Altering the representation of a color from one basis to another is called a color space transformation. A color space transformation commonly occurs when an image illustrated in one color space is transformed into another. Depending on the application, the objective could be a representation capable of desired image analysis.

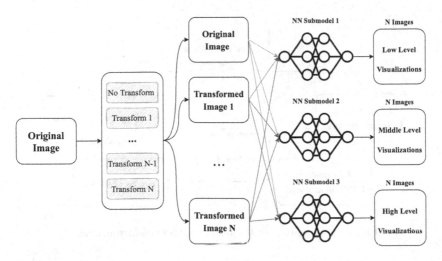

Fig. 1. The visualization process of image transformations block diagram.

Kernel Filters. Using kernel filters, either a blurrier image can be created employing a Gaussian blur filter, or a sharper image along edges can be generated with a high contrast vertical or horizontal edge filter.

Mixing Images. Among the sub-areas of data augmentation, we can mention image mixing. As a result of this transformation, specific characteristics of images are concealed. Therefore, the network will be forced to focus on the overall structure of the object in the image instead. This image-mixing approach has been shown to improve the object detectors' performance.

Random Erasing. During convolutional neural networks (CNNs) training using image data, random erasing selects an area randomly in the image and substitutes its pixels with random values.

We have used the most standard transformations in image classification-based tasks to convert the original image and produce more image samples. Flipping, rotation, translation, cropping, noise injection, and color space (isolating a single color channel) are geometric transformations. When referring to an image, flip transformation is a conversion that lets us reverse an image horizontally/vertically, and cropping is the reduction of undesirable external regions from an image. Moreover, rotation turns an image in a clockwise or counterclockwise direction, and in 3-D coordinate systems, RGB color space is represented by Red, Green, and Blue coordinates. Only one coordinate is preserved in this transformation. Deep neural networks can avoid overfitting by applying salt and pepper noise to the image using noise injection techniques. The translation transformation moves a shape by a specified distance in an image.

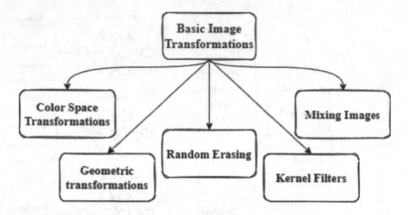

Fig. 2. A taxonomy of the basic image transformations.

We have applied 11 transformations encompassing translation, sharpening, rotation, flipping, cropping, random erasing, Gaussian blur, LAB color space (L*a*b*), Gaussian noise injection, blue channel, mixing images, and gray-scale. The outcomes of these transformations on one of the corel5K images [9] have been illustrated in Fig. 3 and Fig. 4.

3.2 Feature Map Visualizations

Convolutional neural networks process three-dimensional images and classify them according to the class, such as cat or dog. By training, we obtain trained weights, which are data patterns extracted from images. Therefore, after applying the transformations on each image, we feed them to our backbone pre-trained model, VGG-16 [2]. First, we extract three different submodels from the primary pre-trained model to have one of the low convolutional blocks as the low-level output, one of the middle convolutional blocks as the middle-level output, and one of the high convolutional blocks as the high-level output. Then, after feed-forwarding the image to each one of the submodels, we calculate the derivatives and gradients. Finally, we represent these gradients in an image and plot them, as demonstrated in Fig. 5. According to the figure, low-level features are minor details in an image, like lines or dots, that can be detected using a convolutional filter. Next, low-level features construct middle-level features, and high-level features are built on top of low and middle-level features to detect objects and more complex shapes/patterns in the image.

3.3 Implementation Details

We have used the pre-trained model, VGG-16 [2]. All our codes have been implemented in Python using Tensorflow 2 and OpenCV library. The size of the input images is $192 \times 128 \times 3$ (or $128 \times 198 \times 3$), and the size of the output images is $96 \times 96 \times 3$. We have also resized input images to $96 \times 96 \times 3$. The scale of

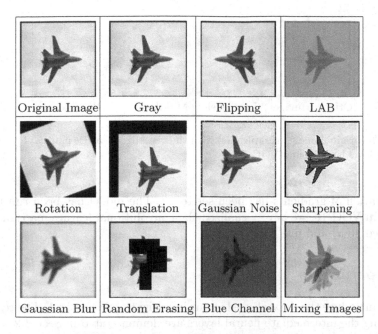

Fig. 3. The results of image transformations function on sample one from corel5k [9] employed as a data augmentation technique in our investigation.

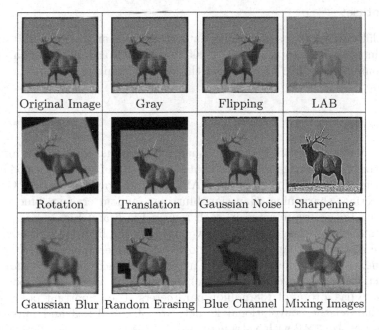

Fig. 4. The results of image transformations function on sample two from corel5k [9] employed as a data augmentation technique in our investigation.

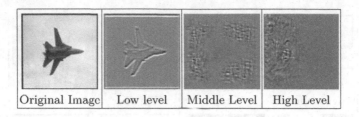

| Original Image | Low level | Middle Level | High Level |

Fig. 5. The original image (sample one) with the visualized feature maps at low, middle, and high-level layers using VGG-16 [2].

magnification of gradients has been set to 10. The model has been run for five epochs. In VGG-16, we have visualized the convolutional feature maps of blocks one, three, four, and five.

4   Experiments

We first introduce the dataset used in our investigation in Sect. 4.1. The results of visualizing the intermediate neural layers are demonstrated in Sect. 4.2. Finally, we further discuss and analyze our results in the mentioned section.

4.1   Dataset

The corel5k dataset [9] is a multi-label dataset from the image domain. It consists of 5,000 images with a total number of 260 tags in the vocabulary. For this paper, we randomly choose five images from the dataset, which are representative of the dataset.

4.2   Results

In this section, we compare the three visualization results (low, middle, and high-level) of the original image with the visualization result of all transformed images. The transformations include flipping, LAB, rotation, gray, translation, Gaussian noise injection, sharpening, Gaussian blurring, random erasing, blue channel, and mixing images represented in each row in Fig. 6 and Fig. 7. Each column represents the input images with low-level, middle, and high-level visualizations. The selected feature maps are from blocks one, three, and five in Fig. 6 and blocks one, three, and four in Fig. 7. The effects of each image transformation on the activation of convolutional neurons at the three blocks are apparent.

VGG-16 has a total of 138 million parameters. The important point to note here is that all the convolutional kernels are of size 3 × 3 and max-pooling kernels are of size 2 × 2 with a stride of two. In this paper, we use three different submodels of VGG-16; therefore, the total parameters for each submodel are less than 138 million. VGG-16 has a total of 138 million parameters. The critical point to note here is that all the convolutional kernels are of size 3 × 3 and max-pooling kernels are of size 2×2 with a stride of two. In this paper, we use three different submodels of VGG-16; therefore, the total parameters for each submodel are less than 138 million. The process of all the transformations of a sample being fed to the three submodels takes approximately 183.7 s.

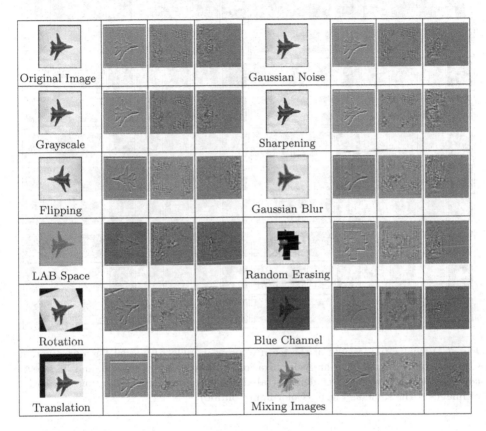

Fig. 6. Visualization results of the feature maps in VGG-16 model for sample one. For VGG-16, the feature maps of block1, block3, and block5 have been extracted. Three visualizations relevant to low, middle, and high-level convolutional layers have been demonstrated for each image transformation. (Color figure online)

4.3   Discussion

Convolutional neural networks are opaque, and visualizing intermediate feature representations across CNN layers enables us to understand how CNNs classify images. To investigate the advantages of using data augmentation techniques, in Fig. 6 and Fig. 7, it is possible to see the activation map of the neurons occurring in VGG-16. Analysis of the visualized feature maps indicates that image transformations can make neural networks more robust to different variations in images, such as translation, rotation, and so forth. Some transformations,

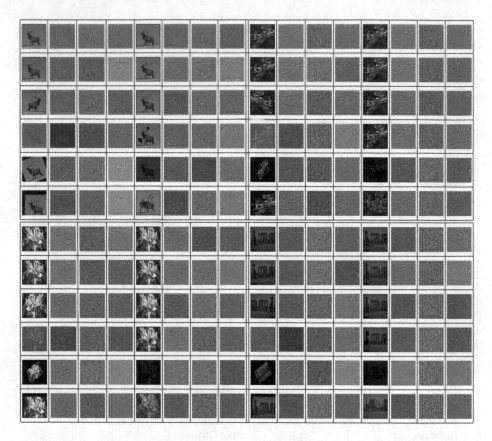

Fig. 7. Visualization results of the feature maps in VGG-16 model for four different samples from corek5k [9]. Three visualizations relevant to low, middle, and high-level convolutional layers have been demonstrated for each image transformation. The order of images is the same as Fig. 6. (Color figure online)

like sharpening, provide more details about objects of interest. It emphasizes differences in adjacent pixel values and makes the image look more vivid than its original one. Transformations, such as rotation or translation, make the network robust to variances that may occur during the test phase. By transforming an image to another color space, such as LAB, it seems that the feature maps contain a more noisy background than the feature map of the original image. Our results have tended towards RGB working better than LAB color space. In the blue channel, based on the visualized feature maps, it can be inferred that some information is lost, and this is true since we ignore two color channels. Mixing images, on the other hand, seems to have distorted the image and the intermediate feature maps are ambiguous. We believe mixing the image features after one or more convolutional layers makes more sense.

There is only one plane of information in gray-scale images instead of three planes in colored images (RGB color space). However, the gray-scale images maintain the demanded shape and texture data from the original RGB images and, thus, are adequate to handle vision tasks such as classification problems where the color does not affect the decision. Since some situations may lead to a blurry image, blurring is often employed as a pre-processing/augmentation step. These circumstances may be when a user scans a letter with a mobile app. Another scenario may be when a drone flies over an object of interest. As presented in Fig. 6, the plane details in the image are missed in the visualized feature maps. On the other hand, occlusion invariance plays an essential role in CNN generalization. Therefore, robust models should be able to determine an object's class if some image segments are not visible. However, limited variation in the training samples prevents the network from annotating occluded objects. A trained CNN performs well on images with no occlusion if all the objects are perceptible. As a result, depending on the percentage of the erased data, random erasing assists the decision process of the neural model, as it is represented in Fig. 6 and Fig. 7. More specifically, the information about the plane's tail is still preserved. However, in sample two, the background of the object is erased and does not affect the decision process. Based on the nature of the dataset samples and the target application, each of these transformations can assist in augmenting the dataset, which leads to more model robustness and high generalization capability to unseen test samples.

5   Conclusion

The advancement of deep neural networks and their demand for large image samples, as well as the existence of different object variations in computer vision tasks, have led to various data augmentation techniques. On the other hand, deep neural networks are opaque, and understanding their internal structure is tricky. A solution to this matter could be visualizing the intermediate layers given the input image. Comprehending these representations, especially convolutional layers, is becoming increasingly important. In this study, we randomly extract two images from the corel5k dataset and then apply various image transformations. The results of these transformations are fed to three deep network submodels at multiple levels to visualize their corresponding feature maps and investigated to see their impacts on the learning process. In our future work, we intend to go beyond these basic transformations and investigate more complicated ones.

References

1. Yosinski, J., Clune, J., Nguyen, A., Fuchs, T., Lipson, H.: Understanding neural networks through deep visualization. arXiv preprint arXiv:1506.06579 (2015)
2. Simonyan, K., Zisserman, A.: Very deep convolutional networks for large-scale image recognition. arXiv preprint arXiv:1409.1556 (2014)
3. Lotfi, F., Jamzad, M., Beigy, H.: Automatic image annotation using tag relations and graph convolutional networks. In: 2021 5th International Conference on Pattern Recognition and Image Analysis (IPRIA), pp. 1–6. IEEE (2021)

4. Lotfi, F., Jamzad, M., Beigy, H.: Automatic image annotation using quantization reweighting function and graph neural networks. In: Hacid, H., et al. (eds.) ICSOC 2021. LNCS, vol. 13236, pp. 46–60. Springer, Cham (2022). https://doi.org/10.1007/978-3-031-14135-5_4

5. Wang, J., Yang, Y., Mao, J., Huang, Z., Huang, C., Xu, W.: CNN-RNN: a unified framework for multi-label image classification. In: Proceedings of the IEEE Conference on Computer Vision and Pattern Recognition, pp. 2285–2294 (2016)

6. Tan, M., Pang, R., Le, Q.V.: EfficientDet: scalable and efficient object detection. In: Proceedings of the IEEE/CVF Conference on Computer Vision and Pattern Recognition, pp. 10781–10790 (2020)

7. Zeiler, M.D., Fergus, R.: Visualizing and understanding convolutional networks. In: Fleet, D., Pajdla, T., Schiele, B., Tuytelaars, T. (eds.) ECCV 2014. LNCS, vol. 8689, pp. 818–833. Springer, Cham (2014). https://doi.org/10.1007/978-3-319-10590-1_53

8. Wong, S.C., Gatt, A., Stamatescu, V., McDonnell, M.D.: Understanding data augmentation for classification: when to warp?. In: 2016 International Conference on Digital Image Computing: Techniques and Applications (DICTA), pp. 1–6. IEEE (2016)

9. Duygulu, P., Barnard, K., de Freitas, J.F.G., Forsyth, D.A.: Object recognition as machine translation: learning a lexicon for a fixed image vocabulary. In: Heyden, A., Sparr, G., Nielsen, M., Johansen, P. (eds.) ECCV 2002. LNCS, vol. 2353, pp. 97–112. Springer, Heidelberg (2002). https://doi.org/10.1007/3-540-47979-1_7

10. Yu, W., Yang, K., Bai, Y., Xiao, T., Yao, H., Rui, Y.: Visualizing and comparing AlexNet and VGG using deconvolutional layers. In: Proceedings of the 33rd International Conference on Machine Learning (2016)

11. Yu, W., Yang, K., Bai, Y., Yao, H., Rui, Y.: Visualizing and comparing convolutional neural networks. arXiv preprint arXiv:1412.6631 (2014)

12. Mahendran, A., Vedaldi, A.: Visualizing deep convolutional neural networks using natural pre-images. Int. J. Comput. Vis. **120**(3), 233–255 (2016)

Object-Centric Predictive Process Monitoring

Wissam Gherissi[(✉)] [iD], Joyce El Haddad[iD], and Daniela Grigori[iD]

Université Paris-Dauphine, Université PSL, CNRS, LAMSADE, 75016 Paris, France
{wissam.gherissi,joyce.elhaddad,daniela.grigori}@dauphine.psl.eu

Abstract. Predictive process monitoring approaches aim to make predictions about the future behavior for running instances of business processes, such as next activity or remaining time. Most of these approaches use single object type event logs as if the business process is operating in isolation. Whereas, in an organization, several instances of different processes related to a set of objects can be executed at the same time and may interact with each other. This paper investigate the use of object-centric event logs as they offer information about events and their related objects, allowing access to a global view about the running processes in an organization. We propose an object-centric predictive approach considering interactions between different object types. The proposed approach is evaluated on a publicly available object-centric log. The analysis of the results shows that using additional features (i.e., several object types' information) can generally help increase prediction performances.

Keywords: Predictive monitoring · Object-centric event log · Process mining

1 Introduction

Process Mining has seen many developments over the last years with the advances of artificial intelligence domain, especially in machine and deep learning. Researchers have adapted innovative machine learning models and architectures to apply them on the different process mining techniques like process discovery, conformance checking and process enhancement. Process mining takes as input an event log recording events related to the execution of a process. The proposed techniques until recently worked on single case identifier event logs. This type of event logs is limited to a single perspective i.e. single type of object of a process whereas real processes can have multiple perspectives and incorporate multiple objects. These event logs have limited the use of process mining to studying a precise aspect of a process rather than all interactions between objects and processes, and also posed other problems like convergence and divergence [1] due to differences between the event logs and the reality of processes. Object-centric event logs (OCEL) are rather different than classic event logs with closer representation of real processes. OCELs store information about the process on

J. Troya et al. (Eds.): ICSOC 2022 Workshops, LNCS 13821, pp. 27–39, 2023.
https://doi.org/10.1007/978-3-031-26507-5_3

multiple aspects in one event log with the use of object types. OCELs allow access to the process covering all the related instances. For example in the case of order management process, an OCEL will contain information about instances ranging from placing the order, products management until the package delivery. Recently, there have been general interest in the use of OCELs for process mining especially in process discovery using Petri nets [4] and performance analysis [9]. But, to the best of our knowledge, there is still no approach tailored for OCEL for predictive process monitoring, especially for behavior prediction. When we try to use OCEL for prediction tasks, the first problem we face is identifying the trace ID. In OCEL, an event is not associated with a single case ID, as in classical logs. While classical logs can be obtained by flattening the log, using these logs in isolation may not take into account the interaction between objects.

In this paper, we analyze the specific challenges that OCEL poses for predictive monitoring and we investigate whether taking into account the interaction between objects may improve the prediction. We propose a first approach for predictive monitoring, more precisely next activity and time prediction (next event and remaining time).

We adapt the LSTM architecture inspired from [17], that have been proven to have very good results on traditional event logs. We extend this architecture to predict instance remaining time and obtain better results than predicting activities iteratively until the end of the sequence. We evaluate our model and approach on a publicly available OCEL[1] and we made available the code on Github[2].

The remainder of the paper is as follows. Section 2 discusses related work on object-centric event logs and predictive process monitoring. Section 3 introduces the basic notions and formal definitions for event logs. Section 4 presents the proposed LSTM model and the approach from data preprocessing to prediction tasks. Section 5 presents the experimental results and Sect. 6 concludes the paper.

2   Related Work

To the best of our knowledge, there are no dedicated works that examine both predictive process monitoring and object-centric event logs. To address this gap, we discuss first some works on object-centric event logs and then some works on predictive process monitoring.

Object-Centric Process Mining. Process mining [3] is a set of techniques that can be applied on event logs such as process discovery to detect patterns and model processes. There are also techniques like conformance checking and process enhancement with the objective of improving the process performance and making sure that the process is conforming to established norms.

---

[1] http://ocel-standard.org/1.0/running-example.jsonocel.zip.
[2] https://github.com/wissam-gherissi/PPM-OC.

Recently, researchers have been studying a new format of event logs called object-centric event logs [10] as an alternative to traditional single case event logs to overcome problems like "convergence" and "divergence" mentioned in [1] and present new insights on processes.

In order to represent multiple processes in the same event log, [2] propose the idea of federated process mining utilizing event data from different sources of information in the same organization or across organizations. Other papers working on this type of event logs evolve around the technique of process discovery by discovering the process Petri net in [4] or the behavioral constraints model in [13], hence discovering the different relations between the activities and multiple object types. Furthermore, the notions of precision and fitness as metrics to evaluate process discovery have been adapted for the case of object-centric event logs in [5].

Predictive Process Monitoring. In predictive process monitoring papers, different approaches and models were applied on traditional event logs for a variety of prediction tasks. For next activity and time remaining predictions, models were proposed such as recurrent neural networks (RNNs) [11,12], convolutional neural networks (CNNs) [8,15], attention mechanisms [16] and transformers [6].

LSTMs were studied in [7,17] and [14] as a solution for sequence prediction given the long memory capacity of this architecture. Precisely in [17], the model is constructed using LSTM layers for multiple prediction tasks (next activity, next event time, suffix prediction, time remaining prediction) using one model with a single training step for different tasks rather than training multiple models divided over the tasks. We choose this architecture for its performances on classic logs. We adapt it for OCEL, by introducing changes in the data preprocessing part and to the model construction, adding a LSTM layer for the remaining time prediction task.

All of these previous works presented in this part have focused on implementing prediction models and studying patterns for traditional event logs rather than object-centric event logs.

Finally, the closest paper to our approach is working on the combination of object-centric event logs and predictive process analytics in [9]. This work, although used object-centric event logs, is focused on predictive analysis and performance indicators using gradient boosting. In this paper, we use neural networks and LSTMs for predicting process behavior, precisely next activity, next event time and remaining time using object-centric event logs.

3   Preliminaries

In this section, we introduce the basic notions for object-centric event logs and LSTMs that will be used in this paper.

3.1   Object Centric Event Logs

These notions are based on the definitions of [10].

Definition 1 *(Universes). The used universes are:* $\mathbb{U}_E$ *the universe of events,* $\mathbb{U}_{act}$ *the universe of activities,* $\mathbb{U}_{att}$ *the universe of attribute names,* $\mathbb{U}_{val}$ *the universe of attribute values,* $\mathbb{U}_{typ}$ *the universe of attribute types,* $\mathbb{U}_o$ *the universe of object identifiers,* $\mathbb{U}_{ot}$ *is the universe of object types,* $\mathbb{U}_{act}$ *the universe of activities,* $\mathbb{U}_{time}$ *the universe of timestamps.*

Definition 2 *(OCEL). An object-centric event log is defined in [10] as a tuple* $L = (E, AN, AV, AT, OT, O, \pi_{typ}, \pi_{act}, \pi_{time}, \pi_{vmap}, \pi_{omap}, \pi_{otyp}, \pi_{ovmap}, <)$ *where,*

- $E \subseteq \mathbb{U}_E$ *is the set of events.* $AN \subseteq \mathbb{U}_{att}$ *is the set of attribute names.* $AV \subseteq \mathbb{U}_{val}$ *is the set of attribute values.* $AT \subseteq \mathbb{U}_{typ}$ *is the set of attribute types.* $O \subseteq \mathbb{U}_o$ *is the set of object identifiers.* $OT \subseteq \mathbb{U}_{ot}$ *is the set of object types.*
- $\pi_{typ} : AN \cup AV \rightarrow AT$ *is the function associating each attribute name or value to the corresponding attribute type.* $\pi_{act} : E \rightarrow \mathbb{U}_{act}$ *is the function associating each event with its activity.* $\pi_{time} : E \rightarrow \mathbb{U}_{time}$ *is the function associating each event with a timestamp.*
- $\pi_{vmap} : E \rightarrow (AN \nrightarrow AV)$ *such that:*

$$\pi_{typ}(n) = \pi_{typ}(\pi_{vmap}(e)(n)) \quad \forall e \in E, \forall n \in \mathrm{dom}(\pi_{vmap}(e))$$

is the function associating an event identifier to its attribute value assignments with the condition that the attribute name and value have the same attribute type.
- $\pi_{omap} : E \rightarrow \mathcal{P}(O)$ *is the function associating an event identifier to a set of related object identifiers. In the case of additional objects identifiers used in the Definition 4, we use the notion of* π_{rmap}
- $\pi_{otyp} \in O \rightarrow OT$ *is the function assigning precisely one object type for each object identifier.*
- $\pi_{ovmap} : O \rightarrow (AN \nrightarrow AV)$ *such that*

$$\pi_{typ}(n) = \pi_{typ}(\pi_{ovmap}(o)(n)) \quad \forall o \in E, \forall n \in \mathrm{dom}(\pi_{vmap}(o))$$

is the function associating an object to its attribute value assignments. Each object is related to attributes with attribute name and value such that the name and the value must have the same attribute type.
- $<$ *is a partial order based on the timestamps of events such that*

$$e_1 < e_2 \iff \pi_{time}(e_1) < \pi_{time}(e_2)$$

An example of an OCEL is shown in Table 1 for the process of ordering products for deliver. As it can be seen, the order have many related objects such as the ordered items and the packages in which the delivery is happening.

Definition 3 *(Single object type event log). Inspired from the Object type Projection definition in [1], a single object type event log (an example is shown in Table 2) is defined as follows:*

Table 1. Example of object centric event log describing order management process

Event identifier	Activity name	Timestamp	Objects			Attributes	
			Order	Item	Package	Price	Weight
...	...	...	...	...	...	...	...
70	place order	$2019-05-22\,10:33:18$	{990018}	{880074, 880075, ...}	$\emptyset$	823.98	1.97
71	confirm order	$2019-05-22\,10:34:00$	{990008}	{880023, 880024, ...}	$\emptyset$	1428.97	3.75
...	...	...	...	...	...	...	...
14230	pick item	$2019-12-31\,17:17:59$	{991296}	{885262}	$\emptyset$	29.99	0.38
14231	item out of stock	$2019-12-31\,17:20:10$	{991291}	{885233}	$\emptyset$	79.99	0.483
...	...	...	...	...	...	...	...
17900	create package	$2020-02-24\,13:45:30$	{991572, 991393, ...}	{886439, 886438, ...}	{661050}	1424.97	2.852
17901	send package	$2019-12-31\,13:52:48$	{991583, 991604, ...}	{886559, 886479, ...}	{661048}	2749.97	3.01
...	...	...	...	...	...	...	...

$(E^{ot}, \leq^{ot})$ *is a projection of the events of an object-centric event log on a single object type, where for a specific* $ot \in \mathbb{U}_{ot}$

$$e \in E^{ot} \text{ such as } e = (ei, act, time, omap, vmap), E^{ot} = \{e \in E \mid \pi_{omap}(e)(ot) \neq \emptyset\} \text{ and}$$

$$\preceq^{ot}_E = \{(e_1, e_2) \in E^{ot} \times E^{ot} \mid e_1 \preceq_E e_2 \wedge \pi_{omap}(e_1)(ot) \cap \pi_{omap}(e_2)(ot) \neq \emptyset\}$$

Table 2. Extracting single object type event log on order object type from Table 1

Case identifier	Activity name	Timestamp
...	...	...
990018	place order	$2019-05-22\,10:33:18$
990008	confirm order	$2019-05-22\,10:34:00$
...	...	...
991296	pick item	$2019-12-31\,17:17:59$
991291	item out of stock	$2019-12-31\,17:20:10$
...	...	...
991572	create package	$2020-02-24\,13:45:30$
991583	send package	$2019-12-31\,13:52:48$
...	...	...

4   Predictive Process Monitoring for Object-Centric Logs

As we have seen in the previous section, multiple object types might interact and influence each other in a process, resulting in multiple case notions. Our goal is to handle these case notions in predictive monitoring. With an object-centric log, user may be interested in:

- P1: making predictions about a given object (next activity for a given item, delivery date of a given package)
- P2: making predictions about the global process (in an order management, what is the next activity concerning the related items, packages, etc.)

For the first type of prediction (P1), it is possible to use the single object type to make predictions for a given object. However, in some cases, user could be interested in defining a custom object life cycle. Thereby, we define a filtered log notion.

For the second type of prediction (P2) for a global process, using the single object type log may not be sufficient, as the interactions between objects are not taken into account. For this reason, we propose the enriched log notion.

Consider the process of ordering products for delivery (whose log is presented in Table 1), where an order is placed first by the customer for the purchase and delivery of products. In order to consider the instance of an order as completed, all the other related objects (items, packages) have to have their instances completed. In this case, the orders is the global process. It is clear that predicting the remaining time until the completion of the order instance should take into account the interactions between objects.

In the following, we define the notions of enriched and filtered log useful for object-centric predictive monitoring.

First, we define a new type of event log where each event, in addition to the single object type projection, is enriched with a set of the other related objects identifiers.

Definition 4 *(Enriched single object type event log). An enriched single object type event log $(E_{enr}^{ot}, \leq_{enr}^{ot})$ (an example is shown in Table 3) is a projection of an object-centric event log on a single object type **ot** with the addition of an event attribute **rmap** describing the set of related object identifiers with types **ro** included in **enr**:*

$$e \in E_{enr}^{ot} \text{ such as } e = (ei, act, time, rmap, vmap)$$

$$E_{enr}^{ot} = \{e \in E \mid \pi_{omap}(e)(ot) = ei, \forall ro \in enr, \pi_{rmap}(e)(ro) \neq \emptyset\} \text{ and}$$

$$\preceq_{enr}^{ot} = \{(e_1, e_2) \in E^{ot} \times E^{ot} \mid e_1 \preceq_E e_2 \wedge \pi_{omap}(e_1)(ot) \cap \pi_{omap}(e_2)(ot) \neq \emptyset\}$$

Table 3. Example of enriched single object type event log on order object type from Table 1

Event identifier	Activity name	Timestamp	Related objects	
			Item	Package
...	...	...	...	...
990018	place order	$2019 - 05 - 22\,10:33:18$	$\{880074, 880075, \ldots\}$	$\emptyset$
990008	confirm order	$2019 - 05 - 22\,10:34:00$	$\{880048, 880049, \ldots\}$	$\emptyset$
...	...	...	...	...
991296	pick item	$2019 - 12 - 31\,17:17:59$	$\{885262\}$	$\emptyset$
991291	item out of stock	$2019 - 12 - 31\,17:20:10$	$\{885233\}$	$\emptyset$
...	...	...	...	...
991572	create package	$2020 - 02 - 24\,13:45:30$	$\{886439, 886438, \ldots\}$	$\{661050\}$
991583	send package	$2019 - 12 - 31\,13:52:48$	$\{886559, 886479, \ldots\}$	$\{661048\}$
...	...	...	...	...

The simple object log is enriched with information about the related objects. Thus object interaction is extracted, allowing to take into account that a specific object type process evolution is affected by the progress made by other related objects processes.

Definition 5 *(Filtered simple object event log).* *A filtered simple object event log is a simple object event log where only events concerning activities of interest for the user are kept.*

This allows an analyst to define the object cycle which is of interest for him for the predictive monitoring, by eliminating activities which do not influence or are not relevant for the object life cycle. An example of a filter is shown in Table 4.

4.1 Pipeline for Predictive Process Monitoring

The workflow of our approach is detailed below. It consists of three main steps: event log preprocessing, feature engineering, and prediction model construction.

Event Log Preprocessing. The first step of the approach is extracting the types of logs we described above by first flattening the OCEL over specific object types. Flattening an object-centric event log is transforming it into a single object type event log as per Definition 3. In the case of an event having multiple objects of the same type, that event is extracted in each separate "flattened" event log maintaining pertinent traces for all objects (this corresponds to the convergence phenomenon which, contrary to process modeling, is not a problem for process analysis).

As explained above, in some cases, an additional filter on the event log must be applied in order to specify the object types of interest for each activity resulting in a filtered log as per Definition 5. An example is shown for further details in the Sect. 5.

Starting from the flattened log for a given object, the enriched single object type event log (Definition 4) will be built by adding an additional attribute, namely the set of objects related to the given object. As for example, in the order management example, an event can refer to multiple object types used like orders, items and packages.

Feature Engineering. In this step, the goal is to prepare the input data for the prediction model. First, in the case of deep learning models, input data has to be of fixed shape. The input will be a multi-dimensional matrix containing features for each activity of each case. After calculating the maximum trace length (i.e., the number activities describing the execution of one case), its dimensions are defined as *number_of_cases* × *max_trace_length* × *number_of_features*.

The features set for the input matrix contain both categorical and numerical attributes. Categorical features describe the activity taking place during each event. Numerical features describe temporal properties of the event (time duration between the event and the start of the sequence, time since the last event, time of the day (since midnight) and the day of the week). These features also describe the related objects set in the enriched event log by calculating their number (in our case, we calculate the number of related items).

Prediction Model Construction. The prediction tasks are multi-class classification for next activity prediction and regression for next event time prediction and instance time remaining. In the first task, for each event and based on a fixed size prefix, the model predicts the probability for each activity being the next event and the activity with the highest probability will be selected as the model's prediction for next activity. For the second task, the model predicts the duration after which the next activity will need to be executed. For the remaining time prediction, the model predicts the duration separating the present time step and the end of the instance. In [17], remaining time can be predicted using the same model by using a loop to predict the next event time until the model predicts the end of the sequence and the remaining time will be the sum of predictions. In this paper, we applied a modification to the model architecture by adding an LSTM layer for predicting the instance remaining time directly instead of looping over the same model for multiple prediction, thus decreasing the error rates.

Our implemented model is inspired by the architecture used in [17]. It is composed of four LSTM layers of size 100, the first layer is shared for all tasks taking on the data matrix as input, the other three layers are divided into the prediction tasks taking in as input the output of the shared layer.

The next activity layer feeds its output to a fully connected layer with softmax activation function[3], the output size is equal to the number of unique activities plus one class that will characterize the end of a trace, thus calculating the probabilities of belonging to each class. The time prediction layers feed the output to a fully connected layer with output of size 1 to predict the time remaining until the next activity or until the end of the sequence.

All performances recorded below are the mean of the performances on all prefixes length ranging from 2 to maximum trace length - 1. For next activity prediction, we use the accuracy metric. For time prediction tasks, we evaluate the model's performance using MAE (Mean Absolute Error) in days.

The implemented model is further summarized in the Fig. 1:

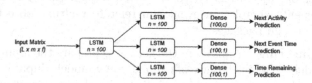

Fig. 1. Model architecture: L: *number of sentences*, m: *maximum trace length*, f: *number of features*, n: *number of neuros*, c: *number of unique*

5   Experimental Results

We implemented the approach presented in previous section in Python and we made the code publicly available (see Footnote 2) for reproducible results.

---

[3] Softmax function: $\sigma(z_i) = \frac{e^{z_i}}{\sum_{j=1}^{K} e^{z_j}}$ $\quad for\ i = 1, 2, \ldots, K.$

The results presented were implemented on the following configuration: HP Elitebook 830 G8, processor: Intel Core i7-1185G7 @3.00 GHz with 64 GB RAM.

Data. We applied the approach proposed above on an order management object-centric event log (see Footnote 1). The event log is composed of 22367 events and 5 objects types: "customers", "items", "orders", "packages" and "products". There are 17 different customers, 8159 items, 2000 orders, 1325 packages and 20 products.

In the enrichment step, we add a numerical feature describing the number of related items for each event. For example, for an event with the activity "place order", we add the number of items ordered during that event. For the package object type, we have the possibility of choosing orders or items or both as related objects. We limit the experiments on the items as related objects for this paper.

We focus on three object types (order, item and package), whose relationships are presented in Fig. 2. We expect that adding the other types (customer and product) would no have significant impact on predictions, given the cardinality of their relationship (one customer per order and one product per item). Furthermore, given these relationships between the items and the other object types (one order/package per item), we limit the enrichment step to the order and package object types. This results in "NA" (Not Applicable) values observed in Table 5 for the enriched event log on item level.

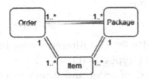

Fig. 2. Object types relationships overview

Prediction Results. We present the prediction results of our approach for the different types of tasks we proposed. First, we suppose that the analyst is interested in making predictions for custom object life-cycle and then we present results on the complete object-life cycle and on the global process. We flatten the event log on the order, item and package object types in addition to a custom filter on the activity-object type combination presented in the Table 4. The prediction results are presented in Table 5A.

Table 5B presents prediction results for complete event logs flattened on object types: order and item (without any filter on activities). For the packages, there are only four related activities; all these activities have been selected in the filter, thus the filtered log and the complete log are the same.

In Table 5A, we observe satisfying results for the accuracy for next activity prediction with over 87% for order and item object types and over 75% for package with improvement for the case of enriched event log. For time prediction, we have order object type sequences with an average trace length of 20 days, we

Table 4. Activity-Object type Filter

Activity	Object type
Place order	Order, item
Confirm order	Order, item
Payment reminder	Order
Pay order	Order
Item out of stock	Item
Reorder item	Item
Pick item	Item
Create package	Item, package
Send package	Item, package
Failed delivery	Item, package
Package delivered	Item, package

observe less than 7 days for next event time and 9 days for remaining time. For package object type, average trace length is 1.55 days. We have MAEs of 0.61 and 0.28 for next event time and remaining time respectively. For the items, we have an average trace length of 15.5 days. Error rates are 1.13 and 1.62 for next event time and remaining time.

Table 5. (A) Prediction results for the filtered event log and enriched flattened on order, item and package object types (left), (B) Prediction results for the complete event log and enriched flattened on order and item object types (right)

Object type	Prediction Task	Single EL	Enriched EL
Order	Next Activity Accuracy	0.87	**0.88**
Order	Next Event Time MAE (days)	**6.70**	6.78
Order	Remaining Time MAE (days)	12.21/**8.70**	11.66/11.71
Package	Next Event Accuracy	0.75	**0.77**
Package	Next Event Time MAE (days)	0.61	**0.59**
Package	Remaining Time MAE (days)	0.85/0.29	0.82/0.28
Item	Next Event Accuracy	0.87	NA
Item	Next Event Time MAE (days)	1.13	NA
Item	Remaining Time MAE (days)	6.04/**1.62**	NA

Object type	Prediction Task	Single EL	Enriched EL
Order	Next Activity Accuracy	0.60	**0.63**
Order	Next Event Time MAE (days)	1.01	**0.95**
Order	Remaining Time MAE (days)	76/8.2	81/14
Item	Next Activity Accuracy	0.78	NA
Item	Next Event Time MAE (days)	1.62	NA
Item	Remaining Time MAE (days)	38/5.62	NA

In Table 5B, in next activity prediction, we observe accuracy over 60% for order and 78% for item. We notice improvement in terms of accuracy for the enriched event log for order object type. In next event time and remaining time predictions, we observe error rates of 0.95 and 8.2 respectively for order object type. For items, we have the following errors rates 1.62 and 5.62 for next event time and remaining time respectively. In the case of remaining time predictions, we observe improvement on error rates with the additional LSTM layer compared to iterative predictions proposed in [17]. We can see that the MAE for item object type is improved up to 10 times with our architecture.

Discussion. Based on the experimental results of Table 5, we get overall improvements for enriched event log in terms of accuracy for next activity prediction and MAE for time predictions. This can be explained by the addition of a numerical feature (number of items) to the input matrix, this feature can help extract the influence of the number of related items in the scheduling of activities and the time remaining until the end of the sequence. The exception for this is the remaining time for the orders, where the enrichment of the log do not seem to improve the results. This may be explained by the fact that Orders is the global process for the considered log, thus already containing all the information about the related objects.

The model with an additional LSTM layer used for remaining time prediction has proven to be more efficient and accurate compared to the iterative model. Based on the experimental results, the proposed approach has enhanced the prediction performances on almost all the object types and event logs.

The proposed approach can be resumed in two steps. First, we tried feature enrichment using the number of related items which has proven experimentally to enhance the model's performances especially on the accuracy for next activity prediction. Second, we added a new LSTM layer dedicated to predict remaining sequence time instead of the classic iterative approach, this change has enhanced the prediction performances and reduced greatly the MAE on almost all object types and event logs both single and enriched. More experiments should be done to validate these preliminary results.

6 Conclusion

In this paper we proposed a first approach for predictive monitoring tailored to object centric logs. Specifically, we addressed the problem of next activity prediction, next event time and remaining time (until the end of process) prediction. A single neural network architecture based on LSTM has been experimentally evaluated for these tasks. We showed that taken into account related objects improve overall its performance. Compared with existing LSTM-based approaches for predictive monitoring, our architecture allows also to predict the remaining time until the end of the instance execution. The experimental results showed that the produced output for remaining time is better than the one computed by iteratively predicting next event time until the end of the process. In future work, we plan to propose new neural network architectures integrating more features of OCEL and compare them with the basic approach proposed in this paper. Our evaluation is based on the single OCEL log publicly available. We intend to extend this evaluation by searching more real-life logs from industrial partners or by building synthetic logs.

References

1. Aalst, W.M.P.: Object-centric process mining: dealing with divergence and convergence in event data. In: Ölveczky, P.C., Salaün, G. (eds.) SEFM 2019. LNCS, vol. 11724, pp. 3–25. Springer, Cham (2019). https://doi.org/10.1007/978-3-030-30446-1_1

2. van der Aalst, W.: Federated process mining: exploiting event data across organizational boundaries, pp. 1–7 (2021). https://doi.org/10.1109/SMDS53860.2021.00011

3. van der Aalst, W., et al.: Process mining manifesto. In: Daniel, F., Barkaoui, K., Dustdar, S. (eds.) BPM 2011. LNBIP, vol. 99, pp. 169–194. Springer, Heidelberg (2012). https://doi.org/10.1007/978-3-642-28108-2_19

4. van der Aalst, W.M., Berti, A.: Discovering object-centric Petri nets. Fund. Inform. **175**(1–4), 1–40 (2020)

5. Adams, J.N., Van Der Aalst, W.M.: Precision and fitness in object-centric process mining. In: 2021 3rd International Conference on Process Mining (ICPM), pp. 128–135 (2021). https://doi.org/10.1109/ICPM53251.2021.9576886

6. Bukhsh, Z.A., Saeed, A., Dijkman, R.M.: ProcessTransformer: predictive business process monitoring with transformer network (2021). https://doi.org/10.48550/ARXIV.2104.00721

7. Camargo, M., Dumas, M., González-Rojas, O.: Learning accurate LSTM models of business processes. In: Hildebrandt, T., van Dongen, B.F., Röglinger, M., Mendling, J. (eds.) BPM 2019. LNCS, vol. 11675, pp. 286–302. Springer, Cham (2019). https://doi.org/10.1007/978-3-030-26619-6_19

8. Di Mauro, N., Appice, A., Basile, T.M.A.: Activity prediction of business process instances with inception CNN models. In: Alviano, M., Greco, G., Scarcello, F. (eds.) AI*IA 2019. LNCS (LNAI), vol. 11946, pp. 348–361. Springer, Cham (2019). https://doi.org/10.1007/978-3-030-35166-3_25

9. Galanti, R., de Leoni, M., Navarin, N., Marazzi, A.: Object-centric process predictive analytics (2022). https://doi.org/10.48550/ARXIV.2203.02801

10. Ghahfarokhi, A.F., Park, G., Berti, A., van der Aalst, W.: OCEL standard (2020). https://ocel-standard.org/1.0/specification.pdf

11. Harl, M., Weinzierl, S., Stierle, M., Matzner, M.: Explainable predictive business process monitoring using gated graph neural networks. J. Decis. Syst. 1–16 (2020). https://doi.org/10.1080/12460125.2020.1780780

12. Hinkka, M., Lehto, T., Heljanko, K.: Exploiting event log event attributes in RNN based prediction. In: Ceravolo, P., van Keulen, M., Gómez-López, M.T. (eds.) SIMPDA 2018-2019. LNBIP, vol. 379, pp. 67–85. Springer, Cham (2020). https://doi.org/10.1007/978-3-030-46633-6_4

13. Li, G., de Carvalho, R.M., van der Aalst, W.M.P.: Automatic discovery of object-centric behavioral constraint models. In: Abramowicz, W. (ed.) BIS 2017. LNBIP, vol. 288, pp. 43–58. Springer, Cham (2017). https://doi.org/10.1007/978-3-319-59336-4_4

14. Lin, L., Wen, L., Wang, J.: MM-Pred: a deep predictive model for multi-attribute event sequence, pp. 118–126 (2019). https://doi.org/10.1137/1.9781611975673.14

15. Pasquadibisceglie, V., Appice, A., Castellano, G., Malerba, D.: Using convolutional neural networks for predictive process analytics. In: 2019 International Conference on Process Mining (ICPM), pp. 129–136 (2019). https://doi.org/10.1109/ICPM.2019.00028

16. Philipp, P., Jacob, R., Robert, S., Beyerer, J.: Predictive analysis of business processes using neural networks with attention mechanism. In: 2020 International Conference on Artificial Intelligence in Information and Communication (ICAIIC), pp. 225–230 (2020). https://doi.org/10.1109/ICAIIC48513.2020.9065057
17. Tax, N., Verenich, I., La Rosa, M., Dumas, M.: Predictive business process monitoring with LSTM neural networks. In: Dubois, E., Pohl, K. (eds.) CAiSE 2017. LNCS, vol. 10253, pp. 477–492. Springer, Cham (2017). https://doi.org/10.1007/978-3-319-59536-8_30

Comparing Ordering Strategies for Process Discovery Using Synthesis Rules

Tsung-Hao Huang$^{(\boxtimes)}$ and Wil M. P. van der Aalst

Process and Data Science (PADS), RWTH Aachen University, Aachen, Germany
{tsunghao.huang,wvdaalst}@pads.rwth-aachen.de

Abstract. Process discovery aims to learn process models from observed behaviors, i.e., event logs, in the information systems. The discovered models serve as the starting point for process mining techniques that are used to address performance and compliance problems. Compared to the state-of-the-art Inductive Miner, the algorithm applying synthesis rules from the free-choice net theory discovers process models with more flexible (non-block) structures while ensuring the same desirable soundness and free-choiceness properties. Moreover, recent development in this line of work shows that the discovered models have compatible quality. Following the synthesis rules, the algorithm incrementally modifies an existing process model by adding the activities in the event log one at a time. As the applications of rules are highly dependent on the existing model structure, the model quality and computation time are significantly influenced by the order of adding activities. In this paper, we investigate the effect of different ordering strategies on the discovered models (w.r.t. fitness and precision) and the computation time using real-life event data. The results show that the proposed ordering strategy can improve the quality of the resulting process models while requiring less time compared to the ordering strategy solely based on the frequency of activities.

Keywords: Process discovery · Synthesis rules · Ordering strategy

1 Introduction

Process mining, a discipline bridging the gap between process science and data science [2], offers techniques and tools to analyze event data, i.e., event logs, generated during the process execution. The analysis generated by process mining techniques provides valuable data-driven insights for the stakeholders.

Process discovery is one of the three main research fields in process mining among conformance checking and process enhancement. Process discovery techniques aim to learn end-to-end process models from the event data. With the discovered models, knowledge workers can apply other process mining techniques to generate further insights for optimization.

J. Troya et al. (Eds.): ICSOC 2022 Workshops, LNCS 13821, pp. 40–52, 2023.
https://doi.org/10.1007/978-3-031-26507-5_4

While various algorithms have been proposed, only a few ensure desirable properties such as soundness and free-choiceness. On the one hand, the soundness property guarantees that (1) it is always possible to finish the process (2) a process can be properly completed (3) no inexecutable transitions exist in the model [1]. On the other hand, the free-choice property separates the choice and synchronization constructs of a process model (Petri net). Such property is desirable as it allows easy conversions from the discovered model to widely-used notations such as BPMN [3]. Moreover, free-choice nets are supported by an abundance of analysis techniques developed from the theory [5].

State-of-the-art techniques, such as the Inductive Miner (IM) [9] family, discover process models guaranteed to be sound and free-choice. IM can provide such guarantees by exploiting its internal process representation - the *process tree*. However, such representation can also be a double-edged sword. Due to the representational bias, the discovered models by IM are doomed to be block-structured, i.e., the model must compose of parts that have a single entry and exit [9]. This implies that only a subset of sound free-choice workflow nets can be discovered by IM.

To provide a more flexible process representation while keeping the same guarantees, we proposed a novel discovery algorithm, the so-called Synthesis Miner in [8]. The Synthesis Miner utilizes the synthesis rules from the free-choice net theory [5]. Activities in the event log are gradually added to a model under construction using predefined patterns. Following the rules ensures that the discovered process models are always sound and free-choice. Moreover, it is shown that the discovered models have compatible quality compared to the ones from Inductive Miner. Nevertheless, the possible applications of synthesis rules are highly dependent on the existing model structure. Different orders of adding activities can result in different models. Therefore, an open research question is the influence of the order in which the activities are added to an existing model on the final process model quality. In this paper, we address the research question by comparing the ordering strategies for the Synthesis Miner and taking a deeper look into the impacts of the activity adding order to the model quality and computation time. The experiment using four publicly available real-life event logs shows that advanced ordering strategies can significantly improve the model quality and the computation time.

The remainder of the paper is structured as follows. Related work is presented in Sect. 2. We introduce the necessary notations and concepts used throughout the paper in Sect. 3. Then, the proposed ordering strategies are introduced in Sect. 4. The evaluation using publicly available real-life event logs is presented in Sect. 5. Finally, Sect. 6 concludes this paper.

2   Related Work

For a general introduction to process mining, we refer to [2]. Additionally, a review and benchmark of the recent development in process discovery can be found in [4]. In this paper, we focus on process discovery techniques that incrementally modify a model under construction to derive the final process.

Incremental process mining allows users to learn a process model from event logs by gradually integrating different traces into an existing model [14]. As the ordering strategy has a significant impact on the model quality, a study [13] is conducted to investigate the interplay. Nevertheless, it is the trace that is added to the algorithm iteratively rather than the activity. Therefore, it is less relevant to this paper.

Dixit et al. [6] were among the first to use synthesis rules from free-choice net theory [5] to discover process models. Inspired by [6,8] introduces the Synthesis Miner that automates the discovery by introducing predefined patterns and a search space pruning mechanism. Both [6] and [8] introduce a few ordering strategies for their approaches. However, the choice of ordering is left to the user as an input parameter. The impact of the ordering strategies on the model quality and computation time is not thoroughly investigated. Furthermore, the interplay between the ordering strategies and the search space pruning has not been explained. Last but not least, a comparison between different ordering strategies is needed. In this paper, we aim to address the open research question and provide users with a rule of thumb.

3 Preliminaries

In this section, we introduce the necessary concepts and notations that are used throughout the paper.

For an arbitrary set A, we denote the set of all possible sequences as A^* and the set of all multi-sets over A as $\mathcal{B}(A)$. Given $\sigma_1, \sigma_2 \in A^*$, $\sigma_1 \cdot \sigma_2$ denotes the concatenation of the two sequences. Let A be a set and $X \subseteq A$ be a subset of A. For $\sigma \in A^*$ and $a \in A$, we define $\lceil_X \in A^* \rightarrow X^*$ as a projection function recursively with $\langle\rangle\lceil_X = \langle\rangle$, $(\langle a \rangle \cdot \sigma)\lceil_X = \langle a \rangle \cdot \sigma\lceil_X$ if $a \in X$ and $(\langle a \rangle \cdot \sigma)\lceil_X = \sigma\lceil_X$ if $a \notin X$. For example, $\langle x, y, x \rangle\lceil_{\{x,z\}} = \langle x, x \rangle$. The projection function can also be applied to a multi-set of sequences. For example, $[\langle x, y, x \rangle^4, \langle x, y \rangle^2, \langle y, x, z \rangle^6]\lceil_{\{y,z\}} = [\langle y \rangle^6, \langle y, z \rangle^6]$. We denote $\mathcal{U}_A$ as the universe of activity labels.

Definition 1 (Trace & Log). *A trace $\sigma \in \mathcal{U}_A^*$ is a sequence of activity labels. A log is a multi-set of traces, i.e., $L \in \mathcal{B}(\mathcal{U}_A^*)$.*

Definition 2 (Log Properties [8]). *Let $L \in \mathcal{B}(\mathcal{U}_A^*)$ and $a, b \in \mathcal{U}_A$ be two activity labels. We define the following log properties:*

- *$\#(a, L) = \Sigma_{\sigma \in L}|\{i \in \{1, 2, ..., |\sigma|\}|\sigma(i) = a\}|$ is the times a occurred in L.*
- *$\#(a, b, L) = \Sigma_{\sigma \in L}|\{i \in \{1, 2, ..., |\sigma|-1\}|\sigma(i) = a \wedge \sigma(i+1) = b\}|$ is the number of direct successions from a to b in L.*
- *$caus(a, b, L) = \begin{cases} \frac{\#(a,b,L)-\#(b,a,L)}{\#(a,b,L)+\#(b,a,L)+1} & \text{if } a \neq b \\ \frac{\#(a,b,L)}{\#(a,b,L)+1} & \text{if } a = b \end{cases}$ is the strength of causal relation (a, b).*
- *$A_c^{pre}(a, L) = \{a_{pre} \in \mathcal{U}_A | caus(a_{pre}, a, L) \geq c\}$ is the set of a's preceding activities, determined by threshold c.*

- $A_c^{fol}(a, L) = \{a_{fol} \in \mathcal{U}_A | caus(a, a_{fol}, L) \geq c\}$ is the set of a's following activities, determined by threshold c.

Definition 3 (Petri Net). Let $N = (P, T, F, l)$ be a Petri net, where P is the set of places, T is the set of transitions, $P \cap T = \emptyset$. $F \subseteq (P \times T) \cup (T \times P)$ is the set of arcs, and $l \in T \rightarrow \mathcal{U}_A \cup \{\tau\}$ is a labeling function that assigns activity labels to transitions. A transition $t \in T$ is invisible (or silent) if $l(t) = \tau$.

Definition 4 (Path & Elementary Path). A path of a Petri net $N = (P, T, F)$ is a non-empty sequence of nodes $\rho = \langle x_1, x_2, ..., x_n \rangle$ such that $(x_i, x_{i+1}) \in F$ for $1 \leq i < n$. ρ is an elementary path if $x_i \neq x_j$ for $1 \leq i < j \leq n$. For $X, X' \in P \cup T$, $elemPaths(X, X', N) \subseteq (P \cup T)^*$ is the set of all elementary paths from some $x \in X$ to some $x' \in X'$.

Definition 5 (Workflow Net (WF-net) [1]). Let $N = (P, T, F, l)$ be a Petri net. $W = (P, T, F, l, i, o, \top, \bot)$ is a WF-net iff (1) it has a dedicated source place $i \in P$: $\bullet i = \emptyset$ and a dedicated sink place $o \in P$: $o \bullet = \emptyset$ (2) $\top \in T$: $\bullet \top = \{i\} \wedge i \bullet = \{\top\}$ and $\bot \in T$: $\bot \bullet = \{o\} \wedge \bullet o = \{\bot\}$ (3) every node x is on some path from i to o, i.e., $\forall_{x \in P \cup T} (i, x) \in F^* \wedge (x, o) \in F^*$, where F^* is the reflexive transitive closure of F.

Definition 6 (Activity Order). Let $L \in \mathcal{B}(\mathcal{U}_A^*)$ and $A = \bigcup_{\sigma \in L} \{a \in \sigma\}$. $\gamma \in A^*$ is an activity order for L if $\{a \in \gamma\} = A$ and $|\gamma| = |A|$.

Synthesis Miner: Process Discovery Using Synthesis Rules. In previous work [8], we introduced the Synthesis Miner that guarantees to discover sound and free-choice workflow nets by applying the synthesis rules defined in [5] with an additional dual abstraction rule [8].

Given a workflow net W, the abstraction rule (ψ_A) allows to add a place p and a transition t between a set of transitions $R \subseteq T$ and a set of places $S \subseteq P$ if they are fully connected, i.e., $(R \times S \subseteq F) \wedge (R \times S \neq \emptyset)$. The linear transition/place rule (ψ_T/ψ_P) allows to add a transition t/place p if it is linearly dependent on the other transitions/places in the corresponding incidence matrix. The dual abstraction rule (ψ_D) can add a transition t and a place p between a set of places S and a set of transitions R if $(S \times R \subseteq F) \wedge (S \times R \neq \emptyset)$. All four rules[1] preserve sound and free-choice properties [5,8]. Figure 1 shows a few examples of rules applications.

Given a log L, the Synthesis Miner first determines an activity order γ. Then, the iteration is initiated. In iteration i (where $1 \leq i \leq |\gamma|$), activity $\gamma(i)$ is added to an existing net[2] from the $i - 1$ iteration. The procedure for every iteration is as follows: (1) use heuristics from the projected log $L_i = L \restriction_{\{\gamma(1), \gamma(2), ... \gamma(i)\}}$ to find the most likely position for the to-be-added activity $\gamma(i)$ on the existing WF-net (W_i), (2) apply predefined patterns (derived from synthesis rules) to get the set of candidate nets, and (3) select the best net (w.r.t. fitness and precision) from the set of candidates for the next iteration.

---

[1] For the formal definitions of the rules, we refer to [5,8].

[2] The existing net in the first iteration is initiated by the initial net, as shown in the example for the abstraction rule in Fig. 1.

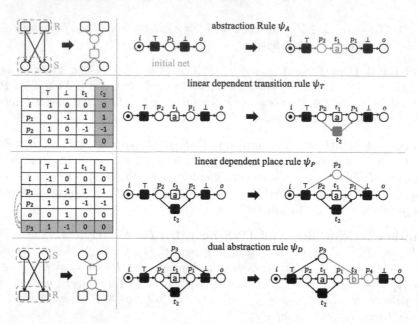

Fig. 1. Some examples of the synthesis rules applications. ψ_A allows to add p_2 and t_1 by $R = \{\top\}$ and $S = \{p_1\}$. t_2 is added by ψ_T as it is linearly dependent on t_1. p_3 is added by ψ_P as it is a linear combination of p_1 and p_2. ψ_D allows to add t_3 and p_4 with $S = \{p_1, p_3\}$ and $R = \{\bot\}$.

As step (1) is directly affected by the ordering strategy, we formally define[3] how the search space is limited to only a subset of the nodes on a workflow net using log heuristics.

Definition 7 (Reduced Search Space). *Let $a \in \mathcal{U}_A^*$ be an activity, $L \in \mathcal{B}(\mathcal{U}_A^*)$ be a log, $W = (P, T, F, l, i, o, \top, \bot)$ be a WF-net, and $0 \le c \le 1$. T^{pre} is the set of transitions labeled by the preceding activities of a in log L. $T^{pre} = \{t \in T | l(t) \in A_c^{pre}(a, L)\}$ if $A_c^{pre}(a, L) \ne \emptyset$, otherwise $T^{pre} = \{\top\}$. T^{fol} is the set of transitions labeled by the following activities of a in log $L.T^{fol} = \{t \in T | l(t) \in A_c^{fol}(a, L)\}$ if $A_c^{fol}(a, L) \ne \emptyset$, otherwise $T^{fol} = \{\bot\}$. The reduced search space is $reduce(a, L, W, c) = \{x \in \rho | \rho \in elemPath(T^{pre}, T^{fol}, W)\}$.*

The function *reduce* first finds the preceding and following activities and the corresponding sets of labeled transitions for the to-be-added activity $\gamma(i)$. Then, it returns the set of nodes, denoted as V_i, that are on the path between the preceding and following transitions. V_i is used to confine the application of synthesis rules. To be more precise, the set of transitions R and the set of places S used as the preconditions for applying rules ψ_A and ψ_D need to be a subset of V_i, i.e., $S \subseteq V \wedge R \subseteq V$. As for rule ψ_T / ψ_P, the new transition/place (t'/p') cannot have arcs connected to any node other than V_i. This step helps us to limit the search space to the most likely nodes on a workflow net to add activity $\gamma(i)$. Figure 2 shows an example for reducing the search space.

---

[3] As the formal definitions of steps (2) and (3) are out of scope, we refer to [8].

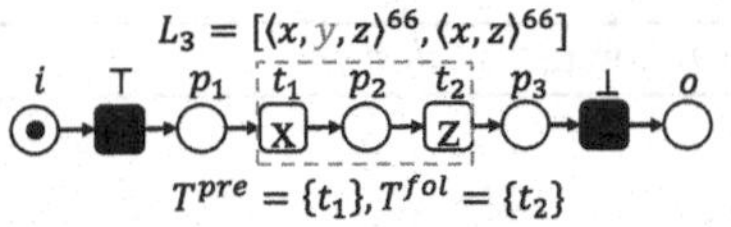

$L_3 = [\langle x, y, z \rangle^{66}, \langle x, z \rangle^{66}]$

$T^{pre} = \{t_1\}, T^{fol} = \{t_2\}$

(a) W_2, the existing net from the last iteration

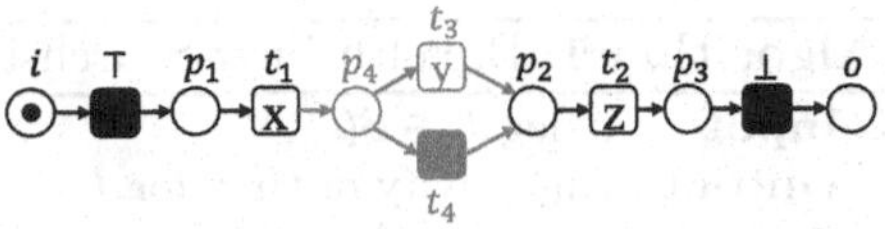

(b) W_3, the net after adding y

Fig. 2. An example showing how the search space is reduced. Consider the log $L_3 = [\langle x, y, z \rangle^{66}, \langle x, z \rangle^{66}]$. y is the activity which we want to add to the net W_2. Using $c = 0.9$, we get $T^{pre} = \{t_1\}$ and $T^{fol} = \{t_2\}$. Therefore, the function *reduce* would return the set of nodes between t_1 and t_2, which means $V_3 = \{t_1, p_2, t_2\}$ as highlighted by the green dashed line in (a). The application of synthesis rules would then only consider these three nodes. Finally, the best net is selected as W_3 from the candidates and is visualized in (b). (Color figure online)

4   Ordering Strategies

In this section, we introduce different ordering strategies. To illustrate the ordering strategy, consider the following log $L_s = [\langle b, c, d, e, f, g \rangle, \langle b, e, c, d, f, g \rangle, \langle b, e, c, f, g, d \rangle, \langle b, e, c, f, d, g \rangle, \langle b, c, e, d, f, g \rangle, \langle b, c, e, f, g, d \rangle, \langle b, c, e, f, d, g \rangle, \langle e, b, c, d, f, g \rangle, \langle e, b, c, f, g, d \rangle, \langle e, b, c, f, d, g \rangle]$.

The corresponding directly follows graph (DFG) is shown in Fig. 3.

The first ordering strategy is frequency-based and it is relatively straightforward. The activities are simply ordered by their frequency in the log.

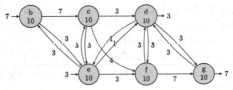

Fig. 3. The DFG for log L_s.

Definition 8 (Frequency-Based Ordering). *Let* $L \in \mathcal{B}(\mathcal{U}_A^*)$. *Frequency-based ordering function is* $order_{freq}(L) = \gamma$ *such that* γ *is an activity order and* $\forall_{1 \leq i < j \leq |\gamma|} \#(\gamma(i), L) \geq \#(\gamma(j), L)$.

If activities have the same frequency, we order them alphabetically. Using the example log L_s for illustration, the order would be $order_{freq}(L_s) = \langle b, c, d, e, f, g \rangle$.

The other ordering strategies are more involved as they consider not only the frequency of activities but also the connections between them. Before introducing the other ordering strategies, we first define a helper function that ranks the directly-follow activities based on the strength of connections.

Definition 9 (Directly-Follow Activities Sorting). *Let* $L \in \mathcal{B}(\mathcal{U}_A^*)$ *and* $a \in \mathcal{U}_A$. $A = \{b \in \mathcal{U}_A | \#(a, b, L) > 0\}$ *is the set of activities directly-follow* a *in* L *at least once and* $\sigma \in A^*$. *Directly-follow activities sorting is* $sortDFA(a, L) = \sigma$ *such that* $\{b \in \sigma\} = A$ *and* $|\sigma| = |A|$ *and* $\forall_{1 \leq i < j \leq |\sigma|} \#(a, \sigma(i), L) \geq \#(a, \sigma(j), L)$.

For example, $sortDFA(b, L_s) = \langle c, e \rangle$. This is because activities c and e have incoming arcs from b and the strength $\#(b, c, L_s) \geq \#(b, e, L_s)$. With the function for sorting directly-follow activities defined, we are now ready to define the Breadth-First-Search-Based ordering strategy in Algorithm 1.

Algorithm 1: Breadth-First-Search-Based Ordering, $order_{BFS}$

Input   : A log $L \in \mathcal{B}(\mathcal{U}_A^*)$
Output : An activity order γ for L
$A \leftarrow \bigcup_{\sigma \in L} \{a \in \sigma\}$;   // the set of activities in L
$A^s \leftarrow \{\sigma(1) \mid \sigma \in L \wedge \sigma \neq \langle\rangle\}$;   // the set of start activities in L
$\sigma \leftarrow order_{freq}(L) \upharpoonright_{A^s}$;   // the sequence of start activities ordered by frequency
$i \leftarrow 1$;
while $|\sigma| \neq |A|$:
$\quad$ $A' \leftarrow A \setminus \{a \in \sigma\}$;   // the set of activities that are not in σ
$\quad$ $\sigma' \leftarrow sortDFA(\sigma(i), L) \upharpoonright_{A'}$;   // sort $\sigma(i)$'s following activities & project on A'
$\quad$ $\sigma \leftarrow \sigma \cdot \sigma'$;   // update σ
$\quad$ $i \leftarrow i + 1$;
$\gamma \leftarrow \sigma$;
return γ;

BFS-based ordering strategy starts by building a sequence of start activities in a log and iteratively append the sequence of directly-follow activities using the function in Definition 9. Applying the function to the example log L_s, we get $order_{BFS}(L_s) = \langle b, e \rangle \cdot \langle c \rangle \cdot \langle f, d \rangle \cdot \langle\rangle \cdot \langle g \rangle = \langle b, e, c, f, d, g \rangle$. σ is initiated with $\langle b, e \rangle$. Then, in iteration i, σ is appended by the sequence of $\sigma(i)$'s directly-follow activities sorted by $sortDFA(\sigma(i), L_s)$ with the set of activities already in σ filtered out. The loop continues until σ includes every activity in the log. As its name suggests, the ordering prioritizes the exploration of the directly-follow activities.

Next, we introduce another ordering strategy in Algorithm 2 that is Depth-First-Search-based. While also considering the connection between the activities as BFS-based ordering strategy, DFS-based ordering prioritizes depth over breadth. That is, the directly-follow activities are not explored thoroughly until activities with higher depth have been explored. Applying DFS-based ordering to log L_s, we get $order_{DFS}(L_s) = \langle b, c, f, g, d, e \rangle$.

Note that although we define the BFS- and DFS-based ordering strategies to start from the start activities, one can also initiate the exploration from another direction, i.e., from the end activities and subsequently explore the directly-precede activities for ordering. Using L_s as an example, if starting from the set of end activities, we would get $\langle g, f, c, b, e, d \rangle$ with DFS-based ordering on log L_s and $\langle g, d, f, c, e, b \rangle$ with BFS-based ordering.

To explain how the progression of the process discovery influenced by the different ordering strategies, Fig. 4 shows all the intermediate nets when applying Synthesis Miner to log L_s using the three different ordering strategies. DFS-based ordering tends to build the process from start to end at the beginning before adding the activities in the parallel/choice branches. On the contrary, BFS-based ordering prioritizes the construction of local control flows. For example, the difference is observable from iteration 1 to 2. While all the ordering strategies produce the same net in iteration 1, BFS-based ordering suggests to add the concurrent activity e for b in iteration 2 and DFS-based ordering adds

Algorithm 2: Depth-First-Search-Based Ordering $order_{DFS}$

Input : A log $L \in \mathcal{B}(\mathcal{U}_A^*)$
Output : An activity order γ for L

$A \leftarrow \bigcup_{\sigma \in L} \{a \in \sigma\}$;   // the set of activities in L
$A^s \leftarrow \{\sigma(1) \mid \sigma \in L \land |\sigma| \neq 0\}$;   // the set of start activities in L
$\sigma^s \leftarrow order_{freq}(L) \restriction_{A^s}$;   // the sequence of start activities ordered by frequency
$\sigma \leftarrow \langle \sigma^s(1) \rangle$;   // initiate the sequence with the most frequent start activity
$\sigma^s \leftarrow \sigma^s \restriction_{\{A^s \setminus \{\sigma^s(1)\}\}}$;   // update σ^s to be the stack
while $|\sigma| \neq |A|$ **:**
$\quad A' \leftarrow A \setminus \{a \in \sigma\}$;   // set of activities that are not in σ
$\quad \sigma^f \leftarrow sortDFA(\sigma(|\sigma|), L) \restriction_{A'}$;   // sort $\sigma(|\sigma|)$'s following activities
$\quad$ **if** $|\sigma^f| = 0$ **:**
$\quad\quad \mid \quad \sigma \leftarrow \sigma \cdot \langle \sigma^s(1) \rangle$;   // append the 1st element from the stack σ^s to σ
$\quad$ **else :**
$\quad\quad \mid \quad \sigma \leftarrow \sigma \cdot \langle \sigma^f(1) \rangle$;   // append the 1st element from σ^f to σ
$\quad \sigma^s \leftarrow (\sigma^f \restriction_{A \setminus \{a \in \sigma \lor a \in \sigma^s\}}) \cdot (\sigma^s \restriction_{A \setminus \{a \in \sigma\}})$;   // update the stack σ^s
$\gamma \leftarrow \sigma$;
return γ;

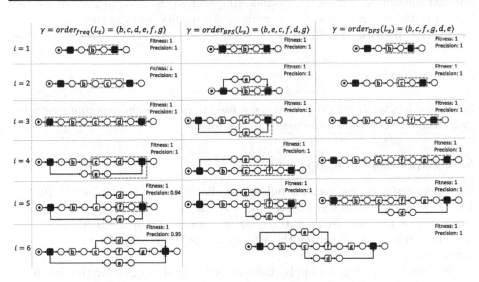

Fig. 4. A comparison of different ordering strategies for log L_s. Each column represents an ordering strategy and each row corresponds to the intermediate workflow net in iteration i after adding $\gamma(i)$. The green dashed lines highlight the nodes representing the reduced search space. The metrics fitness and precision are measured using the corresponding projected log $L_i = L \restriction_{\{\gamma(1), \gamma(2), ... \gamma(i)\}}$. Note that the final model discovered by the BFS- and DFS-based ordering strategies are the same in this example. (Color figure online)

the directly-follow activity c of b first. The frequency ordering doesn't seem to have clear patterns for the discovery.

We expect that the choice of ordering can significantly influence the computation time of discovery. The main difference stems from the time required to check the feasibility of the linear dependency rules. As the WF-net grows, it becomes more expensive (w.r.t. time) to check if a candidate place/transition is linear dependent. Thus, it is preferable to limit the search space as small as possible, especially in the later iterations. Recall that the reduced search space (Definition 7) is a set of nodes confining the application of synthesis rules. The green dashed lines in Fig. 4 highlight the reduced search space V_i in iteration i. As shown in Fig. 4, generally, BFS-based ordering can keep the search space smaller than the other strategies because it prioritizes the connected activities. In contrast, the search space of DFS-based ordering is more likely to be large in the later iterations. As the parallel/alternative activities are added later, the preceding and following activities of the to-be-added activity $\gamma(i)$ is highly likely to be spread across the existing net. Together with the effect of search space reduction, it results in a relatively large search space, which indicates more nodes to be considered. Examples can be seen in iterations 4 and 5 for the DFS-based ordering in Fig. 4.

Although it is assumed that BFS-based ordering would have relatively lower computation time, search space reduction might introduce trade-offs between the optimal solution and time. In the following section, we aim to investigate the impact of the ordering strategy on both model quality and the time to discover the process model in the experiment.

5   Evaluation

In this section, we present the experiment used to evaluate the ordering strategies including the setup and a discussion of the result[4].

5.1   Experimental Setup

For the experiment, we use four publicly available real-life event logs [7,10–12]. The logs are filtered to focus on the mainstream behaviors (at least 95% of the traces) where the most frequent trace variants are used. For the BPI2017 log [7], we split it into three logs using the activity prefix (A, W, O). This results in six logs in total.

For every event log, we apply different ordering strategies for the Synthesis Miner [8] with default values for the other parameters. For the BFS- and DFS-based ordering strategies, we apply the ordering from both directions (start and end activities). Therefore, we evaluate five ordering strategies. To measure the effect of ordering strategies on search space pruning, we keep track of the ratio of reduced search space. This is evaluated by $\frac{|V_i|}{|P_i \cup T_i|-2}$, where V_i is the set of reduced nodes, P_i and T_i are the set of places and transitions in the existing WF-net W_i. The -2 in the denominator is there to exclude the two places (source and sink) that can never be connected by new nodes by Definition 5. Using Fig. 4 as an example, the value of $\frac{|V_3|}{|P_3 \cup T_3|-2}$ for the frequency ordering strategy would be

---

[4]   https://github.com/tsunghao-huang/synthesisRulesMiner.

$\frac{9}{11-2} = 1$ in iteration 3. This indicates that all the possible nodes are considered for the application of synthesis rules to add the next activity. Furthermore, we evaluate the final model in terms of fitness, precision, and F1 score (the harmonic mean of fitness and precision).

5.2   Results and Discussion

Search Space Reduction and Computation Time. Figure 5 shows the result of the comparison among the five ordering strategies regarding their effects on the search space reduction. The value in the y-axis $\frac{|V_i|}{|P_i \cup T_i|-2}$ is the average across six event logs. As indicated, the metric keeps track of the reduced search space ratio for adding the next activity, which indicates the number of possible synthesis rule applications. In general, we can observe from the figure that the ordering strategies behaved as expected. As shown in Fig. 5a, in the later stage of the discovery ($i \geq 8$), the BFS-ordering strategies (bfs_start, bfs_end) keep the ratio of reduced search space at a low level while the value for frequency and DFS-based ordering strategies show that they are more likely to include a large portion of the nodes in the search space.

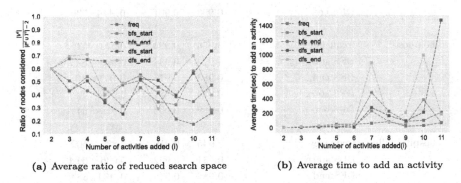

| (a) Average ratio of reduced search space | (b) Average time to add an activity |

Fig. 5. Comparisons of ordering strategies on the effects of search space reduction as well as the computation time for each step. Note that it is preferable to have a lower value for $\frac{|V_i|}{|P_i \cup T_i|-2}$.

Figure 5b shows the average time to add an activity to the existing WF-net for each step of six logs. Comparing the two figures, one can see the effect of search space reduction on the computation time. As shown in Fig. 5b, the bfs_end strategy keeps the average computation time for each step at a fairly low level. This is also the case for the bfs_start strategy despite the two peaks when adding the 7th and 10th activity. The two peaks in the 7th and 10th steps are especially severe for the dfs_end strategy. Both took more than 10 min to add a single activity to the existing model. Also, the longest duration to add an activity also happens in the 11th step of the dfs_start strategy.

In short, due to its interplay with the search space reduction, the BFS-based ordering strategies have significant advantage in terms of computation time.

Table 1. Quality of the models discovered by different ordering strategies.

Log	Ordering Strategy & IMf	Fitness	Precision	F1	time(sec)
BPI2017A	frequency	0.971	0.947	0.958	685
	BFS_start	0.973	1.000	0.986	893
	BFS_end	0.990	0.935	0.961	**334**
	DFS_start	0.963	0.868	0.913	1850
	DFS_end	0.999	0.986	**0.993**	1248
	IMf(0.2)	0.999	0.936	0.967	10
BPI2017O	frequency	0.993	0.962	0.978	537
	BFS_start	0.985	0.963	0.974	**165**
	BFS_end	0.989	1.000	0.995	231
	DFS_start	0.996	1.000	**0.998**	498
	DFS_end	0.993	0.962	0.978	360
	IMf(0.2)	0.997	0.907	0.950	7
BPI2017W	frequency	0.993	0.726	0.838	3617
	BFS_start	0.974	0.864	0.914	1626
	BFS_end	0.993	0.888	0.936	**579**
	DFS_start	0.974	0.864	0.914	1732
	DFS_end	0.993	0.901	**0.944**	5397
	IMf(0.2)	0.923	0.897	0.910	14
helpdesk	frequency	0.974	0.984	0.978	51
	BFS_start	0.974	0.984	0.978	52
	BFS_end	0.983	0.976	**0.979**	**43**
	DFS_start	0.974	0.984	0.978	49
	DFS_end	0.989	0.963	0.976	64
	IMf(0.2)	0.967	0.950	0.958	1
hospital billing	frequency	0.945	0.810	0.879	509
	BFS_start	0.931	0.922	0.936	**314**
	BFS_end	0.988	0.935	**0.961**	383
	DFS_start	0.931	0.970	0.961	2154
	DFS_end	0.943	0.883	0.920	2359
	IMf(0.2)	0.982	0.906	0.943	45
traffic	frequency	0.967	0.930	0.945	274
	BFS_start	0.967	0.930	0.945	**202**
	BFS_end	0.972	0.720	0.825	388
	DFS_start	0.991	0.933	**0.960**	366
	DFS_end	0.942	0.858	0.903	443
	IMf(0.4)	0.904	0.720	0.801	28

Model Quality. Table 1[5] shows the result of the model quality using the five different ordering strategies. As expected, we observe that the BFS-based ordering strategies have the lowest computation time in all six event logs. This corresponds to the findings in the previous section. Moreover, despite the search space being considerably reduced, the models discovered using BFS-ordering strategies have the highest F1 score in two out of the six logs.

As for the DFS-based ordering strategies, they have an apparent disadvantage for computation time but get the highest F1 score in the other four event logs. The result matches our assumption as search space reduction introduces a trade-off between the optimal solution and time. Lastly, the frequency ordering strategy has no significant advantage in model quality and computation time. The results show that the ordering strategies that take the connections between activities into consideration can improve the Synthesis Miner than the frequency-based ordering strategy.

6   Conclusion

In this paper, we introduced five ordering strategies for the process discovery algorithm using synthesis rules [8]. We investigated the impact of ordering strategies on model quality and computation time. The results show that compared to the ordering strategy solely based on the frequency of activities, the proposed ordering strategies considered the connection between activities (Breadth-First-Search-based and Depth-First-Search-based) have superior performance w.r.t. time and model quality respectively. It is shown in the result that the introduced BFS-based ordering strategies can speed up the computation. Nevertheless, the overall discovery time of the Synthesis Miner is still not comparable to the state of the art despite being able to discover models with better quality. Therefore, for future work, we plan to speed up the Synthesis Miner by further exploiting the log heuristics and investigating more sophisticated ordering strategies. Another direction for improvement is the ability to cope with infrequent behaviors as we use the most frequent trace variants to capture the mainstream process. It would be valuable to introduce a filtering mechanism to the Synthesis Miner so that it can directly work on the original log without depending on pre-filtering the log.

Acknowledgements. We thank the Alexander von Humboldt (AvH) Stiftung for supporting our research.

References

1. van der Aalst, W.M.P.: The application of Petri nets to workflow management. J. Circuits Syst. Comput. **8**(1), 21–66 (1998)
2. van der Aalst, W.M.P.: Process Mining - Data Science in Action, 2nd edn. Springer, Heidelberg (2016)

---

[5] To provide a reference to the state of the art, we also present the results from IMf (marked by gray color). The best model generated by IMf (w.r.t. F1 score) is selected from a set of nets using five different values ($[0.1, 0.2, 0.3, 0.4, 0.5]$) for the filter.

3. van der Aalst, W.M.P.: Using free-choice nets for process mining and business process management. In: FedCSIS 2021, vol. 25, pp. 9–15 (2021)
4. Augusto, A., et al.: Automated discovery of process models from event logs: review and benchmark. IEEE Trans. Knowl. Data Eng. **31**(4), 686–705 (2019)
5. Desel, J., Esparza, J.: Free Choice Petri Nets, vol. 40. Cambridge University Press, Cambridge (1995)
6. Dixit, P.M., Buijs, J.C.A.M., van der Aalst, W.M.P.: Prodigy: human-in-the-loop process discovery. In: RCIS 2018, pp. 1–12. IEEE (2018)
7. van Dongen, B.: BPI Challenge 2017 (2017). https://doi.org/10.4121/uuid: 5f3067df-f10b-45da-b98b-86ae4c7a310b
8. Huang, T.H., van der Aalst, W.M.P.: Discovering sound free-choice workflow nets with non-block structures. In: Almeida, J.P.A., Karastoyanova, D., Guizzardi, G., Montali, M., Maggi, F.M., Fonseca, C.M. (eds.) EDOC 2022. LNCS, vol. 13585, pp. 200–216. Springer, Cham (2022). https://doi.org/10.1007/978-3-031-17604-3_12
9. Leemans, S.J.J., Fahland, D., van der Aalst, W.M.P.: Scalable process discovery and conformance checking. Softw. Syst. Model. **17**(2), 599–631 (2018)
10. de Leoni, M.M., Mannhardt, F.: Road Traffic Fine Management Process (2015). https://doi.org/10.4121/uuid:270fd440-1057-4fb9-89a9-b699b47990f5
11. Mannhardt, F.: Hospital Billing - Event Log (2017). https://doi.org/10.4121/uuid: 76c46b83-c930-4798-a1c9-4be94dfeb741
12. Polato, M.: Dataset belonging to the help desk log of an Italian Company (2017). https://doi.org/10.4121/uuid:0c60edf1-6f83-4e75-9367-4c63b3e9d5bb
13. Schuster, D., Domnitsch, E., van Zelst, S.J., van der Aalst, W.M.P.: A generic trace ordering framework for incremental process discovery. In: Bouadi, T., Fromont, E., Hüllermeier, E. (eds.) IDA 2022. LNCS, vol. 13205, pp. 264–277. Springer, Cham (2022). https://doi.org/10.1007/978-3-031-01333-1_21
14. Schuster, D., van Zelst, S.J., van der Aalst, W.M.P.: Incremental discovery of hierarchical process models. In: Dalpiaz, F., Zdravkovic, J., Loucopoulos, P. (eds.) RCIS 2020. LNBIP, vol. 385, pp. 417–433. Springer, Cham (2020). https://doi.org/ 10.1007/978-3-030-50316-1_25

Developing Supply Chain Risk Management Strategies by Using Counterfactual Explanation

Amir Hossein Ordibazar[1(✉)] , Omar Hussain[1] , Ripon K. Chakrabortty[2] ,
Morteza Saberi[3] , and Elnaz Irannezhad[4]

[1] School of Business, UNSW Canberra, Canberra, ACT, Australia
`a.ordibazar@adfa.edu.au`
[2] School of Engineering and Information Technology, UNSW Canberra,
Canberra, ACT, Australia
[3] School of Computer Science, University of Technology Sydney,
Sydney, NSW, Australia
[4] School of Civil and Environmental Engineering, UNSW Sydney,
Kensington, NSW, Australia

Abstract. Supply Chain Risk Management (SCRM) is necessary for economic development and the well-being of society. Therefore, many researchers and practitioners focus on developing new methods to identify, assess, mitigate and monitor supply chain risks. This paper developed the Risk Management by Counterfactual Explanation (RMCE) framework to manage risks in Supply Chain Networks (SCNs). The RMCE framework focuses on monitoring SCN, and in case of any risks eventuating, it explains them to the user and recommends mitigation strategies to avoid them proactively. RMCE uses optimisation models to design the SCN and Counterfactual Explanation (CE) to generate mitigation recommendations. The developed approach is applied to an actual case study related to a global SCN to test and validate the proposed framework. The final results show that the RMCE framework can correctly predict risks and give understandable explanations and solutions to mitigate the impact of the monitored risks on the case study.

Keywords: Supply Chain Risk Management · Recommendations · Counterfactual Explanation · Optimisation · Case study

1 Introduction

The counterfactual Explanation (CE) method is a recent advancement in Explainable Artificial intelligence (XAI). For any given input, the CE alters the features of a prediction model to change the undesirable output to a desirable one. Since there are multiple options for changing the input features, the CE uses an optimisation model to find the option with the minimum effort needed to satisfy the required constraints. So, the objective function of the CE model

© The Author(s), under exclusive license to Springer Nature Switzerland AG 2023
J. Troya et al. (Eds.): ICSOC 2022 Workshops, LNCS 13821, pp. 53–65, 2023.
https://doi.org/10.1007/978-3-031-26507-5_5

includes minimising the effort needed, and the constraints consider that the CE changes the values of those features that can be changed in their allowed range and takes the interdependency between features into account. The output of the CE optimisation model is a perturbation vector.

The CE method optimises the objective functions and recommends changes in the input features of the prediction model. Therefore, It has the capability to take risks occurrence as undesirable outputs into account and give recommendations to mitigate the impact of the risks or proactively avoid them. For instance, if the prediction model forecasts that specific delivery of an item has a delay in future, the CE considers different allowed changes in the input features, which alter the predicted delay into on-time delivery. It then chooses the one with the minimum cost among different options like changing the supplier, vehicle, driver, or route to recommend to the risk manager. If the changes are not allowed by the problem assumptions, then they will not be recommended.

On the other hand, the output of the prediction models, which detects the risks, and the results of the CE, which recommends the mitigation strategies, should be understandable for the human user to improve trust. Therefore, even if the prediction model can identify the risks accurately and the CE can recommend mitigation strategies correctly, the risk manager might not comprehend and consequently trust the recommendations. In this case, the recommender system may not reach the intended achievements despite the proper design.

This paper tries to apply the CE in the SCRM by proposing the Risk Management by Counterfactual Explanation (RMCE) framework to monitor and mitigate the risks in SCNs, which monitors risks and recommends mitigation strategies to avoid them while explaining both risks and recommendations.

In summary, the contributions and motivations of this paper are as follows:

- The inter-dependencies among the features of the SCN are considered in a mathematical optimisation model
- Risks caused by the external events of the SCN are avoided proactively
- The RMCE framework recommends solutions to mitigate the risks of the SCN along with justifications
- The recommendations of the CE are applicable and realistic, and compatible with the SCN requirements

2   Literature Review

The CE method is widely used to change the output of AI models and give recommendations to reach a more desirable output. Many researchers applied the CE method to different applications such as fault detection and diagnosis [1] and financial problems [2]. The CE also has some applications in SCRM [3] as a recommender system to mitigate risks. The main challenge in using CE is generating recommendations that are not applicable and realistic, [4] proposed a feasible and actionable CE model to address the mentioned deficiencies for the considered cases. The XAI methods are more required on black-box AI models like Neural Network (NN), [5] proposed a CE on graphical NN, which is robust to the noise, and the results change the output of the prediction model. [6] considered the feasibility and diversity of the counterfactual actions and applied the model to four case studies. In other cases, CE is used to change the recommended movie to watch for neural commanders [7].

The risk mitigation stage of the SCRM is one of the essential requirements of the current research. Some researchers used machine learning and simulation for supplier selection, and operational indexes like delay were considered for supplier selection, which causes lower risks for the SCN [8]. Some others validated the effectiveness and recognised the influential factors for the adoption of AI in supply chain risk mitigation. e.g., [9] conducted a survey on Indian agriculture companies by structural equation modelling (SEM), and concluded that AI has a significant impact on risk mitigation of the supply chain. To mitigate the risks of the SCN regarding operational disruptions, a two-stage stochastic model of an SCN has been proposed, and some suggestions were recommended by [10]. In this research [11], mathematical optimisation models are employed to make decisions to overcome severe disruptions caused by disasters to lead a robust business continuity management. AI has been progressively proving as an effective tool in reducing risks of the SCN [12].

Therefore, based on the literature review, optimisation and prediction models are considered to design the RMCE framework in this paper. In addition, we tried to increase the explainability of the SCRM mitigation strategies by using the CE optimisation model. To overcome the challenges of recommending non-applicable and non-feasible solutions, the constraints of the SCN are considered in the CE optimisation model. Therefore all recommendations are in accordance with the SCN nature.

3   The Risk Management by Counterfactual Explanation (RMCE) Framework

Researchers in the literature have broadly used the CE method to recommend solutions to avoid unpleasant and undesirable outcomes [2,3]. The CE method's capability can contribute to the planning and decision-making of SCNs in case of mitigation of future undesirable outputs like risks and disruptions. In this paper, we propose a Risk Management by Counterfactual Explanation (RMCE) framework to get the advantage of the CE method and proactively assist risk managers in avoiding risks. In the following sections, first, we describe the SCN optimization model and then explain how the RMCE framework can help in risk management.

3.1   The SCN Optimization Model

In this paper, we considered a two-echelon SCN by considering soft time windows for the delivery time of products to consumers (i.e., transportation of different products from suppliers to consumers). The soft time windows specify a time range for delivery, while violation of the time windows is possible but has some penalties. This SCN model has two input data types: Type 1 and Type 2. The Type 1 input are those parameters that the user enters into the SCN model and can manually be changed (e.g. time windows, the capacity of suppliers, transportation costs, and customers' demands). Type 2 inputs include parameters that machine learning models predict; these inputs will change if the prediction features change. Examples of input data type 2 is the transportation time, which machine learning models can predict by considering different features such as supplier city and customer city.

The main goal is to plan SCN by designing an optimisation model. In this stage, the SCN gives a significant output, the transportation schedule, which includes departure time from suppliers and arrival time for customers' delivery. The first objective function calculates transportation costs, and the second objective function calculates the total violation penalty in case of any violation from time windows. The optimisation model tries to minimise these two objective functions simultaneously. Finally, the optimisation model plans an optimal and feasible schedule of SCN by satisfying all constraints and optimising all objective functions. Figure 1 shows the optimisation process.

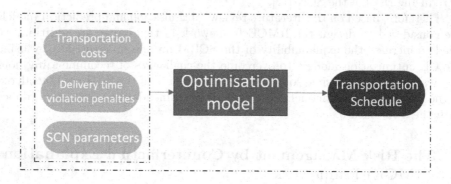

Fig. 1. The optimisation model for planning SCN

This section details SCN optimisation Mixed Integer Linear Programming (MILP) model sets, parameters, variables, objective functions, and constraints. Table 1 defines the sets of the model. Tables 2 and 3 describe the parameters and variables of the MILP model, respectively. Equations (1–2) and Eqs. (3–12) show the Objective functions and constraints of the MILP SCN optimization model, respectively.

Table 1. Set definition of the MILP model

Index set	Description
I	Set of suppliers $i \in \{1, 2, ..., |I|\}$
J	Set of consumers $j \in \{1, 2, ..., |J|\}$
P	Set of products $p \in \{1, 2, ..., |P|\}$

Table 2. The parameters of the MILP model

Parameters	Description
$D_{j,p}$	Demand of consumer j for product p
$SC_{i,p}$	Capacity of supplier i for providing product p
$TT_{i,j}$	Planned transportation time from supplier i to consumer j
$A_{j,p}$	Starting of delivery time window of product p for consumer j
$B_{j,p}$	End of delivery time window of product p for consumer j
$Cost_{i,j}$	The transportation cost from supplier i to consumer j
$Penalty1_{j,p}$	Penalty for delivery before time window for consumer j for product p
$Penalty2_{j,p}$	Penalty for delivery After time window for consumer j for product p
M	A large number

Table 3. The variables of the MILP model

Variables	Description
$X_{i,j,p}$	Integer variable for the amount of transportation from supplier i to consumer j for product p
$Z_{i,j,p}$	binary variable if consumer j received product p from supplier i 1, otherwise 0
$ta_{i,j,p}$	continuous variable for arrival time of product p for consumer j from supplier i
$td_{i,j,p}$	continuous variable for departure time of product p from supplier i for consumer j
$AS_{j,p}$	continuous variable for arrival before time window of consumer j for product p
$AL_{j,p}$	continuous variable for arrival after time window of consumer j for product p

$$\text{Minimize Objective Function 1}: F_1(X_{i,j,p}) = \sum_{i,j,p} Cost_{i,j} * X_{i,j,p} \quad (1)$$

$$\text{Minimize Objective Function 2}: F_2(AS_{j,p}, AL_{j,p}) = \sum_{j,p} Penalty1_{j,p} * AS_{j,p}$$
$$+ \sum_{j,p} Penalty2_{j,p} * AL_{j,p} \quad (2)$$

Subject to

$$X_{i,j,p} \leq M * Z_{i,j,p} \quad \forall i,j,p \quad (3)$$

$$X_{i,j,p} \geq Z_{i,j,p} \quad \forall i,j,p \quad (4)$$

$$\sum_i X_{i,j,p} \geq D_{j,p} \quad \forall j,p \quad (5)$$

$$\sum_j X_{i,j,p} \leq SC_{i,p} \quad \forall i,p \quad (6)$$

$$AS_{j,p} \geq (ta_{i,j,p} - B_{j,p}) - (1 - Z_{i,j,p}) * M \quad \forall i,j,p \quad (7)$$

$$AL_{j,p} \geq (A_{j,p} - ta_{i,j,p}) - (1 - Z_{i,j,p}) * M \quad \forall i,j,p \quad (8)$$

$$ta_{i,j,p} = td_{i,j,p} + TT_{i,j} \quad \forall i, j, p \tag{9}$$

In Eq. (1), the first objective function minimizes transportation costs. In Eq. (2), the second objective function tries to minimize the penalty caused by the delivery out of the allowed time window. Equations (3–4) are logical constraints to relate the amount of transportation with the binary variable of serving a consumer for each product from each supplier. Equation (5) considers the demand satisfaction, i.e., the consumer will receive the predefined demand, and the extra delivery can be controlled by the first objective function in Eq. (1), which tries to minimize transportation costs. Equation (6) ensures suppliers' capacity. Equation (1–8) respectively calculate if delivery arrived sooner or later than the preferred time window. Equation (9) calculates the departure time of transportation from each supplier and arrival time to the consumer using transportation time.

3.2 The Mechanism of Counterfactual Explanation in Decision Making

The next stage considers that the disruptions and changes in constraints and inputs cause risks. Considering the new status caused by changes in inputs and parameters, the user checks the feasibility and optimality of the planned SCN's schedule. If constraints are still satisfied, there is no need for any further action. On the other hand, If the changes in the input data lead to violations of the constraints of the SCN model (e.g. demand satisfaction and on-time delivery), the CE optimization model needs to recommend solutions to avoid risks proactively. The objective function of the CE optimization model calculates the effort needed for the CE-based recommendations. Outputs of the CE model consists of changed transportation schedule and arrival/departure times. The CE optimization model takes all constraints of the SCN optimization model into account to keep the recommended solution feasible in the context of the SCN. Figure 2 shows the schematic process of this stage.

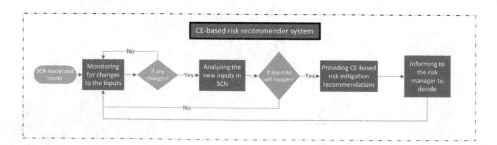

Fig. 2. The RMCE framework for risk mitigation recommendations

This section depicts CE recommender optimization mode. Table 4 shows the new parameters and variables of the CE model.

Table 4. The parameters and variables of the CE optimization model

Symbol	Role	Description
$X_{i,j,p}^{O}$	Parameter	The optimal amount of variable $X_{i,j,p}$
$ta_{i,j,p}^{O}$	Parameter	The optimal amount of variable $ta_{i,j,p}$
$P_{i,j,p}^{X}$	Variable	Integer variable for the recommended perturbation in parameter $X_{i,j,p}^{O}$
$P_{i,j,p}^{T}$	Variable	Integer variable for the recommended perturbation in parameter $ta_{i,j,p}^{O}$
$X_{i,j,p}^{'}$	Variable	Integer variable for the changed amount of variable $X_{i,j,p}$
$ta_{i,j,p}^{'}$	Variable	Integer variable for the changed amount of variable $ta_{i,j,p}$
$Effort_{i,j}$	Parameter	Effort needed for each unit of variable $P_{i,j,p}$
$T\acute{T}_{i,j}$	Parameter	New transportation time for transportation from supplier i to consumer j
$S\acute{C}_{i,p}$	Parameter	Changed capacity of supplier i for providing product p
α	Parameter	Percentage of allowed variation from the first objective function
β	Parameter	Percentage of allowed variation from the second objective function

Equation (11) shows the objective function of CE optimization model. Equation (12–15) show the constraints of the CE model.

Minimize Objective Function CE: $F_3(P_{i,j,p}) = \sum_{i,j,p} Effort_{i,j} * P_{i,j,p}$ (11)

Subject to:

Constraints (3–9)

$$X_{i,j,p}^{'} = X_{i,j,p}^{O} + P_{i,j,p}^{X} \quad \forall i,j,p \tag{12}$$

$$ta_{i,j,p}^{'} = ta_{i,j,p}^{O} + P_{i,j,p}^{T} \quad \forall i,j,p \tag{13}$$

$$F_1^{New}(X_{i,j,p}^{'}) \leq F_1^{Old}(X_{i,j,p}^{O}) * (1+\alpha) \tag{14}$$

$$F_2^{New}(AS_{j,p}, AL_{j,p}) \leq F_2^{Old}(AS_{j,p}, AL_{j,p}) * (1+\beta) \tag{15}$$

It is possible that either the data type 1 (e.g. suppliers capacity $SC_{i,p}$) or the data type 2 (e.g.transportation time$LT_{i,j}$) are changed. As mentioned, in the case of changing the inputs of the SCN, some deviation from constraints may happen. The CE model changes the allowed input data (e.g. the transported amount of products $X_{i,j,p}$ and arrival/departure time $td_{i,p}$ / $ta_{j,p}$) of the SCN to avoid future risks. The objective function of the CE model is to minimize the effort needed to change the transportation schedule, which is shown in Eq. (11). Moreover, it tries to maintain the financial cost of transportation and the penalty of deviation from time windows at the same level as the optimized SCN in stage 1. We defined two allowed limits (e.g. α and β) for the allowed increase in the two objective functions. First, the CE model ensures that the constraints of the SCN are satisfied; therefore, Eq. (3–9) are the constraints of the CE model. Equation (12) calculates the variation of the transported amount from each supplier to each consumer for each product. Equation (13) calculates the variation of the transportation time from each supplier to each consumer for each product. Equation (14–15) ensure that the objective functions of the designed SCN plan in the previous stage will not get worse than the allowed percentage.

Finally, by solving the CE optimization model, the RMCE framework, by considering the changes in the input parameters of the SCN, recommends a new feasible transportation plan in which two objective functions of the SCN are near optimum amounts. In addition, the CE model in providing its recommendations considers the interdependency of parameters; for a solution that is not an outlier since the solved model is feasible.

4   Implementation of RMCE Framework and Case Study

This section will examine the proposed RMCE framework to validate the results. To do that, a two-echelon SCN is considered based on an open-source Data Base (DB) [13] that includes records of delivery of different products from suppliers to consumers worldwide in four years. The scheduled and actual delivery times exist in this DB; therefore, it is possible to predict the actual transportation time for deliveries in the future. This DB has a great capacity to predict the parameters of SCN; therefore, first, the optimised SCN is planned by the model in Sect. 3.1. Then, by considering the predicted transportation time and other disruptions, the CE model considers the probable future risks and recommends mitigation strategies in case of necessity.

4.1   Designing Prediction Model for SCN Parameters

There are 53 features and around 181000 records in the analysed DB. For each record, scheduled TT, Order City, Order Profit Per Order, Product Name, Full Customer Name, order year, order month, order day, and order Hours are used to train the machine. The actual Transportation Times (TT) in the DB is the target of the prediction.

This research uses a classification model to predict TT. The target of the classification model is actual TT. In the DB, actual TT is integer values ranging from 0 to 6 d. Therefore, we consider seven classes for the labels, and the learner should predict each record's class. For instance, if the classification model predicts class 6 for a given input vector, it means that transportation takes six days (Classes start from 0 to 6). We applied different well-known classification learning models, and the Decision Tree (DT) model could predict by the F_1 score of 85%.

Meanwhile, we tested ensemble-based classifiers to improve the accuracy and reduce over-fitting risks: Random Forest (RF) and XGBoost classifiers. The results for the XGBoost were better than other used classifiers by the F_1 of 91%. Therefore, the output of the XGBoost classifier was used for further steps.

4.2   Optimisation Model to Design SCN Schedule

In this section, the parameters of the SCN explained in Sect. 3.1 will be used. To avoid the computational complexity of the optimisation model; we used a subset of the DB that consists of three suppliers, 28 consumers and 13 products to design the SCN schedule. We extracted the demand, supplier capacity and delivery time windows of products from the subset DB. The optimal schedule of transportation is as Table 5.

Table 5. The optimal transportation schedule

Supplier	1	1	1	1	1	1	1	1	1	1	1	1	1	1	1	2	2	2	2	2	2	2	2	2	2	2	2	3	3	3	3	3
Consumer	3	5	8	9	11	12	13	15	16	17	20	22	23	24	26	1	2	4	6	17	18	19	21	24	25	27	28	5	7	10	14	20
Product 1																							151					1				
2																273					1				146							
3		215	140	140				244		53					148					271			151			54						
4																273																
5	105			140					148						118						117			121								
6																			180													211
7															33						110	117										
8					94					53																						
9					186	144	137																					213	24		273	
10																273																
11											109																					
12																	211															
13																														28		

Table 5 shows the departure dates of the vehicles from the suppliers for each product. The consumers will receive the products TT days after the departure dates, which is the transportation time for each pair of supplier-consumer. In total, 32 transportation have been done, and all demands are satisfied. The total transportation cost is 1263 dollars, and there is no deviation in time windows, so there is no penalty cost. Notably, the scheduled transportation times are used to plan the SCN, which may be different in practice. In the next stage, the RMCE predict the possible future risks and recommends mitigation strategies.

4.3   Proposing Recommendations Based on the Counterfactual Explanation Optimisation Model

This section examines the effectiveness of the RMCE framework. In case of disruptions, we solve the CE optimisation model, Sect. 3.2, to recommend some mitigation strategies. These modifications consider the constraints of the SCN and the interdependency of parameters. The actual transportation times may be longer or shorter than the scheduled ones. So, the arrival times may be different from the scheduled ones. Based on the historical data, the RMCE framework predicts transportation times. Departure dates are the same as shown in Table 5. The RMCE calculates new arrival dates for consumers, which are more realistic than the planned ones because they use historical data to predict transportation times.

The probable risks caused by variation of the transportation times are considered. Besides that, the disruption of unavailability of suppliers to provide some products is applied too. The probable risks in the SCN are presented in Table 6. All recommendations to avoid each risk are shown in Table 7; in some cases, there may be multiple choices (e.g. risks 2 and 7). In the case study, changing the departure date has no cost, but changing the supplier may cost.

Table 6. The probable risks predicted by the RMCE

No	Supplier	Consumer	Product	Explanation of the problem	Category of risks
1	2	24	2	If you transport products on day 146, you will probably have two days advanced delivery	Advanced delivery
2	2	6	3	If you transport products on day 271, you will probably have one day advanced delivery	Advanced delivery
3	1	17	11	If you transport products on day 109, you will probably have one day advanced delivery	Advanced delivery
4	3	10	13	If you transport products on day 28, you will probably have two days advanced delivery	Advanced delivery
5	2	27	3	If you transport products on day 54, you will probably have one day advanced delivery	Advanced delivery
6	1	16	3	If you transport products on day 53, you will probably have two days delay in delivery	Late delivery
7	3	20	6	If you transport products on day 211, you will probably have one day delay in delivery	Late delivery
8	1	12	8	Supplier 1 is no longer available for providing product 8, the consumer 12 may confront with unsatisfied demand	Supplier unavailability
9	1	16	8	Supplier 1 is no longer available for providing product 8, the consumer 16 may confront with unsatisfied demand	Supplier unavailability

Table 7. The recommendation generated by the CE model and its explanation

No	Recommendation	Explanation	Recommendation cost	Alternative recommendation	Explanation	Recommendation cost
1	$P^T_{2,24,2} = 2$	Postpone departure date two days later on day 148	No	N.A	No	N.A
2	$P^T_{2,6,3} = 1$	Postpone departure date one day later on day 272	No	$P^X_{2,6,3} = -1$ & $P^X_{1,6,3} = +1$	Changing the supplier 2 to supplier 1 for delivery of product 3	8 dollars
3	$P^T_{1,17,11} = 1$	Postpone departure date one day later on day 110	No	N.A	No	N.A
4	$P^T_{3,10,13} = 2$	Postpone departure date two days later on day 28	No	N.A	No	N.A
5	$P^T_{2,27,3} = 1$	Postpone departure date one day later on day 55	No	N.A	No	N.A
6	$P^T_{1,16,3} = -3$	Bring forward departure date three days sooner on day 50	No	N.A	No	N.A
7	$P^T_{3,20,6} = -1$	Bring forward departure date one day sooner on day 210	No	$P^X_{3,20,3} = -6$ & $P^X_{2,20,6} = +6$	Changing the supplier 3 to supplier 2 for delivery of product 6	12 dollars
8	$P^X_{1,12,8} = -1$ & $P^X_{2,12,8} = +1$	Changing the supplier 1 to supplier 2 for delivery of product 8	1 dollar	N.A	No	N.A
9	$P^X_{1,16,8} = -1$ & $P^X_{2,16,8} = +1$	Changing the supplier 1 to supplier 2 for delivery of product 8	8 dollars	N.A	No	N.A

Three categories of identified risks were monitored: Advanced and delayed deliveries and supplier unavailability. It is noteworthy to mention that it is possible to consider other risks (e.g. demand fluctuation, road closure), monitor them, and try to eliminate their impact on the SCN. The identified risks are based on the nature of the SCN and the players. We just considered these three risk categories in this case study based on the available data.

The CE optimisation model recommends a mitigation strategy to avoid risks. The output of the recommender system is shown in Table 7. In some cases, If the user does not accept the first optimised recommendation, the CE model recommends an alternative mitigation strategy shown in Table 7 (No. 2 & 7). These are the output of the optimisation model of Sect. 3.2 based on the input of the case study. The recommendations are explained to make them more understandable and transparent for the user. Some recommendations lead to extra transportation costs because of changing the supplier.

Advanced and delayed deliveries are more frequent than others. The RMCE recommends postponing or bringing forward the departure date or changing the supplier alternatively. The third category of risks is an external event in which the user manually enters the CE model; supplier 1 is no longer available to provide product 8. So, the RMCE recommend ordering those products from supplier two, which is available for providing product 8. However, these changes may have some increase in transportation costs.

All the changes are validated by the target values of actual transportation times. There are some other deviations from scheduled TT, but they are in the range of the time windows. So, no future risk will happen for them, and no action is required. However, some changes are recommended for those deviations which impact customer satisfaction for the arrival times (e.g. risks 1–7).

There are two advantages of the proposed framework; first, the explainability of the probable risks and the recommendations, and second the intelligence of the recommendations to consider constraints and objectives of the SCN.

5   Conclusion and Future Works

In this paper, the RMCE framework has been explained. It uses optimisation models to plan SCN and improves the accuracy of the SCN plan by using prediction models to forecast future events. Meanwhile, the user can enter some external events into the model manually. If the events impact the profitability or well-being of the players of the SCN, RMCE recommends strategies to avoid them. Both risks and recommendations are explainable to the risk manager. In addition, by getting advantages of the optimisation models, multiple aspects of the SCN are considered to monitor risks and generate recommendations.

For future studies, we recommend considering large-scale SCNs with more players and tires and considering the ripple effect of the risks in SCN.

References

1. Harinarayan, R.R.A., Shalinie, S.M.: XFDDC: eXplainable Fault Detection Diagnosis and Correction framework for chemical process systems. Process Saf. Environ. Prot. **165**, 463–474 (2022)
2. Kanamori, K., Takagi, T., Kobayashi, K., Arimura, H.: DACE: distribution-aware counterfactual explanation by mixed-integer linear optimization. In: IJCAI, pp. 2855–2862 (2020)
3. Ordibazar, A.H., Hussain, O., Saberi, M.: A recommender system and risk mitigation strategy for supply chain management using the counterfactual explanation algorithm. In: International Conference on Service-Oriented Computing, pp. 103–116. Springer, Cham (2022). https://doi.org/10.1007/978-3-031-14135-5_8
4. Poyiadzi, R., Sokol, K., Santos-Rodriguez, R., De Bie, T., Flach, P.: FACE: feasible and actionable counterfactual explanations. In: Proceedings of the AAAI/ACM Conference on AI, Ethics, and Society, pp. 344–350 (2020)
5. Bajaj, M., et al.: Robust counterfactual explanations on graph neural networks. In: Advances in Neural Information Processing Systems, vol. 34, pp. 5644–5655 (2021)
6. Mothilal, R.K., Sharma, A., Tan, C.: Explaining machine learning classifiers through diverse counterfactual explanations. In: Proceedings of the 2020 Conference on Fairness, Accountability, and Transparency, pp. 607–617 (2020)

7. Tran, K.H., Ghazimatin, A., Saha Roy, R.: Counterfactual explanations for neural recommenders. In: Proceedings of the 44th International ACM SIGIR Conference on Research and Development in Information Retrieval, pp. 1627–1631 (2021)
8. Cavalcante, I.M., Frazzon, E.M., Forcellini, F.A., Ivanov, D.: A supervised machine learning approach to data-driven simulation of resilient supplier selection in digital manufacturing. Int. J. Inf. Manag. **49**, 86–97 (2019)
9. Nayal, K., Raut, R., Priyadarshinee, P., Narkhede, B.E., Kazancoglu, Y., Narwane, V.: Exploring the role of artificial intelligence in managing agricultural supply chain risk to counter the impacts of the COVID-19 pandemic. Int. J. Logistics Manag. (2021)
10. Budiman, S.D., Rau, H.: A stochastic model for developing speculation-postponement strategies and modularization concepts in the global supply chain with demand uncertainty. Comput. Ind. Eng. **158**, 107392 (2021)
11. Schätter, F., Hansen, O., Wiens, M., Schultmann, F.: A decision support methodology for a disaster-caused business continuity management. Decis. Support Syst. **118**, 10–20 (2019)
12. Gupta, S., Modgil, S., Meissonier, R., Dwivedi, Y.K.: Artificial intelligence and information system resilience to cope with supply chain disruption. In: IEEE Transactions on Engineering Management (2021)
13. Tiwari, S.: DataCo smart supply chain for big data analysis. www.kaggle.com/datasets/shashwatwork/dataco-smart-supply-chain-for-big-data-analysis

Explainable Predictive Decision Mining for Operational Support

Gyunam Park[1]([⊠]), Aaron Küsters[2], Mara Tews[2], Cameron Pitsch[2], Jonathan Schneider[2], and Wil M. P. van der Aalst[1]

[1] Process and Data Science Group (PADS), RWTH Aachen University, Aachen, Germany
{gnpark,wvdaalst}@pads.rwth-aachen.de
[2] RWTH Aachen University, Aachen, Germany
{aaron.kuesters,mara.tews,cameron.pitsch, lennart.schneider}@rwth-aachen.de

Abstract. Several decision points exist in business processes (e.g., whether a purchase order needs a manager's approval or not), and different decisions are made for different process instances based on their characteristics (e.g., a purchase order higher than €500 needs a manager approval). Decision mining in process mining aims to describe/predict the routing of a process instance at a decision point of the process. By predicting the decision, one can take proactive actions to improve the process. For instance, when a bottleneck is developing in one of the possible decisions, one can predict the decision and bypass the bottleneck. However, despite its huge potential for such operational support, existing techniques for decision mining have focused largely on describing decisions but not on predicting them, deploying decision trees to produce logical expressions to explain the decision. In this work, we aim to enhance the predictive capability of decision mining to enable proactive operational support by deploying more advanced machine learning algorithms. Our proposed approach provides explanations of the predicted decisions using SHAP values to support the elicitation of proactive actions. We have implemented a Web application to support the proposed approach and evaluated the approach using the implementation.

Keywords: Process mining · Decision mining · Machine learning · Operational support · Proactive action

1 Introduction

A process model represents the control-flow of business processes, explaining the routing of process instances. It often contains decision points, e.g., XOR-split gateway in BPMN. The routing in such decision points depends on the data attribute of the process instance. For instance, in a loan application process, the assessment of a loan application depends on the amount of the loan, e.g., if the amount is higher than €5,000, it requires *advanced assessment* and, otherwise, *simple assessment*.

© The Author(s), under exclusive license to Springer Nature Switzerland AG 2023
J. Troya et al. (Eds.): ICSOC 2022 Workshops, LNCS 13821, pp. 66–79, 2023.
https://doi.org/10.1007/978-3-031-26507-5_6

Decision mining in process mining aims to discover a decision model that represents the routing in a decision point of a business process [8]. The discovered decision model can be used for 1) describing how decisions have been made and 2) predicting how decisions will be made for future process instances. While the focus has been on the former in the literature, the latter is essential to enable proactive actions to actually improve business processes [13]. Imagine we have a bottleneck in *advanced assessment* due to, e.g., the lack of resources. By predicting the decision of a future loan application, we can take proactive action (e.g., suggesting to lower the loan amount to conduct *simple assessment*), thus facilitating the process.

To enable such operational support, a decision model needs to be both 1) predictive (i.e., the model needs to provide reliable predictions on undesired/ decisions) and 2) descriptive (i.e., domain experts should be able to interpret how the decision is made to elicit a proactive action). Figure 1 demonstrates these requirements. Figure 1(a) shows a decision point in a loan application process, and there is a bottleneck in *advanced assessment*. Our goal is to accurately predict that a loan application with the amount of €5,500 and interest of 1.5% needs *advanced assessment*, which is undesired due to the bottleneck, and recommend actions to avoid the bottleneck. Figure 1(b) shows four different scenarios. First, if we predict a desired decision (i.e., predicting the simple assessment), no action is required since the simple assessment has no operational issues. Second, if we predict an undesired prediction incorrectly (e.g., incorrectly predicting the advanced assessment), we recommend an inadequate action. Third, if we predict the undesired decision correctly but no explanations are provided, no action can be elicited due to the lack of explanations. Finally, if we predict the undesired decision, and the corresponding explanations are provided (e.g., the amount/interest of the loan has a positive/negative effect on the probability of conducting the advanced assessment, respectively), we can come up with relevant actions (e.g., lowering the amount or increasing the interest rate).

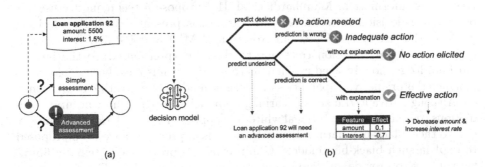

Fig. 1. (a) Decision point in a process model. (b) Different scenarios showing that decision mining needs to be predictive and descriptive to enable operational support.

Existing work has focused on the descriptive capability of decision models by deploying highly interpretable machine learning algorithms such as decision trees [8,11,15]. However, it leads to limited predictive capability due to the limitation of decision trees, such as overfitting and instability (i.e., adding a new data point results in regeneration of the overall tree) [16]. In this work, we aim to enhance the predictive capabilities of decision mining, while providing explanations of predicted decisions. To this end, we estimate the decision model by using machine learning algorithms such as support vector machines, random forests, and neural networks. Next, we produce explanations of the prediction of the decision model by using SHAP values.

We have implemented the approach as a standalone web application. Using the implementation, we have evaluated the accuracy of predicted decisions using real-life event logs. Moreover, we have evaluated the reliability of explanations of predicted decisions by conducting controlled experiments using simulation models.

This paper is structured as follows. First, we discuss related work on decision mining and explainability in Sect. 2. Next, we introduce process models and event logs in Sect. 3. In Sect. 4, we provide our proposed approach. In Sect. 5, we explain the implementation of a web application based on the approach. Sect. 6 evaluates the approach based on the implementation using simulated and real-life event logs. We conclude this paper in Sect. 7.

2   Related Work

Several approaches have been proposed to learn decision models from event logs. Rozinat et al. [15] suggest a technique based on Petri nets. It discovers a Petri net from an event log, identifies decision points, and employs classification techniques to determine decision rules. De Leoni et al. [8] extend [15] by dealing with invisible transitions of a Petri net and non-conforming process instances using *alignments*. These methods assume that decision-making is deterministic and all factors affecting decisions exist in event logs. To handle non-determinism and incomplete information, Mannhardt et al. [11] propose a technique to discover overlapping decision rules. In [2], a framework is presented to derive decision models using Decision Model and Notation (DMN) and BPMN. All existing approaches deploy decision trees due to their interpretability. To the best of our knowledge, no advanced machine learning algorithms have been deployed to enhance the predictive capabilities of decision models along with explanations.

Although advanced machine learning approaches provide more accurate predictions compared to conventional white-box approaches, they lack explainability due to their black-box nature. Recently, various approaches have been proposed to explain such black-box models. Gilpin et al. [4] provide a systematic literature survey to provide an overview of explanation approaches. The explanation approaches are categorized into *global* and *local* methods. First, global explanation approaches aim to describe the average behavior of a machine learning model by analyzing the whole data. Such approaches include Partial Dependence Plot (PDP) [6], Accumulated Local Effects (ALE) Plot [1], and global surrogate models [3]. Next, local explanation approaches aim to explain individual predictions by individually examining the instances. Such approaches include Individual Conditional Expectation (ICE) [5], Local Surrogate (LIME) [14], and Shapley Additive Explanations (SHAP) [10]. In this work, we use SHAP to explain the predictions produced by decision models due to its solid theoretical foundation in game theory and the availability of global interpretations by combining local interpretations [10].

3   Preliminaries

Given a set X, we denote the set of all multi-sets over X with $\mathcal{B}(X)$. $f\!\restriction_X$ is the function projected on X: $dom(f\!\restriction_X) = dom(f) \cap X$ and $f\!\restriction_X(x) = f(x)$ for $x \in dom(f\!\restriction_X)$.

3.1   Process Models

Decision mining techniques are independent of the formalism representing process models, e.g., BPMN, YWAL, and UML-activity diagrams. In this work, we use Petri nets as the formalism to model the process.

First, a Petri net is a directed bipartite graph of places and transitions. A labeled Petri net is a Petri net with the transitions labeled.

Definition 1 (Labeled Petri Net). *Let* $\mathbb{U}_{act}$ *be the universe of activity names. A labeled Petri net is a tuple* $N=(P,T,F,l)$ *with* P *the set of places,* T *the set of transitions,* $P \cap T = \emptyset$, $F \subseteq (P \times T) \cup (T \times P)$ *the flow relation, and* $l \in T \nrightarrow \mathbb{U}_{act}$ *a labeling function.*

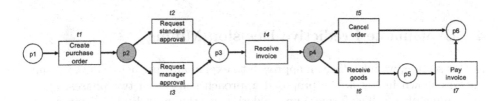

Fig. 2. An example of Petri nets highlighted with decision points.

Figure 2 shows a Petri net, $N_1 = (P_1, T_1, F_1, l_1)$, where $P_1 = \{p1, \ldots, p6\}$, $T_1 = \{t1, \ldots, t7\}$, $F_1 = \{(p1, t1), (t1, p2), \ldots\}$, $l_1(t1) = $ *Create purchase order,* $l_1(t2) = $ *Request standard approval,* etc.

The state of a Petri net is defined by its marking. A marking $M_N \in \mathcal{B}(P)$ is a multiset of places. For instance, $M_{N_1} = [p1]$ represents a marking with a token in $p1$. A transition $tr \in T$ is *enabled* in marking M_N if its input places contain at least one token. The enabled transition may *fire* by removing one token from each of the input places and producing one token in each of the output places. For instance, $t1$ is *enabled* in M_{N_1} and *fired* by leading to $M'_{N_1} = [p2]$.

Definition 2 (Decision Points). *Let $N=(P,T,F,l)$ be a labeled Petri net. For $p \in P$, $p\bullet = \{t \in T \mid (p,t) \in F\}$ denotes it outgoing transitions. $p \in P$ is a decision point if $|p\bullet| > 1$.*

For instance, $p2$ is a decision point in N_1 since $p2\bullet = \{t2, t3\}$ and $|p2\bullet| > 1$.

Table 1. An example of event logs.

Case id	Activity	Timestamp	Resource	Total-price	Vendor
PO92	Create purchase order	09:00 05.Oct.2022	Adams	1,000	Apple
PO92	Request standard order	11:00 07.Oct.2022	Pedro	1,000	Apple
PO93	Create purchase order	13:00 07.Oct.2022	Peter	1,500	Samsung
...	...	...	...	...	...

3.2 Event Logs

Definition 3 (Event Logs). *Let $\mathbb{U}_{event}$ be the universe of events, $\mathbb{U}_{attr}$ the universe of attribute names ($\{case, act, time, res\} \subseteq \mathbb{U}_{attr}$), and $\mathbb{U}_{val}$ the universe of attribute values. An event log is a tuple $L = (E, \pi)$ with $E \subseteq \mathbb{U}_{event}$ as the set of events and $\pi \in E \to (\mathbb{U}_{attr} \nrightarrow \mathbb{U}_{val})$ as the value assignments of the events.*

Table 1 shows a part of an event log $L_1 = (E_1, \pi_1)$. $e_1 \in E_1$ represents the event in the first row, i.e., $\pi_1(e_1)(case) = PO92$, $\pi_1(e_1)(act) = Create\ Purchase\ Order$, $\pi_1(e_1)(time) = $ 09:00 05.Oct.2022, $\pi_1(e_1)(res) = Adams$, $\pi_1(e_1)(total\text{-}price) = 1,000$, and $\pi_1(e_1)(vendor) = Apple$.

4 Explainable Predictive Decision Mining

In this section, we introduce an approach to explainable predictive decision mining. As shown in Fig. 3, the proposed approach consists of two phases: *offline* and *online* phases. The former aims to derive decision models of decision points, while the latter aims at predicting decisions for running process instances along with explanations. In the offline phase, we compute *situation tables* based on historical event logs and estimate decision models using the *situation tables*. In the online phase, we predict decisions for ongoing process instances and explain the decision.

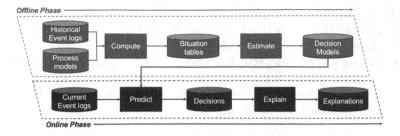

Fig. 3. An overview of the proposed approach.

4.1 Offline Phase

First, we compute situation tables from event logs. Each record in a situation table consists of features (e.g., total price of an order) and a decision in a decision point (e.g., $t2$ at decision point $p2$ in Fig. 2), describing how the decision has been historically made (e.g., at decision point $p2$ in Fig. 2, standard approval (i.e., $t2$) was performed when the total price of an order is €1,000).

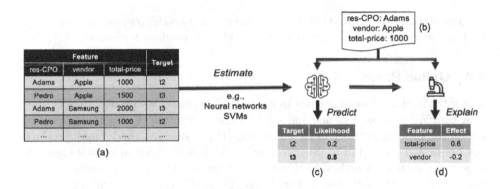

Fig. 4. An example of the proposed approach.

Definition 4 (Situation Table). *Let $\mathbb{U}_{feature}$ be the universe of feature names and $\mathbb{U}_{fmap} = \mathbb{U}_{feature} \nrightarrow \mathbb{U}_{val}$ the universe of feature mappings. Let $N=(P,T,F,l)$ be a labeled Petri net and $p \in P$ a decision point. $sit_p \in \mathbb{U}_L \mapsto \mathcal{B}(\mathbb{U}_{fmap} \times p\bullet)$ maps event logs to situation tables (i.e., multi-sets of feature mappings and decisions). $S_p=\{sit_p(L) \mid L \in \mathbb{U}_L\}$ denotes the set of all possible situation tables of p.*

The table in Fig. 4(a) represents a situation table of $p2$ in Fig. 2 derived from the event log depicted in Table 1. For instance, the first row in Fig. 4(a) describes that *request standard approval* ($t2$) was executed when human resource *Adams* performed *create purchase order* (i.e., *res-CPO*) for the order of €1,000 (i.e., *total-price*) with *Apple* (i.e., *vendor*). Formally, $s_1 = (fmap_1, t2) \in sit_{p2}(L1)$

where $fmap_1 \in \mathbb{U}_{fmap}$ such that $fmap_1 = \{(res\text{-}CPO, Adams), (vendor, Apple),$ $(total\text{-}price, 1{,}000)\}$. Note that, s_1 corresponds to event e_2 in Table 1 and $fmap_1$ is derived from all historical events of $PO92$.

A decision model provides the likelihood of each transition in a decision point based on a given feature, e.g., when the total price of an order (i.e., feature) is €1,800, standard approval will be performed with the likelihood of 0.2 and manager approval with the likelihood of 0.8.

Definition 5 (Decision Model). *Let $N=(P,T,F,l)$ be a labeled Petri net and $p \in P$ a decision point. Let $dmap_p \in p\bullet \to [0,1]$ be a decision mapping that maps decisions to likelihoods such that the sum of all likelihoods adds up to 1, i.e., $\Sigma_{p' \in p\bullet} dmap_p(p') = 1$. D_p denotes the set of all possible decision mappings. $DM_p \in \mathbb{U}_{fmap} \to D_p$ is the set of all possible decision models of p that map feature mappings to decision mappings.*

We estimate decision models based on situation tables.

Definition 6 (Estimating Decision Models). *Let $N=(P,T,F,l)$ be a labeled Petri net and $p \in P$ a decision point. $estimate_p \in S_p \to DM_p$ is a function estimating a decision model from a situation table.*

The estimation function can be built using many machine learning algorithms such as neural networks, support vector machines, random forests, etc.

4.2   Online Phase

Using the decision model derived from the offline phase, we predict the decision of a running process instance and explain the prediction. Using the feature of a running process instance depicted in Fig. 4(b), a decision model may produce the prediction shown in Fig. 4(c), leading to the final decision of *request manager approval* that has the highest likelihood. Next, we compute an explanation for the decision (i.e., the effect of each feature on the prediction) as shown in Fig. 4(d), e.g., *total-price* has a positive effect of 0.6 while *vendor* has a negative effect of 0.2. In other words, *total-price* increases the likelihood of predicting the decision of *request manager approval* by the magnitude of 0.6 and *vendor* decreases it by the magnitude of 0.2, respectively.

In this work, we use SHAP values [10] to provide explanations of decisions. SHAP values are based on *Shapley* values. The concept of *Shapley* values comes from *game theory*. It defines two elements: a game and some players. In the context of predictions, the game is to reproduce the outcome of the model, and the players are the features used to learn the model. Intuitively, Shapley values quantify the amount that each player contributes to the game, and SHAP values quantify the contribution that each feature brings to the prediction made by the model.

Definition 7 (Explaining Decisions). *Let $fmap \in \mathbb{U}_{fmap}$ be a feature mapping and $F = \{f_1, f_2, \ldots, f_i, \ldots\} = dom(fmap)$ denote the domain of $fmap$.*

Let $N=(P,T,F,l)$ be a labeled Petri net, $p \in P$ a decision point, and dm_p a decision model. Let $t \in p\bullet$ be a target transition. The SHAP value of feature f_i for predicting t is defined as:

$$\psi_{f_i}^t = \sum_{F' \subseteq F \backslash \{f_i\}} \frac{|F'|!(|F|-|F'|-1)!}{|F|!}(dm_p(fmap\lceil_{F' \cup \{f_i\}})(t) - dm_p(fmap\lceil_{F'})(t))$$

For $fmap$, $exp_{dm_p,t}(fmap) = \{(f_1, \psi_{f_1}^t), (f_2, \psi_{f_2}^t), \dots\}$ is the explanation of predicting t using dm_p.

As shown in Fig. 4(d), for feature mapping $fmap'$ described in Fig. 4(b), the explanation of predicting $t3$ (i.e., request manager approval) using decision model dm_{p2}' is $exp_{dm_{p2}',t3}(fmap') = \{(total\text{-}price, 0.6), (vendor, -0.2)\}$. In other words, $total\text{-}price$ has a positive effect with the magnitude of 0.6 on the decision of $t3$ and $vendor$ has a negative effect with the magnitude of 0.2.

Moreover, we can provide a global explanation of a decision model by aggregating SHAP values of multiple running instances. For instance, by aggregating all SHAP values of $total\text{-}price$ for predicting $t3$, e.g., with the mean absolute value, we can compute the global effect of $total\ price$ to the prediction.

5 Implementation

We have implemented a Web application to support the explainable decision mining with a dedicated user interface. Source code and user manuals are available at https://github.com/aarkue/eXdpn. The application comprises three functional components as follows.

Discovering Process Models. This component supports the discovery of process models based on inductive miner [7]. The input is event data of the standard XES. The discovered accepting Petri net is visualized along with its decision points.

Decision Mining. This component supports the computation of situation tables from event logs and the estimation of decision models from the computed situation table. First, it computes situation tables with the following three types of features:

- *Case features*: Case features are on a case-level and used for predicting all decisions related to that case.
- *Event features*: Event features are specific to an event and used for predicting decisions after the occurrence of the event.
- *Performance features*: Performance features are derived from the log. It includes *elapsed time of a case* (i.e., time duration since the case started) and *time since last event* (i.e., time duration since the previous event occurred).

Next, the estimation of decision models uses the following machine learning algorithms: *Random Forests*, *XGBoost*, *Support Vector Machines (SVMs)*, and *Neural Networks*.

Visualizing Decisions and Explanations. This component visualizes the F1 score of different machine learning algorithms and suggests the best technique based on the score. Moreover, it visualizes the explanation of the decision both at local and global levels. Local explanations are visualized with *force plot* (cf. Fig. 5(a)), *decision plot* (cf. Fig. 5(b)), and *beeswarm plot* (cf. Fig. 5(c)), whereas global explanations are visualized with *bar plot* (cf. Fig. 5(d)), *force plot* (cf. Fig. 5(e)), and *beeswarm plot* (cf. Fig. 5(f)). We refer readers to [9] for the details of different plots.

6   Evaluation

In this section, we evaluate the approach by conducting experiments using the implementation. Specifically, we are interested in answering the following research questions.

- RQ1: Does the advanced machine learning algorithm efficiently predict the decisions?
- RQ2: Does the approach provides reliable explanations for the predictions?

6.1   RQ1: Prediction Accuracy

In order to answer RQ1, we conduct experiments using real-life event logs: Business Process Intelligence Challenge (BPIC) 2012[1] and BPIC 2019[2]. For each event log, we first discover a process model and determine decision points. Then we estimate different decision models for each decision point and compare the performance of the decision models using 5-fold cross-validation. To measure the performance of the decision model, we use F1 scores. Each model is instantiated with suitable, event-log-specific parameters, which have largely been obtained from a parameter grid search on each decision point as well as manual test runs. For decision tree algorithms, we apply pruning steps to avoid too many splits that result in decision trees harder to interpret in practice due to their complexity.

Table 2 shows the F1 score of different machine learning algorithms in different real-life event logs[3]. The top two scores for each decision point are highlighted with bold fonts. *XGBoost* shows good scores for all decision points except $p14$ in BPIC 2012 and $p4$ in BPIC 2019. The scores for *Support Vector Machine* belong to the top two scores for most of the decisions except $p4$ and $p6$ in BPIC 2012

---

[1] https://doi.org/10.4121/uuid:3926db30-f712-4394-aebc-75976070e91f.

[2] https://doi.org/10.4121/uuid:d06aff4b-79f0-45e6-8ec8-e19730c248f1.

[3] The experimental results are reproducible in https://github.com/aarkue/eXdpn/tree/main/quantitative_analysis along with the corresponding process model.

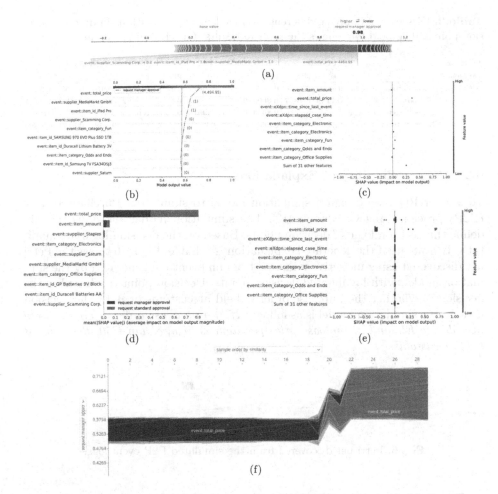

Fig. 5. Local explanations: (a) Force plot, (b) Decision plot, and (c) Beeswarm plot explain how the model arrived at the decision of a running instance (i.e., *request manager approval* with the likelihood of 0.98). For instance, (a) visualizes the positive (red-colored) and negative (blue-colored) features with increasing magnitudes. **Global explanations**: (d) Bar plot, (e) Beeswarm plot, and (f) Force plot explain how the model arrived at the decision of all running instances (both on *request standard approval* and *request manager approval*). For instance, (d) visualizes the mean absolute SHAP value for each feature on predicting *request standard approval* (blue-colored bar) and *request manager approval* (red-colored bar), showing that total-price has the highest impact on both predictions. (Color figure online)

and p8 and p11 in BPIC 2019, whereas the ones for *Neural Network* belong to the top two scores in p4, p6 and p14 in BPIC 2012 and p4 and p8 in BPIC 2019. *Decision Tree* shows the top two scores only for p16 in BPIC 2012 and p11 in BPIC 2019.

Table 2. F1 scores of applying different machine learning algorithms in different decision points. The bold font shows the top two results in each decision point.

Event logs		BPI challenge 2012 (only offers)						BPI challenge 2019 (filtered)			
Decision point		p4	p6	p12	p14	p16	p19	p3	p4	p8	p11
Algorithms	Decision tree	0.6888	0.7545	0.7955	0.9633	**0.9612**	0.9263	0.9555	0.9948	0.8135	**1.0000**
	XGBoost	**0.7189**	0.7897	**0.8004**	0.9697	**0.9612**	**0.9407**	0.9632	0.9948	**0.8293**	**1.0000**
	Support vector machine	0.7151	0.7799	**0.8023**	0.9701	**0.9612**	**0.9414**	0.9649	**0.9950**	0.8096	0.9997
	Neural network	**0.725**	**0.8048**	0.7955	**0.9698**	0.9607	0.9317	0.9583	**0.9981**	**0.8191**	0.9949

6.2   RQ2: Reliability of Explanations

To answer RQ2, we design a simulation model to simulate a Purchase-To-Pay (P2P) process using CPN tools [12]. The simulation model allows us to fully define the decision logic of decision points. Based on the decision logic, we qualitatively evaluate if the generated explanation is reliable. Figure 6 shows the Petri net discovered using inductive miner [7] from an event log generated by the simulation model, with highlighted decision points. Decision point (c) describes the decision of whether the purchase order is held at customs or not. The decision logic in the simulation model is as follows: *If 1) a purchase order originates from outside the EU and 2) the base price per item is higher than €50, the order is held at customs.*

Fig. 6. Petri net discovered from the simulated P2P event logs.

The beeswarm plot in Fig. 7(a) explains the decision at decision point (c). The Non-EU origin (high value of `origin_Non EU`) has a strong positive impact on the probability of being held at customs according to the decision model. Moreover, the existence of items in category `Odds and Ends`, which have low base prices, has a negative impact on the probability, whereas the existence of items in category `Electronics`, which have high base prices, has a positive impact on the probability. When the individual product names, categories, and vendors are excluded (see Fig. 7b), the four most impactful features that remain are exactly the ones used in the logic of the underlying simulation model: The EU or Non-EU origin, the total price and the number of items in the order. Overall the decision logic as interpretable through the plots corresponds to the underlying logic applied in the simulation model, showing that the explanation obtained is reliable.

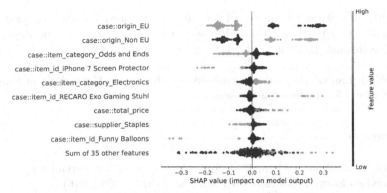

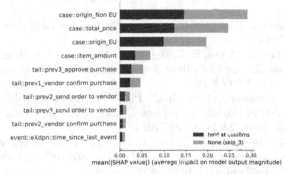

(a) Beeswarm plot visualizing the impact of high or low feature values on the model probability of being held at customs. The Non-EU origin (high value of origin_Non EU) has a strong positive impact on the probability of being held at customs.

(b) Bar plot visualizing the mean absolute SHAP value of each selected feature, per output class

Fig. 7. Qualitative analysis showing the explanation plots of decision point (c) using a neural network model.

7   Conclusions

In this paper, we proposed an approach to explainable predictive decision mining. In the offline phase of the approach, we derive decision models for different decision points. In the online phase, we predict decisions for running process instances with explanations. We have implemented the approach as a web application and evaluated the prediction accuracy using real-life event logs and the reliability of explanations with a simulated business process.

This paper has several limitations. First, the explanation generated by the proposed approach is less expressive than the logical expression generated by traditional decision mining techniques. Also, we abstract from the definition of features that can be used to construct the situation tables, focusing on explaining several possible features in the implementation. In future work, we plan to extend the approach with a taxonomy of features to be used for the comprehensive construction of situation tables. Moreover, we plan to connect the explainable predictive insights to actual actions to improve the process.

Acknowledgment. The authors would like to thank the Alexander von Humboldt (AvH) Stiftung for funding this research.

References

1. Apley, D.W., Zhu, J.: Visualizing the effects of predictor variables in black box supervised learning models. CoRR arXiv:abs/1612.08468 (2016)
2. Bazhenova, E., Weske, M.: Deriving decision models from process models by enhanced decision mining. In: Reichert, M., Reijers, H.A. (eds.) BPM 2015. LNBIP, vol. 256, pp. 444–457. Springer, Cham (2016). https://doi.org/10.1007/978-3-319-42887-1_36
3. Frosst, N., Hinton, G.E.: Distilling a neural network into a soft decision tree. CoRR arXiv:1711.09784 (2017)
4. Gilpin, L.H., Bau, D., Yuan, B.Z., Bajwa, A., Specter, M.A., Kagal, L.: Explaining explanations: An approach to evaluating interpretability of machine learning. CoRR arXiv:1806.00069 (2018)
5. Goldstein, A., Kapelner, A., Bleich, J., Pitkin, E.: Peeking inside the black box: visualizing statistical learning with plots of individual conditional expectation. J. Comput. Graph. Stat. **24**(1), 44–65 (2015)
6. Greenwell, B.M., Boehmke, B.C., McCarthy, A.J.: A simple and effective model-based variable importance measure. CoRR arXiv:1805.04755 (2018)
7. Leemans, S.J.J., Fahland, D., van der Aalst, W.M.P.: Discovering block-structured process models from event logs - a constructive approach. In: Colom, J.-M., Desel, J. (eds.) PETRI NETS 2013. LNCS, vol. 7927, pp. 311–329. Springer, Heidelberg (2013). https://doi.org/10.1007/978-3-642-38697-8_17
8. de Leoni, M., van der Aalst, W.M.P.: Data-aware process mining: discovering decisions in processes using alignments. In: Shin, S.Y., Maldonado, J.C. (eds.) 28th Annual ACM Symposium on Applied Computing, pp. 1454–1461. ACM (2013)
9. Lundberg, S.: Shap library documentation. https://shap.readthedocs.io/en/latest/index.html#. Accessed 05 Aug 2022
10. Lundberg, S.M., Lee, S.: A unified approach to interpreting model predictions. In: Guyon, I., et al. (eds.) NeurIPS 2017, pp. 4765–4774 (2017)
11. Mannhardt, F., de Leoni, M., Reijers, H.A., van der Aalst, W.M.P.: Decision mining revisited - discovering overlapping rules. In: Nurcan, S., Soffer, P., Bajec, M., Eder, J. (eds.) CAiSE 2016. LNCS, vol. 9694, pp. 377–392. Springer, Cham (2016). https://doi.org/10.1007/978-3-319-39696-5_23
12. Park, G., van der Aalst, W.M.P.: Towards reliable business process simulation: a framework to integrate ERP systems. In: Augusto, A., Gill, A., Nurcan, S., Reinhartz-Berger, I., Schmidt, R., Zdravkovic, J. (eds.) BPMDS/EMMSAD -2021. LNBIP, vol. 421, pp. 112–127. Springer, Cham (2021). https://doi.org/10.1007/978-3-030-79186-5_8
13. Park, G., van der Aalst, W.M.P.: Action-oriented process mining: bridging the gap between insights and actions. Prog. Artif. Intell. (2022). https://doi.org/10.1007/s13748-022-00281-7

14. Ribeiro, M.T., Singh, S., Guestrin, C.: "why should I trust you?": explaining the predictions of any classifier. In: Krishnapuram, B., Shah, M., Smola, A.J., Aggarwal, C.C., Shen, D., Rastogi, R. (eds.) 22nd SIGKDD, pp. 1135–1144. ACM (2016)
15. Rozinat, A., van der Aalst, W.M.P.: Decision mining in ProM. In: Dustdar, S., Fiadeiro, J.L., Sheth, A.P. (eds.) BPM 2006. LNCS, vol. 4102, pp. 420–425. Springer, Heidelberg (2006). https://doi.org/10.1007/11841760_33
16. Safavian, S.R., Landgrebe, D.A.: A survey of decision tree classifier methodology. IEEE Trans. Syst. Man Cybern. **21**(3), 660–674 (1991)

A Blockchain Oracle-Based API Service for Verifying Livestock DNA Fingerprinting

Amirmohammad Pasdar[1]([✉]), Young Choon Lee[1], Paul Ryan[2],
and Zhongli Dong[2]

[1] School of Computing, Macquarie University, Sydney, Australia
amirmohammad.pasdar@hdr.mq.edu.au, young.lee@mq.edu.au
[2] Aglive Pty Ltd., Geelong, Australia
{paul,andrew}@aglive.com

Abstract. Blockchain, a type of distributed ledger technology, has revolutionized the digital economy such as cryptocurrencies and supply chain management with its transparency, immutability, and decentralization properties. In addition, smart contracts are introduced to the blockchain to provide programmability removing third parties for administration. Although promising, blockchains and smart contracts are closed technologies meaning they have no interaction with the external world where real-world data and events exist, i.e., off-chain data. It becomes more challenging when the off-chain data is unstorable onto the blockchain due to data volume and privately maintained by third parties for security and confidentiality. In this paper, we address the problem of enabling a private blockchain platform to access privately owned sensitive off-chain data (i.e., DNA fingerprinting). This off-chain data is used for the traceability of products (i.e., products' origin) along the supply chain with a real-world livestock use case. To this end, we present a livestock blockchain oracle (LBO) as a service to mitigate the accessibility issue and automate the process of verifying purchasable products for livestock DNA fingerprinting verification. We have conducted an evaluation study using real-world livestock data from third-party service providers. Results based on the livestock product information and registered DNA service providers show that LBO is a reliable and responsive decentralized oracle blockchain for verification.

Keywords: Blockchain · Smart contracts · Blockchain oracles · DNA fingerprinting service

1 Introduction

Blockchain is a distributive technology revolutionizing the digital economy and decentralized finance (Defi) ecosystem. The use of blockchain can be seen in decentralized applications (DApps), including but not limited to food security [5]. A blockchain is a distributed ledger technology where transactions are permanently stored on many nodes. Transactions are messages digitally signed by cryptographic techniques for storing parameters/results and are immutable records collected in the form of blocks chained together through the hash. These blocks are appended to the ledger by consensus algorithms such as proof of work (PoW) or proof of stake (PoS) [15]. In addition, smart contracts are event-driven and self-executable programs that are compiled into bytecode. They are executed on the blockchain by employing available resources that attract transaction fees.

Smart contracts and blockchain technology have connectability issues meaning they have no access to real-world information and events (off-chain data). This information can be publicly available data (e.g., stock market data and exchange rates) or privately owned sensitive information in high volumes, such as DNA fingerprinting in the agriculture industry. Hence, they are closed technologies meaning they have no interaction with the external world; therefore, the usability of smart contracts is limited to the data on the blockchain (on-chain data). There should be a mechanism referred to as the "blockchain oracle" to bring real-world data into the blockchain and broaden the scope of smart contract operation. Oracles (or *data feeds*) are third-party services in the form of smart contracts deployed on the blockchain that send and verify the external information to the smart contracts [20]. They may consult with single or multiple sources (decentralized oracles) for fetching the required information.

There have been several studies on blockchain oracles, e.g., [4,6,9,20], for transferring data to the blockchain, but most if not all of them did not examine it from the private *industry* perspective. Chainlink [9] is a general-purpose and token-based framework for building secure decentralized input and output oracles. Town Crier [20] is an enclave-based oracle that employs Intel software guard extension (SGX) technology for ensuring data integrity. Adler et al., [4] present a general-purpose decentralized oracle referred to as Astraea that deals with binary queries, and Al Breiki et al., [6] propose a decentralized access control for the internet of things (IoT) data that is assisted by blockchain and trusted oracles.

This paper addresses the problem of enabling the private blockchain platform to access sensitive off-chain data through an API service with a case study for livestock DNA fingerprinting verification. DNA fingerprinting provides the traceability of livestock products (e.g., beef) at any point along the supply chain by comparing its DNA profile with an initial privately maintained sample. Third-party DNA services are already used on livestock farms, and DNA testing units fitted to smartphones can test and return a result in minutes without the need to send it out to the lab. The challenge is to connect the blockchain platform with these third-party DNA service providers holding privately owned sensitive data to provide a trusted and convenient way of verifying purchasable products.

To this end, we develop a livestock blockchain oracle (LBO shown in Fig. 1) as a service for DNA fingerprinting verification automation with real-world livestock data provided by third-party service providers. In particular, LBO employs three smart contracts: Oracle, Request, and Response. Oracle contract is in charge of registering the third-party APIs to be assigned to the queries submitted to the blockchain. The Request contract handles these queries and employs oracle reputation/performance metrics for selection to obtain the requested data. Returned results from the selected oracles are aggregated by the Response

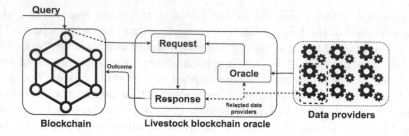

Fig. 1. Livestock blockchain oracle consists of three smart contracts; Oracle, Request, and Response.

contract, where the performance and reputation metrics of participated data providers are adjusted.

We design and implement LBO service that employs Web3j [3] as a lightweight Java and Android library for working with smart contracts and the Ethereum blockchain. We evaluate the performance of LBO based on real-world meat product information and a verified DNA service provider in terms of gas[1] consumption and turnaround time. Results present LBO as a reliable and responsive decentralized blockchain oracle.

The paper is organized as follows: Sect. 2 briefly overviews the related works on blockchain oracles and their design patterns. In Sect. 3, we present the livestock blockchain oracle in detail. In Sect. 4, the oracle is evaluated and we conclude the paper in Sect. 5.

2   Related Work

Blockchain oracles can be classified into three overlapping categories in terms of source, information direction, and trust. The source represents the origin of data, and the information direction implies how information flows (inbound or outbound) from/to external resources. Finally, trust can be centralized (single source) or decentralized (multiple sources).

In addition, from a technical perspective, blockchain oracles can be divided into two main groups based on how the outcome is finalized and saved onto the blockchain. They are referred to as voting-based oracles and reputation-based ones. Voting-based oracles, e.g., [4,7,8,10,13,14,16] employ participants' stakes for outcome finalization while the reputation-based oracles, e.g., [6,9,12,17–19] consider reputation or performance metrics in conjunction with authenticity proof mechanisms for data correctness and integrity.

Astraea [4] is a general-purpose decentralized oracle for binary queries. This oracle has entities such as submitter, voter, and certifier, each holding stakes. Voters play low-risk/low-reward games while certifiers play high-risk/high-reward games, and based on their outcomes and whether they are matched, rewards or

---

[1] Gas refers to the computational efforts required to execute specific operations on the Ethereum network.

penalties are distributed. Kamiya [13] provides an extension to Astraea, and in the extended version, two propositions are submitted, and rewards are distributed based on the different responses. Also, Merlini et al., [14] present a paired-question oracle that employs two antithetic questions for queries. If responses to queries are matched, the submitter reclaims the bond, and voters are rewarded or penalized if they agree or disagree with the majority of answers. Nelaturu et al., [16] provide a framework that employs a crowd-sourced voting mechanism that uses strategies for oracles like Astraea [4].

Cai et al., [8] present a peer prediction-based protocol that employs a nonlinear stake scaling with a lightweight scoring rule to control the rewards for the voters. Each report receives a score, that rewards are distributed to the top-scored voters by considering the accuracy and degree of agreement with peers. Buterin [7] shows a mechanism based on the Schellingcoin concept for creating decentralized data feeds. In this mechanism, submitted responses are sorted, rewards are distributed to the users who provide correct responses, and it is between specific percentiles. Velocity [10] is a decentralized market for trading a custom type of derivative option and uses a smart contract called PriceGeth to fetch the price information in real time.

He et al., [12] present a scalable data feed service that uses a reputation evaluation strategy assisted by TLSNotary [17] to detect malicious nodes. Woo et al., [19] propose a distributed oracle to import time-variant data into the blockchain by employing multiple oracles, and data integrity is assessed with the help of Intel SGX. Al Breiki et al., [6] present a decentralized access control for IoT data that is assisted by trusted oracles. Wang et al., [18] propose an oracle based on Application-Specific Knowledge Engines (ASKE) framework to acquire and analyze information. It automatically employs data analysis methods on the collected data managed by authoritative websites via web crawlers. Last but not least, Chainlink [9] is a general-purpose and token-based framework that employs a blockchain-agnostic token that can simultaneously run on different blockchains via external adapters for various data sources.

3   Livestock Blockchain Oracle (LBO) Service

This section describes the livestock blockchain oracle service structure, formulating the problem.

3.1   The Blockchain Events

The Ethereum blockchain employs events and logs to facilitate the communication between smart contracts and decentralized applications as events are methods to understand contract state changes. Contracts are allowed to log these changes by the Ethereum blockchain, and the Ethereum virtual machine (EVM) can retrieve and filter the events and their data about the state change.

In this regard, smart contracts emit events and record logs to the blockchain when a transaction is mined. In this case, the decentralized application (or the smart contracts) is notified to continue the process of a specific action. The livestock blockchain oracle uses blockchain events (e) as a means of communication.

Oracle Smart Contract Events. The Oracle smart contract events (o_e) can be grouped into two classes; registration events and controlling events. The former notifies the blockchain oracle, particularly the Request smart contract, that a new data provider is registered on the blockchain and can be employed to fetch requested query information. The latter refers to *controlling* events that restrict the registered data provider(s) in case of performance and trust issues. The controlling events trigger functions that activate/deactivate the registered data providers on the blockchain and inform the decentralized application.

Since the blockchain oracle relies on performance metrics, the participating data providers may be banned from being involved in the process for a certain time due to intermittent issues, e.g., being unresponsive to the queries or being unqualified to retrieve the data. These data providers might be activated again after screening their performance.

Request Smart Contract Events. Incoming requests to the blockchain oracle are managed by the Request smart contract, which emits two main events (r_e). When a request is created, the corresponding event is emitted that mostly maintains the information about the product identifier and associated information.

Once a request is created, it should be assigned to registered and qualified data providers for fetching the information notifying the Response contract to take over the process. In addition, it includes information about selected data providers for the specific request.

Response Smart Contract Events. When the Request events (p_e) are emitted, the Response contract will be in charge of fetching the required information by the involved data providers. It finalizes the feedback, returns the result to the blockchain, and updates the participant data providers' performance metrics. Thus, the Response smart contract emits events about when data providers return responses and whether the corresponding request becomes finalized.

Once data providers provide their responses, responses should be aggregated to return the final feedback to the blockchain and the application. The response contract will emit an event notifying the application that the corresponding request is finalized, attaching the final feedback and the corresponding data provider.

3.2   Smart Contracts

The overall structure of the designed blockchain oracle (Fig. 1) presents how smart contracts interact with each other through emitted events on the blockchain. The designed oracle has three smart contracts; Oracle, Request, and Response. It is a form of a reputation-based oracle, meaning metrics of data providers are computed and assessed for selection. It employs *trusted* data providers for fetching data and submitting it to the blockchain.

Oracle. This smart contract is responsible for registering third-party data providers and maintaining their reputation metrics. These reputation metrics are kept to assist requests with selecting eligible data providers to obtain data.

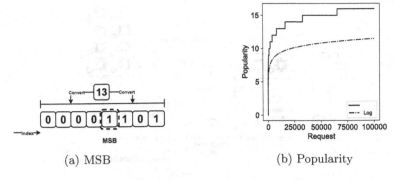

(a) MSB   (b) Popularity

Fig. 2. MSB and popularity of data providers; (a) MSB definition and (b) comparison between MSB and the natural logarithm for behavior.

Data providers are initially registered in the system, given zero popularity value, and each data provider can be accessed by its address. Each registered data provider has a deterministic address on the blockchain whose popularity value is managed by a function that employs the most significant bit (MSB) procedure to increase/decrease the value with respect to the performance of data providers.

Figure 2 illustrates how MSB is calculated; in Fig. 2a, the MSB is the largest index value in the binary format representation. Figure 2b shows the comparison between MSB and the natural logarithm, and the MSB mimics the logarithmic behavior in the real world as Solidity yet to support fixed-point number functionality. Hence, to control the popularity, MSB is employed that gradually and efficiently manages the value. This technique has two main benefits; firstly, the difference between the popularity of data providers is not prone to sudden spikes and immediate changes. This feature enables the blockchain oracle to rely fairly on the median value of its popularity. Secondly, by considering Fig. 2b, the sensitivity of updating the popularity is not linear or scaled to the number of served requests.

The Oracle contract also maintains the status of registered data providers and the monetary incentives/penalties in the form of balance they may be given. Suppose the data provider is untruthful or has low performance. In that case and regardless of their popularity value (recall the events of smart contracts; p_e and o_e), the data provider is deregistered and is not employed in the list of eligible data providers for fetching data.

Request. This smart contract maintains the requested query and holds information about assigned data providers with their provided stakes. This smart contract also relies on the Oracle contract to access the registered data providers.

Upon creating a request, an event will trigger the blockchain function to assign registered data providers to the request. Data providers are assigned to specific requests based on their popularity values and registration status.

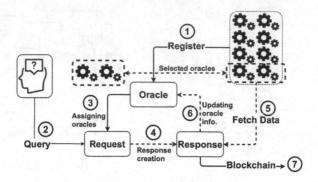

Fig. 3. Processing a request on the livestock blockchain oracle service.

The Request contract employs the median value (m) technique for selecting data providers within a set and has been used in the literature [7]. Per each request, the registration status of data providers is checked, the popularity values of the eligible data providers are sorted, and the median value is selected. This median value will act as a threshold for assigning data providers to the request to fetch the data. Hence, data providers with a larger popularity value than the median will be selected to retrieve data. As the median value is not affected by smaller or larger values, it becomes a suitable metric for choosing the data providers.

$$\mathbb{O}_i^r \leftarrow \{\forall\, o_i \in \mathbb{O} \,\exists\, m \text{ s.t. } \phi_i \geq m\} \tag{1}$$

In Eq. 1, m is the median value, and $\mathbb{O}_i^r$ is the list of eligible data providers to be assigned to the request (r_i). Once the list of data providers is ready, the Response contract will fetch the result for finalizing the outcome.

Response. The smart contract deals with fetching and storing responses of data providers and returning the final result (i.e., outcome) to the application.

Each response (p_i) maintains the block time, defined as a data provider's response arrival time. There is a response time window (ω) to ensure the data providers are responsive in a reasonable time. Otherwise, they will be penalized (i.e., reducing their popularity and holding their stakes) and may be deactivated after repeatedly being unresponsive.

Selected data providers by the Request smart contract will be in charge of retrieving data for the Response contract. If responses are not received within a specified time window, they will be discarded, and their data providers will be penalized. In addition, data providers will also be penalized when their outcomes do not match with the majority. The majority rule is a decision for choosing the one that more than half of the outcomes support. Hence, for $|\mathbb{P}|$ outcomes received in the specified time window, there is ξ_p representing the outcome that more than half of data providers agree with. Equation 2 illustrates the increase ($\uparrow$) or decrease ($\downarrow$) of popularity (ϕ_i) and their corresponding stakes considering the least arrival time (τ_p) and the response arrival time of a data provider (τ_i^p).

Algorithm 1: Livestock blockchain oracle (LBO)

Data: Data providers ($\mathbb{O}$), request (r_i), responses ($\mathbb{P}_i$), response time window (ω)

Result: Outcome (γ_i^r)

1 Register new data providers, update $\mathbb{O}$, and emit o_e

2 Check the registration status of data providers in $\mathbb{O}$ and sort the list w.r.t. popularity in ascending order

3 Compute median value $m \leftarrow Median(\mathbb{O})$ and notify the Response contract by emitting r_e

4 Initialize $\mathbb{P}_i^r \leftarrow \emptyset$, $\tau_i^r \leftarrow \emptyset$ & $\mathbb{O}_i^r$ w.r.t. Equation 1

5 **for** $o_i \in \mathbb{O}$ **do**

6 $\quad | \quad \mathbb{P}_i^r \leftarrow p_i^o$ & $\tau_i^r \leftarrow Time(p_i^o)$

7 **end**

8 $\tau_p \leftarrow \min\limits_{\forall \tau \ in \ \tau_i^r} \tau^r$

9 Compute $\xi_p \leftarrow \{\forall \ p_i \in \mathbb{P} \ s.t. \ |\tau_i^r - \tau_p| \leq \omega\}$

10 $\mathbb{P}_i^r \leftarrow \{\forall \ p_i \in \mathbb{P} \ \exists \ \tau_i^r \ s.t. \ |\tau_i^r - \tau_p| \leq \omega$ & $p_i = \xi_p\}$

11 $\gamma_i^r \leftarrow Median(\mathbb{P}_i^r)$ and emit p_e

---

$$\phi_i = \begin{cases} \uparrow \forall \ p_i : |\tau_i^p - \tau_p| \leq \omega \ \& \ p_i = \xi_p \\ \downarrow Otherwise. \end{cases} \tag{2}$$

Algorithm 1 in conjunction with Fig. 3 illustrates how a request is processed by the livestock blockchain oracle. Figure 3 shows that per each incoming request, eligible data providers should be selected, and this eligibility is managed by Eq. 1. Once the data providers are assigned to the request, the Response contract is notified by the event. The Response contract will maintain information about data retrieved by data providers and their arrival times. Per a specified time window, the least arrival time of responses is detected and is used to filter non-responsive data providers. These data providers will be penalized by reducing their popularity and withholding their stakes based on Eq. 2, and these updates will be saved onto the blockchain.

4   Evaluation

In this section, we evaluate the livestock blockchain oracle performance. We first explain the simulation setup and then discuss the LBO performance result.

4.1   Simulation Setup

The smart contracts of the livestock blockchain oracle are written in the Solidity programming language (v0.6.0 and compatible with higher versions) and are converted into Java classes by Web3j library [3] to be compatible with a mobile application. Web3j is a lightweight Java and Android library for working with smart contracts and integrating with nodes on the Ethereum blockchain [11].

Moreover, Ganache CLI is employed as a local Ethereum blockchain to test the decentralized application. It uses ethereumjs for simulating full client behavior and remote procedure calls (RPC) functions [1].

We use a sample real-world dataset that consists of essential livestock information, including the product identifier code (PIC), RFID, and comprehensive analysis of its minerals. Also, a third-party service provider recognized in industry traceability is used as a trusted and registered data provider for the blockchain oracle. The dataset is privately owned and securely stored in their database due to the sensitivity of the information. Hence, an API is provided for passing the product identifier for the dataset to output a binary result, i.e., valid or invalid. The API URL structure is shown in Eq. 3 in which φ is the product RFID to be passed to the URL.

$$curl - X\ GET$$
$$"https://tracebaseapi.azurewebsites.net/ \qquad (3)$$
$$RFID/\varphi" - H\ "accept:text/plain"$$

Randomly selected requests from the dataset are submitted to the blockchain for verification. We evaluate the performance of the designed blockchain oracle in terms of turnaround time and gas usage on the local Ethereum blockchain.

4.2 Simulation Results

We evaluate the livestock blockchain oracle service based on a scenario in which the number of data providers is increased for scalability, and the consumed gas is reported. The consumed gas mainly shows that the designed blockchain oracle will not hit the existing gas limit for execution. Due to the limitation of the provided datasets, their sensitiveness, and the way products are verified by the third party, the same provider is re-registered for each scenario. Since Request and Response contracts rely on the Oracle contract for interactions, the Oracle smart contract is deployed first, followed by the Request and Response smart contracts.

We consider increasing the number of data providers to 5 to evaluate the scalability, and requests are randomly chosen from the dataset. The scalability evaluation will provide insights into how it may affect the performance of the designed oracle. Per each finalized request, the consumed gas on the Ethereum blockchain and the request turnaround time is reported. Since the responsiveness of the third-party API affects the designed blockchain oracle performance, the delay of queries is computed and shown in Fig. 4.

Figure 4 presents how responsive the data provider is in fetching the query data as the server load (i.e., the response time) affects the turnaround time of the livestock blockchain oracle. Hence, Fig. 4a shows a significant delay in returning the feedback for the initial request(s) submitted to the API due to execution of underlying components, e.g., database query execution, with the average ∼710 ms. Apart from the initial delays (with a volatile average latency between ∼680 ms and ∼730 ms), the API has an average latency of ∼430 ms with volatile

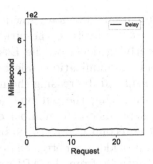
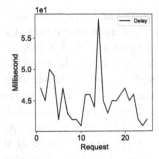

(a) The data provider API latency with (b) The latency after the short initial the very first request(s).   spike period.

Fig. 4. Query response time of the third party API. The significant delay at the beginning in Fig. 4a is due to the execution of underlying components, e.g., database query execution. Figure 4b can be seen as a microscopic view of Fig. 4a after the short initial spiky delay.

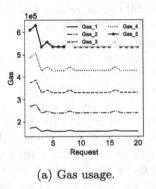
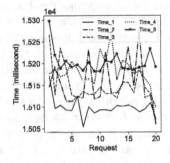

(a) Gas usage.   (b) Outcome turnaround time.

Fig. 5. Livestock blockchain oracle performance, (a) gas usage, (b) the scalability evaluation, and how long it takes to process a request. The number of participating data providers is shown as x in Gas_x (and $Time\_x$).

response time, including spikes that are shown in Fig. 4b. Figure 4b points out that improving the response time explicitly affects the user experience achieved via optimizing the database and the web server performance.

Figure 5 presents the livestock blockchain oracle service performance in consumed gas and the outcome's turnaround time. Figure 5a illustrates the consumed gas for all the scenarios where the number of data providers is increased. This Fig. 5a demonstrates that by increasing the number of data providers for retrieving data, the gas consumption also increases, and the gas consumption nearly has a linear relationship with the number of data providers in the system. The initial spike seen in the Figure could be related to the significant delay for requests (Fig. 4a) and the underlying delays between components of the blockchain oracle such as Web3j, Ganache CLI, and mining time.

Moreover, Fig. 5b presents the scalability evaluation and shows how long the livestock blockchain oracle takes to finalize a request. On average, the turnaround time for requests is ~15 s considering the underlying delay on the Ethereum blockchain for mining. In addition, the overhead communication time between the application and the blockchain should be considered. Increasing the number of data providers did not significantly impact finalizing the outcome and its turnaround time. The turnaround time seldom depends on the number of data providers, and it can be seen from Fig. 5b, for the second half of the submitted requests (≥ 10), the turnaround time of 5 data providers is better than 2 or 4 data providers. In addition, the spikes in Fig. 5b can be from the API response delay shown in Fig. 4b as well as underlying performance issues with the Web3j and Ganache CLI [2]. In other respects, the designed oracle has the potential to be converted into a reliable and fast decentralized blockchain oracle.

5   Conclusion

Blockchain technology has revolutionized the digital economy and has changed the financial market in the last few years. This disruptive technology is a distributed ledger technology where data is shared among nodes connected over the internet. Data state changes on the blockchain are permanently saved onto the immutable ledger in a decentralized way. Blockchain is enabled by smart contracts to provide programmability; although promising, blockchains and smart contracts do not have access to the external world. Hence, blockchain oracles are introduced to resolve blockchain connectability and expand the usability of smart contracts. This paper presented the livestock blockchain oracle (LBO) service as a use case study for the automation of livestock DNA fingerprinting verification evaluated by real-world livestock datasets. The challenge was to connect the blockchain platform with these third-party DNA service providers holding privately owned sensitive data to provide a trusted and convenient way of verifying purchasable products. The designed blockchain oracle provided the connectability feature and employed the performance metrics of third-party data providers for finalizing the outcome. Results showed that the LBO is a responsive decentralized oracle.

References

1. Ganache. https://www.trufflesuite.com/ganache (2021)
2. Performance regression in ganache-cli. https://github.com/trufflesuite/ganache-cli/issues/677 (2021)
3. Web3j: Web3 java ethereum dapp api. https://github.com/web3j (2021)
4. Adler, J., Berryhill, R., Veneris, A., Poulos, Z., Veira, N., Kastania, A.: Astraea: a decentralized blockchain oracle. In: 2018 IEEE International Conference on Internet of Things (iThings) and IEEE Green Computing and Communications (GreenCom) and IEEE Cyber, Physical and Social Computing (CPSCom) and IEEE Smart Data (SmartData), pp. 1145–1152. IEEE (2018). https://doi.org/10.1109/Cybermatics_2018.2018.00207

5. Ahmed, S., Ten Broek, N.: Blockchain could boost food security. Nature **550**(7674), 43–43 (2017)
6. Al Breiki, H., Al Qassem, L., Salah, K., Habib Ur Rehman, M., Sevtinovic, D.: Decentralized access control for IoT data using blockchain and trusted oracles. In: 2019 IEEE International Conference on Industrial Internet (ICII), pp. 248–257. IEEE (2019). https://doi.org/10.1109/ICII.2019.00051
7. Buterin, V.: Schellingcoin: a minimal-trust universal data feed. https://blog.ethereum.org/2014/03/28/schellingcoin-a-minimal-trust-universal-data-feed/ (2014)
8. Cai, Y., Fragkos, G., Tsiropoulou, E.E., Veneris, A.: A truth-inducing sybil resistant decentralized blockchain oracle. In: 2020 2nd Conference on Blockchain Research Applications for Innovative Networks and Services (BRAINS), pp. 128–135. Wiley (2020). https://doi.org/10.1109/BRAINS49436.2020.9223272
9. Ellis, S., Juels, A., Nazarov, S.: Chainlink a decentralized oracle network. https://link.smartcontract.com/whitepaper (2017)
10. Eskandari, S., Clark, J., Sundaresan, V., Adham, M.: On the feasibility of decentralized derivatives markets. In: Brenner, M., et al. (eds.) FC 2017. LNCS, vol. 10323, pp. 553–567. Springer, Cham (2017). https://doi.org/10.1007/978-3-319-70278-0_35
11. Ethereum: https://ethereum.org/en/whitepaper/ (2020)
12. He, J., Wang, R., Tsai, W., Deng, E.: SDFS: a scalable data feed service for smart contracts. In: 2019 IEEE 10th International Conference on Software Engineering and Service Science (ICSESS), pp. 581–585. IEEE (2019). https://doi.org/10.1109/ICSESS47205.2019.9040803
13. Kamiya, R.: Shintaku: An end-to-end-decentralized general-purpose blockchain oracle system. https://gitlab.com/shintakugroup/paper/blob/master/shintaku.pdf (2018)
14. Merlini, M., Veira, N., Berryhill, R., Veneris, A.: On public decentralized ledger oracles via a paired-question protocol. In: 2019 IEEE International Conference on Blockchain and Cryptocurrency (ICBC), pp. 337–344. IEEE (2019)
15. Mingxiao, D., Xiaofeng, M., Zhe, Z., Xiangwei, W., Qijun, C.: A review on consensus algorithm of blockchain. In: 2017 IEEE International Conference on Systems, Man, and Cybernetics (SMC), pp. 2567–2572. IEEE (2017). https://doi.org/10.1109/SMC.2017.8123011
16. Nelaturu, K., et al.: On public crowdsource-based mechanisms for a decentralized blockchain oracle. IEEE Trans. Eng. Manage. **67**(4), 1444–1458 (2020). https://doi.org/10.1109/TEM.2020.2993673
17. TLSnotary: Tlsnotary a mechanism for independently audited https sessions. https://tlsnotary.org/TLSNotary.pdf (2014)
18. Wang, S., Lu, H., Sun, X., Yuan, Y., Wang, F.: A novel blockchain oracle implementation scheme based on application specific knowledge engines. In: 2019 IEEE International Conference on Service Operations and Logistics, and Informatics (SOLI), pp. 258–262. IEEE (2019). https://doi.org/10.1109/SOLI48380.2019.8955107
19. Woo, S., Song, J., Park, S.: A distributed oracle using intel SGX for blockchain-based IoT applications. Sensors **20**(9), 2725 (2020)
20. Zhang, F., Cecchetti, E., Croman, K., Juels, A., Shi, E.: Town crier: an authenticated data feed for smart contracts. In: Proceedings of the 2016 aCM sIGSAC Conference on Computer and Communications Security, pp. 270–282. ACM (2016)

ASOCA: Adaptive Service-oriented and Cloud Applications

Introduction to the 6th Workshop on Adaptive Service-Oriented and Cloud Applications (ASOCA 2022)

The ASOCA 2022 workshop addressed the adaptation and reconfiguration issues of service-oriented and cloud applications and architectures.

An adaptive and reconfigurable service-oriented application can repair itself if any execution problems occur, in order to successfully complete its own execution, while respecting functional and non-functional agreements. In the design of an adaptive and reconfigurable software system, several aspects have to be considered. For instance, the system should be able to predict or to detect degradations and failures as soon as possible and to enact suitable recovery actions.

Topics

The main topics of the ASOCA 2022 workshop were devoted to the design and the implementation of adaptive and reconfigurable service-oriented and cloud applications and architectures. Specifically, the relevant topics include, but are not limited to:

- Distributed and centralized solutions for the diagnosis and repair of service-oriented and cloud applications;
- Design for diagnosability and repairability;
- Monitoring simple and composite architectures, components and services;
- Semantic (or analytic) architectural and behavioral models for monitoring of software systems;
- Dynamic reconfiguration of service-oriented and cloud applications;
- Planning and decision making;
- Technologies for ensuring autonomic properties;
- Predictive management of adaptability;
- Management of autonomic properties;
- Experiences in practical adaptive and reconfigurable service-oriented and cloud application;
- Tools and prototypes for managing adaptability.

Accepted Papers

The program committee selected 6 papers from 12 received papers based on the originality, quality, and relevance to the topics of the workshop. Each submission was reviewed by at least three reviewers. The list of accepted papers is as follows:

- Marwa Chaabane and Bruno Koller. *A Systematic Literature Review on Multi-modal Medical Image Registration.*

- Mamadou Lamine Gueye and Ernesto Exposito. *Education 4.0: Proposal of a Model for Autonomous Management of Learning Processes.*
- Daniel Friis Holtebo, Jannik Lucas Sommer, Magnus Mølgaard Lund, Alessandro Tibo, Junior Dongo and Michele Albano. *EXOGEM: Extending OpenAPI Generator for Monitoring of RESTful APIs.*
- Jiyoung Oh, Claudia Raibulet and Joran Leest. *Analysis of MAPE-K Loop in Self-Adaptive Systems for Cloud, IoT and CPS.*
- Gary White, Leonardo Lucio Custode and Owen O'Brien. *SASH: Safe Autonomous Self-Healing.*
- Imen Jdey. *Trusted Smart Irrigation System based on Fuzzy IoT and Blockchain.*

Acknowledgement

We are grateful to all program committee members and the external reviewers for their effort to read and discuss the papers in their area of expertise. We would also like to thank the authors for their submissions and for ensuring the success of this track.

November 2022   ASOCA 2022 Workshop Organizers

A Systematic Literature Review on Multi-modal Medical Image Registration

Marwa Chaabane[1,2]([✉]) and Bruno Koller[2]

[1] Department of Computer Science, University of Kiel, Kiel, Germany
marwa.mchaabone@gmail.com
[2] Scanco Medical AG, 8306 Brüttisellen, Switzerland

Abstract. Context: In today's health care, multi-modal image registration increasingly important role in medical analysis and diagnostics. Multi-modal image registration is a challenging task because of the different imaging conditions that changes from one imaging modality to another.
Objective: The purpose of this work is to determine the current state of the art in the field of medical image registration shedding light on techniques that have been used to register medical image combinations from different modalities and the importance of combining different modalities in automatic way in the medical domain.
Method: To fulfill this objective we chose a Systematic Literature Review (SLR) as method to follow. Which allows to collect and structure the information that exists in the field of multi-modal image registration.
Results: Several automatic solutions based on different registration techniques were proposed according to each specific modality combination.
Conclusion: The results provide the following conclusions: First, the machine learning in the recent years plays an important role in the automatic registration process. An important number of research propose a learning-based registration solution. Second, There few solutions in literature that tackle the automatic registration of histology - CT modality combination. Finally, the existing research work propose registration solutions for only combination of two modalities. A very few number of work suggest a tri-modality combining.

Keywords: Systematic Literature Review · SLR · Medical image registration · Multi-modal image · Registration

1 Introduction

Image registration is the process of transforming different image data sets into one coordinate system with matched imaging contents, which has significant applications in the medical domain. Registration improves the analysis of a pair of images that were performed from different viewpoints or based on different modalities [9,15]. Until recently, image registration was a manual tasks done by

J. Troya et al. (Eds.): ICSOC 2022 Workshops, LNCS 13821, pp. 97–105, 2023.
https://doi.org/10.1007/978-3-031-26507-5_8

the expert of the medical domain. On the other hand, several image registration tasks are quite challenging. Thus, the quality of manual matching is almost dependent upon the expertise of the user which can lacks accuracy. In order to fulfill the previously motioned limits of manual registration, a verity of automatic registration methods has been developed.

This paper presents an SLR on multi-modal medical image registration. A systematic review is a means of identifying, evaluating and interpreting all available research relevant to a particular research question (RQ), topic area, or phenomenon of interest in an unbiased and repeatable manner [10]. There are a number of different reasons to follow systematic reviews. Namely, providing a detailed summary of the current literature relevant to a RQ; to identify where there are limitations in current research work and help to decide where further study might be needed. The aim of this review is to aggregate the published knowledge on the topic of medical image registration.

2   Method

In this section, we describe the RQ and search strategy aiming to find all primary studies related to multi-modal medical image registration.

2.1   Research Questions

With the aim of finding all relevant primary studies that handles with the medical image registration from different modalities, we established the following research questions:

- RQ1: How the literature has addressed the multi-modal medical image registration?
- RQ2: Which automatic techniques and methods have been used to match 2D and 3D medical images?
- RQ3: What is the purpose of processing the image registration automatically?
- RQ4: Is the automatic image registration particular to specific modalities?

2.2   Search Strategy

Our search strategy is an organized structure of key words, related to the broad concepts of our search question, used to search a database.

Adding the different variations, and related terms to these key words we obtained three groupes:

- Groupe1: ("image", "images", "imaging")
- Groupe2: ("multi-modal", "multi modal", "multimodal", "multi modality", "multimodality", "multi-modality")
- Groupe3: ("matching", "registration", "registering")

Then, Boolean operators (AND and OR) allow us to try different combinations of search terms. Our final search string is: (**"image" OR "images" OR "imaging"**) AND (**"multi-modal" OR "multi modal" OR "multimodal" OR "multi modality" OR "multimodality" OR "multi-modality"**) AND (**"matching" OR "registration" OR "registering"**).

After establishing the search string, we selected the most commonly used publication databases to conduct SLR in computer science and image processing, namely: ACM Digital Library, IEEE Xplore, and Scopus. Springer was not considered in this SLR as it is already indexed by Scopus. It is important to notice that all databases required minor changes to the search string. In addition, we limited the search scope to **title, abstract, and keywords** of primary studies.

The selected sources are shown in Table 1.

Table 1. Literature sources.

Source	Type of source	Search URL
ACM Digital Library	Peer-reviewed paper	https://dl.acm.org
IEEE Xplore Digital Library	Peer-reviewed paper	https://ieeexplore.ieee.org
Springer	Peer-reviewed paper	www.springer.com
Science direct	Peer-reviewed paper	www.sciencedirect.com
Hyper Articles en Ligne (HAL)	Open archive	https://hal.archives-ouvertes.fr
Google Scholar	Meta search engine includes peer reviewed paper and grey literature	https://scolar.google.com

2.3   Selection Criteria

The selection criteria help in the identification of relevant primary studies. Therefore, Inclusion Criteria are used to select those primary studies that handles with the registration of multi-modal medical images. Conversely, Exclusion Criteria are useful to avoid the primary studies that do not address the main topics covered in this SLR, are not available, or are directly related to an included primary study of the same author.

The selection of relevant primary studies was further broken down into two steps: (i) selection of primary studies based on their title and abstract; (ii) selection of primary studies based on their full text.

In our selection process, we use the following Inclusion Criteria and Exclusion Criteria:

Inclusion Criteria:

- Publications that match one of the search items
- Publications that relate to the research questions
- Publications that do not have best practices examples

Exclusion Criteria:

- Publications are published before 2010
- Publications that do not match one of the search items
- Publications that do not relate to the search questions
- Publications that have best practices examples/results assessments

2.4 Data Collection

The number of papers resulting from the search is summarized in Table 2. After filtering irrelevant, duplicate and incomplete papers, a total of 45 papers were selected for the reviewing process. Table 3 presents the filtering process.

The state of the art is presented according to the different cases as follows. The selected papers per resources are distributed as shown in Table 4.

Table 2. Search results by resource.

Resource	Number of papers
Springer	70
IEE Xplore Digital Library	17
ACM Digital library	264
Google Scholar	54
Science Direct	28
Hyper Articles en Ligne (HAL)	16
Total	**449**

Table 3. Filtered search results.

Selection criteria	Number of papers
Irrelevant and duplicates	3
Incomplete and not related to RQ, Excluded by reading title and abstract	315
File not found	9
Total for Introduction reading	**122**
Not related to RQ, Excluded by reading Introduction	77
Total for reading	**45**

3   Findings

Out of 449 papers, 122 selected for introduction reading and were thus opened and inspected, yielding 45 relevant papers.

Table 4. Filtered search results by resource.

Resource	Number of papers
Springer	8
IEE Xplore Digital Library	3
ACM Digital library	20
Google Scholar	7
Science Direct	4
Hyper Articles en Ligne (HAL)	3

3.1 Multi-modal Medical Image Registration Techniques

This section deals with the RQ1 and explore the techniques that have been used for image registration from different modalities in the medical field. The image registration is divided into tow main categories: **"rigid registration"** which includes the intensity based techniques and **"non-rigid registration"** which includes the feature-based techniques [9]. The learning-based technique that belongs in some work to rigid registration and in some other work to non-rigid registration is the top used technique in the recent work with 11 articles [2, 4–6, 8, 11, 13, 14, 16, 19, 21].

In literature, there are some work dealing with 2D to 3D image registration -with the aim of combining histological sections to CT volumes-, and 3D to 3D image registration to combine CT to CT volumes over time, MRI to CT volumes and PET to CT volumes: The work of Huanjie et al. [20] proposes an algorithm to perform the image registration of 3D bone images coming from different modalities (MR, SPECT and CT) to combine anatomical and functional information. This algorithm aims to improve the image registration accuracy based on feature-based image registration method. Also, the research of Sabokrohiyeh et al. [18] is interested in image registration of 4D flow MRI (poor quality) to 3D cine MRI; multi 2D slices (high quality) following a sketch-based image registration method to improve registration accuracy. With the same objective of achieving a high accuracy, the work of Liu at al. [12] suggests a weighed image registration method based on curvature feature. In addition, the research of Albers et al. [2] is a recent work dealing with registration of 2D histological data to 3D CT volume based on an elastic image registration. This type of registration requires to be performed following 2 steps: Fist, retrieve the orientation of the 2D histology section to extract the appropriate section within the CT volume (manually). Then perform an automatic 2D to 2D registration. Even though the previously mentioned work are interested in performing 2D/3D to 3D image registration semi-automatically or automatically, they still limited to perform the registration image by image.

On the other hand, medical analysis rely on a big amount of imaging data. In this context, Xamflow[1] is a workflow-based framework proposed by Lucid.

---
[1] https://xamflow.lucid.ch/.

It enables to execute a workflow e.g. registration, on a vast imaging data set. This framework, allows to execute static workflows which fits to process imaging data which have the same characteristics, e.g. image registration of a set CT volumes scanned overtime with the same machine.

Thus, the existing solutions are limited to process data that have the same characteristics. The current solutions are time consuming and require the user's intervention along the steps of the registration process to adjust the registration parameters properly to the given data set characteristics.

3.2 Purpose of Multi-modal Medical Image Registration

Medical image registration is more and more gaining importance in several clinical applications namely Computer assisted Diagnosis, Computer aided Therapy, and Computer assisted Surgery [3,22,23]. The importance and usefulness of the automatic multi-modal image registration is coming from the growth and diversity of medical imaging modalities. I the medical domain each modality provide different types of information. For instance anatomical information about the underlying tissues is provided by Computed Tomography (CT) modality through the X-ray attenuation coefficient from X-ray. While proton density can be obtained with the Magnetic Resonance Imaging (MRI) modality. This kind of images allows the expert of the domain to quantify and visualize the size, shape and spatial relationship between anatomical structures and any pathology.

On the other hand there are other modalities that provide functional information such as the blood flow or glucose metabolism e.g.: Positron Emission Tomography (PET) modality. Which allows the experts of the domain to study the relationship between anatomy and physiology. In addition to that, microscopy images collected either in-vivo or ex-vivo as histology images provide another important source of information which illustrate structures at microscopic level [17].

Thus the automatic multi-modal image registration techniques importance arises from their ability to help the experts in the diagnosis [1,7].

3.3 Modalities Used in Automatic Image Registration Techniques

This section deals with the third RQ and looks at work what are the modality combinations tackled by the automatic image registration techniques. We found 27 over 45 papers that dealt with this RQ. Figure 1 reveals that a large majority of the papers contribute to CT to MRI modality combination (33%). On second place, histology to CT modality combination is addressed by a one fifth of the papers (20%). 16% of addressed papers are interested in the image registration of CT to US modality combination as well as US to MRI modality combination and 10% of studies handling PET to CT modality combination. Finally, image registration work devoted for tri-modality combination are addressed by only (5%) of the papers.

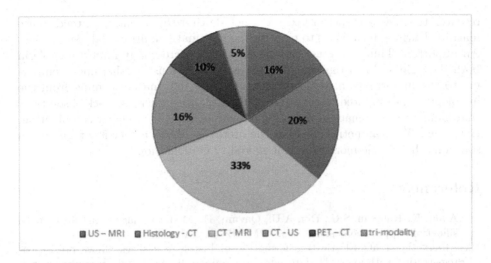

Fig. 1. Percentage of research studies addressing automatic image registration techniques for each modality.

4 Threats to Validity

This section is devoted to analyze the threats to validity regarding the conclusions of our SLR. The main threats to the validity of our review we have identified are these: *Choice of Papers:* relevant papers may not be identified because they do not match to the search criteria. To resolve this problem, we have taken into consideration the recommendations of the experts at each stage of our SLR to avoid. *Unbalanced Results:* Impartiality in such papers can affect the interpretation of the results. In fact, the rather low number of existing research materials about modality combinations and the increased prevalence other modality combinations. Thus, the papers analyzed for those modality combinations were not entirely numerically balanced. Nevertheless, the fact that our choice of papers is validated by experts, ensures that our interpretation reflects the reality of the literature this threat to validity

5 Conclusion and Discussion

The goal of this review is to run the published knowledge about automatic multi-modal image registration. To start, we defined our RQ aiming to find the relevant primary studies related to automatic multi-modal image registration. After establishing our RQ, we created a set of keywords that our audience might be searching on. Then, we established a search strategy to follow, based on our set of keywords. Using this search strategy, we search manually on specific online databases. Among 449 papers, 112 was selected for introduction reading and were thus opened and inspected, yielding 45 relevant papers. We selected only papers that deal with our RQ. As result, we obtained 41 over 45. From the research that has been performed, we conclude that the recent work tend to use machine learning techniques to perform the automatic multi-modal registration. An important Thus, machine learning is playing increasingly important role in both the rigid and non-rigid image registration solutions. Furthermore, comparing to the importance of the combination of the information coming from the histology and Computed tomography (CT) modalities, there is a lack of solutions that handle the automatic registration of histology to CT modality combination. In the end, WE can notice also that the literature shows a very few registration solutions that tackle more than ome modality combination.

References

1. Alam, F., Rahman, S.U., Din, A.U., Qayum, F.: Medical image registration: classification, applications and issues. JPMI **32**(4), 300 (2018)
2. Albers, J., et al.: Elastic transformation of histological slices allows precise co-registration with microCT data sets for a refined virtual histology approach. Sci. Rep. **11**, 10846 (2021)
3. Arimura, H.: Image-Based Computer-Assisted Radiation Therapy. Springer, Cham (2017)
4. Bashiri, F.S., Baghaie, A., Rostami, R., Yu, Z., D'Souza, R.M.: Multi-modal medical image registration with full or partial data: a manifold learning approach. J. Imaging **5**(1), 5 (2018)
5. Cao, X., Yang, J., Wang, L., Xue, Z., Wang, Q., Shen, D.: Deep learning based inter-modality image registration supervised by intra-modality similarity. In: Shi, Y., Suk, H.-I., Liu, M. (eds.) MLMI 2018. LNCS, vol. 11046, pp. 55–63. Springer, Cham (2018). https://doi.org/10.1007/978-3-030-00919-9_7
6. Cheng, X., Zhang, L., Zheng, Y.: Deep similarity learning for multimodal medical images. Comput. Methods Biomech. Biomed. Eng.: Imaging Vis. **6**(3), 248–252 (2018)
7. El-Gamal, F.E.Z.A., Elmogy, M., Atwan, A.: Current trends in medical image registration and fusion. Egypt. Inf. J. **17**(1), 99–124 (2016)
8. Ferrante, E., Oktay, O., Glocker, B., Milone, D.H.: On the adaptability of unsupervised CNN-based deformable image registration to unseen image domains. In: Shi, Y., Suk, H.-I., Liu, M. (eds.) MLMI 2018. LNCS, vol. 11046, pp. 294–302. Springer, Cham (2018). https://doi.org/10.1007/978-3-030-00919-9_34
9. Hill, D.L., Batchelor, P.G., Holden, M., Hawkes, D.J.: Medical image registration. Phys. Med. Biol. **46**(3), R1 (2001)
10. Kitchenham, B.: Procedures for performing systematic reviews. Keele UK Keele Univ. **33**(2004), 1–26 (2004)
11. Liao, R., Miao, S., de Tournemire, P., Grbic, S., Kamen, A., Mansi, T., Comaniciu, D.: An artificial agent for robust image registration. In: Proceedings of the Thirty-First AAAI Conference on Artificial Intelligence, AAAI 2017, pp. 4168–4175. AAAI Press (2017)
12. Liu, B., Gao, X., Liu, H., Wang, X., Liang, B.: A fast weighted registration method of 3d point cloud based on curvature feature, pp. 83–87. ICMIP 2018, Association for Computing Machinery, Guiyang, China (2018)
13. Liu, Q., Leung, H.: Tensor-based descriptor for image registration via unsupervised network. In: 2017 20th International Conference on Information Fusion (Fusion), pp. 1–7. IEEE (2017)

14. Ma, K., et al.: Multimodal Image Registration with Deep Context Reinforcement Learning. In: Descoteaux, M., Maier-Hein, L., Franz, A., Jannin, P., Collins, D.L., Duchesne, S. (eds.) MICCAI 2017. LNCS, vol. 10433, pp. 240–248. Springer, Cham (2017). https://doi.org/10.1007/978-3-319-66182-7_28
15. Maintz, J.A., Viergever, M.A.: A survey of medical image registration. Med. Image Anal. **2**(1), 1–36 (1998)
16. Miao, S., et al.: Dilated FCN for multi-agent 2d/3d medical image registration. In: Proceedings of the AAAI Conference on Artificial Intelligence, vol. 32 (2018)
17. Rueckert, D., Schnabel, J.A.: Medical image registration. In: Deserno, T. (eds) Biomedical image processing, pp. 131–154. Springer, Berlin (2010). https://doi.org/10.1007/978-3-642-15816-2_5
18. Sabokrohiyeh, S., Ang, K., Elbaz, M., Samavati, F.: Sketch-based registration of 3D cine MRI to 4D flow MRI. In: Proceedings of the Association for Computing Machinery, Stockholm, Sweden, ICBBT 2019, pp. 14–21 (2019)
19. Stergios, C., et al.: Linear and deformable image registration with 3D convolutional neural networks. In: Stoyanov, D., et al. (eds.) RAMBO/BIA/TIA -2018. LNCS, vol. 11040, pp. 13–22. Springer, Cham (2018). https://doi.org/10.1007/978-3-030-00946-5_2
20. Tao, H., Lu, X.: A new 3d multi-modality medical bone image registration algorithm. In: Proceedings of the Association for Computing Machinery, Singapore, ICVIP 2017, pp. 140–145 (2017)
21. Uzunova, H., Wilms, M., Handels, H., Ehrhardt, J.: Training CNNs for image registration from few samples with model-based data augmentation. In: Descoteaux, M., Maier-Hein, L., Franz, A., Jannin, P., Collins, D.L., Duchesne, S. (eds.) MICCAI 2017. LNCS, vol. 10433, pp. 223–231. Springer, Cham (2017). https://doi.org/10.1007/978-3-319-66182-7_26
22. Valsecchi, A., Damas, S., Santamaria, J., Marrakchi-Kacem, L.: Genetic algorithms for voxel-based medical image registration. In: 2013 Fourth International Workshop on Computational Intelligence in Medical Imaging (CIMI), pp. 22–29. IEEE (2013)
23. Zheng, L., Qian, G.: A sift-based approach for image registration. In: Yang, Y., Ma, M. (eds.) Green Communications and Networks, vol. 113, pp. 277–287. Springer, Dordrecht (2012)

Education 4.0: Proposal of a Model for Autonomous Management of Learning Processes

Mamadou Lamine Gueye(✉) and Ernesto Exposito

Universite de Pau et des Pays l'Adour, E2S UPPA, LIUPPA, Anglet, France
{mamadou.gueye,ernesto.exposito}@univ-pau.fr

Abstract. From antiquity until nowadays, educational systems have evolved in parallel with major social and economic changes, integrating pedagogical and technological innovations into the educational ecosystem and leading to the advent of a new educational revolution, called Education 4.0. The Education 4.0 paradigm allows both, to support educational organizations in the adoption of pedagogical and digital transformations, and at the same time to meet the needs of new generations of learners and teachers. The increasing use of ICT and the power of the Internet have fostered the emergence of a new generation of learners for whom technology is an integral part of their lives and therefore of their learning style. To respond effectively to the specific needs of these new learner profiles, educational organizations must adopt significant and ongoing transformations in the way we teach and learn. Enabling student-centered teaching, personalized learning paths, and access to a variety of heterogeneous educational resources have made educational processes too complex for the educator to effectively monitor the individual progress of each student. It becomes necessary to automate the management of learning processes to provide better answers to the evolving and specific needs of the different actors (students, educators, training program managers, companies, etc.). This research project aims at proposing an autonomous architecture of Cyber-Physical systems for Education 4.0. This architecture responds to the needs of educational systems, integrating digital technologies for the development of heterogeneous learning environments, capable of meeting the needs of a plurality of learners with different profiles and supporting teachers and training managers in the management of learning processes. This architecture offers the possibility of autonomous management of learning processes to analyze the progress of students and to prescribe the necessary recommendations to increase the chances of success, facilitating the mission of teachers.

Keywords: Education 4.0 · Cyber-physical systems · Autonomic computing · Learning process · Learning analytics

1 Introduction

The current context of educational organizations is characterized by an increasing evolution The current context of educational organizations is characterized by an increasing

© The Author(s), under exclusive license to Springer Nature Switzerland AG 2023
J. Troya et al. (Eds.): ICSOC 2022 Workshops, LNCS 13821, pp. 106–117, 2023.
https://doi.org/10.1007/978-3-031-26507-5_9

evolution of the need for continuous improvement of learning and the environments in which it occurs to provide effective responses to the expectations of the various stakeholders. Nowadays, Education 4.0 also promotes the ubiquitous availability of information with learning systems making learning processes and pathways more dynamic [1]. The sources of knowledge and competencies are increasingly heterogeneous and complex, making it sometimes difficult to effectively exploit resources in relation to learning outcomes and pathways to better guide the learner's evolution and facilitate the teacher's task. Moreover, the growing integration of ICT and the power of the Internet has encouraged the emergence of a new generation of learners with different profiles, interests, and learning rhythms. This makes it extremely complex for the teacher to optimally manage the learning process, adapt, and personalize the learning paths, and evaluate the quality and effectiveness of the educational content. For this reason, these organizations need to transform the process paradigm of technology-supported mass education into a new digital transformation approach, centered on automated management of learning processes. In this paper, we propose an architecture for autonomous management of learning processes to meet the challenges of Education 4.0, based on Learning Analytics methodologies. This model allows educational organizations to evolve towards the Education 4.0 paradigm, to automate and digitalize learning processes and pathways to increase the chances of success for learners and facilitate the work of the teacher. This document is structured around five main sections. Section 2 presents a state-of-the-art on the different educational evolutions. Section 3 provides a survey of related work in our research area. Section 4 presents an autonomic architecture for Education 4.0. Section 5 presents the implementation of the architecture and the analysis of the results obtained in the framework of the PIA-3 HyPE-13 project (*Hybridation et Partage des Enseignements*) within a consortium of 12 French higher education institutions and EdTech companies.

2   State of Art

From antiquity to nowadays, educational systems have evolved in parallel with major social and economic changes, as well as pedagogical and technological innovations in the educational ecosystem leading to the advent of a new educational revolution called Education 4.0. To understand the expected challenges of Education 4.0, it is important to review previous educational revolutions from antiquity to today [2]:

- **First educational revolution: Education 1.0** could be defined as the period from antiquity to the Middle Ages, during which the educational system was characterized by an informal mode of teaching, developed mainly within religious institutions. Each educator constructed his or her teachings according to his or her knowledge, expertise, and what he or she felt was important for the learners. During this period, it was possible for the educator to ensure quality teaching with personalized follow-up of each learner, but the transmission of knowledge and competencies was reserved for small groups of learners from a privileged socio-economic level, the majority of whom were male.
- **Second educational revolution: Education 2.0** appeared in response to society's need to democratize education and to train the largest number of individuals giving

rise to education open to the public with advanced and formal teaching methods, within schools, colleges, and universities. During this period, the mode of teaching was guided by a program-oriented approach with the exit profile of the learners as a reference. Learning activities and content, as well as assessments, were decided in accordance with the learner's graduation profile. The increase in the number of learners makes it more and more difficult to provide personalized follow-ups to each learner to ensure success.

- **Third educational revolution: Education 3.0** is characterized by the increasing integration of Information and Communication Technologies for Education (ICTE). Education 3.0 is a direct consequence of the availability of information, the massive deployment of computers, and mobile devices, and the power of the internet encouraging the adoption of new methods of access and dissemination of knowledge with new paradigms of interaction between human beings. New models of open and online education such as Massive Online Open Courses (MOOC), Corporate Online Open Course (COOC), and Small Private Online Courses (SPOC) have completely disrupted our way of learning and teaching giving origin to mass education without constraints of space, time, and place. However, with a plurality of learners with different profiles and rhythms, it becomes difficult, if not impossible, for the teacher to provide each learner with a personalized follow-up. The heterogeneity of the sources of knowledge makes it more difficult to see the learning paths of the learners and makes it difficult for the teacher to evaluate the quality of the educational content. Education 3.0 has had a huge impact on the educational ecosystem by encouraging the emergence of new generations of learners who are using new forms of interaction and adopting new cognitive models that are setting the stage for the next educational revolution.

To better understand the challenges of Education 4.0, it is important to understand how the various industrial revolutions have led to major upheavals in all activities of human life, including education. Nowadays, we are witnessing the fourth industrial revolution (Industry 4.0) which is mainly based on the integration of cutting-edge technologies such as Artificial Intelligence, Robotics, Big Data, Cloud Computing, Internet of Things, Internet of Services, and 3D printing in the industry, with the aim of automating and digitizing manufacturing processes and next-generation services. Industry 4.0 encourages a fusion between the physical and digital worlds to improve the management of products, business processes, and services [3]. It is also characterized by a shift from mass production or service offering to customized production focused on the individual requirements of each customer [4]. Educational organizations are also moving towards the fourth educational revolution, entitled Education 4.0.

- **Fourth educational revolution: Education 4.0** could be defined based on two emerging trends, one of which is the integration of advanced technologies driven by Industry 4.0 in education and the other the pedagogical innovations and changes needed to meet the new challenges of tomorrow's learners and society. On the one hand, Education 4.0 is considered a direct consequence of the emergence of Industry 4.0, with a view to preparing future generations of learners for the fourth industrial revolution and aligning education with Industry 4.0 [5]. It involves integrating the technological advances of Industry 4.0 for educational purposes [1]. With this new trend, Education

4.0 encourages the transformation of the process of integrating technological advances into teaching and learning to encourage an alignment between education and Industry 4.0 [8]. On the other hand, Education 4.0 is a vision of the future of education that encourages the use of the potential of digital technologies, personalized data, and the opportunities offered by this connected world to encourage lifelong learning [6, 7]. It is an educational revolution that allows learners to be architects of their learning, through the personalization of flexible, dynamic, and adaptive learning paths [2]. With this second trend, Education 4.0 launches educational organizations into a dynamic of adopting new technological and pedagogical transformations to better meet the specific needs of each learner. Education 4.0 is a continuation of the process of integrating digital technology into education to use the potential of digital technology and encourage continuous innovation (Fig. 1).

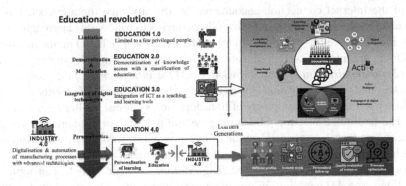

Fig. 1. Evolution towards the Education 4.0 paradigm.

3 Related Works

Nowadays, proposals of application or examples of implementation of the Education 4.0 paradigm are increasingly developing in educational organizations. Most of the related works are proposals of models or cases of application of the Education 4.0 paradigm that is oriented on the adoption of new technological and pedagogical transformations. These transformations aim to encourage the personalization of learning with flexible, dynamic, and adaptive learning paths. There are also application cases focused on the integration of advanced Industry 4.0 technologies in education for better preparation of learners for the fourth industrial revolution.

Fisk [6] proposes general innovations and mutations needed to implement the Education 4.0 paradigm. This proposal is based on the adoption of nine trends in the world of learning which are *(1) learning in diverse times and places, (2) personalization of learning, (3) adaptive and dynamic learning processes, (4) project-based learning, (5) field experience, (6) data interpretation, (7) formative assessments, (8) student ownership,* and *(9) mentoring system.* In this approach, the nine trends of Education 4.0 contribute significantly to the transformation of the current teacher role by putting the learner at the center of learning concerns.

Hussin [7] implements the nine trends of Education 4.0 proposed by [6] in a language course based on the use of several digital tools with varied content formats (text, video, file, and website links). The author uses educational technologies (*OpenLearning, Mentimeter, Padlet* and *Kahoot*) allowing him to implement flipped classroom, activity-based learning, diagnostic and formative assessments, active pedagogy, as well as badges to reward learners' participation and creativity. According to the author, despite the instability of the Internet connection encountered by the students, the approach was well appreciated by the latter who would like other courses to follow this approach.

Intelitek [5] develops an implementation of Education 4.0, based on the transformation of four paradigms of current education which are *(1) the empty brain paradigm to be filled, (2) the requirement of basic knowledge, (3) the interference of the computer with the thinking* and *(4) the individual learning mode.* The learning environments are inspired by Industry 4.0 and the development of transportation systems, healthcare systems, and more. The Intelitek Education 4.0 learning system is based on fundamental principles of Education 4.0 such as personalization of learning paths, formative assessment mode, mentoring, and divergence and plurality of learner profiles.

Mourtzis et al. [8] present *"The Teaching Factory Concept"* which is an application of the Education 4.0 paradigm in manufacturing education. This developed approach is based on the integration of Cyber-Physical systems and Industry 4.0 technologies in teaching. This concept is applied to a use case of a remote-control car manufacturing course based on a combination of traditional manufacturing techniques with technologies introduced by Industry 4.0. This application introduces students to advanced manufacturing techniques, integration, and analysis of data collected from design to prototype manufacturing to better perform performance testing during the process.

These related works are proposals and cases of application of the Education 4.0 paradigm that is mostly oriented to an alignment of education with Industry 4.0 or a set of technological innovations and pedagogical mutations. However, to the best of our knowledge, there is not yet an architectural framework to support educational organizations in their processes towards the implementation of the Education 4.0 paradigm.

4 Proposal

In this paper, our contribution aims to provide an architecture for the autonomic management of learning processes to support educational organizations in their transformations towards Education 4.0. The autonomic character of the system refers to the automation of monitoring and remediation processes, based on observations and diagnosis of the learner's evolution and the proposal of resources or activities to anticipate failure and increase the chances of success. This solution proposes an architectural framework of the Education 4.0 paradigm to support educational organizations in their transformation to automate and digitalize the process and flexible, dynamic, and adaptive learning paths for mass but also individualized education. It allows for improvement and optimize learning processes, personalizes, and adapts learning paths, and ensures an evaluation of the quality and effectiveness of educational content through the implementation of Learning Analytics methodologies. With our approach, we aim to enable educational institutions to face the complexity and inefficiency of manual management of learning processes. The high-level architecture of our contribution is presented in Fig. 2, based on the *ARCADIA* (Architecture Analysis and Design Integrated Approach) methodology.

4.1 Actors

To better ensure this transition to Education 4.0, we will propose a system that considers the issues related to Education 4.0 actors such as people, connected objects, and services. The system is based on the operational needs of the actors, the activities to be performed, as well as the entities, roles, and concepts related to the application of the Education 4.0 paradigm.

4.2 Common Semantic Space

To automate learning processes, it is necessary to have a format for the de-scription of all entities (resources, actors, properties, relations, events, etc.) with a language that can be understood and interpreted by both humans and machines for automated management of learning processes. It is for these reasons that we have adopted a representation of the information in the format of the xAPI standard [9]. This will allow us to have a shared conceptualization resulting in a standard and explicit specification language understandable by humans and machines.

4.3 Autonomous Learning Management

The autonomic management of learning processes requires a system able to implement functions of description (complete description of actors, events, and actions performed), diagnosis (identify problems in learning processes), prediction (able to make a prediction about what will happen in the future, for example predicting the failure or success of a student) and prescription (propose actions or recommendations to the student or teacher in order to improve the results and learning outcomes). This allows the automation (or semi-automation) and optimization of the management of learning processes, as well as the ability to adapt to dynamic and unpredictable changes in learning environments; for this reason, we have adopted an approach, in-spired by the concept of the *IBM MAPE-K* reference architecture of *Autonomic Computing* [10, 11] to provide our system with autonomous manager modules: *Description, Diagnosis, Prediction, Prescription*.

4.4 Autonomous Management Architecture

The architecture of the solution we propose is based on data sources coming from the learning environment which can be composed of one or more LMS (Learning Management System), learning objects, virtual learning environments, as well as the interaction traces of the actors. After the collection and storage of learning data using a Learning Record Store (LRS), this data is destined for the autonomous learning management system based on autonomous manager modules around an LRS, provided by the LA levels of analysis methodologies [12–14]:

- **Description (What happened?):** This is the first level of analysis, based on observations and reporting. Once the learning traces have been collected and processed, the system provides, through a descriptive analysis, the progress, participation, and performance, as well as the different interactions of the learners describing their individual learning paths. As a result, we can visualize the learning path followed by each learner, organized by learning outcomes, or also by learning objects. We can visualize the link between the resources and the related activities, in other words the learning objects and their respective learning outcomes.
- **Diagnostic (Why did it happen?):** This is the second level of analysis that provides an explanation of the descriptive elements to critically evaluate why an out-come occurred. It is in the diagnostic analysis that the system allows for correlations between each learner's learning path and the results of their progress, participation, and performance assessments. With this additional information, we can quickly identify learners who need help and study their individual learning paths to understand the "Why" of their current situation.
- **Prediction (What will happen in the future?):** This is the third phase of the analysis methodology whose objective is to make predictions about what will happen in the future. The learning traces can link each learning object (resource, activity, or assessment) used by the learner to the expected learning outcomes, for which he/she might also have prerequisites. This information allows more specific predictions to be made based on the prerequisites for each learning outcome. This would also offer the possibility of predicting the success or failure of a learner based on visual indicators (semaphore model based on green, yellow, and red indicators) related to his/her progression, participation, and performance in a course.
- **Prescription (What should be done to improve?):** this is the most advanced level of analysis that will allow the implementation of action plans in the form of recommendations to the teacher or learner to help them improve their learning. Since it is possible to clearly identify the learning objects in which the learners encounter difficulties, it becomes possible for the teacher to be able to evaluate the quality of the learning content. As a result, it can be recommended to the learner that before starting a learning resource consult the content of another resource that is essential in the acquisition of a learning outcome. It also offers the possibility of recommending to the learner a learning path to follow to effectively use the learning resources.

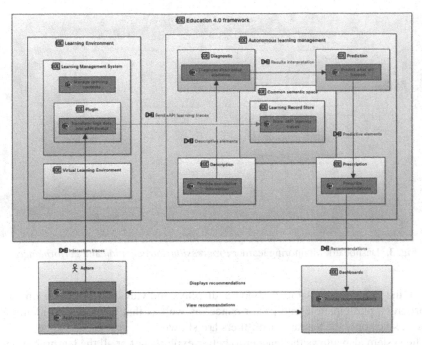

Fig. 2. Cyber-Physical Systems autonomic architecture for Education 4.0.

5 Results

The architecture proposed in this research project has been adopted in the design and implementation of a SPOC intended to train more than 200 teachers who are part of the consortium of 12 French universities participating in the HyPE13 project (ANR-PIA3: *Hybrider et Partager les Enseignements*). The goal of this SPOC was to train teachers in the design of hybrid courses integrating the analysis of digital learning traces. It also aimed to present the foundations of methods and tools for analyzing and interpreting digital learning data to help teachers provide personalized support to their students. In addition, this SPOC offered a general introduction to Learning Analytics (LA) to raise teachers' awareness and provide a methodological framework for designing lessons with LA integration. The SPOC consists of 6 learning paths (LP), each of which is composed of at least 5 learning objects (LO). The SPOC was launched in June 2021 and proposed 6 h of training, including 4 h of asynchronous learning activities spread over 5 learning paths and 2 of synchronous learning activities proposed during the 6th and last learning path, in the form of a workshop. The target audience was teachers, students, training managers, and university staff. This case study allowed us to implement and evaluate our architecture, thanks to the deployment of learning traces sensors within the learning objects and learning paths that were processed within MAPE loops. For each student loop, a dashboard is able to show in real time the learning analytics results: describing, diagnosing, and predicting the progression, participation, and performance of each learner. Teachers have access to a global dashboard presenting the analysis results for the student's cohort (see Fig. 3).

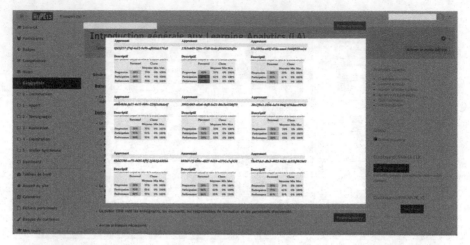

Fig. 3. Dashboard: Monitoring learner *Progression*, *Participation* and *Performance*.

For the student, the same dashboard displays individual information on his or her progress, participation, and performance, as well as that of other non-identifiable learners, since only the learner's identifiers are shown.

The system also allows the teacher to better explore part or all the learning process, to have general information on the progress of the learning process, to see the frequency of consultation of learning resources, the transition time between resources, etc. (see Fig. 4., Fig. 5, Fig. 5, and Fig. 7). Larger loops were used to identify learning patterns, based on Process Mining techniques, using the Celonis platform [15].

Fig. 4. General information about the learning process.

The teacher can view the learning paths followed by all learners during the learning process with visibility into the path of each learner. Based on the information used in the learning process, the system can recommend an optimal learning path (Fig. 6).

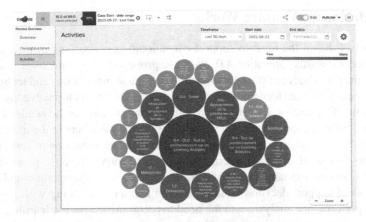

Fig. 5. Frequency of use of learning resources.

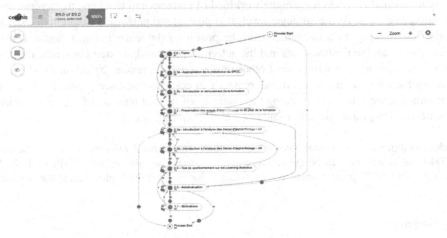

Fig. 6. Visualization of the learning paths of learners

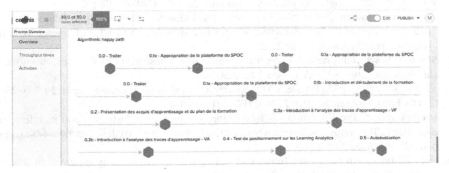

Fig. 7. Recommendation of optimal learning path

6   Conclusion and Future Works

This paper has shown the need to support educational organizations in their transformation process towards Education 4.0. We have proposed an architectural framework that allows the progressive implementation of pedagogical innovations and technologies to support the digital transformation of educational organizations to evolve towards the new paradigm of Education 4.0. This architecture allows to answer the needs of personalization and optimization of learning, as well as to support teachers in the improvement of learning. It offers an incremental approach allowing organizations to progressively integrate the 4 levels of analysis (descriptive, diagnostic, predictive, and prescriptive) to implement autonomous management of learning processes. At the operational level, the results obtained support decision-making through learner monitoring with descriptive indicators, performance analysis, and the need to recommend specific learning paths or resources to meet certain prerequisites. At the management level, these results showed that it is possible to ensure overall management of the training program with the possibility to reschedule or even share the workload of learners and teachers, to increase and encourage success. At the strategic level, it is possible to perform a qualitative evaluation of the training, to better understand the profile of the learners and to know if it is necessary to evolve the resources and the activities proposed, in their content and form. In our future work, we will present other implementation results based on the deployment of the solution in courses of our master's in computer science programs. In these experiments, we will work more on the maturity of the automation of the prescription function by integrating the recommendation of learning contents.

Acknowledgment. The authors would like to thank the *Conseil Départemental des Landes* (CD40) for its support in carrying out this research project. The partners in the HyPE13, UNITA and Connect UNITA projects are also acknowledged for enabling the deployment of the solution.

References

1. Halili, S.H.: Technological advancements in education 4.0. Online J. Distance Educ. e-Learn. **7**(1) (2019). https://tojdel.net/journals/tojdel/articles/v07i01/v07i01-08.pdf
2. Federation of Indian Chambers of Commerce and Industry: Leapfrogging to Education 4.0: Student at the core (2017). http://www.moe.gov.mm/sites/default/files/Leapforgging_to_Education_4.0.pdf. Accessed 2 June 2022
3. Mecalux News: Industrie 4.0: la quatrième révolution industrielle (2020). https://www.mecalux.fr/blog/industrie-4-0. Accessed 2 June 2022
4. Vaidya, S., Ambad, P.M., Bhosle, S.M.: Industry 4.0 – a glimpse. Procedia Manuf. **20**, 233–238 (2018). https://doi.org/10.1016/J.PROMFG.2018.02.034
5. Intelitek report: The Education 4.0 Revolution. Analysis of Industry 4.0 and its effect on education (2018). https://e4-0.ipn.mx/wp-content/uploads/2019/10/the-education-4-0-revolution.pdf. Accessed 23 Sept 2022
6. Fisk, P.: Education 4.0 ... the future of learning will be dramatically different, in school and throughout life (2017). https://www.peterfisk.com/2017/01/future-education-young-everyone-taught-together/. Accessed 2 July 2022
7. Hussin, A.A.: Education 4.0 made simple: ideas for teaching. Int. J. Educ. Literacy Stud. **6**, 92–98 (2018). https://doi.org/10.7575/AIAC.IJELS.V.6N.3P.92

8. Mourtzis, D., Vlachou, E., Dimitrakopoulos, G., Zogopoulos, V.: Cyber-physical systems and Education 4.0-the teaching Factory 4.0 concept. Procedia Manuf. **23**, 129–134 (2018). https://doi.org/10.1016/j.promfg.2018.04.005
9. Advanced Distributed Learning Initiative: Experience API Standard. https://adlnet.gov/projects/xapi/. Accessed 30 Sept 2022
10. Kephart, J.O., Chess, D.M.: The vision of autonomic computing. Computer **36**(1), 41–50 (2003). https://doi.org/10.1109/MC.2003.1160055
11. Sinreich, D.: An architectural blueprint for autonomic computing. IBM (2006). https://citeseerx.ist.psu.edu/viewdoc/download?doi=10.1.1.150.1011&rep=rep1&type=pdf
12. Gartner Research: Best Practices in Analytics: Integrating Analytical Capabilities and Process Flows. https://www.gartner.com/en/documents/1964015/best-practices-in-analytics-integrating-analytical-capab. Accessed 3 Sept 2022
13. Katie, L.: The 4 Levels of Learning Analytics (2014). https://schoolleadership20.com/forum/topics/the-4-levels-of-learning-analytics-by-katie-lepi. Accessed 23 Sept 2022
14. SOLAR.: What is Learning Analytics?. https://www.solaresearch.org/about/what-is-learning-analytics/. Accessed 4 Aug 2022
15. Process Mining and Execution Management Software: Celonis. https://www.celonis.com/. Accessed 15 Sept 2022

EXOGEM: Extending OpenAPI Generator for Monitoring of RESTful APIs

Daniel Friis Holtebo, Jannik Lucas Sommer, Magnus Mølgaard Lund,
Alessandro Tibo, Junior Dongo, and Michele Albano[✉][iD]

Department of Computer Science, Aalborg University, Aalborg, Denmark
{dholte18,jsomme18,mlund18}@student.aau.dk,
{alessandro,jdongo,mialb}@cs.aau.dk

Abstract. The creation of adaptive and reconfigurable Service Oriented Architectures (SOA) must take into account the unpredictability of the Internet and of potentially buggy software, and thus requires monitoring subsystems for detecting degradations and failures as soon as possible. In this paper we propose EXOGEM, a novel and lightweight monitoring framework for REpresentational State Transfer (REST) Application Programming Interfaces (APIs). EXOGEM is an extension to the mainstream code generator OpenAPI Generator, and it allows to create a monitoring subsystem for generated APIs with limited changes to the usual API development workflow. We showcase the approach on a smart grid testbed, where EXOGEM monitors the interaction of a heatpump with a system that optimizes its operations. Our measurements estimate EXOGEM's comparable to the usage of HTTPS when the server is not flooded with requests. Moreover, in one experiment EXOGEM was used to identify high load, and to activate computational elasticity. Together, this suggests that EXOGEM can be a useful monitoring framework for real-life systems and services.

Keywords: Monitoring · OpenAPI generator · Service level agreement · Quality of Service · ReST

1 Introduction

With the emergence of Software as a Service (SaaS) and distributed applications architectures, the use of RESTful APIs and Service Oriented Architectures (SOA) in the software industry is ever increasing. Growing competition led to the need for fast development and robust maintenance of novel APIs and services, and to the creation of standards and tools to satisfy these needs. OpenAPI specifications (OAS) are among the most accepted approaches to APIs description and services formalization [17]. Among the tools that make use of an OAS, the spotlight is currently on OpenAPI Generator [15], which is one of the most accepted code generators for APIs, and it is in fact used by a large number of industry leaders [16].

J. Troya et al. (Eds.): ICSOC 2022 Workshops, LNCS 13821, pp. 118–129, 2023.
https://doi.org/10.1007/978-3-031-26507-5_10

However, offering services of a verifiable quality can be challenging, especially when a contractual Service Level Agreement (SLA) is part of the picture. The demand of services can fluctuate leading to perceived service degradation, and it is just one of the unpredictable variables describing common scenarios and which present hindrance to respecting required Quality of Service (QoS). Approaches involving the service reconfiguration, such as elasticity [3], require knowledge on the state of the distributed systems. The challenge then becomes how to know the load of the services and their health status. Monitoring also allows for different measurement techniques of the QoS depending on the monitoring implementation, such as using timing data to monitor a time constraint or monitoring the usage of system resources. Monitoring mechanisms are often implemented as standalone applications, thus requiring that they get maintained as any other software component, leading to more work for the developers.

In this paper we propose EXOGEM, which is a lightweight framework for the co-development of RESTful APIs and their monitoring subsystems through the extension of OpenAPI Generator. The main novelties of EXOGEM are:

- the monitoring framework is generated together with the RESTful APIs from an OAS. Our target audience makes already use of code generation from an OAS, thus our approach minimizes both the effort to include EXOGEM in an existing development process for APIs, and the steepness of the learning curve;
- monitoring data regarding the server is collected and cached concurrently with the execution of the services, and it is piggybacked to the client. Thus the server is not required to send any extra messages;
- the client sends data regarding both server and client to a specific monitoring server, which checks a set of configurable properties, and raises events if conditions are not satisfied.

The rest of the paper is organized as follows. Section 2 provides background information regarding existing solutions as well as the main tools EXOGEM utilizes. Section 3 describes the general approach of EXOGEM, and it is thus of interest for users of EXOGEM. Implementation details are explained in Sect. 4, for the benefit of developers interested into extending EXOGEM or to customize its mechanisms. Section 5 describes a case study that makes use of an API generated and monitored using EXOGEM, as well as the results of testing the case study. Section 6 wraps up the paper and proposes future work.

2   Background Information

2.1   Related Work

Existing approaches to service monitoring focus on a few trends, which allow to identify general cons and pros.

In [11] Katsaros *et al.* propose a two-layered monitoring framework that enables the collection and aggregation of monitoring data, which is used to determine whether or not the overall system complies with a set of soft real-time constraints. The rationale for a two-layered framework is to control the cost of the monitoring operations, with a layer controlling when the other layer is allowed to collect and communicate monitoring data. Collected data include high-level application-specific data as well as data related to the system where the application is executed, such as CPU speeds, bandwidth and hard disk usage.

In [7], Ferreira *et al.* describe their approach to implement a QoS architecture in Arrowhead-compliant [6] systems of systems inside local clouds. Their approach monitors in real-time data relevant to QoS such as delay, bandwidth usage, and resource limits such as CPU and memory load. Then, their solution compares the monitored data with a SLA to assess if current performance satisfies hard-coded requirements.

The mainstream solution *Nagios* [2] is an open source monitoring toolkit. Nagios offers a spectrum of monitoring capabilities for services, operating systems, and network infrastructure. The solution is quite mature and it can be deployed out of the box to detect out of bounds data and alert administrative staff if needed. NEB2REST is an extension of Nagios, proposed in [12], in which Nagios transmits data to a monitoring service via the NEB2REST component each time data are collected. Their approach provides flexibility and scalability due to its service-oriented architecture and aims at a small overhead load via the small amount of data NEB2REST transmits to the monitoring service.

In [4], Chowdhury *et al.* propose a real-time customizable network monitoring framework for software defined networks called Payless. The middleware offers a RESTful API to collect dataflow information and metrics, and it promises no significant network overhead based on its RESTful structure. Some of the available measurement targets are performance, security and fault-tolerance.

The EXOGEM monitoring framework is targeted at RESTful APIs that are generated with OpenAPI Generator, and it offers benefits over existing works. For example, [7] focuses on using a service-oriented middleware that must be configured and deployed, while EXOGEM minimizes the extra work required to the developers since the monitoring subsystem is part of the generated API code. Other works [4,11,13] discuss the cost of monitoring functionalities, but propose no solution. EXOGEM optimizes its operations by scheduling and caching resources data collection, and by offloading to the client the transmission of monitoring data. Finally, many approaches make use of external software [2,12] executed in parallel to the business logic to collect information to satisfy quite general use cases. On the other hand, EXOGEM code is executed as part of the API calls themselves, and it limits data collection to the configured use case.

2.2   OpenAPI

OpenAPI Generator [15] is an open source tool that allows generation of RESTful client API libraries and server stubs in many different programming languages, as well as documentation, given an OpenAPI specification (OAS) [14], which defines a REST API in terms of its operations, models, etc.

To generate the code, the OpenAPI Generator's engine parses an OAS into a tree. Then the engine uses Mustache [19] files as templates. Mustache is a logic-less template system that uses tags marked as placeholders which can be replaced with zero, one or multiple values given a tree. Figure 1 shows an example, where an OpenAPI specification was parsed into a data structure (left), represented as JSON for the sake of readability. The data jointly with the mustache template (middle) produces the results depicted to the right.

Fig. 1. The data (left) and the mustache template (middle) produce the results to the right.

We make use of the same notion of *paths* as Sferruzza *et al.* in [18] to indicate elements in a OAS tree. As the name *paths* is already used in OpenAPI, this notion will be referred to as *Sferruzza-paths* in this paper. In `operations > operation` the '>' indicates that `operation` is a child of `operations`. For example, from the root of an OAS, operations are accessible via the *Sferruzza-path* `apiInfo > apis > operations > operation`.

The OpenAPI standard allows developers to customize generated code by modifying *mustache* templates [19] and adding specification extensions to the OAS. To access custom OpenAPI tags implemented using specification extensions, the `vendorExtensions` node must be entered at the location of the custom tag. For example, to access a tag called `x-custom-tag` in the operation tag specified previously, the *Sferruzza-path* would be `apiInfo > apis > operations > operation > vendorExtensions > x-custom-tag`.

Specification extensions provide a wide range of opportunities for extending OpenAPI with new features. An example is [18] wherein Sferruzza *et al.* allow developers to define and generate working web services using only an OAS as a way of merging the REST API generation and the web service development processes. In [10] Karlsson *et al.* generate automated property tests alongside the REST APIs from an OAS in order to find faults in a system at a low cost.

3 Proposed Approach

The EXOGEM approach considers that the monitoring subsystem for an API is generated together with the server and client code from an OAS. In a scenario, we consider that there are three actors, the client that initiates the communication, the server that is contacted, and the monitoring server that receives monitoring data.

The development and deployment approach is depicted in Fig. 2, where the square boxes are files, the ones with a blue gradient not being developed by the user, the ones with a yellow gradient containing changes when EXOGEM is part of the picture, and the circle represents the action of generating the client library and the server skeleton. Subfigure 2a considers the usual development of API client and server, comprising the generation of a client library and a server skeleton from an OAS, the development of client and server business logic, and their configuration. Subfigure 2b represents the same process when EXOGEM is part of the picture. The only change needed in the OAS is the specification of which API endpoints and operations must be monitored. In the client configuration it is possible to specify the URL of the monitoring server. Finally, even though the skeleton of the monitoring server is shipped by us, it is reasonable that the developer defines its own business logic, for example to activate elasticity when the total service time is higher than a threshold.

A visual representation of the communication flow for a client's full request can be seen in Fig. 3, where (a) shows the flow without monitoring and (b) with monitoring. On the figure the numbers 1 through 4 represent the sequence in which data are transmitted between the components.

The EXOGEM approach proposes to generate the monitor subsystems of an API together with the client and server from an OAS; the server answers requests with a message containing both the response body for the request and monitoring data for the server; thereafter the client will send the monitoring data for itself and for the server to a monitoring server at each RESTful interaction. The rationale behind the approach is that we piggyback server's monitoring data over an existing communication channel to save communication bandwidth, and thus the client will be the one in charge of performing one more data communication operations to reach out to the monitoring server.

The monitoring server has one endpoint only called exogem_log, which all clients will target with their monitoring data. We are providing also the OAS

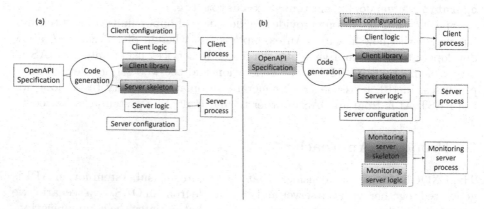

Fig. 2. Development and deployment of client and server, without (subfigure (a)), and with EXOGEM (subfigure (b)).

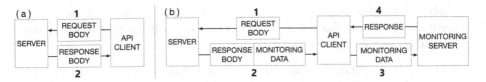

Fig. 3. Communication flow of a normal REST request made with the API client library (subfigure **(a)**), and with EXOGEM (subfigure **(b)**).

of the monitoring server, to make it easier for developers to customize it. By default, whenever the server receives a request, it immediately collects a timestamp. After the response is ready to be sent to the client, the server collects one more timestamp and sends the service result, the two timestamps and a custom monitoring data structure to the client. The client collects a timestamp just before sending the service request, and one when the response is received. After the response is received, the client composes the monitoring data from the server request with its own monitoring data (at least the contacted endpoint and API request parameters) and timestamps, and ships that to the monitoring server.

We consider that the server can be developed without EXOGEM in mind, and thus it does not always provide any monitoring data and timestamp to the client. Even in that case, the client generated by OpenAPI Generator | monitoring subsystem will send to the monitoring server its own timestamps and monitoring data.

Finally, the framework also offers an option to change the communication flow by "choking" the communication with the monitoring server, leading back to the flow in Subfig. 3a. In this case, the developer will still have access to the monitoring data returned by the server and the timestamps on the client side, and it will be in charge of managing the monitoring data in its business logic. The aim of this feature is to allow complex and not foreseen strategies to communicate and use monitoring data.

4   Implementation

This section provides implementation details regarding the EXOGEM plugin for OpenAPI Generator, comprising the new features and specification extensions that were implemented. EXOGEM targets the Javascript programming language, since it is arguably one of the most popular for API client and server programming. In order to accommodate the features provided by EXOGEM, the templates for the "Javascript" client generator, and for the "nodejs-express-server" generator were modified.

EXOGEM introduces new tags in OpenAPI specifications, as follows:

- *x-monitor-server* - A **string** specifying the URL for the monitoring server.
- *x-monitor* - A OpenAPI **object** specifying which API operations must be monitored by EXOGEM. In first instance, it is interpreted as a boolean, thus anything except a *false* leads to an operation to be monitored.

– *choke* - A **boolean** that can be contained into the *x-monitor* object. If it is
present and it is not *false*, it means that the monitoring activities are choked,
see end of Sect. 3.

By default, EXOGEM implements two timestamp properties in the data
structures used for monitoring when a RESTful request is performed and
answered. With regards to the server generation, the code to collect the timing data is generated and two timestamps are added to an attribute map, and
secondly, the properties with accompanying setter methods are added to the
class. For the client, monitoring code is generated for any operations that, in the
OpenAPI document, contains the *x-monitor* tag, that is, if the *Sferruzza-path*
`apiInfo > apis > operations > operation > vendorExtensions > x-monitor`
exists for the specific operation. The "choking" functionality (see Sect. 3) requires
that the user implements its own method for manual transmission of monitoring
data.

Listing 1.1 shows an excerpt of the mustache template code for the generation of the monitoring subsystem of the server. Lines 4 and 9 collect timestamps
regarding the service execution. Later on, the request is augmented of the monitoring data and the timestamps. Finally, the controller sends the response to
the service client. The tags `x-monitor` on line 3, 5, 8 and 18 are used to skip the
generation of the augmented data structure if monitoring is not enabled. Thus,
if EXOGEM is not enabled, all the code that takes care of augmenting the server
response is not executed, and there will be no slowdown in the API call. When
the request is finished on the server side, the response data, which contains both
the monitoring data and the response body, is returned to the client.

Listing 1.1: Mustache code added to controller.mustache file. We abbre-
viate **request**, **response**, **serviceOperation**, and **serviceResponse** as
req, **res**, **serOp**, and **serRes**, respectively.

```
1   static async handleRequest(req, res, serOp) {
2     try {
3       {{#vendorExtensions}}{{#x-monitor}}
4         let tts_start = + new Date();
5       {{/x-monitor}}{{/vendorExtensions}}
6
7       let serRes = await
            serOp(this.collectRequestParams(req));
8
9       {{#vendorExtensions}}{{#x-monitor}}
10        let tts_end = + new Date();
11        let stats = global.server_stats_array;
12        serRes.payload["exogem_stats"] = {};
13        serRes.payload.exogem_stats["srv_resources"]
            = stats;
14        serRes.payload.exogem_stats["srv_start"] =
            tts_start;
```

```
15      serRes.payload.exogem_stats["srv_end"] =
            tts_end;
16      {{/x-monitor}}{{/vendorExtensions}}
17
18      Controller.sendResponse(res, serRes);
19    } catch (error) {
20      Controller.sendError(res, error);
21    }
22  }
```

With regards to the monitoring data, the client will merge the data received from the server with its own data, see Listing 1.2. After this procedure the monitoring data is sent to the monitoring server, by performing an extra API call.

Listing 1.2: Merging procedure of client and server monitoring data, prior to contacting the monitoring server.

```
1  let cln_info = {
2    basePath: this.apiClient.basePath,
3    endpoint: '<&path>',
4    ...
5    cln_start: cln_start,
6    cln_end: cln_end
7  }
8  let srv_info = data["exogem_stats"];
9  let exogem_data = {
10   srv_info: srv_info,
11   cln_info: cln_info
12 }
```

5   Case Study and Experimental Results

The EXOGEM approach was showcased on a smart heat pump scenario, which is a device powered by electricity and that transfers heat to provide comfort in an apartment or a house. Some algorithms have been implemented for optimal control of heat pumps to save energy and improve comfort. We consider a heat pump that decides its optimal setpoints by using the Uppaal Stratego tool [5] to compute the optimal strategy [1,9].

5.1   Scenario

Mathematically, the problem is described as a set of timed automata. The client input includes the indoor temperature of the room managed by the heat pump, the outdoor temperature, weather forecast, etc. Further details regarding how these functions work are out of this paper's scope. The technique proved to

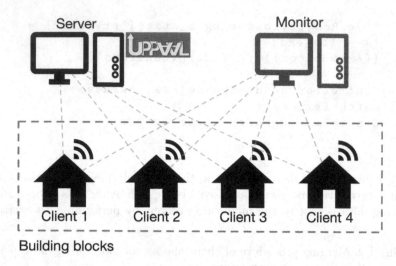

Fig. 4. Overall communication channels of the use case. Requests/Response are represented with dashed green lines. (Color figure online)

be able to minimize the energy expenditure while heating an apartment or a house while guaranteeing comfort constraints set by the user [8]. Even though the approach can be effective to optimize energy usage, it is computationally heavy, thus it is necessary to monitor the performance of the involved systems to ensure that the load is not excessive for the computational platform at hand.

The interconnectedness of the system components is depicted in Fig. 4. We consider a demo site with building blocks composed of a set of apartments equipped with heat pumps, which is the client in our architecture, and it uses an API client library to send current data to a *server* that receives the data, and then it spawns a process running Uppaal Stratego. The rationale for using the EXOGEM monitoring framework in the scenario is that Uppaal Stratego is a memory and CPU hungry application. Suppose the number of requests by the heat pumps is more significant than what can be executed in real-time. In that case, it will probably happen that the requests will accumulate on top of each other, which can lead to memory overflows on the server, and at least to timeouts in response to the clients.

The *monitoring* server included in the system receives timing data and server resource information are received, they are analyzed, processed and saved locally. If needed, the monitoring server will issue commands to the virtual machine where the server is running to scale up its computational capabilities to control the execution delays.

5.2 Results

The use case is used to test the system and benchmark EXOGEM. The system is configured on a local network with the server and monitoring server being on

Table 1. Results from the overhead test in seconds.

Monitoring	Total time	Average time
Enabled	1,448	1.45 ± 0.37
Disabled	1,387	1.39 ± 0.23

separate machines, and the clients are all run from a single computer. To make sure that the clients are not bottlenecked by hardware limitations, they are run on a 24 thread CPU. A downside to the setup, is that every client has to use the same network interface for communication, which may influence the timings. Two scenarios were experimented with, one with monitoring enabled and one without monitoring. For each scenario, 10 tests were performed, and for each one the client sent 100 requests to the server.

Table 1 compares the results. We get that the EXOGEM overhead is on average 60 ms, which amounts to 4.3% of the total service time. For sake of comparison, running 1,000 requests with HTTP rather than HTTPS on the local network incurred in an average overhead of 22 ms, or 1.5% for each request sent. The left part of Fig. 5 shows the cumulative distribution function of the data for the response time with and without EXOGEM, and it confirms that they are very similar.

To test the scalability of the approach when the system load increases, multiple clients were instantiated, to send requests to the server concurrently. In the test, each client sends 50 requests with a period of 1 s, which is slightly lower than the average time to process a request. The right side of Fig. 5 shows how the total service time grows as time passes by. It can be argued that the "without elasticity" server would not able to support the client requests within a reasonable timeframe. The graph stops after 24 requests since it starts thrashing its memory and starts issuing timeouts to the client requests. On the other hand, after the delay grows over 10 s, the "with elasticity" experiments is able to come back to reasonable total service times.

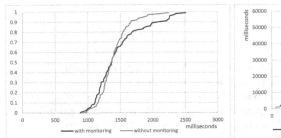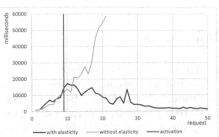

Fig. 5. Cumulative distribution function of the total service time with and without EXOGEM (left) and elasticity experiment (right). The red line indicates the time when the EXOGEM server activates the elasticity on the application server. (Color figure online)

6   Conclusion

In this paper we proposed a solution to the problem of monitoring RESTful APIs and web services. Our approach, called EXOGEM, allows to co-generate a monitoring subsystem from the same OpenAPI specification that is used to generate the code for API client and API server. Our approach was implemented by extending the mainstream OpenAPI Generator, which is well-known in the industry and thus does not force the developer to learn new tools and platforms to implement monitoring functionalities. By bestowing communication responsibilities to the client, we save on the computational load on the server in a client/server architecture, thus contributing to the light weight of the solution.

The framework was tested on a use case featuring a set of heat pumps requiring an optimized strategy to heat apartments with minimal energy expenditure while respecting comfort constraints. The system components were generated by OpenAPI Generator with EXOGEM, where customized monitoring data structures were used for application specific data. The use case was then used to benchmark the implementation. The first test shows the overhead introduced with EXOGEM to be around the tens of milliseconds, which is comparable with the overhead of well-accepted functionalities such as making use of the HTTPS protocol. The second test showed how EXOGEM is able to protect a server from overloads by activating the elasticity capabilities of the underlying cloud.

Future work will improve the support for custom data structure, will extend the supported platforms (currently we support Windows and Linux only), and will provide mechanisms to monitor external processes on the machine executing the server, thus allowing for agent-based monitoring strategies.

Moreover, we plan to deploy EXOGEM on a real large-scale smart grid to monitor how the different components of the architecture interact with each other by means of API calls.

Acknowledgment. Research funded in part by the ERC Advanced Grant LASSO; by the Villum Investigator Grant S4OS; by the European Union through the Horizon 2020 project DomOS (grant agreement 894240).

References

1. Agesen, M.K., Enevoldsen, S., Le Guilly, T., Mariegaard, A., Olsen, P., Skou, A.: Energy consumption forecast of photo-voltaic comfort cooling using UPPAAL Stratego. In: Aceto, L., Bacci, G., Bacci, G., Ingólfsdóttir, A., Legay, A., Mardare, R. (eds.) Models, Algorithms, Logics and Tools. LNCS, vol. 10460, pp. 603–622. Springer, Cham (2017). https://doi.org/10.1007/978-3-319-63121-9_30
2. Barth, W.: Nagios: System and Network Monitoring. No Starch Press (2008)
3. Brabra, H., Mtibaa, A., Gaaloul, W., Benatallah, B.: Model-driven elasticity for cloud resources. In: Krogstie, J., Reijers, H.A. (eds.) CAiSE 2018. LNCS, vol. 10816, pp. 187–202. Springer, Cham (2018). https://doi.org/10.1007/978-3-319-91563-0_12

4. Chowdhury, S.R., Bari, M.F., Ahmed, R., Boutaba, R.: PayLess: a low cost network monitoring framework for software defined networks. In: 2014 IEEE Network Operations and Management Symposium (NOMS), pp. 1–9. IEEE (2014). https://doi.org/10.1109/NOMS.2014.6838227

5. David, A., Du, D., Guldstrand Larsen, K., Legay, A., Mikučionis, M.: Optimizing control strategy using statistical model checking. In: Brat, G., Rungta, N., Venet, A. (eds.) NFM 2013. LNCS, vol. 7871, pp. 352–367. Springer, Heidelberg (2013). https://doi.org/10.1007/978-3-642-38088-4_24

6. Delsing, J., et al.: The arrowhead framework architecture. In: IoT Automation, pp. 79–124. CRC Press (2017)

7. Ferreira, L.L., Albano, M., Delsing, J.: QoS-as-a-service in the local cloud. In: 2016 IEEE 21st International Conference on Emerging Technologies and Factory Automation (ETFA), pp. 1–8. IEEE (2016). https://doi.org/10.1109/ETFA.2016.7733699

8. Golmohamadi, H., Larsen, K.G., Jensen, P.G., Hasrat, I.R.: Integration of flexibility potentials of district heating systems into electricity markets: a review. Renew. Sustain. Energy Rev. **159**, 112200 (2022)

9. Hasrat, I., Jensen, P., Larsen, K., Srba, J.: End-to-end heat-pump control using continuous time stochastic modelling and uppaal stratego. In: Aït-Ameur, Y., Crăciun, F. (eds.) TASE 2022. LNCS, vol. 13299, pp. 363–380. Springer, Cham (2022). https://doi.org/10.1007/978-3-031-10363-6_24

10. Karlsson, S., Čaušević, A., Sundmark, D.: QuickREST: property-based test generation of OpenAPI-described restful APIs. In: 2020 IEEE 13th International Conference on Software Testing, Validation and Verification (ICST), pp. 131–141. IEEE (2020). https://doi.org/10.1109/ICST46309.2020.00023

11. Katsaros, G., Kousiouris, G., Gogouvitis, S., Kyriazis, D., Varvarigou, T.: A service oriented monitoring framework for soft real-time applications. In: 2010 IEEE International Conference on Service-Oriented Computing and Applications (SOCA),D pp. 1–4. IEEE (2010). https://doi.org/10.1109/SOCA.2010.5707182

12. Katsaros, G., Kübert, R., Gallizo, G.: Building a service-oriented monitoring framework with rest and nagios. In: 2011 IEEE International Conference on Services Computing, pp. 426–431. IEEE (2011). https://doi.org/10.1109/SCC.2011.53

13. Klitgaard, A.S., Alexander Sønderby, A., Jørgensen, H.S., Walstrøm Petersen, K., Dongo, J., Albano, M.: Resilience-focused monitoring framework for edge systems. In: 2022 IEEE International Conference on Edge Computing and Communications (EDGE), pp. 153–158 (2022). https://doi.org/10.1109/EDGE55608.2022.00030

14. The OpenAPI specification. https://github.com/OAI/OpenAPI-Specification/blob/master/README.md

15. OpenAPI generator. https://openapi-generator.tech/

16. Who is using this? https://openapi-generator.tech/users

17. Schwichtenberg, S., Gerth, C., Engels, G.: From open API to semantic specifications and code adapters. In: 2017 IEEE International Conference on Web Services (ICWS), pp. 484–491. IEEE (2017)

18. Sferruzza, D., Rocheteau, J., Attiogbé, C., Lanoix, A.: Extending openapi 3.0 to build web services from their specification. In: International Conference on Web Information Systems and Technologies (2018)

19. Wanstrath, C.: Mustache manual. https://mustache.github.io/mustache.5.html

Analysis of MAPE-K Loop in Self-adaptive Systems for Cloud, IoT and CPS

Jiyoung Oh[1], Claudia Raibulet[1,2(✉)] [iD], and Joran Leest[1]

[1] Faculty of Sciences, Department of Computer Science, Vrije Universiteit Amsterdam, De Boelelaan 1111, 1081 HV Amsterdam, The Netherlands
j2.oh@student.vu.nl, {c.raibulet,j.g.leest}@vu.nl
[2] DISCo - Dipartimento di Informatica, Sistemistica e Comunicazione, Universitá degli Studi di Milano-Bicocca, Viale Sarca 336, 20126 Milan, Italy
claudia.raibulet@unimib.it

Abstract. Self-adaptive approaches aim to address the complexity of modern computing generated by the runtime variabilities and uncertainties. In this context, MAPE-K loop is considered today a major approach for the design and implementation of self-adaptive solutions because it captures in a systematic way the main steps of the adaptation process: (1) Monitor the execution context, (2) Analyze the monitored context, (3) Plan the appropriate adaptation strategy, (4) Execute the adaptation strategy, all these steps using a common Knowledge about the context. Implementations of MAPE-K loops may be particularly complex, domain specific, as well as case study dependent. In this paper, we provide a preliminary analysis of MAPE-K loops in various artifacts in different application domains (i.e., cloud - Hogna and TMA, cyber-physical systems - TRAPP and AMELIA, Internet of Things - DeltaIoT). Our main objective is to outline the similarities and differences among the available implementations of MAPE-K control feedback loops in self-adaptive systems. Additionally, the application domains of the considered examples are highly related, so that solutions in one domain may trigger developments in others. We also provide an insight into MAPE-K loops to enable researchers and practitioners to use, re-use, improve the available solutions.

1 Introduction

The complexity of sustainable software and resource distribution of networks has increased because of the spiked usage of mobile and embedded devices with relatively high-speed wireless networking [11]. Moreover, the Internet of Things (IoT) and cloud computing exploit the distribution and availability of these paradigms and apply them in various application domains, such as smart city, home automation, and wearable devices, resulting in more complexity. All these utilizations of IoT and cloud computing demand frequent network environment changes, which increase network dynamicity. The network dynamicity stresses

J. Troya et al. (Eds.): ICSOC 2022 Workshops, LNCS 13821, pp. 130–141, 2023.
https://doi.org/10.1007/978-3-031-26507-5_11

a network, and it makes the network vulnerable to maintaining its quality [21]. Thus cost- and time-consuming maintenance is required during execution [23].

Self-adaptive systems (SAS) [11,14,16,18,23] can cope with this problem. SAS are software-intensive systems that can modify themselves autonomously to various changes in the environment. They respond at the execution time for efficient use of resources, time, and cost [4]. SAS can minimize human intervention and supervision, reduce costs and resource usage. They also reduce recovery time by responding to the change immediately and automatically during their execution.

To respond to internal and external changes, SAS use the Monitor-Analyze-Plan-Execute-Knowledge (MAPE-K) feedback control loop [10], and especially self-adaptation for cyber-physical systems (CPS) utilize it dominantly [14]. The architecture of the SAS that utilize the MAPE-K loop consists of two types of systems: the *managed* system and the *managing* system. The MAPE-K loop is located in the managing system, hence the managing system is also called *the controller*. MAPE-K monitors and controls the managed system, which provides the domain-specific functionality, to adjust a program to fit its desired state [5]. The sensors and actuators of the MAPE-K loop are located in the managed system for monitoring the system and for applying the adaptations.

For further progress, there is a need to analyze available solutions in similar or related application domains to enable their use, re-use and enhancement. The research question (RQ) leading our work of this paper is:

What are the applications of the MAPE-K loop in the available self-adaptive systems and how can they be analyzed?

To answer this research question, this paper investigates five SAS in the IoT, sCPS, and Cloud application domains, which are related fields; Cloud supports IoT operations and sCPS utilizes IoT.

The MAPE-K loop monitors internal failures and unpredictable external events, then analyzes the situation and devises an adaptation plan to achieve its desired state. Finally, it executes the plan. The plan can be varied by the domain and the adaption preferences of its operators [4], the decentralization level of managed systems, managing systems, and control activities of the MAPE-K loop [5]. Besides the MAPE-K components, usually, the MAPE-K loop includes a Knowledge component. A Knowledge saves data from the managed system, adaptation objectives, and information processed and shared by the MAPE-K components [1]. The name of the knowledge can be different from system to system (e.g., database, knowledge).

Because of these traits, the MAPE-K loop is implemented in diverse domains for the automation of the adaptation process. This paper deals with how SAS approaches are applied to IoT, smart CPS (sCPSs), and Cloud, which are emerging techniques affecting human lives and computing paradigms.

sCPS performs autonomously in the real world, interacts with users, or controls the real world through physical devices or vehicles. IoT [20,24] enables millions of sCPS devices to be network-connected to sense, gather, process, and exchange data. For example, sCPS using drones [13], submarines [6], and cars

[22] have their own physical devices and offer advanced services cooperating with their devices through a network, with IoT approaches.

For the analysis of SAS in the IoT domain, DeltaIoT [9] is investigated. Seamless cooperation of devices in a fluctuating network environment is one of the challenges that SAS for IoT have to solve with autonomous tuning. To handle various network environment changes, DeltaIoT suggests self-adaptive approaches to configure the network in order to minimize the loss of packet delivery and energy in an offline environment.

For examples of self-adaptive navigation systems in the sCPS domain, AMELIA and TRAPP are examined. AMELIA provides a technique that generates a graphic model from a set of trajectories made by spatially distributed IoT devices [25]. Self-adaptation is used to combine the spatial information of each distributed device and create a graphic model based on this information. This approach is useful for navigating a vehicle in a continuously changing external environment. On the other hand, TRAPP [7] makes simulations of urban traffic and comes up with optimized navigation for each driver, preventing a vehicle from getting caught in a traffic jam. The self-adaptive framework of TRAPP combines two frameworks; SUMO for traffic scenarios and EPOS for calculating the best route based on the simulation. TRAPP's MAPE-K loop controls EPOS to get the desired status on the SUMO simulation.

Cloud computing is a prominent and popular technology due to its flexibility and scalability of resources and ubiquitous access to high-quality applications [2]. Therefore, cloud computing has been used to support IoT workflows that process complex handling of time-series data [24]. Cloud systems in and of themselves are SAS, taking into account that cloud service providers grant as many resources as users ask and pay for [15]. However, since the public cloud does not provide enough resources for develop self-adaptive applications, the Hogna platform facilitates the implementation of self-adaptive applications and the comparison to other available similar solutions [2]. Meanwhile, the TMA platform implements a self-adaptive approach for cloud systems to manage trustworthiness (trustworthy quality of service and provider) among other factors [15].

To summarize, the contribution of this paper consists in the analysis of the MAPE-K application in five SAS (DeltaIoT, AMELIA, TRAPP, Hogna, TMA) in three related application domains (IoT, CPS, Cloud). We outline the similarities and differences among them with the objective to provide an insight into available MAPE-K solutions and enable their adoption, adaptation, and further improvement in future SAS.

The structure of the paper is as follows; Sect. 2 introduces the five SAS provided by the SEAMS community[1] DeltaIoT, AMELIA, TRAPP, Hogna, and TMA. Section 3 compares and outlines the similarities and differences of the SAS approaches by focusing on the architectural aspects and each MAPE-K phase. Section 4 discusses the limitations and future works. Lastly, Sect. 5 concludes the paper.

---

[1] SEAMS   artifacts   -   https://www.hpi.uni-potsdam.de/giese/public/selfadapt/exemplars/.

2   Overview

We present here an overview of the five SAS artifacts analyzed in this paper: Hogna and TMA (cloud computing), DeltaIoT (IoT), AMELIA and TRAPP (CPS). All these artifacts use the MAPE-K loop for their self-adaptation.

Hogna [2] is a framework for the cloud environment supporting self-adaptive applications by enabling to skip the prototype creation. The artifact includes functions of self-adaptation and dynamic deployment of the cloud. Hogna also evaluates the health of an application with declaration and configuration of the instances and review of the application performance.

TMA [15] addresses trustworthiness in a cloud environment considering the worthiness of the service and its providers. A self-adaptive approach evaluates trustworthy properties. Trust is achieved through its lifecycle before and after deployment. Hence, TMA, a self-adaptive framework that can support these qualities is introduced with flexibility that existing self-adaptive solutions did not offer.

DeltaIoT [9] optimizes a multi-hop network. Tiny embedded computers, called motes, collect context information such as temperature, battery level, occupancy. Because of the size of the motes, the built-in battery provides limited energy and resources. Therefore, to use efficiently their battery, strategic distribution of the motes is critical, and optimization of motes interaction through self-adaptation is required.

AMELIA [25] creates a dynamically and continuously changing geographical model during runtime of trajectories. A trajectory is created when the recordings of longitude and latitude from radio navigation sensors create a sequence from prior observations. The self-adaptive approach of AMELIA creates geographical models by probing topological relations in a discrete space based on a set of trajectories made by distributed IoT devices.

TRAPP [7] Based on a given map, TRAPP: Traffic Reconfigurations via Adaptive Participatory Planning presents decentralized solutions to traffic management by using realistic simulations. It is build on: SUMO (Simulation of Urban Mobility) and EPOS (Economic Planning and Optimized Selections).

3   Analysis of SAS

To answer the RQ defined in the Introduction section, i.e., *What are the applications of the MAPE-K loop in the self-adaptive artifacts and how can they be analyzed?*, we have identified several aspects and features of SAS meaningful for their understanding and comparison. We present these features based on the main steps of the MAPE-K. They emerged from the insight into the MAPE-K loops applied in the five SAS artifacts.

3.1   General/Architectural Aspects

The architectural aspects of SAS have common properties, as well as differences (as summarized in Table 1). Hogna, TMA, and DeltaIoT focus on the environmental settings, while AMELIA and TRAPP are about traffic and navigation of their agents.

All the systems are multi-agent models, but cloud adaptation systems can operate with only one agent. Cloud self-adaptive systems control the environment for their agents' (website or application in the cloud) performance. Therefore, the number of agents does not affect the operation of the system in the case of Hogna and TMA. However, IoT and sCPS require a number of agents for their execution. In detail, DeltaIoT needs some agents to structure the network (motes). AMELIA uses multiple agents to receive temporal-spatial information. TRAPP provides routes to its agents according to each agent's preference hence, TRAPP requires the information of all the drivers in the domain.

Four out of the five considered systems (TRAPP excluded), implement their MAPE-K loop in the cloud and Internet, allocating only observing and actuating tasks to their agents, which is simpler and lighter compared to the MAPE-K main functions. In other words, heavy computing that requires high energy consumption can be dealt efficiently in the cloud without depleting agents' resources. The method of transferring observed information to the MAPE-K on the cloud differs depending on the optimization strategy; sensors transfer directly via wireless Internet, or some other components collect the information from each agent and send it to the MAPE-K loop. For example, TMA's API interface collects the information and sends it to the MAPE-K loop. Moreover, it encrypts the data for security.

Knowledge is the repository for saving the observed information from the sensors, as well as analyzed results and plans. It continuously communicates with other MAPE-K components to provide and save data. Some systems name it differently; the Knowledge of DeltaIoT is the Statistics engine, and that of Hogna is the database. According to the purpose of the self-adaptation loop, the saving frequency in one iteration of the loop is different; some MAPE-K loops save all the actions from every phase while others record only at the monitoring phase. Hence, the frequency and the amount of storage in the Knowledge, and the communication method between the Knowledge and other MAPE-K components can affect the performance of the MAPE-K loop.

Self-adaptive approaches also provide an abstraction for extensibility and customizability. DeltaIoT's Web Service Engine is the interface that connects the website with the MAPE-K loop and DeltaIoT. Through the website, users can access DeltaIoT, and modify the self-adaptive strategies to their objectives. TRAPP allows modularity in the form of a Python class that inherits from the `Strategy` by offering every MAPE-K phase as a method. Hogna provides its MAPE-K functions in independent components and enables researchers to replace any component with a customized one. In this way, Hogna secures high freedom of data types and logic. TMA uses a similar modularity approach but in the form of a pod in Kubernetes. To sum up, for reusability, developing each MAPE-K phase in an independent constituent is the main method to enable the user to fine-tune the process or the logic.

Table 1. Architectural aspects of SAS

	Goal	Model type	MAPE-K location	Transferring method	Knowledge	Abstraction
Hogna	Optimized deployment of topology through metric optimization	Multi agents or single agent	Cloud (primary subsystem)	Not available	Exists (database)	Replaceabe components
TMA	Trustworthy properties combination and scale up and down	Multi agents or single agent	TMA platform in cloud	API interface	Exists	Pod
DeltaIoT	New network settings to make a mote reach the gateway	Multi agents	Internet web service (Managing system tier)	Wireless internet	Exists (Statistics engine)	Webservice engine
AMELIA	Optimization with various conditions	Multi agents	Software enabled systems	Wireless internet	Exists	Not available
TRAPP	Real-time distributed traffic optimization	Multi agents	Not available	Not available	Exists	Python method

Table 2. Features of the monitoring phase of SAS

	External context	Sensor type	Observed data	Data handling	Handling tool	Processed data type	Knowledge saves the observed data
DeltaIoT	Wireless network with motes	RFID Sensor	Packet delivery performance of a link	Does not exist	Not available	Not available	Yes
AMELIA	Continuously changing space	IoT devices with radio navigation sensors	Time-stamped coordinates	Exists	External tool with two algorithms	Geographical model	Yes
TRAPP	Simulated traffic	Not available	SUMO framework parameters	Does not exist	Not available	Not available	Yes
Hogna	CPU usage of instances on the cloud	Amazon EC2 ActiveWatch	Time and metrics	Exists	Proxy and internal loop	List of recently used metrics	Yes
TMA	Web applicationon the sloud	Not available	Measurements and events	Exists	Knowledge	Normalized metrics	Yes

3.2 Features of the Monitoring Step

The monitoring step collects the observed data from sensors. To stabilize the performance of the adaptation loop before analyzing the data, pre-processing is required to resolve the complexity of data types or build new attributes using raw data. Therefore, the types of sensors and data handling of each self-adaptive approach are analyzed in this section (see Table 2).

All SAS have sensors, but TRAPP and TMA do not mention details about the sensors they use. In the case of TRAPP, its environment is generated by a simulating framework, and properties for analysis are sent directly to the Monitor without using sensors. AMELIA and DeltaIoT use physical sensors to observe real-life properties, while Hogna utilizes software sensors to check the cloud environment.

Usually, the collected data is saved with time information. Therefore, the records of the data changes over time are used for predicting the future situations or specific occasions. Further, the differences during some periods are measured and traced. For instance, DeltaIoT calculates the transmission duration with the time records and diagnoses a bottleneck on the mote network. TRAPP uses time records to predict repetitive traffic situations at specific times, then evaluates its plan and the outcome after execution.

Table 3. Features of analyzing phase of SAS

	Data types for analysis	Extra tool	Triggering factor
DeltaIoT	Packet performance	Not availbale	Under/over performing links
AMELIA	Spatial-temporal properties	Spatio-temporal model checker	TRUE(Boolean)
TRAPP	Median of properties	Does not exist	Higher median values than the threshold
Hogna	Recently used metrics	Does not exist	Higher metrics values than the threshold
TMA	Score of a group	The Knowledge	Different scores from the threshold

Table 4. Features of planning phase of SAS

	What the planner generates	How the plan works	Methods	Plan is saved
DeltaIoT	New network settings to make a mote reach the gateway	Adjust power setting or distributing factor	Assign new value in the range	No
AMELIA	Provide a new position or route to each agent	Not available	Not available	No
TRAPP	A decentralized route for each agent by its preference	Adjust EPOS parameters	Assign new value in the range	Yes
Hogna	Assign one more worker to the cluster	Not available	Add a worker to the cluster	No
TMA	Adjust the number of pod to reach the required trustworthiness level	Scale up when the score is low Scale down when the score is high	Add or subtract a pod	No

AMELIA, Hogna, and TMA have data pre-processing procedures that show distinctive traits. Hogna's Monitoring component contains the internal feedback loop which produces the list of recently used metrics. AMELIA's data processing uses an external tool to generate a geographical model from the time-stamped coordinates with its two algorithms. Therefore AMELIA's external tool handles more complex tasks than Hogna's internal feedback loop. TMA uses the Knowledge for both data processing and normalizing since the Knowledge contains the algorithm for these processes. Two subcomponents in the Knowledge handle each procedure. The quality model (QM) handles the data process of scalable metrics, and DataLoader normalizes processed data into the range of 0 to 1.

All five considered systems save the data in the Knowledge during the monitoring phase. The saved data in the Knowledge is provided to the Analyzer or Planner to make optimisation plans or compare the performance of the last iterations plan.

3.3 Features of the Analysing Step

The analysing phase verifies the data for the validation of requirements. Although the monitoring step accepts values in the correct form, the analysis phase has to check whether there is a violation of restrictions; such as abnormal values, in detail, an instance that must be smaller than the other instance or not in the normal range.

Some systems perform simple data processing to compare the value with the pre-decided threshold (see Table 3). In the case of TRAPP, its analyzer calculates the average of properties. The spatio-temporal model checker of AMELIA confirms if the model from the monitoring step satisfies the given conditions

Table 5. Features of executing phase of SAS

	Actuator type	Actuators are distinct From sensors	Actions
DeltaIoT	Motes	No	Actuators follows the plan by adjusting methods
AMELIA	IoT devices (taxi)	No	Actuators follows the plan
TRAPP	Drivers in the simulation	No	Change the type of objectives by the plan
Hogna	Execution engine	Yes	Migrate, resize, and pause instances by the plan
TMA	Kubernetes-actuator email-actuator, API-actuator	Yes	Scale up/down the number of modes by the plan

with STREL [3], which validates complicated spatial-temporal requirements. The Knowledge of TMA uses the quality model (QM) to find the group's highest trustworthiness score, assigning different weights to each attribute.

In most cases, the analysing step uses threshold violation to trigger. There are three types of threshold violations found. The first type is made when the analyzer verifies higher or lower values from the monitor than the threshold. DeltaIoT and TMA are in this case. The analyzer of DeltaIoT determines under- or over-performing links that do not meet the desired signal-to-noise ratio, the power setting, and the distribution factor and invoke the planner. TMA also activates its planner when the score is not the same as the threshold. The second type of violation is when the observed result is higher than the threshold. It is regarded as a situation that needs optimization so it does trigger the planner. TRAPP and Hogna use this type of violation. Hogna's analyzer acts uniquely; if the violation is not found, it does not trigger the planning phase but removes one worker. The last type is when the result has to be the same as the threshold. AMELIA triggers its planner only when the analyzer result is TRUE since it means the planner can optimize the situation, otherwise it cannot.

3.4 Features of the Planning Step

The adaptation plans generated during the planning step illustrate how SAS optimize the performance with self-adaptation (see Table 4). The common approach of planners is tuning parameters so the next observed value can reach the desired value: meet the thresholds. The planner of DeltaIoT devises a plan for an under or over-performing mote to reach its destination node with reasonable energy consumption by adjusting the power setting or distributing factor if there are two destination nodes. TRAPP marks crowded streets and generates a route for each agent. DeltaIoT and TRAPP have a similar controlling method; increase the settings when the current value is lower than the threshold, or decrease it in the opposite situation. The difference between them is that TRAPP saves all the parameter changes in the Knowledge. Hogna and TMA have similar plans: when an agent is in need of more workers/pods, they assign one more worker/pod. However, when its agent requires fewer resources, only TMA subtracts a pod in the planning phase, since Hogna removes a worker during the analyzing phase. AMELIA does not deliver the exact operation of its planner, but provides the possible goals of the planner, which are the optimized distribution of taxis or assessing distribution approaches.

3.5 Features of the Execution Step

Systems are divided into three types of actuators by their architectural aspect (see Table 5). The first type is when actuators are part of sensors. TRAPP's SUMO framework performs as a sensor, observing almost every aspect of the simulation and the actuators are simulated drivers in the simulation made by SUMO. The second case is when sensors are part of actuators. The second case is normally used for sCPS systems that use physical devices like sensors and actuators, e.g., drones in Dragonfly [13]. The sensors of DeltaIoT are in the motes, but DeltaIoT's actuators are the motes themselves. Taxis are AMELIA's actuators but they also perform as sensors. Moreover, not all AMELIA's sensors are actuators, any kind of distributed IoT device can be used as a sensor, for instance, people's smartphones. The last case is when sensors and actuators are distinctive components. The SAS for cloud environment settings are in this case. One common aspect of the actuators of Hogna and TMA is that for system extensibility, they modularized the actuators. Hognavs Execution Engine is its actuator. It is separated from the MAPE-K loop to enable different cloud providers. TMA also has a separated actuator from sensors, and there are three kinds of actuators. The Kubernetes-actuators apply the plan from the planner, the email actuator informs `FaultTolerantQueue` through the email that the Kubernetes-actuator executed the plan since the score was not in the required range. Lastly, the API-actuator provides extensibility to a third-party API.

4 Discussion and Further Studies

In this paper, there have been identified some aspects or features for the analysis of SAS which may be considered as preliminary guidelines for development, analysis, and comparison of MAPE-K steps for self-adaptive systems.

In the last decade, several studies have concerned various aspects of self-adaptive systems [8,11,12,16,17,19,23]. However, none of them had as objective the analysis of the MAPE-K steps in available self-adaptive systems. The importance of MAPE-K loop in self-adaptive systems is outline also by Arcaini et al. [1], who proposed a conceptual and methodological framework for formal modeling, validating, and verifying MAPE-K loops in distributed self-adaptive systems. They specify the MAPE-K loops in an abstract stateful language, i.e., Abstract State Machines.

We consider there is an increasing need to examine self-adaptation tendencies and various strategies, since it will help researchers to use and re-use the part which is already well-defined and focus on their objectives. Therefore, this section discusses some of the aspects that need to be studied more and the five systems' strategies to effectively construct each phase of the MAPE-K loop.

The MAPE-K loop is utilized in a variety of ways across several domains. In this paper, self-adaptive strategies in the IoT, sCPS navigation, and Cloud were inspected. Depending on their domains, the five systems showed similarities and differences. From the domain point of view, the cloud environment self-adaptive systems, i.e., Hogna and TMA, were distinctive from the other domains in their modularization method and optimization plan actions. The five systems are all multi-agent, with two cloud systems also supporting the single-agent operation (see Table 1, Model Type). However, there was no mention of the minimal or ideal number of agents. As a result, in order to respond to changes in the number of agents that may occur in the real world and provide a stable service, research on the number of agents of a multi-agent model is required.

In most systems, since the MAPE-K loop is located on the cloud or the Internet (see Table 1, MAPE-K Location), it communicates with sensors and actuators via the Internet, and during the monitoring phase, if the system is using physical sensors, the transmission is through wireless Internet (see Table 1, Transferring Method). Research about minimizing energy consumption or wireless recharging batteries will give more freedom in the usage of sensors and actuators of sCPS self-adaptive systems.

Data processing is common during the monitoring phase (see Table 2, Data Handling), but it can also happen during the analyzing phase. For data handling, internal or external feedback tools and specific languages are used (see Table 3, Extra Tool). During the monitoring phase, Hogna and TMA's data processing is simple compared to AMELIA. While, AMELIA's external tool performs more complicated tasks, with time-stamped coordinates, it makes a geographical model (see Table 2, Handling Tool). Then the model is checked with a language that validates spatial-temporal conditions during analysis step. Like this, various tools, algorithms, and language can be used strategically.

The triggering factors of the analysis phase vary by the violation type (see Table 3, Triggering Factor). As explained in the analyzing step section, there are three types of violations found in the five systems. The violation is decided by the pre-decided threshold to reach the desired status. However, in the case of finding the most optimized status in a given situation, the application of the self-adaptive approach to set the threshold should be studied.

The procedures held in the executing phase are tuning the parameters, or adding or subtracting a worker in the cloud (see Table 4, How the plan works and Methods). However, TRAPP and TMA have distinguishing characteristics. TRAPP changes its execution objective by the plan type (see Table 5, Actions). TMA is the only system that uses multiple kinds of actuators, one for implementing the plan (see Table 5, Actuator Type), and two others for extended usage. Therefore, implementing variations during the execution phase is possible and it enables a more detailed execution of plans for various situations.

5   Conclusions and Further Work

As far as concerns our knowledge, there is no similar work that compares SEAMS self-adaptive artifacts based on their implementation of the MAPE-K steps by identifying various features. This paper depicted each aspect of the five self-adaptive systems' MAPE-K process and introduced common or distinctive features that are observed throughout each phase and have to be considered when building a self-adaptive system. This is the first step in understanding and learning from available solutions, as well as for having a common view on the MAPE-K steps. Further work will consider the analysis of the MAPE-K loops in all the thirty available SEAMS artifacts, as well as the inclusion of other examples of self-adaptive systems. The objective is to extract principles and patterns for the design and implementation of MAPE-K loops for self-adaptive systems.

References

1. Arcaini, P., Riccobene, E., Scandurra, P.: Modeling and analyzing MAPE-K feedback loops for self-adaptation. In: 10th Intl Symposium on Software Engineering for Adaptive and Self-Managing Systems, pp. 13–23 (2015). https://doi.org/10.1109/SEAMS.2015.10
2. Barna, C., Ghanbari, H., Litoiu, M., Shtern, M.: Hogna: a platform for self-adaptive applications in cloud environments. In: 10th International Symposium on Software Engineering for Adaptive and Self-Managing Systems, pp. 83–87 (2015). https://doi.org/10.1109/SEAMS.2015.26
3. Bartocci, E., Bortolussi, L., Loreti, M., Nenzi, L.: Monitoring mobile and spatially distributed cyber-physical systems. In: 15th International Conference on Formal Methods and Models for System Design, pp. 146–155 (2017). https://doi.org/10.1145/3127041.3127050
4. Cámara, J., de Lemos, R., Laranjeiro, N., Ventura, R., Vieira, M.: Testing the robustness of controllers for self-adaptive systems. J. Braz. Comput. Soc. **20**(1), 1–14 (2014). https://doi.org/10.1186/1678-4804-20-1
5. Garces, L., Martinez-Fernandez, S., Graciano Neto, V.V., Nakagawa, E.Y.: Architectural solutions for self-adaptive systems. Comput. J. **53**(12), 47–59 (2020). https://doi.org/10.1109/MC.2020.3017574
6. Gerasimou, S., Calinescu, R., Shevtsov S., Weyns, D.: UNDERSEA: an exemplar for engineering self-adaptive unmanned underwater vehicles. In: 12th Intl Symposium on Software Engineering for Adaptive and Self-Managing Systems, pp. 83–89 (2017). https://doi.org/10.1109/SEAMS.2017.19
7. Gerostathopoulos, I., Pournaras, E.: TRAPPed in Traffic? A self-adaptive framework for decentralized traffic optimization. In: 14th International Symposium on Software Engineering for Adaptive and Self-Managing Systems, pp. 32–38 (2019). https://doi.org/10.1109/SEAMS.2019.00014
8. Gerostathopoulos, I., Raibulet, C., Alberts, E.: Assessing self-adaptation strategies using cost-benefit analysis, In: 19th International Conference on Software Architecture Companion, pp. 92–95 (2022). https://doi.org/10.1109/ICSA-C54293.2022.00023
9. Iftikhar, M.U., Ramachandran, G.S., Bollansée, P., Weyns, D., Hughes, D.: DeltaIoT: a Self-adaptive internet of things exemplar. In: 12th Intl Symposium on Software Engineering for Adaptive and Self-Managing Systems, pp. 76–82 (2017). https://doi.org/10.1109/SEAMS.2017.21
10. Iglesia, D.G.D.L., Weyns, D.: MAPE-K formal templates to rigorously design behaviors for self-adaptive systems. In: ACM Transactions on Autonomous and Adaptive Systems, vol. 10, no. 3, pp. 1–31 (2015). https://doi.org/10.1145/2724719
11. Krupitzer, C., Roth, F.M., VanSyckel, S., Schiele, G., Becker, C.: A survey on engineering approaches for self-adaptive systems. Pervasive Mobile Comput. J. **17**, 184–206 (2015). https://doi.org/10.1016/j.pmcj.2014.09.009
12. Krupitzer, C., Temizer, T., Prantl, T., Raibulet, C.: An overview of design patterns for self-adaptive systems in the context of the Internet of Things. IEEE Access **8**, 187384–187399 (2020). https://doi.org/10.1109/ACCESS.2020.3031189

13. Maia, P.H., Vieira, L., Chagas, M., Yu, Y., Zisman, A., Nuseibeh, B.: Dragonfly: a tool for simulating self-adaptive drone behaviours. In: 14th International Symposium on Software Engineering for Adaptive and Self-Managing Systems, pp. 107–113 (2019). https://doi.org/10.1109/SEAMS.2019.00022

14. Muccini, H., Sharaf, M., Weyns, D.: Self-adaptation for cyber-physical systems: a systematic literature review. In: 11th International Symposium on Software Engineering for Adaptive and Self-Managing Systems, pp. 75–81 (2016). https://doi.org/10.1145/2897053.2897069

15. Pereira, J.D., et al.: A platform to enable self-adaptive cloud applications using trustworthiness properties. In: 15th International Symposium on Software Engineering for Adaptive and Self-Managing Systems, pp. 71–77 (2020). https://doi.org/10.1145/3387939.3391608

16. Raibulet, C., Arcelli Fontana, F., Carettoni, S.: A preliminary analysis of self-adaptive systems according to different issues. Softw. Qual. J. 28(3), 1213–1243 (2020). https://doi.org/10.1007/s11219-020-09502-5

17. Raibulet, C., Arcelli Fontana, F., Capilla, R., Carrillo, C.: Chapter 13 - an overview on quality evaluation of self-adaptive systems. In: Mistrik, I., Ali, N., Kazman, R., Grundy, J., Schmerl, B.: Managing Trade-Offs in Adaptable Software Architectures, Morgan Kaufmann, pp. 325–352 (2017). ISBN: 9780128028551, https://doi.org/10.1016/B978-0-12-802855-1.00013-7

18. Raibulet, C., Arcelli Fontana, F.: Evaluation of self-adaptive systems: a women perspective. In: 11th European Conference on Software Architecture, Companion, 23–30 (2017). https://doi.org/10.1145/3129790.3129825

19. Raibulet, C.: Hints on quality evaluation of self-systems. In: 8th International Conference on Self-Adaptive and Self-Organizing Systems, pp. 185–186 (2014). https://doi.org/10.1109/SASO.2014.36

20. Rana, M.M., Bo, R.: IoT-based cyber-physical communication architecture: challenges and research directions. IET Cyber-Phys. Syst.: Theory Appl. 5(1), 25–30 (2020). https://doi.org/10.1049/iet-cps.2019.0028

21. Reggiani, A., Schintler, L., Czamanski, D., Patuelli, R. (eds.): Handbook on Entropy, Complexity and Spatial Dynamics. The Rebirth of Theory? Edward Elgar, Cheltenham (2021)

22. Ruiz, A., Juez, G., Schleiss, P., Weiss, G.: A safe generic adaptation mechanism for smart cars. In: 26th International Symposium on Software Reliability Engineering, pp. 161–171 (2015). https://doi.org/10.1109/ISSRE.2015.7381810

23. Salehie, M., Tahvildari, L.: Self-adaptive software: landscape and research challenges. ACM Trans. Auton. Adapt. Syst. 4(2), 1–42 (2009). https://doi.org/10.1145/1516533.1516538

24. Serhani, M.A., Kassabi, H.T., Shuaib, K., Navaz, A.N., Benatallah, B., Beheshti, A.: Self-adapting cloud services orchestration for fulfilling intensive sensory data-driven IoT workflows. Future Gener. Comput. Syst. 108, 583–597 (2020). ISSN: 0167–739X. https://doi.org/10.1016/j.future.2020.02.066

25. Tsigkanos, C., Nenzi, L., Loreti, M. Garriga, M. Dustdar, S., Ghezzi, C.: Inferring analyzable models from trajectories of spatially-distributed Internet of Things. In: 14th International Symposium on Software Engineering for Adaptive and Self-Managing Systems, pp. 100–106 (2019). https://doi.org/10.1109/SEAMS.2019.00021

SASH: Safe Autonomous Self-Healing

Gary White[(✉)], Leonardo Lucio Custode, and Owen O'Brien

Huawei Ireland Research Centre, Townsend St, Dublin 2 D02 R156, Ireland
{gary.white,leonardo.lucio.custode,owen.obrien}@huawei.com

Abstract. With the large scale and user demands on modern cloud systems there is a need for autonomous approaches to self-healing. When there is no operator in the loop for self-healing actions, it is crucial to ensure that the actions taken are safe and effective. In this paper we propose SASH: Safe Autonomous Self-Healing, which uses surrogate models to estimate the safety and effectiveness of self-healing actions. SASH uses system metrics, configuration parameters, domain information and available actions to decide on the best fault remediation action or combination of actions. The performance of the action(s) are then verified through a validation block that updates the knowledge base with how the actions performed for that fault. This data is then used to update the safety and effectiveness estimation algorithm. The results show the framework is able to successfully remediate faults with a low number of actions and with protection against unsafe actions.

Keywords: Self-healing · Cloud computing · Effectiveness estimation · Safety estimation · Causal inference

1 Introduction

Due to the advantages it offers in terms of availability, lower cost and quality of service, cloud computing has become increasingly popular [16]. However, there are many challenges associated with managing these large-scale cloud environments. They require many human operators to respond to faults that must be remediated quickly to ensure availability guarantees [6]. Four nines of availability gives you 4.38 min of downtime per month, which leaves very little time for a human operator to identify, analyse and solve the problem. Due to the variety of faults that can happen, there is no standardization in the way each operator can handle a new fault if it has not been experienced before and alternative solutions to faults can become siloed between teams [10].

Autonomous systems are needed to achieve this high level of reliability and must be able to function on their own without operator input [7]. An autonomous system has many self-components, such as self-healing, self-protecting, self-optimization and self-configuration [4]. This paper focuses on self-healing, to discover, diagnose and react to disruptions. To enable effective self-healing it should be combined with root cause analysis to ensure that we are healing the root cause and not a symptom of the problem [21].

© The Author(s), under exclusive license to Springer Nature Switzerland AG 2023
J. Troya et al. (Eds.): ICSOC 2022 Workshops, LNCS 13821, pp. 142–153, 2023.
https://doi.org/10.1007/978-3-031-26507-5_12

A number of approaches have been proposed to manage these self-healing systems. Multi-agent systems can be used to manage these self-healing systems, but can require a large amount of communication between agents [15]. Deep reinforcement learning has also been used to manage these self-healing systems, but these methods require a large amount of data and can have long training times [22]. Standard machine learning approaches are also being used to provide some additional approaches for self-healing systems [20]. Artificial immune systems are a biologically inspired approach to deal with self-healing using vertebrae immune system as a source of inspiration modelling the use of B-cells and T-cells in computational problems [14].

In this paper we present SASH: a safe autonomous self-healing framework. The framework is tested on a Markov Decision Process (MDP), created using cloud data, which models common faults in cloud computing in a repeatable way. We test multiple configurations for the components of SASH and study the outcomes in terms of: number of actions needed to solve the problem, percentage of safe actions taken and the amount of faults resolved. The paper is organised as follows, Sect. 2 presents the related work that has been conducted on self-healing, Sect. 3 presents the design of our approach and a description of the algorithms used. Section 4 presents the experimental setup that was used to evaluate different configurations in our self-healing framework and the end-to-end results using an ablation study. Section 5 presents the results of those experiments and Sect. 6 concludes the paper and presents some future work.

2 Related Work

To provide the robustness and availability needed in modern cloud systems, self-healing has been used to be able to automatically react to faults and recover the system to normal functioning behaviour [5]. With the development of autonomous self-healing approaches, without a human in the loop it is crucial to understand how the remediation actions will perform when deployed in the environment [19]. We can understand self-healing actions by the effectiveness of the action in solving a problem and the safety associated with taking that action [13]. These scores can be combined and weighted for a specific application, increasing the level of safety for critical applications.

There are many different approaches that can be used to calculate the effectiveness of self-healing actions. Active learning approaches that require operator input are difficult to scale [1]. Machine learning-based approaches have become a popular way to replace the operator and achieve zero-touch self-healing. Naïve Bayes has been used classify the effectiveness of the actions [5], neural networks have also been used to make prediction for potential self-healing actions [9] as well as more recent deep learning approaches [8].

A very important requirement for any action taken in a production system is that it is safe, especially if the system is autonomous. There has been growing research in this area to leverage machine learning for risk assessment [13]. This is especially important for critical applications, such as autonomous vehicles where taking an unsafe action can lead to a loss of life [17]. Due to the risks associated with taking these actions simple rule based approaches have often been used in combination with Monte Carlo tree search to ensure that no actions are taken that would introduce risk into the system [12]. Some approaches have introduced a shielding module at the end of the decision making process, which uses static-rules to ensure no unsafe actions are deployed [2]. In our approach we use an LSTM to predict the safety and effectiveness of the action before they are deployed in the environment, in combination with a threshold and a validation component. This ensures that we only deploy actions that have been validated to be safe and effective without having to use static rules, which can become outdated as the system evolves.

3   SASH Design

3.1   Overall Architecture

The overall design of SASH is presented in Fig. 1. There are a number of key components in the overall SASH architecture: validation, knowledge base, safety and effectiveness estimation and the domain. The domain is used to subdivide the cloud into manageable areas of expertise, such as database, northbound interfaces and schedulers. This allows us to deal with specific problems that only appear in one domain. From the domain we get the fault id, list of potential actions, system metrics and configuration parameters. These are all fed into the safety and effectiveness estimation block, which predicts the safety and effectiveness of each of the available actions. The two metrics are then combined with equal weight into a final score that is used to rank the actions and find the best available. If there is an individual action above the threshold that can solve the problem then we take this action. If there is no individual action above the threshold then we search for a combination of actions to solve the problem. Once the action is deployed the validation block is used to identify that the problem has been solved and the knowledge base is then updated with the safety and effectiveness from deploying the action in the environment. The safety and effectiveness estimation algorithm is then updated using these new values.

3.2   Safety and Effectiveness Estimation

The goal of this component is to estimate two key properties for the actions that SASH can perform: *safety* and *effectiveness*. Safety, in our framework, is defined as the probability that a given action will lead to another state which is safe, i.e., allows to transition to other states. Formally, we can define the set of safe states as follows:

$$\mathcal{S}^s = \{s \in \mathcal{S} : s \in \mathcal{S}^g \vee \sum_{s' \neq s} \mathcal{P}(s', \cdot | s) > 0\} \tag{1}$$

where $\mathcal{S}^g$ is the set of goal states.

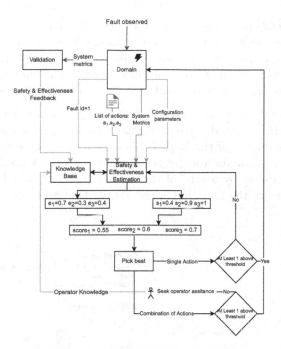

Fig. 1. Detailed SASH architecture

On the other hand, we define the *effectiveness* as the probability that a given action will lead to the goal state. From this point of view, the effectiveness can be seen as a $\mathcal{Q}$ function learned on a reward function $\mathcal{R}$ in a Markov Decision Process. In our case $\mathcal{R}$ can be defined as follows:

$$\mathcal{R}(s, a, s') = \begin{cases} 1 & s' \in \mathcal{S}^g \\ 0 & else \end{cases} \tag{2}$$

Machine Learning Models

LSTM: this model consists of an LSTM cell followed by a two-hidden-layers neural network. The inputs required by this model are: One-hot encoding of the fault, System metrics, Configuration parameters, List of previously-executed actions (each action is one-hot encoded) and One hot encoding of the action that we want to evaluate. The loss function used for this model is the mean squared error between the prediction and the target.

DQN: this model consists of a two-hidden layer neural network trained by means of Deep Q Learning [11]. DQN-based models do not need an input of the list of actions previously executed, since they can learn the value of each action by learning the expected future discounted reward. Thus, this model takes in input the following values: One-hot encoding of the fault, System metrics and Configuration parameters. Then, the model simultaneously returns the estimates for all the possible actions.

Pre-attention DQN: this model consists an attention module that computes an embedding of the current state and feeds it to the DQN described above. Compared with DQN alone, this approach should return better estimates, because the attention module is expected to produce a better embedding from the data. This model takes the same inputs as the DQN and returns the same output.

Post-attention DQN: this model consists of a DQN in parallel with an attention module. In this case, the attention module computes a mask that is then multiplied to the output of the DQN. This approach is expected to "filter" out the actions that are not suitable for the current context. Attention-based DQN provides explainability by means of the attention scores, which we can use to understand what are the most important inputs that were used for computing the Q-values.

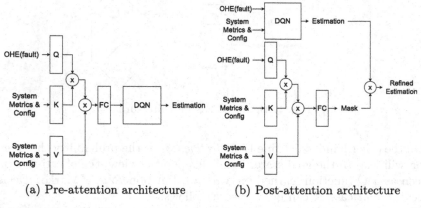

(a) Pre-attention architecture   (b) Post-attention architecture

Fig. 2. Proposed architectures. "OHE" stands for one-hot encoding, while "FC" stands for "fully-connected layer".

Pretraining. Since our goal is to train a *safe* autonomous system, we need to pretrain the agent before deploying it to the cloud service. To do so, we collect a number of $(\mathcal{S}, \mathcal{A}, \mathcal{R}, \mathcal{S}')$ tuples from the environment, that can come either from human interactions with the system or from chaos testing in a test environment. Then, we use these tuples to pretrain the models. More specifically, for the non-DQN-based models, we compute the discounted reward for each trajectory and use it as a target. On the other hand, for the DQN-based models, we use the target network to estimate the maximum future reward of the agent.

Deployment. After the pretraining phase, the neural networks are ready to be deployed in the actual environment together with the SASH framework. Then, at each time step, when an update is triggered by the *validation* component (see Sect. 3.3), we perform online Q-learning to refine the Q-values.

3.3 Validation

Once we have taken an action in the environment, we want to ensure that the action was causal to the problem being solved and not due to some random fluctuation in the environment. It can also be the case that taking an action can lead to a new fault, which is different to the one that we were trying to solve. Figure 3a shows more detail of the validation component. A fault trigger is used to start the self-healing algorithm, the fault id is observed to identify if it is a new fault, the same fault or the fault has been fixed. This is then weighted with the strength of the causal relationship to identify how confident we are that the action performed was the one that solved the fault.

Figure 3b shows the overall flow of SASH. After the validation there are three possible outcomes: the fault is solved, there is a new fault or we still have the same fault. If we have solved the problem then there are no more actions to take. For the same fault case, we update the effectiveness of the action to be lower as it has not solved the problem. If we get a new fault after taking the action, then the safety of the action that was taken is reduced.

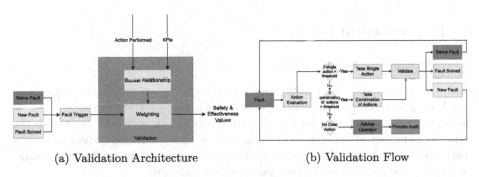

(a) Validation Architecture   (b) Validation Flow

Fig. 3. Validation design

The causal relationship is evaluated between the action performed and the KPI's. When an action is taken there should be a change in the KPI's that were causing the anomaly to be generated, with them returning to their normal operating behaviour. Figure 4a shows an example of Interrupted Time Series. We can see how in this case the red line, which indicates the action taken has lead to a change in the behaviour of the bounce rate time series.

We evaluate a range of different approaches to identify their suitability for our problem. Granger causality is a well established statistical hypothesis test, which is used to determine whether one time series is useful in forecasting another, showing a relationship between the two time series [3]. We also compare time series-based validation approaches, such as regression discontinuity and interrupted time series shown in Fig. 4a. These methods calculate the difference in trend an slope before and after an action was taken. We also compare some of the latest deep learning approaches, such as X-Learner, T-Learner and Treatment-Agnostic Representation Network (TARNet) [18]. The TARNet architecture is shown in Fig. 4b. These approaches use deep causal inference to create a shared representation that can be used to predict the conditional average treatment effect (CATE) of taking or not taking the action.

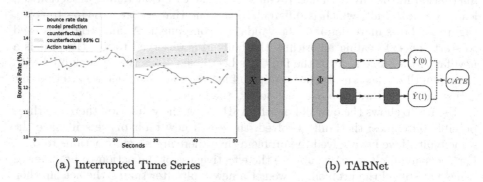

(a) Interrupted Time Series   (b) TARNet

Fig. 4. Validation approaches

4   Experimental Setup

4.1   Repeatable Environment

In order to compare the performance of the system on a generic, repeatable benchmark, we designed a synthetic task with the goal of comparing several properties that are crucial for the system's working: to solve the fault with the minimum number of actions, to avoid an action that leads the system to a risky state, to deal with a moderately large number of actions that are domain specific and have a measurable effect only on specific conditions.

The task is described by the MDP shown graphically in Fig. 5 and is based on our experience in dealing with faults in cloud systems. The MDP consists of three potential starting states, i.e., faults: f_1, f_2, f_3. In this task, SASH has to choose 1 of 14 actions at each timestep to solve the problem. The execution of an action can lead to the following outcomes: the action has no effect on the current fault and the system stays in the same state, the action leads to another state in which the fault is still not solved, the action leads to an unrecoverable state or the action solves the problem. The MDP has stochastic transitions that can lead the system into an unsafe state. This models the many external factors that cannot be taken into account that can drastically change the outcome of an action. Finally, there are faults that can be solved with a single action (f1), faults that can be solved with a combination of actions (f3), and faults that are intrinsically unsafe (f2).

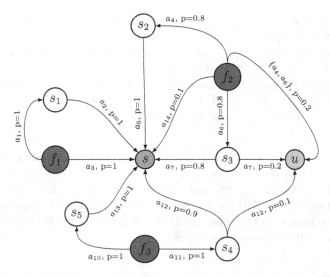

Fig. 5. Markov Decision Process (MDP) for the task used to evaluate and compare our approach. The states with red backgrounds are entry points for different faults. The green state is the "operational" state where no fault is present. Finally, the gray state represents an unrecoverable state to avoid. In all the edges the action triggering the transition (a.) and its probability (denoted by p) are shown. The edges that loop on the same state are hidden to improve readability. (Color figure online)

The state for this task consists of the following features: fault ID and three system metrics. At each timestep, the agent has to choose an action to be performed in the environment. The agent cannot execute a previously-executed action to avoid hysteresis. The two rewards, in terms of safety ($\mathcal{R}_s$) and effectiveness ($\mathcal{R}_e$) are defined as follows:

$$\mathcal{R}_s(s, a, s') = \begin{cases} 1 & s' \neq u \\ -1 & otherwise \end{cases} ; \mathcal{R}_e(s, a, s') = \begin{cases} 1 & s' = s \\ 0 & otherwise \end{cases}. \tag{3}$$

The episode is terminated whenever one of the following conditions is met: the current state is s, the current state is u, there are no more actions that the agent can perform.

4.2 Metrics

Safety and Effectiveness Estimation. To evaluate the quality of the estimation, we compare the methods described in Sect. 3.2 in the environments described in Sect. 4.1 without using the validation method. At the end of the experiments we conduct an ablation end-to-end evaluation combining the safety and effectiveness estimation with the validation algorithm. The metrics we take into account are the following:

- Faults solved (%), the percentage of faults that have been solved over the number of faults presented to the system
- Safety (%), the percentage of simulations that did not end in an unsafe state over the total number of simulations
- Mean number of steps, the mean number of steps needed to solve a fault
- Inference time, the time needed to make a prediction
- Update time, the time needed to update the model.

Validation. To evaluate the validation approach we use a number of traditional metrics to evaluate how well the models perform. We compare the precision, recall and F1 score of the different models to evaluate their performance at identifying the causal relationship. As the scalability of the approaches is also an important requirement to ensure that we get a fast self-healing action we evaluate how well each approach scales.

5   Results

5.1   Safety and Effectiveness Estimation

A comparison of the results obtained on the synthetic task can be seen in Table 1. The results show the performance of the different algorithms in terms of the faults resolved, average solving steps, unsafe actions and the inference time. From the results we can see that LSTM has been able to solve the most amount of faults with the lowest average solving steps. It was also able to solve the faults without taking any unsafe actions, which is important for safety critical applications. The results of the pre-attention and post-attention DQN are disappointing as they had a lower percentage of faults resolved, while taking an increased average number of steps. The LSTM has the largest inference time, but it is less than 0.02s, which is low enough for self-healing cloud applications.

Table 1. Safety & effectiveness results

Method	Faults resolved	Avg solving steps	Unsafe actions	Inference time (s)
DT	67%	9.1	3%	$3.4 * 10^{-4}$
NN	92%	7.3	2%	$3.95 * 10^{-4}$
LSTM	96%	4.7	0%	$1.4 * 10^{-2}$
DQN	78%	6.4	4%	$3.45 * 10^{-4}$
Pre-Attention DQN	73%	6.8	3%	$5.62 * 10^{-4}$
Post-Attention DQN	80%	6.9	2%	$4.34 * 10^{-4}$

5.2 Validation

Table 2 and Fig. 6 show the results of the experiment to evaluate a number of different validation approaches on the experimental setup. The F1 score shows the harmonic mean of the precision and recall giving a good indication of the overall performance on the different validation models. Table 2 shows that Granger Causality has very high precision, but lower recall due to an increased amount of false negatives. The regression discontinuity and interrupted time series have the best performing F1 score overall and achieve very good recall performance. The neural network approaches of S-Learner, T-Learner and TARNet had quite disappointing results. The data set that we used is challenging due to having limited amount of observations before and after interventions.

The scaling of the approaches to an increase in the amount of metrics is shown in Fig. 6. There is a separation between the neural network-based approaches and the more traditional statistical-based approaches. The neural network-based approaches have a much steeper gradient meaning it takes them longer to train on an increased amount of metrics.

Table 2. Validation accuracy

Metric	Precision	Recall	F1 score
Granger causality	1	0.5	0.66
Regression discontinuity	0.83	1	0.91
Interrupted time series	0.82	0.9	0.85
S-learner	0.85	0.32	0.46
T-learner	0.4	0.75	0.52
TARNet	0.39	0.85	0.53

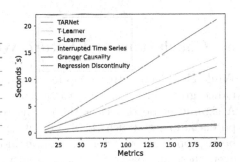

Fig. 6. Validation scale

5.3 End-to-End Results

Figure 7 shows the results of the end-to-end experiments combining the safety and effectiveness estimation module with the validation block. We evaluate the methods in terms of the percentage of faults solved, percentage of safe actions taken and the number of steps to solve the problem. Our hypothesis was that the validation block should help to remove any spurious correlations and only train the model on the actions that have had a positive change, which should improve the quality of the actions taken.

Figure 7a shows the percentage fault solved, in this figure we can see an improvement by using the validation block. Validation ensures that the model is only updated on actions that have been validated to solve the fault, which leads to less false positives and all of the faults being solved. The safety of the actions taken is shown in 7b. The safety was already at 100%, with no change by including the validation block. Finally, Fig. 7c shows the number of steps or actions that were needed to solve the problem. We can see that there has been a reduction in the steps to solve the problem, which would results in shorter self-healing times. The validation block helps to remove any actions in the sequence that don't contribute to solving the problem, which leads to a lower number of steps. As the validation approach is lightweight the end-to-end approach is able to scale linearly with an increased number of metrics.

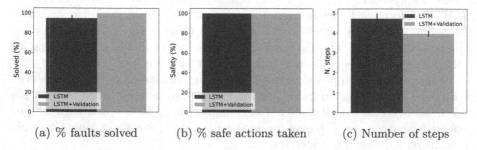

(a) % faults solved   (b) % safe actions taken   (c) Number of steps

Fig. 7. Comparison of only using LSTM and combination with the validation

6   Conclusions and Future Work

While cloud computing adoption continues to grow, its operation and maintenance grows in complexity to support demand for availability and reliability. A significant bottleneck is the reliance on human operators, hindering the full potential of zero touch cloud computing. In recent years, some approaches have been proposed for performing autonomous self-healing in cloud systems. However, these approaches do not take into account the safety of the system, which is a crucial aspect for self-healing. In this paper, we propose a lightweight safe and autonomous self-healing framework, which makes use of two estimators, one of which is explicitly focused on safety estimation. Moreover, we perform a comparison of different methods for each of the core components of SASH, proving that it is an efficient, safe and effective approach to autonomous self-healing. In future work we plan to deploy our work in a production system and add a shielding module to the current architecture.

References

1. Ali-Tolppa, J., Kocsis, S., Schultz, B., Bodrog, L., Kajo, M.: Self-healing and resilience in future 5G cognitive autonomous networks. In: 2018 ITU Kaleidoscope: Machine Learning for a 5G Future (ITU K), pp. 1–8. IEEE (2018)
2. Alshiekh, M., Bloem, R., Ehlers, R., Könighofer, B., Niekum, S., Topcu, U.: Safe reinforcement learning via shielding. In: Proceedings of the AAAI Conference on Artificial Intelligence, vol. 32 (2018)
3. Bressler, S.L., Seth, A.K.: Wiener-granger causality: a well established methodology. Neuroimage **58**(2), 323–329 (2011)

4. Computing, A., et al.: An architectural blueprint for autonomic computing. IBM White Pap. **31**(2006), 1–6 (2006)
5. Dai, Y., Xiang, Y., Zhang, G.: Self-healing and hybrid diagnosis in cloud computing. In: IEEE International Conference on Cloud Computing, pp. 45–56 (2009)
6. Dang, Y., Lin, Q., Huang, P.: AIOps: real-world challenges and research innovations. In: 2019 IEEE/ACM 41st International Conference on Software Engineering: Companion Proceedings (ICSE-Companion), pp. 4–5. IEEE (2019)
7. Gulenko, A.: Autonomic self-healing in cloud computing platforms. Technische Universitaet Berlin, Germany (2020)
8. Jin, Y., et al.: Self-aware distributed deep learning framework for heterogeneous IoT edge devices. Futur. Gener. Comput. Syst. **125**, 908–920 (2021)
9. Magalhaes, J.P., Silva, L.M.: A framework for self-healing and self-adaptation of cloud-hosted web-based applications. In: 2013 IEEE 5th International Conference on Cloud Computing Technology and Science, vol. 1, pp. 555–564. IEEE (2013)
10. Mariani, L., Monni, C., Pezzé, M., Riganelli, O., Xin, R.: Localizing faults in cloud systems. In: 2018 IEEE 11th International Conference on Software Testing, Verification and Validation (ICST), pp. 262–273. IEEE (2018)
11. Mnih, V., et al.: Playing atari with deep reinforcement learning. arXiv preprint arXiv:1312.5602 (2013)
12. Mo, S., Pei, X., Wu, C.: Safe reinforcement learning for autonomous vehicle using Monte Carlo tree search. IEEE Trans. Intell. Transp. **23**, 6766–6773 (2021)
13. Paltrinieri, N., Comfort, L., Reniers, G.: Learning about risk: machine learning for risk assessment. Saf. Sci. **118**, 475–486 (2019)
14. Petrenko, S.: Developing a Cybersecurity Immune System for Industry 40. CRC Press, Boca Raton (2022)
15. Rajput, P.K., Sikka, G.: Multi-agent architecture for fault recovery in self-healing systems. J. Ambient. Intell. Humaniz. Comput. **12**(2), 2849–2866 (2021)
16. Sadiku, M.N., Musa, S.M., Momoh, O.D.: Cloud computing: opportunities and challenges. IEEE Potentials **33**(1), 34–36 (2014)
17. Schwarting, W., Alonso-Mora, J., Rus, D.: Planning and decision-making for autonomous vehicles. Annu. Rev. Control Robot. Auton. Syst. **1**(1), 187–210 (2018)
18. Shalit, U., Johansson, F.D., Sontag, D.: Estimating individual treatment effect: generalization bounds and algorithms. In: International Conference on Machine Learning, pp. 3076–3085. PMLR (2017)
19. Shirazi, E., Jadid, S.: Autonomous self-healing in smart distribution grids using agent systems. IEEE Trans. Industr. Inf. **15**(12), 6291–6301 (2018)
20. Tamim, I., Saci, A., Jammal, M., Shami, A.: Downtime-aware O-RAN VNF deployment strategy for optimized self-healing in the O-cloud. In: 2021 IEEE Global Communications Conference (GLOBECOM), pp. 1–6. IEEE (2021)
21. White, G., Diuwe, J., Fonseca, E., O'Brien, O.: MMRCA: multimodal root cause analysis. In: Hacid, H., et al. (eds.) ICSOC 2021. LNCS, vol. 13236, pp. 177–189. Springer, Cham (2022). https://doi.org/10.1007/978-3-031-14135-5_14
22. Zhou, G., Tian, W., Buyya, R.: Deep reinforcement learning-based methods for resource scheduling in cloud computing: a review and future directions. arXiv preprint arXiv:2105.04086 (2021)

Trusted Smart Irrigation System Based on Fuzzy IoT and Blockchain

Imen Jdey[✉] [ID]

Faculty of Science and Techniques of Sidi Bouzid, University of Kairouan,
Kairouan, Tunisia
imen.jdey@fstsbz.u-kairouan.tn

Abstract. Water scarcity has become a global issue affecting many
countries, particularly in rural and desert areas. In this research, a fuzzy
computational analysis is proposed for IoT smart irrigation systems.
With the increase in the number of connected devices, security and data
privacy are becoming an important challenge in today's IoT applications,
especially as most of these tools are increasingly vulnerable. We present
a combination of fuzzy logic for decision analysis and secure real-time
data collection. Various sensors are distributed in the fields for data collection: temperature as well as humidity. The transfer of these data is
ensured following a secured distributed architecture via Blockchain. A
decision concerning the position of the valve is taken following the analysis through the Mamdani fuzzy logic model. For the design of the fuzzy
system, a rule base as well as a modelling of the different input and output parameters are proposed. The Blockchain technology allows access
to trusted devices only. The results obtained are promising in terms of
water consumption, which has been reduced by more than 60% compared to manual irrigation. On the security side, our solution ensures
the transparent identification of the different trusted nodes.

Keywords: Smart irrigation · Water management · Internet of
things · Fuzzy logic · Blockchain

1 Introduction

Water is becoming increasingly scarce [1,2], and unfortunately few people are
aware of this. According to a report released by the United Nations Children's
Fund (UNICEF) in 2021, more than 36 countries are currently experiencing
water supply problems. Again, according to the UN, the demand for water will
increase by 50% by 2030 [3], due to the growing needs of industry, agriculture,
electricity, population growth and especially with the Russian-Ukrainian war. It
is in this context that our research takes place.

In effect, we are interested in smart agriculture as an alternative ensuring
the water consumption reduction. Farmers used to put a lot of emphasis on
evaluating soil composition and coming up with novel ways to boost crop yields

[16]. Farmers aren't always aware of the water content of their fields, the amount of water they need to irrigate them, or the present climatic conditions that impact them. In this way, the traditional research on soil moisture content is no longer sufficient to boost agricultural yields due to the major changes in climate. This is because soil moisture, temperature, and humidity levels fluctuate during the day in different places of the planet.

Drip farming, sprinkler farming and other conventional technologies are examples of traditional methods that are manually managed and time consuming. When adopting automated irrigation [17], other agricultural operations may be completed at the same time, saving time and money. Watering needs change throughout the day, requiring a method that acts in real time to take these changes into consideration for irrigation. Because of recent developments in sensors for agricultural irrigation systems, as well as the evolution of Machine Learning (ML) that can be used in the development of these systems [18]. Our proposition IrrigControl aims to improve water resource management by offering a smart system that decides on the irrigation process using trustworthy devices. Small and medium agricultural producers will be able to monitor and gather data on climatic and soil variables, store it, process it using fuzzy tools, techniques, and algorithms, and finally manage it over the Internet thanks to its three-level architecture. The proposed smart farm system's privacy will be protected using Blockchain technology. The farmer will be able to see data in tables and statistical graphs through the IrrigControl system's interface. It will also send out email and notifications about a specific event. Mamdani's fuzzy logic method, designed through the rule base and the modelling of input and output variables, allows irrigation decision making. Sensors implemented in the field ensure the collection of real-time data. Several users can be connected at the same time to control the climate parameters. Each transmission of climate parameter value is considered as a transaction between the server and other IoT devices. Blockchain is used in its Ethereum version to secure all these transactions. The effectiveness of our approach is evaluated not only through the irrigation precision in real time but also through privacy preservation and security.

The main contributions of this work are focused on the following topics.

- Increase irrigation precision and reduce costs: collect environmental data received from sensors in real time, using not only temperature but also climatic factors for irrigation planning.
- Based on trusted devices, use the valuable data collected to be more efficient while considering the security and privacy preservation aspect.
- Manage Irrigation Events: automated farm events with personalized notifications. It is possible to get critical alerts on operational problems as they occur and, at the same time, create personalized events.
- Get insightful data analytics: Analyse data with personalized and dynamic graphical reports.

The remainder of the paper is laid out as follows. The background of the study is found in Sect. 2. In the third section, similar research projects will be presented. The proposed smart System IoT platform is described in Sect. 4. The experimental results are discussed in Sect. 5. Section 6 concludes the paper with a discussion as well as conclusions and recommendations for further research.

2   Background Study

2.1   Internet of Things

Smart agriculture uses the Internet of Things to reduce usages such as duration, manpower, and resources. Sensors can talk with one another and transfer signals using a web connection. This smart irrigation system is built to monitor production using sensors such as humidity sensors, and temperature sensors [7,8].

2.2   Fuzzy Learning

Fuzzy logic is one of the unsupervised techniques of machine learning and has emerged alongside big data technologies [13]. The fuzzifier transforms input data into linguistic values of fuzzy sets, while the rule base is made up of a set of rules that express the expert knowledge control policy as "IF - THEN" statements [5,14] as shown in Fig. 1. In order to determine a fuzzy control action, the inference engine must compare the output of the fuzzifier with the fuzzy logic rules and conduct fuzzy implication and approximation reasoning. In order to produce a nonfuzzy (crisp) control action from an inferred fuzzy control action, the defuzzifier completes the operation of defuzzification using preset output membership functions. The definitions and ideas of a fuzzy logic controller are described in further depth in [5].

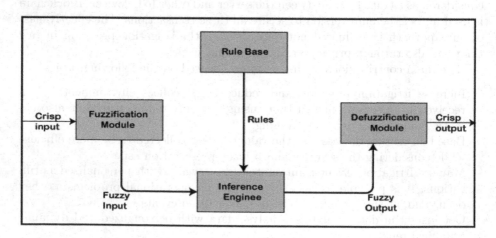

Fig. 1. Architecture of a fuzzy logic system [6].

2.3 Blockchain

The word "Blockchain" means a chain of interconnected blocks and permits the storing of data while generating and updating the distributed ledger using consensus procedures, as well as encrypting the data during transmission [12]. The meaning of the word "blockchain" is obvious [15]. [5] describes Blockchain as a distributed database without a centralized management system. In its peer-to-peer network, it controls how its members communicate. Transfer of data cannot be irreversible.

A node, a computational device, requests a transaction and the other nodes in the network receive this via broadcast. A validation algorithm is used to validate the transaction before it joins the network. The previously completed transaction is updated with the validated transaction(s) They unite to make a block, which is then merged into the larger chain. The new block is added to the current Blockchain using a consensus mechanism [5].

3   Related Works

To achieve the principles of sustainable agriculture, technology, research, and development must be exploited to the utmost extent possible. There were three key revolutions in agricultural development two years ago, notably *machine learning, the internet of things* and *Blockchain* according to the artificial intelligence research tool **Semantic Scholar**. The number of published papers presenting irrigation systems during the last two years is indicated in the figure below Fig 3.

Only 10% of the research has been focused on water management, whereas over 61% has been focused on crop management. Furthermore, crop management relies heavily on water management, including water quality and irrigation [1]. The total number of publications with keywords: "smart irrigation" and "IoT" since 2020 is about 346 papers. But as soon as we add the keyword "Blockchain" or "security", in our search, the number is reduced to 11 i.e., by 97% including 80% of papers submitted in conference.

Among 11 papers selected, we have chosen the 5 most cited papers to summarise the applied methods, the contributions and the limitations.

Table 1. Research findings and shortcomings of smart agriculture systems

Reference	Contribution	Climatic parameter	Research gap
[2] 2021	Deep learning neural network-based IoT	– Soil moisture	– No security – Duration of data collection is only one month
[8] 2021	Edge Computing and IoT	– Temperature – Humidity – Light – soil moisture	– The valve can only be opened or closed (On/Off) by the user – The system can only transfer certain particular data to the main IoT server to predict the watering needs of a crop field
[9] 2022	Real-time monitoring and auto watering system based on predicting mathematical models	– Temperature – Humidity	– No security – Manual ON/OFF switch for the motor
[10] 2022	IoT system using fuzzy logic and Blockchain technologies	– Temperature – Humidity – Soil moisture – Light intensity	– Only 8 plant species are evaluated in the system – Manual ON/OFF switch for the motor
[11] 2020	Blockchain Based fish farm platform	– Temperature – Dissolved Oxygen PH	– For average farmers, the application is too complicated

The main challenges faced by automated irrigation systems, as shown in the Table 1 above; are mainly summarized in the following points:

– Limited use of knowledge-based ML techniques
– Filtering of some important agricultural parameters
– Testing of systems only for a few plants
– Need for expert knowledge for manual irrigation
– Providing medium- and large-scale farmers with precision irrigation monitoring and control systems.

Many networks security and communication performance issues exist in precision agriculture networks, making it difficult to build secure IoT networks. Farmers, for example, need to defend their smart greenhouse networks from cyber threats by securing supply chain systems for the exchange of their crops. They also need a secure environment in which they can manage and access their IoT agricultural machines without risking their identity, privacy, or the integrity of the data processed by these units.

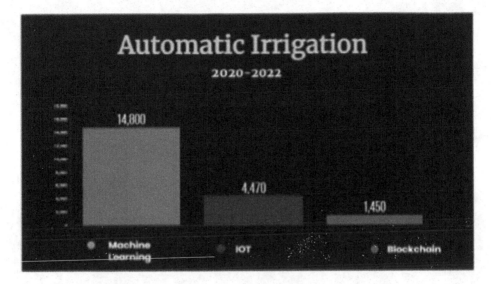

Fig. 2. Number of published papers presenting machine learning, IoT and Blockchain systems for smart irrigation.

Precision agriculture network systems, on the other hand, present network performance issues such as communication speed with many heterogeneous devices and sensors, device power consumption, bandwidth and latency, and data storage limitations. Therefore, Blockchain technology can improve the security, transparency and tamper-resistance of IoT communications. In addition, real-time data tracking in faster end-to-end transaction processes would boost digital agricultural processes. Therefore, Blockchain technology can provide good solutions for security and performance of IoT networks in precision agriculture systems.

4   The Proposed Approach

This study is conducted to solve the irrigation precision and security issues as it was mentioned in previous sections. The research solution concept is described as follows:

- The Fuzzy Learning (FL) can be adopted to address the prediction of the valve position. It allows processing collected sensors' data. Such approach guarantees Increasing irrigation precision and reduce costs.
- To ensure data integrity, the Blockchain technology seems to be an efficient solution. Its ability to ensure immutable transfer data transactions provides a stable environment to safeguard data integrity against manipulative attacks.

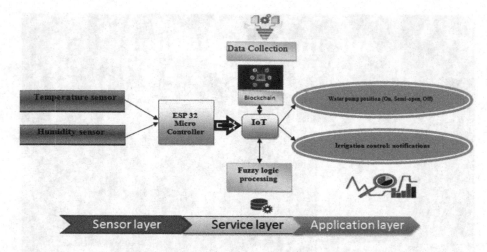

Fig. 3. Block diagram of irrig control.

As shown in the diagram, our proposal is built around 4 layers. The first sensor layer is composed of the following sensors: The installed sensors' specs are listed below:

– Esp32
– DHT11 sensor
– Humidity sensor

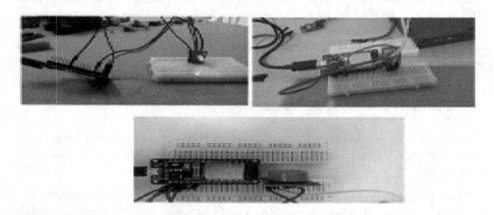

Fig. 4. The component of the sensor layer

A wireless sensor network of sensor nodes is established for data collection. The ESP32 receives the output from these sensors. A Python program is used to collect data from sensors on an hourly basis, store it in an SQLite database, and transfer it to the server over a web service.

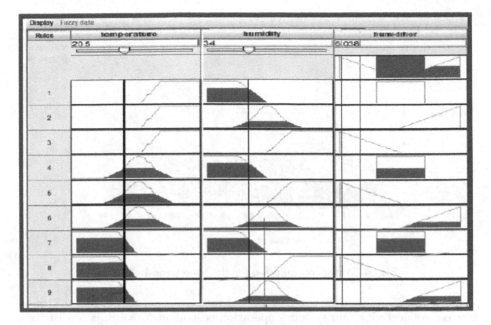

Fig. 5. Window for fuzzy rule viewer: variation of valve position (output) depending on the variation of temperature and humidity (inputs).

The built web service reads the projected data and saves it to the server's MySQL database, which is used in the fuzzy prediction method.

The study employs Blockchain technology to manage the data storage than a centralized server. A smart contract (SC) is used to implement the backup procedure. The SC gathers the climatic parameters from the related distributed ledgers.

The prediction is made using a fuzzy logic inference system. This operation requires a large database for learning, something impossible to do by saving only half season data corresponding to the duration of our study. For this reason, we have resorted to an external database available since 2019:

http://www.emy.gr/emy/en/climatology/climatology-city

The membership functions associated to the inputs and outputs are as shown in the Table 2.

By combining several values of temperature and humidity, we obtain different levels of electric valve opening. Example: for a temperature of 25° and 69% humidity, we have an electric valve opening of 58.3%. The result can be displayed in the form of the following graph 5:

5   Discussion

The major goal of this research is to create a smart trusted system including the processing of various climatic information, the display, actuator control, and

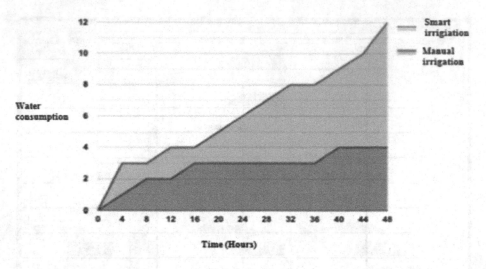

Fig. 6. Water consumption for the time period of 48 h.

wireless connectivity. Our system's operation is straight-forward; it consists of a settings or control component and a measuring component. The system is set to run on autopilot. When the ground is dry, the system is activated automatically by the ESP32 sending a signal to the pump in response to an alert from the humidity and temperature sensors. The planning of this observation framework was made to allow the monitoring of crop parameters during field deployment at different locations on the farm. The designed application allows storing and retrieving data at any time from any remote location. Its objective was to analyse relevant information in real time on weather parameters while helping to organize daily irrigation tasks. In addition, data collected through sensors are integrated in the Blockchain to provide security so that no one will be able to change the values that influence the decision of the valve position. The automatism is translated by the recovery of the climatic values of the sensors and to actuate the output of the valve. Intelligence manifests itself in the analysis of the different parameters and the decision for the output by fuzzy logic. Because of its dual significance, fuzzy logic is used in this module.

The proposed design was shown to effectively control and monitor agricultural conditions while minimizing water waste in empirical tests. As a result, establishing an automatic-sensor-enabled architecture system could be a viable approach for reducing water consumption. As we can see (Fig. 6) after 48 h of testing the reduction in water consumption between manual irrigation and irrigation following our proposal is considerable.

Table 2. The membership functions associated to input and output variables

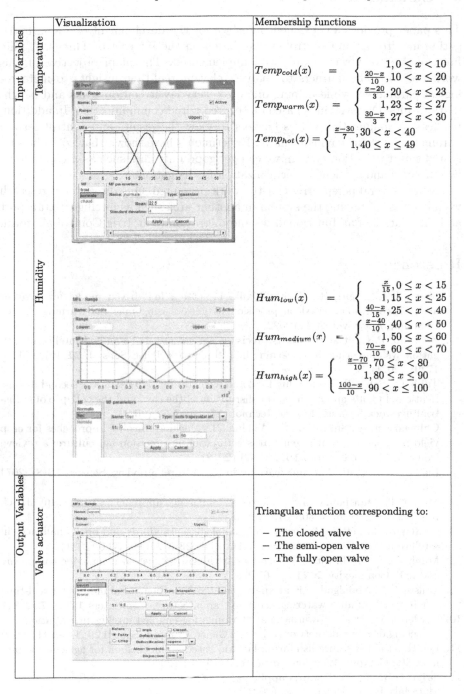

		Visualization	Membership functions
Input Variables	**Temperature**		$Temp_{cold}(x) = \begin{cases} 1, 0 \leq x < 10 \\ \frac{20-x}{10}, 10 < x \leq 20 \end{cases}$ $Temp_{warm}(x) = \begin{cases} \frac{x-20}{3}, 20 < x \leq 23 \\ 1, 23 \leq x \leq 27 \\ \frac{30-x}{3}, 27 \leq x < 30 \end{cases}$ $Temp_{hot}(x) = \begin{cases} \frac{x-30}{7}, 30 < x < 40 \\ 1, 40 \leq x \leq 49 \end{cases}$
	Humidity		$Hum_{low}(x) = \begin{cases} \frac{x}{15}, 0 \leq x < 15 \\ 1, 15 \leq x \leq 25 \\ \frac{40-x}{15}, 25 < x < 40 \end{cases}$ $Hum_{medium}(r) = \begin{cases} \frac{x-40}{10}, 40 \leq r < 50 \\ 1, 50 \leq x \leq 60 \\ \frac{70-x}{10}, 60 \leq x < 70 \end{cases}$ $Hum_{high}(x) = \begin{cases} \frac{x-70}{10}, 70 \leq x < 80 \\ 1, 80 \leq x \leq 90 \\ \frac{100-x}{10}, 90 < x \leq 100 \end{cases}$
Output Variables	**Valve actuator**		Triangular function corresponding to: − The closed valve − The semi-open valve − The fully open valve

6   Conclusion

This paper provides a convenient interface for the development of a smart irrigation monitoring and control system based on the Internet of Things. A fully functional system was created and implemented. The main objective of this work was to enable farmers to analyse relevant real-time insights to meteorological parameters while helping organize everyday irrigation tasks and benchmark results. Our system is based on secured wired communication. In addition, wireless communication allows farmers to view the results and control certain parameters without having to move. Experiments have shown that with the suggested smart irrigation system, we can get good outcomes such as cheap manual labour costs and efficient water utilization for irrigation.

We see several perspectives for the work presented. One direction of research would consist of testing the system in another area such as intelligent transport and Integration of all functionalities and migration to an Irrig Control platform.

References

1. Singh, D.K., Sobti, R., Kumar Malik, P., et al.: IoT-driven model for weather and soil conditions based on precision irrigation using machine learning. Secur. Commun. Netw. vol. 2022 (2022)
2. Kashyap, P.K., et al.: Towards precision agriculture: IoT-enabled intelligent irrigation systems using deep learning neural network. IEEE Sens. J. **21**(16), 17479–17491 (2021)
3. Tubb, C., Seba, T.: Rethinking food and agriculture 2020–2030: the second domestication of plants and animals, the disruption of the cow, and the collapse of industrial livestock farming. Ind. Biotechnol. **17**(2), 57–72 (2021)
4. Chlingaryan, A., Sukkarieh, S., Whelan, B.: Machine learning approaches for crop yield prediction and nitrogen status estimation in precision agriculture: a review. Comput. Electron. Agric. **151**, 61–69 (2018)
5. Liakos, K.G., et al.: Machine learning in agriculture: a review. Sensors **18**(8), 2674 (2018)
6. Mitiku, T., Manshahia, M.S.: Neuro fuzzy inference approach: a survey. Int. J. Sci. Res. Sci. Eng. Tech. **4**, 505–519 (2018)
7. Centenaro, M., et al.: A survey on technologies, standards and open challenges in satellite IoT. IEEE Commun. Surv. Tutorials **23**(3), 1693–1720 (2021)
8. Munir, M.S., et al.: Intelligent and smart irrigation system using edge computing and IoT. Complexity **2021**, 1–16 (2021)
9. Yousif, J.H., Abdalgader, K.: Experimental and mathematical models for real-time monitoring and auto watering using IoT architecture. Computers **11**(1), 7 (2022)
10. Cordeiro, M., et al.: Towards smart farming: fog-enabled intelligent irrigation system using deep neural networks. Future Gener. Comput. Syst. **129**, 115–124 (2022)
11. Lei, H., et al.: A secure fish farm platform based on blockchain for agriculture data integrity. Comput. Electron. Agric. **170**, 105251 (2020)
12. Sajja, G.S., et al.: Towards applicability of blockchain in agriculture sector. In: Materials Today: Proceedings (2021)

13. Kale, S.S., Patil, P.S.: Data mining technology with fuzzy logic, neural networks and machine learning for agriculture. In: Balas, V.E., Sharma, N., Chakrabarti, A. (eds.) Data Management, Analytics and Innovation. AISC, vol. 839, pp. 79–87. Springer, Singapore (2019). https://doi.org/10.1007/978-981-13-1274-8_6
14. Dumitrescu, C., Ciotirnae, P., Vizitiu, C.: Fuzzy logic for intelligent control system using soft computing applications. Sensors **21**(8), 2617 (2021)
15. Gligor, D.M., et al.: Utilizing blockchain technology for supply chain transparency: a resource orchestration perspective. J. Bus. Logistics **43**(1), 140–159 (2022)
16. Brock, C., Jackson-Smith, D., Culman, S., Doohan, D., Herms, C.: Soil balancing within organic farming: negotiating meanings and boundaries in an alternative agricultural community of practice. Agric. Human Values **38**(2), 449–465 (2020). https://doi.org/10.1007/s10460-020-10165-y
17. Koech, R., Langat, P.: Improving irrigation water use efficiency: a review of advances, challenges and opportunities in the Australian context. Water **10**(12), 1771 (2018)
18. Mekonnen, Y., et al.: Machine learning techniques in wireless sensor network based precision agriculture. J. Electrochem. Soc. **167**(3), 037522 (2019)

FMCIoT: Architectures for Future Mobile Computing and Internet of Things

Introduction to the 3rd International Workshop on Architectures for Future Mobile Computing and Internet of Things (FMCIoT 2022)

Mobile phones and Internet of Things (IoT) devices are the top two most significant categories of connected devices in 2022. With a more than 15% compound annual growth rate, they are one of today's hottest trends in academia and industry. Both mobile phones and IoT devices integrate significant technologies such as cloud services, big data, cloud computing, and wireless networking (Bluetooth, Wi-Fi, 5G, etc.) in one platform that services end-users. Regardless of the COVID-19 pandemic and different issues with general supply chain disruptions, in 2021, the number of global IoT active endpoints grew by 8% and is expected to grow by 18% to 14.4 billion active connections in 2022. Despite this rapid growth, many issues at the intersection of Mobile Computing and IoT are still challenging and need to be addressed. These challenges are related to the underlying communication networks, interaction with cloud services, security, the required Quality of Service, the availability of services, integration with next-generation Internet technologies, and many others.

Held in conjunction with ICSOC 2022, the International Workshop on Architectures for Future Mobile Computing and Internet of Things (FMCIoT 2022) solicited original ideas in the broad area of Mobile and IoT architectures, including challenges and opportunities, concepts, applications, and future trends that address the challenges mentioned earlier. The workshop aimed to facilitate discussions among academics and industry to bridge Mobile Computing and IoT practitioners and make positive contributions to the field.

Workshop Overview

We are pleased that the workshop included two keynote talks from two invited speakers.

Prof. Dominique Gabioud is a professor at the University of Applied Sciences and Arts Western Switzerland, Sion, Switzerland. He is conducting research and teaching activities in the field of Operational Technology and Internet of Things applied to energy systems and smart grids. He is the coordinator of the HORIZON 2020 project domOS, whose goal is to develop and prototype a "digital connector" for buildings to be used by various energy and non-energy services. The so-called domOS ecosystem enables decoupling between the infrastructure layer in buildings and the service layer. That was the focus of his talk titled "Decoupling the smart infrastructure in buildings and smart services : the domOS approach" that opened the workshop.

Later in the day, we heard "Internet of Medical and Artificial Intelligence of Things" from Dr Anand Nayyar, who received his Ph.D. (Computer Science) from Desh Bhagat University in 2017 in the area of Wireless Sensor Networks, Swarm Intelligence and Network Simulation. He is currently working at the School of Computer Science-Duy

Tan University, Da Nang, Vietnam, as an Assistant Professor, Scientist, Vice-Chairman (Research) and Director of the IoT and Intelligent Systems Lab. His talk covered how combining the Internet of Things with Artificial Intelligence makes it possible to solve medical issues. The workshop accepted four papers out of seven, giving a 57% acceptance rate. The papers' topics were centered on applied research that focused on platforms built on IoT devices or mobile phones, spanning from how to orchestrate an efficient update of IoT devices in an industrial setting, to how to deploy network functions to optimize energy usage.

Smart Edge Service Update Scheduler: An Industrial Use Case addresses big-scale software updates and the service interruptions they cause due to the need to restart some services after a successful update. It proposes a scheduling algorithm for software updates that clusters edge locations based on edge connections between them and then assigns a weight to each location depending on the impact a software update would have on it. This paper, by Sergio Moreschini et al., received the Best Paper Award.

Energy-aware placement of network functions in edge-based infrastructures with Open Source MANO and Kubernetes addresses Energy consumption (EC) by Network Virtual Functions (NVFs) on Edge devices, which are typically power-constrained; it achieves an overall reduced EC by improving the placement of NVFs on the compute nodes.

People counting in the times of Covid-19 proposes a machine learning-based estimation of the number of people within a public building with multiple entrances. Determining the occupancy of a building is a very valid problem, and such a solution is helpful in many cases, such as emergency situations, waiting lines for restaurants, etc.

A service-oriented middleware enabling decentralised deployment in mobile multihop networks proposes a decentralized and automatized deployment strategy enabling distributed computing in distributed conditions (e.g. IoT/fog/edge) that relies on open-source middleware

Acknowledgement

The workshop was organized thanks to the support from our sponsors: the European Union through the Horizon 2020 project domOS (grant agreement 894240) and the engineering R&D company LEUVILLE OBJECTS. The organizers would like to thank ICSOC 2022 for providing the venue for this workshop to take place, and a special thanks to Raffaela Mirandola and Elena María Navarro Martínez for their intensive help in the process.

November 2022   FMCIoT 2022 Workshop Organizers

Smart Edge Service Update Scheduler: An Industrial Use Case

Sergio Moreschini[1]([✉]), Francesco Lomio[1], David Hästbacka[1], and Davide Taibi[1,2]

[1] Tampere University, Tampere, Finland
{sergio.moreschini,francesco.lomio,davidhastbacka,davide.taibi}@tuni.fi
[2] University of Oulu, Oulu, Finland
davide.taibi@oulu.fi

Abstract. Software systems need to be maintained and frequently updated to provide the best possible service to the end-users. However, updates sometimes, cause the system or part of it to restart and disconnect, causing downtime and potentially reducing the quality of service.

In this work we studied and analyzed the case of a large Nordic company running a service-oriented system running on edge nodes, and providing services to 270K IoT devices. To update the system while minimizing downtime, we develop a smart edge service update scheduler for a service-oriented architecture, which suggests the best possible update schedule that minimizes the loss of connections for IoT devices.

Our approach was validated by applying the scheduling algorithm to the whole system counting 270k edge nodes distributed among 800 locations.

By taking into account the topology of the software system and its real-time utilization, it is possible to optimize the updates in a way that substantially minimizes downtime.

Keywords: Edge computing · Provisioning · Update scheduling · Service-oriented · IoT

1 Introduction

Software systems constantly need to be updated. Modern agile methods allow the continuous development and deployment of changes. However, the deployment of updates can require the restart of the system or part of it.

When considering widely used software systems, and in particular critical systems, downtime is usually unacceptable, and different strategies should be considered to avoid or minimize downtime as much as possible.

In our case, a very large Nordic company[1] is running a service-based system. The system is running 24/7 and it is deployed on edge and cloud, in multiple

---

[1] For reasons of NDA, we are not allowed to disclose the name of the company, nor the low-level details of the use case.

© The Author(s), under exclusive license to Springer Nature Switzerland AG 2023
J. Troya et al. (Eds.): ICSOC 2022 Workshops, LNCS 13821, pp. 171–182, 2023.
https://doi.org/10.1007/978-3-031-26507-5_14

countries. Among different countries, the system has more than 800 locations, with an average of 336 edge nodes for each location for a total of $\sim 270k$ edge nodes. Each edge node provides a service to 100–1000 users connected simultaneously totaling 270 million connected Internet of Things (IoT) devices.

The company is continuously developing the system using an agile methodology and the continuous building of the system needs to deploy a new version of the code every day. However, the deployment of the new version requires the restart of each location, taking an average of 30 min, and impacting all the edge nodes and related services provided to the connected IoT. During this time, all the end users connected to the edge nodes in the location, need to be rerouted to another edge node in a different location, to minimize the number of dropped service calls. However, the IoT devices can access only adjacent locations, due to the wireless technology adopted, increasing the complexity of the updates.

Given the daily upgrade time frame and the number of nodes, it would not be feasible to have a sequential upgrade schedule, as it would require more than 405 h ($\sim$16 days).

Therefore, we intervened to support the company in identifying a smart update algorithm to schedule the updates of each location while reducing the number of service call drops as much as possible, maximizing the quality of service.

For this purpose, we defined a smart scheduling algorithm, validated it, and finally deployed it in production. The goal of the scheduling systems is to provide the suggested timing at which each location should start the provisioning process.

As a result, the company is now able to continuously deploy new updates, dropping only once a day, for 30 min, 20% of the calls to the service APIs.

The result of this work can be useful to researchers to validate the scheduling algorithm and to further extend it. Moreover, companies can benefit from this work by applying and extending it in production. It is important to remember that this algorithm is currently deployed in production, on a very large-scale system.

The remainder of this paper is structured as follows. In the next section, we introduce the necessary background and related work. In Sect. 3 we introduce the smart edge service update scheduler, explaining its characteristics and its rationale. In Sect. 4 we describe how the performance of the scheduling algorithm is measured. Section 5 includes the validation of the algorithm and the smart edge provisioning scenario. Section 6 finally presents our conclusions and draws future works.

2   Background and Related Works

2.1   Provisioning

The term provisioning is usually referred to as the process of preparing and equipping a software system to provide the best possible services to its users. However, since a system needs to be updated constantly, a vital part of the provisioning process is related to the updates and eventual restart of the applications.

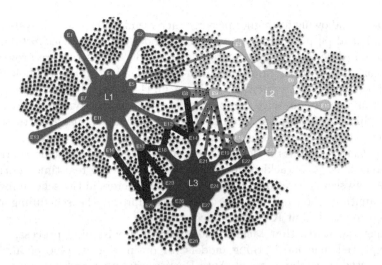

Fig. 1. Example of a system with multiple *locations* (L1, L2, and L3), each with multiple *edge nodes* (E1, E2, ..), and a variety of *IoT devices* connected to the edge nodes of the closest location (squares with same colors as locations). Moreover, the lines connecting edge nodes of different locations indicate the possibility to handover the connections of the IoT devices.

In this work, we use the term provisioning exactly to describe the update process of edge nodes (with consequent rebooting) to provide the best QoS to the system's users (Fig. 1).

2.2 Edge Computing

With the term Edge computing, we refer to a system where the computation is brought closer to the end user and the source of the data [1]. By keeping the majority of the data closer to the end users, there is a significant advantage in terms of lower latency and improved bandwidth compared to centralized systems. For this reason, whenever real-time processing is needed, edge computing allows bringing computation and data storage closer to the client.

2.3 Related Works

The increase in usage of edge technology and computing, including the proliferation of IoT devices, has increased the need for additional care needed to guarantee a sufficient quality of service. This system decentralizes the use of computational resources, bringing new issues in the management of the overall network.

Most of the research has therefore focused on how to optimize the provisioning of the resources for edge systems. Kherraf et al. [2], for example, proposed an approach that decomposes the resource provisioning and workload assignment into subtasks, allowing for higher performance trends in the overall system. Similarly, Cai et al [3] proposed a provisioning model called *edge federation*, which allows to schedule of resources among multiple edge infrastructure providers by characterizing the provisioning as a linear programming problem. Their method resulted in significantly reduced costs. Xu et al. [4] also tried to optimize the provisioning of resources in edge computing, by proposing a dynamic provisioning method which, besides optimizing the resource scheduling, also tries to optimize energy consumption and the completion time. Another issue in resource provisioning is that sometimes it doesn't take into account edge-specific characteristics. Ogbuachi et al. [5] tackled this problem by integrating real-time information regarding physical, operational, and network parameters in the scheduling of 5G edge computing, showing that this approach improves the scheduling process compared to the default Kubernetes scheduler.

Among the works that tackled the resource provisioning process, some of them exploited machine learning models for optimizing it. Guo et al. [6], for instance, used a combination of Auto-Regressive Integrated Moving Average (ARIMA) and Back-Propagation Neural Network (BPNN), to predict the load and optimize the resource provisioning of an edge system. Similarly, Li et al. [7] used the same ARIMA and BPNN models to forecast the load and proposed a location for new requests to be filled, reducing the cost of provisioning.

3   The Scheduling Algorithm

The proposed smart scheduling algorithm is based on three different contribution factors, as described below.

- **Static Weight:** a factor relates to the information which is not going to change in the near future and, therefore, *static* in time. It is computed taking into account the topology of the system.
- **Dynamic Weight:** this factor, in contrast, includes all of the information which is not static in time and therefore related to throughput among different nodes. Specifically, in this model, the Dynamic weight is related to the number of active connections each location has at different time slots.
- **Cluster ID:** this factor assigns a value to each location showing which are similar and can be considered in the same cluster.

3.1   Static Weight

The topology of the network is presented as a structured file including the Edge Source and the Destination Edge for each different possible service. This means that between different couple of locations it is possible to have multiple edge-based connections. Moreover, we also know that different locations have a different number of edge nodes. As we believe that different information has different importance when impacting the topology of the network we computed the static

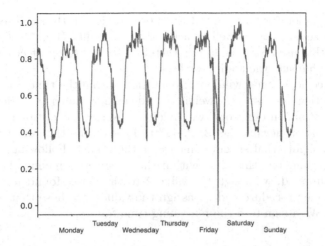

Fig. 2. Seasonality of the active traffic for a specific location.

weight s_w of each location as a weighted sum of this different information so that:

$$s_w = \alpha * W_E + \beta * W_L, \qquad (1)$$

where α and β are two factors assigned to the different weights, W_E is the weight computed based on the number of edges within a single location and W_L is the weight computed based on how many connections there are between two different locations.

More in particular we compute W_E as:

$$W_E(x_E) = \sum_{i=1}^{n} [l_i = x_E], \qquad (2)$$

where l_i is the list of the unique edges, having the location as the prefix.

We compute W_L as:

$$W_L(x_E) = \sum_{i=1}^{n} [lS_i = x_E | lD_i = x_E], \qquad (3)$$

where lS_i is the list of all source locations and lD_i is the list of all destination locations.

3.2 Dynamic Weight

The information related to the temporal evolution of the traffic for each location is especially useful in understanding which location to update (and therefore disconnect) first. The information is presented as a structured file that includes time series for each edge.

From an exploratory analysis of the aforementioned, the time series present an intra-day seasonality as well as a weekly seasonality (Fig. 2). The objective of the algorithm used for this data is therefore to find the perfect time for each location that impacts the traffic the least.

In the specific, given a window of operation within the time series provided, for each location, we assign a weight based on how much provisioning would affect the location. In our work, we divide the weights as optimal, suboptimal, acceptable, and irrelevant (i.e. 3, 2, 1, 0). This means that once we find the minima we assign to that specific time frame the value 3. Following, we compute the minima again, but this time within the time series having the previously time-frame dropped; we assign the value 2 to the newly found minima(s). We repeat the same procedure and we assign the value 1 to those that are found as 3rd minima. We assign 0 to the remaining time frames.

3.3 Cluster ID

A fundamental part of the algorithm is related to the process of clustering the different locations. To compute the clustering we rely on the python package NetworkX [8], used for the analysis of complex networks. NetworkX is mostly known in the literature for its ability to create a visual representation of a network, however, one of its less known but powerful strengths is the ability to compute cluster coefficients. In short, the cluster ID is the ID assigned to a location and used for grouping the locations sharing the highest number of edge connections between them.

The cluster coefficients have therefore been computed through the NetworkX Clustering function giving as an input W_L and the maximum number of allowable clusters. Once the coefficients are computed we created the clusters by computing evenly spaced areas and assigning each area based on the coefficients computed in the previous step.

3.4 Smart Edge Scheduling Algorithm

Given two files related to Topology (TN) and to the temporal evolution of the traffic (TS) we develop our algorithm as shown in Algorithm 1.

More in detail, for each of the possible i locations (l_i) in TN, we compute both the Edge-Based weight (W_E) and the location-based weight (W_L) as previously described in Eq. 2 and 3 respectively. Once both of those are computed, we retrieve the static weight s_w for each possible location.

Then, by making use of W_L, we compute the cluster numbers using NetworkX.

Following, for each specific location, we assigned the dynamic weights DW by finding the minima (first, second and third) in TS. This means that the time frame with the minimum amount of data sent will have the highest dynamic weight assigned (3), the second minimum will have the second highest dynamic weight assigned (2), and so on until the weights are assigned.

Algorithm 1: Smart Edge Provisioning Algorithm

---

for l_i *in* TN **do**
$\quad W_E(x_E) = \sum_{i=1}^{n}[l_i = x_E];$
$\quad W_L(x_E) = \sum_{i=1}^{n}[lS_i = x_E | lD_i = x_E];$
$\quad s_w(x_E) = \alpha + W_E(x_E) + \beta * W_L(x_E);$
end
$C = NetworkX(W_L)$
$DW = AssignDynamicWeights(TS)$
$SW = sort(sw)$ ▷ From lowest to highest value of x_E
for x_E *in* SW **do**
$\quad TF(x_E) \leftarrow \max(DW(x_E))$
$\quad$ **if** $SC(C(TF))$ *is empty* **then**
$\quad\quad | \quad SC(C(TF)) = TF(x_E)$
$\quad$ **else**
$\quad\quad TF2(x_E) \leftarrow \max(DW(x_E), 2)$
$\quad\quad$ **if** $SC(C(TF2))$ *is empty* **then**
$\quad\quad\quad | \quad SC(C(TF2)) = TF2(x_E)$
$\quad\quad$ **else**
$\quad\quad\quad TF3(x_E) \leftarrow \max(DW(x_E), 3)$
$\quad\quad\quad$ **if** $SC(C(TF3))$ *is empty* **then**
$\quad\quad\quad\quad | \quad SC(C(TF)) = TF(x_E)$
$\quad\quad\quad$ **end**
$\quad\quad$ **end**
$\quad$ **end**
end

Once the dynamic weights are assigned, we sort s_w from the lowest to the highest value. The reason behind this choice is that we want to prioritize locations that have the less amount of edges and connections as we will have fewer chances to redirect the connections to adjacent edges and therefore, impact more users.

Then for each location x_E in s_w we search for the maxima in DW, and most importantly, the time-frame ($TF(x_E)$) when the maxima in DW is found. Once the $TF(x_E)$ has been detected we search if that specific TF has been assigned to any location within the same cluster C. If the TF for the specific cluster is vacant, then it is assigned to x_E, if not we repeat the same procedure for the second and third maxima. If all the possible detected TF have been already reserved, we move to the next location.

The reason for using TF is to maximize the degree of parallelism. We want to schedule inter-cluster parallel updates so that we have one update per node for each cluster, which means that the degree of parallelism depends the number of clusters created in the previous step.

Once all the locations have been served we have a clear schedule of which location should perform provisioning at each TF. On the other side, we will also have a list that reports which one is the correct TF to perform provisioning for each location. Inevitably, there are locations for which no suggested TF can be detected. This means that these locations (usually less than 5%), can be assigned to empty TF for their C without varying the impact.

4 Measuring the Scheduling Performance

To properly validate our algorithm it was fundamental for us to understand the performance of the model proposed. Moreover, it was important for us to take into account some key factors such as the number of intra-edge connections broken while provisioning, and the amount of data lost in the same phase. For this reason, we created two metrics based on such factors: the intra-edge impact and the traffic impact.

4.1 Intra-edge Impact

The first factor to take into account when measuring the performance of the network is the number of multiple connections between different locations. A fundamental part of the algorithm relies on the creation of clusters composed of locations that are strictly related to each other. The reason behind the choice is to reduce the number of parallel unavailable locations which share multiple connections. We know that different countries are composed of a different number of locations, therefore, countries with a higher necessity of connection are less demanding. For this reason, we need a factor that shows the ability of the proposed algorithm to keep dense active connections alive when the throughput is high and heavily penalize situations where suggested scheduling cannot be proposed.

The intra-edge impact takes as input the proposed scheduling and the topology of the network: the first provides information related to *when* a specific location is shut down, while the second about *which* connections are going to be impacted by the provisioning. To penalize a situation where scheduling was not possible, all the locations without a suggested schedule are grouped in the same time frame.

4.2 Traffic Impact

The second factor to take into account when measuring the performance of the network is the amount of data lost during the provisioning. The goal of the algorithm is to minimize such an amount through optimal scheduling so that precise handovers can be performed and the chance of failure is reduced to the minimum.

In our environment, the information related to the traffic is provided in time frames of 15 min each. The provisioning time is set so that out of 30 min required, for the first 10 min (i.e. 1/3 of the time) the system runs at lower capability and tries to perform handovers, during the following 5 min the system is inaccessible, and for the last 15 min the location runs again at lower capability.

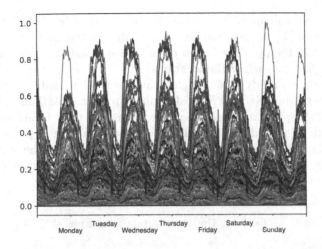

Fig. 3. Seasonality of the active traffic for all the locations considered.

Knowing this, we try to schedule handovers during the whole provisioning time, however, we know from the literature [9] that usually 20% of handovers fail. When creating the traffic impact factor, we grouped all of this information and created a factor that takes as input the proposed scheduling and the temporal evolution of the traffic. This means that for each specifically scheduled provisioning in the first input we search a correspondence for the TF, once the traffic information is found we store it as $v1$ and the following TF as $v2$. Then, we compute the traffic impact for the specific location as:

$$TI = \frac{\frac{1}{3} * v1 + (\frac{2}{3} * v1 + v2)/5}{5} \tag{4}$$

This means that we try to perform handovers all the time. However, statistically, 1 out of 5 times the handover fails and we need to compute the value we would lose in such an event. The traffic impact is composed of two parts, in the first we compute the complete outage which is taking one-third of the time of $v1$, in the second we compute the partial outage, which is taking two third of the time of $v1$, and the full $v2$. In our environment, during a partial outage the system can run at 80%, which means that during that period we lose 1/5 of the traffic.

5 Validation

To validate our scheduling algorithm, we used a system composed of 800 locations, with 270,000 edge nodes in total, averaging around 336 edge nodes for each location.

First of all, we calculated the static weights as described in Sect. 3.1. We obtained a value for each location; such value is only depending on the locations and the Edge devices, therefore, it is not changing, unless the architecture of the network itself would change.

Following, we calculated the dynamic weights described in Sect. 3.2. As it can be seen from Fig. 3, there is a clear seasonality in the data, which allowed us and consider the temporal evolution of the system and therefore calculate the dynamic weights, for each of the locations.

Once the static and dynamic weights have been calculated, we calculated the cluster number using NetworkX as described in Sect. 3.3. This allowed us to have a modeled representation of the edge nodes and their location.

Our smart edge update scheduler produced therefore a proposed update scheduling. In Table 1 it is possible to see an example of the scheduling for some of the locations. As it can be seen, for each of the locations we have a time that represents the moment in which the update is scheduled.

Table 1. Update scheduling example.

Location	Update schedule
235	2022-03-30 02:15:00 UTC
268	2022-03-30 02:30:00 UTC
224	2022-03-30 02:30:00 UTC
318	2022-03-30 02:45:00 UTC
362	2022-03-30 02:45:00 UTC
388	2022-03-30 02:45:00 UTC
402	2022-03-30 03:00:00 UTC
455	2022-03-30 03:00:00 UTC
469	2022-03-30 03:00:00 UTC

6   Conclusion

In this work, we provide a smart edge provisioning algorithm to minimize the number of dropped services and maximize the quality of service in a service-oriented architecture. We developed this algorithm to tweak at its best the environment provided resulting in a reduced amount of time necessary to perform a full upgrade of the elements composing the network and, therefore, not impacting availability of service in the hours with the highest demand. Such an environment is composed of a worldwide network divided into multiple locations, each one composed of multiple EDGE devices providing instruction to multiple IoT devices.

Ideally, the best possible outcome would be to update all the available locations without dropping any information provided to the IoT devices. This would mean that when performing the provisioning (update and restart), the amount of IoT devices connected to the location would be 0.

A possible way to achieve this condition would be by performing handovers to different locations. When performing handover we need to take into account two conditions:

- Network availability: when performing handover we need to make sure that the neighbor locations which are going to provide the service to the IoT devices will not be overpopulated by those. This would risk the malfunctioning of two locations.
- Failed handover: as described in Sect. 4.2, we know for sure that an average of 20% of handovers fail.

Therefore, it is very important to search for the time frame where each location has the minimum amount of throughput.

Given the latter as an input, we developed an algorithm tailored to this environment and impact values to validate it.

As the singular location-based provisioning would be impractical due to a large number of locations, our first goal has been to understand how to cluster different locations so that those could be updated in parallel. For this reason, we calculated weights based on the topology of the locations (and the edge nested in those) and the throughput of each location at each specific time frame.

By jointly analyzing the calculated weights we were able to understand which of these locations have more importance (some locations have fewer connections to other locations and therefore need to be carefully provisioned), and at what time there is less stream of information in the whole environment.

Our algorithm suggests schedules for most of the locations in the network. For some of them, it was not possible to provide an optimal schedule for two reasons:

- impact: the amount of information that they transmit is lower compared to other locations.
- overconnected: they have a high amount of connections to other locations and therefore the handover is easier

For these locations, the overall impact on the network between upgrading in different time frames can be neglected.

Acknowledgments. This work was partially supported by the Adoms grant from the Ulla Tuominen Foundation (Finland) and the MuFAno grant from the Academy of Finland (grant n. 349488).

References

1. Satyanarayanan, M.: The emergence of edge computing. Computer **50**(1), 30–39 (2017)
2. Kherraf, N., Alameddine, H.A., Sharafeddine, S., Assi, C.M., Ghrayeb, A.: Optimized provisioning of edge computing resources with heterogeneous workload in IoT networks. IEEE Trans. Netw. Serv. Manage. **16**(2), 459–474 (2019)

3. Cao, X., Tang, G., Guo, D., Li, Y., Zhang, W.: Edge federation: towards an integrated service provisioning model. IEEE/ACM Trans. Netw. **28**(3), 1116–1129 (2020)
4. Xu, X., Cao, H., Geng, Q., Liu, X., Dai, F., Wang, C.: Dynamic resource provisioning for workflow scheduling under uncertainty in edge computing environment. Concurr. Comput. Pract. Exp. **34**, e5674 (2020)
5. Ogbuachi, M.C., Gore, C., Reale, A., Suskovics, P., Kovács, B.: Context-aware K8S scheduler for real time distributed 5G edge computing applications. In: 2019 International Conference on Software, Telecommunications and Computer Networks (Soft-COM), pp. 1–6. IEEE (2019)
6. Guo, J., Li, C., Chen, Y., Luo, Y.: On-demand resource provision based on load estimation and service expenditure in edge cloud environment. J. Netw. Comput. Appl. **151**, 102506 (2020)
7. Li, C., Bai, J., Ge, Y., Luo, Y.: Heterogeneity-aware elastic provisioning in cloud-assisted edge computing systems. Futur. Gener. Comput. Syst. **112**, 1106–1121 (2020)
8. Schult, D.A.: Exploring network structure, dynamics, and function using NetworkX. In: Proceedings of the 7th Python in Science Conference (SciPy). Citeseer (2008)
9. Legg, P., Hui, G., Johansson, J.: A simulation study of LTE intra-frequency handover performance. In: 2010 IEEE 72nd Vehicular Technology Conference - Fall, pp. 1–5 (2010)

Energy-Aware Placement of Network Functions in Edge-Based Infrastructures with Open Source MANO and Kubernetes

Angel Cañete[1,2(✉)] , Alberto Rodríguez[3], Mercedes Amor[1,2] ,
and Lidia Fuentes[1,2]

[1] Universidad de Málaga, Campus de Teatinos, Málaga, Spain
{angelcv,pinilla,lff}@lcc.uma.es
[2] ITIS Software, Amplicación del Campus de Teatinos, Málaga, Spain
[3] 3intech, Polo de Contenidos Digitales, Málaga, Spain

Abstract. The virtualization of network functions aims to replace traditional network functions running on proprietary middleboxes with software instances running on general-purpose virtualization solutions, looking for more flexible, scalable and sustainable networks. However, despite the availability of platforms and technologies that enable its realisation, there are still technical challenges that have to be addressed to obtain those benefits. One of the challenges is the efficient placement of network functions, considering, for instance, the energy footprint among other constraints and available resources. This paper proposes an energy-aware virtual network function placement and resource-allocation solution for heterogeneous edge infrastructures that considers the computation and communication delays according to the virtual network functions' location in the infrastructure. The solution has been integrated with the ETSI-sponsored project Open Source Management and Orchestration (OSM) as an extension that allows the configuration of virtual network functions and their subsequent resource allocation and deployment at the edge, minimizing energy consumption and ensuring the quality of service. Applied to the deployment of augmented reality services in different scenarios, the results show up to a 51% reduction in energy consumption compared to the default OSM placement and quality of service compliance in all scenarios considered.

Keywords: Edge computing · Energy efficiency · B5G · VNF placement · Open source mano · Feature models

1 Introduction

The execution of traditional network functions (NFs) on proprietary middleboxes has several drawbacks, mainly in terms of high capital, operating and maintenance costs, long deployment cycle, high energy consumption (EC) and

© The Author(s), under exclusive license to Springer Nature Switzerland AG 2023
J. Troya et al. (Eds.): ICSOC 2022 Workshops, LNCS 13821, pp. 183–195, 2023.
https://doi.org/10.1007/978-3-031-26507-5_15

the need for expert personnel to manage and configure the plethora of existing equipment. The replacement of traditional network functions running in middleboxes by software instances running on general-purpose virtualization solutions leads to more flexible, scalable and sustainable networks. Network Function Virtualization (NFV) also meets the evolution in networking required by modern technologies such as Beyond 5G (B5G) and the Internet of Things (IoT), which are looking for more flexible, scalable and sustainable networks. However, although it is widely recognized that NFV solutions need to run as efficiently as possible to address sustainability concerns, existing NFV solutions and enabling virtualization technologies focus mainly on legacy network performance metrics, such as ensuring service availability and neglecting in some way the energy footprint. The efficient realization of NFV poses new challenges to enabling virtualization technologies and NFV platforms solutions [12] to guarantee network performance, NFs dynamic instantiation, their efficient placement and energy footprint reduction.

This paper presents an energy-aware approach n for the optimal placement of Virtual Network Functions (VNFs). Our solution is integrated with the Open Source Management and Orchestration (OSM) platform, which provides a VNF manager, and NFV orchestrator and supports connection to third-party Virtualized Infrastructure Managers (VIMs) (e.g., OpenStack). In addition, OSM supports container technology (via Kubernetes [3]) to enable the design and implementation of Kubernetes-based Network Functions (KNFs) [14] running inside containers. Our solution, named HADES, extends OSM by enabling the optimal placement and configuration of VNFs/KNFs and their subsequent resource allocation and deployment at the edge, minimizing EC and ensuring the quality of service (QoS). To this end, HADES provides an energy-ware scheduler for the open-source Kubernetes container orchestrator which assigns VNFs to nodes taking into account the energy consumption (EC), the computation and the communication delay within an NFV infrastructure. The solution has been integrated as an extension of the project [14] and tested in real (not simulated) scenarios of the deployment of typical augmented reality (AR) services (implemented as KNFs). Using a physical energy meter, the EC of the HADES placement solutions are compared with the default OSM placement scheduler. Furthermore, the QoS obtained with both deployments is tested. The results show up to a 51% reduction in EC and QoS compliance in all scenarios considered.

The remainder of this document is organized as follows. Section 2 introduces the related work and exposes the limitations of existing VNF placement approaches. Section 3 presents HADES and its integration with OSM, while Sect. 4 details the different modules that make up our proposal. Section 5 applies our proposal to the deployment of an augmented reality application on a physical edge infrastructure and evaluates the reduction in the EC obtained. Finally, Sect. 6 concludes the paper and presents future work.

2 Related Work

Both industry and academia have devoted much attention to the development of NFV and edge computing [13].

In the industry, there are several NFV solutions for the management and orchestration of VNF, both proprietary and open source. Concerning open source solutions, on which we will focus in this paper, the most widely used options are OSM (Open Source MANO) [14], Open Platform for NFV (OPNFV, now mixed with CNTT-Cloud iNfrastructure Telco Taskforce) as a new solution called Anuket) [6], and ONAP (Open Network Automation Platform) [4]. Although all of them are very similar, they differ in the amount of resources required for their operation. A deep comparison of installation and operation requirements shows that OPNFV [6] and ONAP [4] require more vCPUs (virtual Central Processing Unit), RAM (Random Access Memory) and disk than OSM, which has a minimum requirement of 2 vCPUs, 6 GB of RAM and 40 GB of disk [14]. This makes OSM the best candidate to integrate with our approach, as the aim of this work is to minimize the EC of VNF deployments in edge infrastructures.

Released in 2016, OSM is primarily developed in Python and runs on Linux operating systems. OSM uses three functional blocks (NFVO, VNFM and VIM) of the NFV MANO to perform VNF configuration and abstraction, and infrastructure orchestration and management. Some of the operations natively supported by OSM are: (i) orchestration service for VNFs; (ii) the possibility of performing complex services; (iii) management of infrastructures with several VIMs associated; (iv) software-defined network (SDN) controllers; (v) monitoring tools. The OSM proposes an open-source implementation of the ETSI (European Telecommunications Standards Institute) NFV architecture publicly available.

Intending to minimize the EC, in [15] authors formulate the VNF placement problem as a decision tree search. The parameters considered during the process are the nodes' CPU, their type and the bandwidth of the links. In [15], the amount of CPU required by the VNFs is fixed, which weakens the applicability of the proposal in heterogeneous infrastructures. With the same objective, authors in [7] propose an NFV scheduling heuristic algorithm to map and schedule traffic flows. Neither [15] nor [7] allows to adapt the nodes in which energy reduction is prioritised according to the needs of the infrastructure.

The work in [16] proposes a Multi-access Edge Computing (MEC)-based VNF placement and scheduling scheme for AR applications, whose objective is to improve the QoS. It deploys AR applications in a simulated environment, regardless of the dependency on peripherals or sensor units. Furthermore, both the cloud and the edge are considered as a set of homogeneous nodes, which simplifies the problem of deciding whether to run the VNFs on the edge, on the cloud or to reject the request. The work in [11] presents a VNF placement model to minimize the end-to-end delays, which is solved using Integer Linear Programming (ILP) and a heuristic algorithm. In [8], authors address the VNF-PC satisfying the delay constraints and reducing the consumption of network resources. The Service Function Chain (SFC, an ordered sequence of VNFs

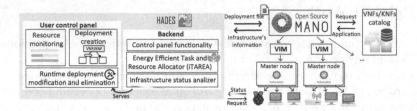

Fig. 1. General overview of our approach.

and subsequent steering of flows through them to provide end-to-end services) placement is solved as a Mixed Integer Nonlinear Programming (MINLP) and a heuristic algorithm is proposed based on the relaxation and delay check. However, the models presented in these works only consider CPU and bandwidth, while other aspects such as disk or RAM are considered. Considering peripherals within the proposal itself (as ours does) and not only in the deployment descriptors allows not only to take into account their presence but also their characteristics (e.g., GPU frequency) to provide solutions that ensure QoS.

3 Our Approach

Figure 1 shows the integration of our platform HADES with Open Source MANO [14]. HADES is a platform that makes use of OSM and Kubernetes functionality for managing VNFs and KNFs deployments, automating and optimizing the deployment process in order to minimize EC. HADES is composed of two main parts: the Web-based back-end module that provides the main functionalities of HADES; and the front-end control panel, which provides the administrator with a GUI to control, monitor and consult the functions of the back-end. Using the control panel, the infrastructure administrator can initiate the deployment by selecting the VNF/KNF and the configuration of its characteristics. The administrator can also modify and remove existing deployments at runtime. The monitoring module displays the status of the infrastructure resources in real-time. Each module is explained in more detail in Sect. 4. To carry out these processes, HADES collects and uses information of the infrastructure provided by the OSM API, while it generates and sends OSM-understandable deployment files to OSM (see Fig. 1). Specifically, HADES endows OSM with the following capabilities:

- *Minimization of energy consumption of the deployments.*
- *Generation of application configuration,* allowing the infrastructure manager to select both application and QoS-related features before deployment.
- *QoS assurement of the deployments.*
- *Resource allocation optimization,* establishing a minimum and maximum range of resource usage to ensure QoS while minimizing resource waste.
- *Deployments considering multiple VIMs* (not natively supported by OSM).
- *Easy modification of deployments, keeping unmodified application parts intact.*

4   HADES Platform

This section presents the operation of the HADES platform and its integration with the rest of the OSM components shown in Fig. 1.

4.1   Deployment Creation Module

The infrastructure manager first selects the VNF/KNF to be deployed from the catalogue to which OSM has access. Then, uses the application feature model (FM) to configure it. Commonly used in software product lines, FMs represent, in terms of features, which elements of a family of software products are common, which are variable and the relationships between them. FMs are represented as a set of hierarchically ordered features, composed of parent-child relationships and a set of constraints which represent the relationships among features. The number of VNFs/KNFs (or tasks) that form the application and their characteristics will depend on the configuration of the application FM. Once configured, the resulting application (formed by a set of VNFs/KNFs) is sent to the iTAREA module (described later), which returns the most energy-efficient assignment of VNFs/KNFs to nodes and the allocation of resources that satisfies the functional and non-functional requirements of the application. Finally, this solution is used to create deployment files, understandable by OSM, with the optimized deployment of the application. As introduced in Sect. 3, HADES allows considering the entire infrastructure (i.e., several clusters), as well as excluding specific nodes or clusters from the solution.

Once the deployment is done, the location information of each task is stored to assure the correct communication between VNFs/KNFs. If the location of a task changes, this information is updated. This mode of operation is based on the Mediator design pattern [9].

Efficient Task and Resource Allocator (iTAREA). The efficient TAsk and REsource Allocator (iTAREA) module is responsible for deciding where each VNF/KNF should be executed and the amount of RAM (Mb), disk (Mb), bandwidth, and percentage of CPU to allocate to each of them. This module is based on the concept that some nodes are more energy efficient than others.

Energy Consumption and Latency Models: The iTAREA uses the following expressions to calculate the latency of the application execution (left) and EC (right), to minimize EC while ensuring the QoS [13]:

$$eCompu_{i,n} = (1 - \alpha_n)(eMax_n v_{i,n} + eIdle_n)tCompu_{i,n}ew_n$$

$$eIdle_n = \alpha_n eMax_n$$

$$tCompu_{i,n} = \frac{w_i}{CPU_n v_{i,n}}$$

$$cSend_{c_{i,j},n,z,ct} = x_{i,n}h_{i,j}P_{n,ct}^{Tx}\frac{c_{i,j} + c_{i,j}pR}{Min(R_{n,ct}^{Tx}, R_{z,ct}^{Rx})}ew_n$$

$$tCommu_{i,j,n,z,ct} = \frac{c_{i,j} + c_{i,j}pR}{Min(R_{n,ct}^{Tx}, R_{z,ct}^{Rx})} + t_{n,z}^{prop}$$

$$eRecp_{c_{i,j},n,z,ct} = x_{j,z}h_{i,j}P_{z,ct}^{Rx}\frac{c_{i,j} + c_{i,j}pR}{Min(R_{n,ct}^{Rx}, R_{z,ct}^{Tx})}ew_z$$

where the computation time of task i in node n ($tCompu_{i,n}$) is obtained by the ratio between the number of CPU cycles (w_i, collected using tools like Linux *perf*) required by task i and the CPU frequency of the node per core (CPU_n) multiplied by the percentage of CPU allocated to the task on the node ($v_{i,n}$). Meanwhile, the communication time is calculated by the ratio between the amount of data to transmit between tasks i and j ($c_{i,j}$)– pR being the probability of retransmission due to packet loss–and the transmission/reception speed (using connection type ct, e.g., *WiFi 2.4, 4G*). The propagation delay $t_{n,z}^{prop}$ is set as the half of the mean round trip time (RTT) obtained by pinging from n to z, and considered like constant [13].

EC (right side of the above equation) at the nodes is influenced by several factors, such as CPU, storage and RAM usage, the CPU being the most influential factor and the most commonly used in the literature [13]. $eCompu_{i,n}$ calculates the computational EC (J) required by the node n to compute task i, while $eIdle_n$ represents the idle EC of a node. The energy consumed by task i to communicate with task j is calculated in the third and fourth expressions of the right side of the equation, which calculate the EC for sending and receiving data from node n to z [13]. Concretely, $eMax_n$ is the EC of node n when it is fully-utilized (in terms of CPU); v the CPU utilization ratio (from 0 to number of node cores); and α, whose value is between 0 and 1, represents the fraction of the idle EC (e.g., 60%) [13]. This model is based on the observation that the EC is linear to the CPU utilization ratio which depends on the computation load [13,15]. The third and fourth expressions of the right-hand side of the above equation denote the EC for data sending and receiving respectively from node n to z [13]. P^{Tx} and P^{Rx} represent the transmission powers, while R^{Tx} and R^{Rx} denote the transmission rates for data transmitting and receiving. $x_{i,n}$ is 1 if task i is assigned to node n, 0 otherwise; $h_{i,j}$ is 0 if tasks i and j are assigned to the same node, 1 otherwise. The variable ew (energy weight), whose value is between 1 and 0, represents the importance of energy saving in each node. The higher its value, the more important it is to save energy at that node. This allows customizing the importance of energy savings according to the needs of the infrastructure, unlike other approaches [13]. An example of practical use is to prioritize the assignment in devices powered by solar panels, thus reducing the carbon footprint.

Implementation:
As the CPU depends on the computing capacity of the node, the variable *CPU-Partitions* contains the portions of CPU that can be assigned to each task by each core; this reduces the search range (and therefore the problem complexity). Therefore, if this variable has a value of 10, the CPU will be allocated in portions of 0.1 cores (100 millicores). Concerning QoS assurance, applications have sets of tasks with time constraints (i.e., they must be completed within a maximum time), which are part of the problem constraints.

This module receives as input the information of the nodes (set N), the tasks (τ), the nodes to exclude (*nodesToAvoid*), the set of time restrictions (Tr), and the CPU portions ($CPUPartitions$). As an output, it returns the task assignment and the amount of resources that the node must reserve for each assigned task.

$$
\begin{aligned}
\textbf{Input:} \quad & N, Tr, \tau, nodesToAvoid, CPUPartitions \\
\textbf{Minimize:} \quad & energy \rightarrow \forall (n, m) \epsilon N, i \epsilon \tau : x_{i,n} eCompu(i, n) + \\
& \sum_{j \epsilon \tau} \left(h_{i,j} eSend(c_{i,j}, n) + x_{j,m} eRecp(c_{i,j}, m) \right)
\end{aligned}
$$

Subject to: $N = N \setminus nodesToAvoid$	(1)
$\forall i \epsilon \tau : \sum_{n \epsilon N} x_{i,n} = 1$	(2)
$\forall n \epsilon N : \sum_{i \epsilon \tau} x_{i,n} {}^i RAM \leq {}^n RAM$	(3)
$\forall n \epsilon N : \sum_{i \epsilon \tau} x_{i,n} {}^i disk \leq {}^n disk$	(4)
$\forall n \epsilon N : \sum_{i \epsilon \tau} x_{i,n} {}^i bandwidth \leq {}^n bandwidth$	(5)
$\forall n \epsilon N, i \epsilon \tau : x_{i,n} RAM_{i,n} \geq {}^i RAM x_{i,n}$	(6)
$\forall n \epsilon N, i \epsilon \tau : x_{i,n} disk_{i,n} \geq {}^i disk x_{i,n}$	(7)
$\forall n \epsilon N, i \epsilon \tau : x_{i,n} bandwidth_n \geq {}^i bandwidth$	(8)
$\forall n \epsilon N : \sum_{i \epsilon \tau} x_{i,n} CPU_{i,n} \leq CPUPartitionsCores_n$	(9)
$\forall n \epsilon N, i \epsilon \tau : CPU_{i,n} \epsilon \mathbb{N}$	(10)
$\forall n \epsilon N, i \epsilon \tau : x_{i,n} \wedge meets(n, i) \vee \neg x_{i,n}$	(11)
$\forall tr \epsilon Tr, (n, m) \epsilon N, i \epsilon \tau : x_{i,n} tCompu(i, n) +$	
$\sum_{(j) \epsilon tr} h_{i,j} x_{j,m} tCommu(c_{i,j}, n, m) \leq time_{tr}$	(12)
Return: $\forall i \epsilon \tau, n \epsilon N : x_{i,n} \rightarrow RAM_{i,n}; x_{i,n} \rightarrow disk_{i,n};$	
$x_{i,n} \rightarrow bandwidth_{i,n}; x_{i,n} \rightarrow CPU_{i,n}$	

$$\text{(1)}$$

The iTAREA module, formalized in Eq. 1, does the following: first, it excludes the nodes to be avoided from the set N (1); (2) checks that each task has a node assigned; (3–5) ensure that nodes have RAM, disk and bandwidth enough to execute their assigned tasks, while (6–8) assure to assign enough resources to properly execute each task; (9–10) check that nodes do not allocate more CPU than available (limiting the search range according to the $CPUPartitions$ variable); (11) checks that the nodes fulfil the task requirements (in terms of peripherals and sensing units); (12) verifies the fulfilment of the time restrictions, considering execution and communication times; finally, the iTAREA returns the solution (task assignment, RAM, disk, bandwidth and CPU assigned to each task). To implement the iTAREA module we use the *Gurobi Parallel Mixed Integer Programming* solver. Thus, (1) the algorithm always returns a solution (differently from heuristic algorithms), which guarantees that the deployment is feasible or the impossibility to deploy the application if no solution is found; while both SMT (Satisfiability Modulo Theories) solvers and MILP (Mixed Integer Linear Programming) allow handling the variables required by the problem at hand (unlike others), MILP solvers return the solution faster than SMT solvers [17]; and (3) Gurobi supports multi-threading, which aids problem scalability. Nevertheless, it could be possible to use other solutions to our approach.

4.2 Resource Monitoring

This module tracks the status of the infrastructure. Its functions include checking the number of VIMs, their characteristics and their associated cluster (if any); and obtaining real-time information about the node's workload (CPU, RAM, disk and bandwidth). Its functions are mainly two: (1) provides the iTAREA module with the necessary information about the infrastructure to perform its function; and (2) allows HADES to be aware of the most demanded nodes, or of those that should be excluded from some deployments. Regarding its implementation, it is a process that periodically makes requests to the Kubernetes clusters to know their status in real-time. This information is stored at the backend, which keeps a log that could be used for different purposes (e.g., to apply auto-scaling).

4.3 Runtime Deployment Modification and Elimination

This module allows both deleting and modifying existing deployments. The elimination of deployments causes the application to stop running and the nodes to release the resources allocated to its execution. For its part, the modification of deployments allows extending, reducing or modifying the functionality of the applications, keeping intact those parts of the application that are not involved.

Deletion is a relatively simple process: the infrastructure manager selects a deployment from among the active ones and orders to delete it, while, the amount of available resources for each node is updated. Application modifications are carried out using the application FMs. The VNFs/KNFs whose functionality has been modified are deleted and the new VNFs/KNFs are deployed instead. Sometimes, it is not necessary to remove existing tasks, and new tasks are added. The resulting SFC remain connected following the location log maintained at the backend.

5   Proof of Concept

In this section, we apply our proposal to the deployment of a distributed application based on KNFs.

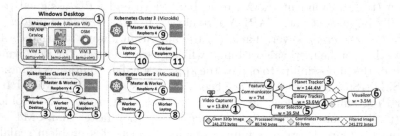

Fig. 2. Experimentation setup (left) and SFC of PlanetARium (right)

5.1   Infrastructure

Figure 2 (left) shows the edge infrastructure used. It consists of eleven hetero-geneous nodes, a manager and the other ten distributed in three Kubernetes clusters (that use Microk8s (v1.23), a lightened version of Kubernetes to reduce EC and improve the applicability of the proposal). The manager node (Node 1) contains instances of HADES, OSM (its most up-to-date release, ELEVEN), the application repository and three virtualized VIMs (virtualized using OSM's native *emu-vim tool*). This node runs Ubuntu 20.04 LTS and has 2 cores of CPU (4.2 GHz) and 8 Gb of memory. Cluster 1 has four nodes: a Raspberry Pi 4 (Node 2) running Ubuntu Mate 20.04.1 (4 cores of up to 1.5 GHz, 4 Gb of RAM) as the master node (which is also a worker) and three worker nodes. Node 3 (desktop) runs Ubuntu 20.04 LTS, having 4 cores of CPU (3.10 GHz) and 12 GB of RAM. Node 4 (laptop) runs Ubuntu 20.04 LTS, and has 4 cores of CPU (2.30 GHz) and 4 GB of RAM. Node 5 (Raspberry Pi 3 B+) runs Ubuntu Server 20.04, 4 cores of CPU (1.4 GHz) and 1 GB of RAM. Cluster 2 is formed by three nodes: Node 6 (Raspberry Pi 4, same configuration as Node 2) operating as master and worker node that manages two worker nodes: Node 7 (desktop) runs Ubuntu 20.04 LTS, has 4 cores of CPU (up to 3.70 GHz) and 12 GB of RAM; and Node 8 (laptop) running Ubuntu 20.04 LTS with 4 cores of CPU (2.20 GHz) and 4 GB of RAM. Finally, Cluster 3 contains three nodes: Node 9 (Raspberry Pi 4, the same configuration as Nodes 2–6) operating as master and worker; Node 10 (laptop), with the same configuration as Node 4; and Node 11, a Raspberry Pi 3 B+ (same characteristics as Node 5). Nodes have a clean installation of the operating system, trying to minimize the number of background tasks.

To carry out an efficient task allocation, HADES uses the idle and busy EC of the nodes. Therefore, the EC of the nodes has been analyzed both at idle (with the Microk8s installed) and during a 1-min CPU matrix stress test. The matrix stressor is a good way to exercise CPU floating-point operations, as well as the memory and data cache of the processor. To measure the EC we use Watts Up? Pro [10], a physical meter that allows real-time monitoring of the amount of energy supplied to the device connected to the power supply.

Regarding communication, the round-trip time between nodes is obtained by pinging from node a to b (considering the average of sending 1000 small pack-ets). The transmission rate has been analyzed using *iPerf* [2] (considering the average transmission rate of sending packages during 100 s). Finally, the power transmission is given directly from the characteristics of the nodes' network cards.

5.2   Case Study: Augmented Reality Services

As case study, we have implemented *PlanetARium*, an application that uses augmented reality (AR) services to display virtual planets, constellations, etc., according to the information obtained from a camera. AR applications are widely used in edge computing approaches, as they are computationally intensive and

delay-sensitive, and processing all the information on devices with low computational capacity is prohibitively expensive because it would affect users' expectations in terms of QoS [13].

PlanetARium is composed of several interconnected micro-services, each of
them being a KNF of the same SFC (see right side of Fig. 2). The desired QoS
stipulated by the infrastructure manager in the deployment module is 15 FPS
(frames per second). Concretely, the KNFs that form the SFC are the following:

- **Video capturer (KNF 1)**: captures video from a camera (required) and
  adapts the resolution to the one selected by the infrastructure manager.
- **Feature Communicator (KNF 2)**: receives the video stream and converts
  it to black-and-white video for easy element detection.
- **Filter Selector (KNF 3)**: applies a filter to reduce the brightness of the
  received video and a blur, assimilating the image to a night sky.
- **Planet Tracker (ArUco Detector, KNF 4)**: searches for ArUco codes in
  the received video, identifying each one and determining its coordinates.
- **Galaxy Tracker (QR Detector, KNF 5)**: searches for QR codes in the
  received video, obtaining their coordinates.
- **Visualizer (KNF 6)**: receives the processed video stream and the coordinates of planets and galaxies and overlays the corresponding virtual elements,
  creating a server accessible through a browser.

All tasks run as Docker containers and communicate through sockets. For
video capture and element detection, PlanetARium uses the open source tool
OpenCV [5] for Python 3, while for 3D element rendering NodeJS and Three
JS. Concerning their requirements in terms of RAM and disk, they are obtained
by using the Linux command *htop* and Docker Stats [1]. To assure the desired
QoS, we extract the computational cost and amount of data to transmit for one
iteration of each task. Then, knowing the time it takes for the deployment to
perform a complete iteration (i.e. to execute each task once), we calculate the
maximal time per iteration (15 iterations per second in our case, 0.067 s per
iteration as maximum). Our model uses the number of CPU cycles to determine
the computational load of the VNFs/KNFs (see Sect. 4.1). Using the Linux tool
perf and a traffic sniffer, we launch 2000 iterations of each task (using different
inputs) for each node and establish an average number of CPU cycles and an
average amount of data transmitted to avoid the bias that could exist by considering only one type of input for each task. PlanetARium KNFs do not reserve
or limit node bandwidth.

5.3 Experiments on Energy Saving

This section compares the EC of the default Kubernetes deployment with that
of HADES for the infrastructure and application presented in Sects. 5.1 and 5.2.
We will consider the deployment of PlanetARium in four scenarios: in Cluster 1,
in Cluster 2, in Cluster 3, and in the complete infrastructure (Clusters 1–3). In
Scenarios 1–3 we will use both the default Kubernetes scheduler (kube-scheduler)

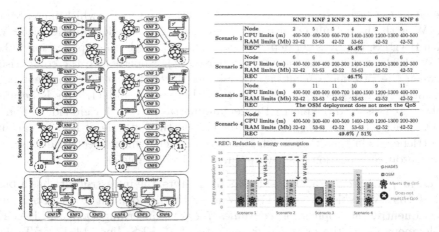

Fig. 3. Task assignment (left), Table 1 (upper right corner), and energy consumption for the different scenarios (lower right corner)

and HADES, while in the fourth one we will perform the deployment only with HADES (OSM only allows to consider one cluster). Finally, we will measure the EC of the nodes before and after deploying the application, thus obtaining the deployment EC. To check compliance with the minimum FPS set at 15, we introduce an on screen frame counter. For a fair comparison of results, all tests were performed at the same location and on the same day, under the same temperature conditions and node status.

Left side of Fig. 3 shows the resulting KNF assignments:

Scenario 1 (Cluster 1): The base consumption (before the application deployment) of Cluster 1 is 77.9 W, being 92.2 W after the PlanetARium deployment. Therefore, the application EC with kube-scheduler is 14.3 W. When deployed with HADES, the EC after the deployment drops to 85.7 W, which means an application EC of 7.8 W. Regarding QoS, both deployments meet the non-functional requirement of 15 FPS. To achieve this, it is crucial to allocate the correct amount of resources to each KNF. Lines 2–5 of Table 1 (upper right corner of Fig. 3) contain the resource allocation of HADES for Scenario 1. Kubernetes does not set a maximum resource usage margin (so QoS cannot be assured as deployments increase), as HADES does. Note that HADES assigns KNF 1, which requires a camera, to Node 2 because the Node 2 camera supports video capture at 15 FPS (the minimal QoS desired); the same check would be performed for any other peripheral that could compromise the QoS.

Scenario 2 (Cluster 2): The base EC of this cluster is 76.9 W, increasing to 91.6 W after the deployment using kube-scheduler (see left side of Fig. 3). Thus, the application EC is 14.7 W. As for deployment with HADES, the EC is 84.8 W, resulting in an application EC of 7.9 W. Concerning QoS, both deployments meet the QoS of 15 FPS established in the configuration phase. Lines 6–9 of Table 1 show the HADES resource allocation.

Scenario 3 (Cluster 3): The base EC of Cluster 3 is 14.9 W, which increases to 20.7 W with the default OSM deployment, giving an application EC of 5.8 W. With HADES, the EC after deployment is 22.6 W, which is an application EC of 7.7 W (1.9 W over the default OSM deployment). Nonetheless, the comparison between the two deployments is not fair, as the Kubernetes deployment does not meet the expected QoS; FPS fluctuate between 3 and 11. This is because Kubernetes assigned the most CPU demanding task (KNF 4, right side of Fig. 2) to the least CPU powerful node (Node 11, see the left side of Fig. 3), causing a bottleneck. On the other hand, the HADES deployment meets the expected QoS (resource allocation is shown in lines 10–13 of Table 1).

Scenario 4 (Clusters 1–3): Considering all clusters, the infrastructure has a base EC of 169,7 W, which rises to 176,9 W after the deployment of PlanetARium. Consequently, the application consumes 7.2 W. Concerning QoS, the HADES deployment meets the expected frame rate of 15 FPS; lines 14–17 of Table 1 contain the resource allocation in the case of HADES.

Lower right corner of Fig. 3 collects the EC obtained for the different scenarios. Experiments reveal that the HADES' deployments have reduced the EC compared with kube-scheduler in all the scenarios considered for the same QoS (Scenarios 1,2 and 4). Specifically, in Scenario 1 HADES has obtained a reduction in EC of 6,4 W, which means a decrease of 45.4%. For Scenario 2, the EC reduction obtained was 6 W (46.7%). Applied to Scenario 4, HADES has obtained a reduction of 7.2 W, being the most energy-efficient deployment. This represents a 49.6% reduction in EC compared to deployment using kube-scheduler in Scenario 1, and a 51% for Scenario 2–the scenarios in which the frame rate with kube-scheduler is as desired. Likewise, has been proved that the allocation of resources made by HADES has fulfilled the minimum QoS of 15 FPS established in all cases, while the deployment of kube-scheduler in Scenario 3 has not.

6   Conclusions and Future Work

NFV and edge computing have established themselves as the key technologies in the adoption of B5G communication technology. Nevertheless, there are still technical challenges to be addressed such as guaranteeing network performance, efficient placement and energy footprint reduction.

This paper presents HADES, a solution developed to work in conjunction with OSM. The result is a platform that optimizes the assignment of VNFs and resources to minimize energy consumption, addressing the problem of NF chaining considering factors typically ignored as disk, RAM or peripherals [12], while assuring the QoS. HADES consists of different modules that allow the creation, modification and elimination of VNFs deployments in edge infrastructures, and resource monitoring. Our proposal has been applied to the deployment of AR services on a heterogeneous edge infrastructure, obtaining a reduction of up to 51% in the EC compared with the default deployment proposed by OSM.

QoS has been measured after deployment, demonstrating that the deployment of HADES met the desired QoS.

In future work, we will work on automating the collection of data needed for deployment optimization by HADES.

Acknowledgements. This work is supported by the European Union's H2020 research and innovation program under grant agreement DAEMON 101017109 and by the projects co-financed by FEDER funds LEIA UMA18-FEDERJA-15, MEDEA RTI2018-099213-B-I00 (MCI/AEI) and RHEA P18-FR-1081.

References

1. Docker's docs. https://docs.docker.com. Accessed 27 Oct 2022
2. iperf tool. https://iperf.fr. Accessed 27 Oct 2022
3. Kubernetes' docs. https://kubernetes.io/docs/home/. Accessed 27 Oct 2022
4. Onap's docs. https://docs.onap.org/. Accessed 27 Oct 2022
5. Opencv's docs. https://docs.opencv.org/4.x/. Accessed 27 Oct 2022
6. Opnfv's docs. https://docs.opnfv.org/. Accessed 27 Oct 2022
7. Assi, C., et al.: Energy-aware mapping and scheduling of network flows with deadlines on VNFs. IEEE Trans. Green Commun. Netw. **3**(1), 192–204 (2019)
8. Cheng, Y., et al.: Deployment of service function chain for NFV-enabled network with delay constraint. In: ICET, pp. 383–386 (2018)
9. Gamma, E., et al.: Design Patterns: Elements of Reusable Object-Oriented Software Addison-Wesley Longman Publishing Co. Inc, USA (1995)
10. Hirst, J.M., et al.: Watts up? pro ac power meter for automated energy recording. Behav. Anal. Pract. **6**(1), 82–95 (2013). https://doi.org/10.1007/BF03391795
11. Luizelli, et al.: Piecing together the NFV provisioning puzzle: efficient placement and chaining of virtual network functions. In: 2015 IFIP/IEEE International Symposium on Integrated Network Management (IM), pp. 98–106 (2015)
12. Mach, P., Becvar, Z.: Mobile edge computing: a survey on architecture and computation offloading. IEEE Commun. Surv. Tutorials **19**(3), 1628–1656 (2017)
13. Mao, Y., et al.: A survey on mobile edge computing: the communication perspective. IEEE Commun. Surv. Tutorials **19**(4), 2322–2358 (2017)
14. Reid, et al.: Osm scope, functionality, operation and integration guidelines. ETSI, White Paper (2019)
15. Soualah, et al.: Energy efficient algorithm for VNF placement and chaining. In: IEEE/ACM CCGRID, pp. 579–588 (2017)
16. Tseng, H.W., et al.: An mec-based vnf placement and scheduling scheme for ar application topology. In: 2021 IEEE Wireless Communications and Networking Conference (WCNC), pp. 1–6 (2021)
17. Wimmer, R., Jansen, N., Ábrahám, E., Becker, B., Katoen, J.-P.: Minimal critical subsystems for discrete-time markov models. In: Flanagan, C., König, B. (eds.) TACAS 2012. LNCS, vol. 7214, pp. 299–314. Springer, Heidelberg (2012). https://doi.org/10.1007/978-3-642-28756-5_21

People Counting in the Times of Covid-19

E. Maione, S. Forti(✉)(iD), and A. Brogi(iD)

Department of Computer Science, University of Pisa, Pisa, Italy
stefano.forti@unipi.it

Abstract. Estimating the number of people within a public building with multiple entrances is an interesting problem, especially when limitations on building occupancy hold as during the Covid-19 pandemic. In this article, we illustrate the design, prototyping and assessment of an open-source distributed Cloud-IoT service that performs such a task and detects crowd formation via EdgeAI, also accounting for privacy and security concerns. The service is deployed and thoroughly assessed over a low-cost Fog infrastructure, showing an average accuracy of 94%.

1 Introduction

Counting people in public spaces got increasingly important in recent years with applications to logistics, marketing and security [20]. Indeed, estimating the number of people inside a building could help enforcing rules on maximum building occupancy, and provides a useful piece of information in emergency situations, e.g. fires or earthquakes. Besides, it could be useful to manage people flows entering or exiting the building through determined entrances and not others. Last, it can provide input to smart ambient services, e.g. to efficiently manage lights or temperature inside specific building areas based on their occupancy.

Considering the Covid-19 pandemic situation, estimating the number of people turns out crucial when limitations on public space occupancy need to be enforced to reduce the risk of contagion. If performed with cameras, the people counting infrastructure can enable a plethora of other useful services to tackle pandemic times, e.g. crowd detection, check on facial-masks. All of the above tasks can be automated by exploiting Internet of Things (IoT) video-cameras and processing video footage with machine learning techniques.

However, foreseeing such a deployment as a Cloud-based service shows limitations related to transmitting video from edge cameras to the cloud to be processed, which could involve high latency, require large bandwidth, and suffer from temporary network disconnections or degradation [5]. Since video footage contains personal images, transmission also involve security and privacy issues. To mitigate such issues, Cloud, Edge, and IoT resources can be suitably combined and exploited. This can be achieved by decentralising low-latency and data processing tasks to edge devices connected to the IoT and exploiting Cloud resources

---

Work partly supported by project *GIÒ: a Fog computing testbed for research & Education* funded by the Department of Computer Science, University of Pisa, Italy.

J. Troya et al. (Eds.): ICSOC 2022 Workshops, LNCS 13821, pp. 196–208, 2023.
https://doi.org/10.1007/978-3-031-26507-5_16

for long-term storage or more resource-demanding tasks. Such is precisely the aim of next-gen Cloud-IoT computing paradigms, e.g. Fog computing [3].

Recently, many proposed to extend edge capabilities with specialised hardware (e.g. GPU co-processors) to support machine learning tasks, leading to the new EdgeAI paradigm [19]. The possibility to send already elaborated/aggregated data enables desirable features for a people counting system such as avoiding leak of sensitive information by elaborating data *in situ*, mitigating network disruption issues by caching results at edge nodes, reducing latency and needed bandwidth by only transmitting relevant updates to the Cloud.

Exploiting EdgeAI to perform people counting in public spaces represents both an interesting use case for Cloud-IoT paradigms and a cost-effective alternative to expensive proprietary solutions that often rely on public Cloud deployments and on costly sensor technologies [7]. However, to the best of our knowledge, no open-source EdgeAI-based service exists that can be deployed onto a low-cost Cloud-IoT infrastructure, considering data privacy and security.

In this context, the main contribution of this article is to illustrate the design (Sect. 2), prototyping (Sect. 3) and assessment (Sect. 4) of GióPeopleCounter, a novel open-source EdgeAI-based service, capable of: (*i*) estimating the number of persons inside a public building with multiple entrances, and (*ii*) detecting crowd formation by setting up and experimenting with a low-cost Cloud-IoT infrastructure. As GióPeopleCounter processes sensitive data, we follow *privacy-by-design* and *security-by-design* principles [4]. We conclude the article by discussing some related work (Sect. 5) and some lines for future work (Sect. 6).

2   System Requirements

Objectives and Stakeholders. Our prototype service, GióPeopleCounter, pursued the two following objectives, related to Covid-19 anti-contagion rules:

(**O1**) *People counting.* The first identified objective of GióPeopleCounter was to estimate the number of people within the Department of Computer Science so to guarantee not to trespass an overall occupancy threshold (e.g. 50%). Such functionality can be useful to estimate the presence of people in the building in non-pandemic times, e.g. in case of emergency evacuations, or to turn on/off the electric appliances depending on people presence.

(**O2**) *Crowd detection.* The second identified objective was to detect crowds in front of the Department doors. Crowd detection can help reception staff to better monitor crowded situation so to dissipate crowds, which were not allowed during the Covid-19 pandemics, when needed.

Besides, we set the objective of deploying GióPeopleCounter over a low-cost Fog infrastructure, made from edge and cloud resources and enabled with EdgeAI capabilities. According to **O1** and **O2**, we identified three main stakeholder roles that we used throughout the requirements elicitation phase:

- *DeptHead*. The first identified stakeholder role was that of the Head of Department, i.e. the person in charge of enforcing Covid-19 rules and regulations, and safety measures within the Department facilities. Indeed, by helping reception personnel in monitoring the number of people within the building, in avoiding crowded situations, and in checking the correct usage of masks, GióPeopleCounter would help enforce anti-contagion rules. Besides, it could help in handling emergency evacuation/rescue situations as well as in detecting unauthorized accesses to the building (e.g. during closing times), and in energy savings related to systems that can be turned off when nobody is within the building (e.g. lights, printers, heating).
- *Receptionist*. The second identified role was that of the reception personnel, delegated by the *DeptHead* to enforce Covid-19 countermeasures at the entrance of the building. Similarly to what was stated above, the *Receptionist* has an interest in all monitoring functionalities envisioned for GióPeopleCounter.
- *SysAdmin*. The last identified role was the system developer and administrator, viz. *SysAdmin*. Such role needs access all system functionalities, being capable of monitoring their correct functioning and acting to guarantee it. This role is interested in system maintenance functionalities, such as users credentials management, system counters reset, service configurations, as well as in the correct functioning of all system components.

Requirements Elicitation. User stories are a technique for requirement elicitation in a non-technical format, as per a feature-driven software development [17]. By interviewing actual persons impersonating the roles identified above, we elicited requirements in the form of 20 user stories as per the template: "*As a* ⟨ who ⟩ *I want to* ⟨ what ⟩ *so that* ⟨ why ⟩". Figure 1 lists all collected user stories.

Privacy and Security. As the system depicted by the elicited user stories involved processing potentially sensitive data, i.e. people images, we have started an analysis of those requirements with the support of the Legal Office of our University. Our goal was to understand how to properly handle/elaborate images and personal data in accordance with laws and regulations on privacy and labour [2]. Particularly, we aimed at ensuring that GióPeopleCounter did not configure as a video-surveillance system to control employees.

We then revised the requirements for GióPeopleCounter following *privacy-by-design* principles. As a result, some user stories of Fig. 1 were modified, some were added and finally others were removed before implementing GióPeopleCounter.

First, two user stories from *DeptHead* and *SysAdmin* were modified as follows:

US4 As a *DeptHead* I want to visualise the **anonymous** logged events (entrance/exit) in a specific time range I can analyse people flows.

US19 As a *SysAdmin* I want to be able to manage users accounts (e.g. emails, **passwords**) so that I can update them in case of **password leaks or** user changes.

AS A	I WANT TO	SO THAT	US id
DeptHead	visualise an estimate of the number of people inside the building	I know how many there are	US1
	visualise the number of people that entered/exited the building from 8 to 20 and from 20 to 8	I can monitor building occupancy live	US2
	to retrieve the estimated number of people that entered/exited the building for each door in a specific time range	I can analyse people flows	US3
	visualize the logged events (entrance/exit) in a specific time range	I can analyse people flows	US4
	visualise the video stream on the entrances	can detect safety-critical situations in real-time	US5
	be able to always access the system and its data	I can always use it even in the presence of crashes, network, or power interruptions	US6
	the people counting is as accurate as possible	I do not incur in false alarms	US7
	to be notified with an email when any person enters the building during the closing time	I know if someone enters without authorisation	US8
	be notified with an email with a recap-report of entrances/exits at last closing-time	I have an overview on activities at closing-time	US9
	all system data not to be lost	I can be sure it is available in case of rescue needs or emergency	US10
Receptionist	visualize the video stream on the entrances	I can intervene in case of need (e.g. crowds)	US11
	be alerted in case there is a crowd in front of one entrance	I can intervene to disperse it	US12
	visualize the number of people inside the building	I know how many there are	US13
SysAdmin	visualize the live streaming from the video cameras	I can understand if there is a malfunctioning	US14
	visualize debug data on live streaming videos	I can better tune the system deployment	US15
	be able to specify daily closing time-ranges and extra closing time days ranges	I can define the closing-time of the building	US16
	be notified about disconnections of videocameras	I can repair them	US17
	to be able to reset people counters	I can install and reset the system when needed	US18
	be able to manage users accounts (e.g. emails)	I can update them in case of user changes	US19
	to know daily the system accuracy	I know the system works properly	US20

Fig. 1. User stories collected for GióPeopleCounter.

In detail, US4 was integrated to make it sure that the system did not configure as a tool to monitor workers, and US22 was enriched so to enable password-based access control for GióPeopleCounter's users.

Similarly, US5 and US11 were removed as live images contain personal data, which only as few users as possible should be authorised to see. As *DeptHead* and *Receptionist* were interested in the estimate of the number of people in the Department, their access to video footage was considered unnecessary.

Finally, two user stories for *DeptHead* were added with objective to enforce privacy protection and compliance with the European GDPR:

US21 As a *DeptHead* I want to be sure that no personal data is stored by the system so that it is not a video surveillance system.
US22 As a *SysAdmin* I want to be sure that no data leaks from the system so that I incur no legal issues.

These user stories prevent any user of the system from accessing any information but only anonymous aggregated data and enforce data protection by minimising the chance of data leaks. Particularly, US21 enforces that our prototype does not store any video recording. To comply with US22, following a *security-by-design* approach, we identified the following security countermeasures needed by GióPeopleCounter deployments:

- *VPN-restricted access.* Videocameras must not connect to the public Internet, so to reduce the risk of external attacks. Therefore, we required to only connect to a LAN within the domain of our University.
- *Authentication.* GióPeopleCounter must be accessible only by authenticated users, being capable of visualising only data they have been granted permission to access according to system requirements.
- *VM Firewall.* The system backend must be deployed to a host machine protected by a firewall employing a *default-deny* policy so to prevent attacks targeting unused ports and to accept only the incoming connections allowed by customized rules, e.g. from within the domain of our University.
- *Encrypted communication.* All communication between system components must be encrypted using secure protocols, i.e. HTTPS and SSL/TLS, to reduce the risk of *man-in-the-middle* attacks. Involved private and public keys must be emitted by a reliable Certification Authority, e.g. *Let's Encript*.

3 System Architecture and Functioning

System Architecture. The collected user stories led to defining the system architecture in Fig. 2 and the associated technical requirements. Such architecture includes five main components:

- *Monitoring Unit.* It is the system component[1] that detects people's entrances and exits. There must be one MU installed at each entrance of the building. MUs are composed of a general-purpose single-board computer (*RaspberryPI 3B+*), a specialised neural co-processor for EdgeAI computation (*Intel Neural Compute Stick 2*) , and a video-camera (*PiCamera*). MUs exploit real-time images of one building entrance, elaborate them to detect human silhouettes to be tracked on the following frames, and finally detect if they cross the entrance to enter or exit the building. Their business logic is implemented in

---

[1] Open-sourced at: https://github.com/di-unipi-socc/GPC-MonitoringUnit.

Python using the OpenVINO[2] framework and pre-trained models for human silhouette identification and silhouette tracking. Each MU currently costs around 200 euro, which meets the objective of being low-cost.

– *Collector.* It is the core backend service[3] of GióPeopleCounter, implemented as a Flask microservice. It features REST APIs to upload count updates and video streaming from the MUs, and provides the access to authenticated users. The Collector interacts with the Database to store aggregated data and performs routine tasks such as monitoring MU disconnections, updating the computation of estimate accuracy, and to send notifications about entrances/exits at closing times.

– *Database.* It stores all data produced by the system such as timestamped entrance/exit events, MU connections/disconnections, closing daytimes, and cumulative daily counts offered to the users. The Database was designed to prevent data loss by relying on Bitnami's PostgreSQL replicas.

– *API Gateway.* It is a HAproxy gateway that handles all incoming HTTP and TCP traffic. When backend services are scaled, it acts as a load-balancer, forwarding the requests to specific instances. The gateway also provides SSL/TLS Termination functionalities, decrypting/encrypting traffic between clients (WebGUI and MUs), and backend services.

– *WebGUI.* It offers access to a dynamic HTML web page, providing dedicated views for each different user role, viz. *DeptHead*, *SysAdmin*, *Receptionist*.

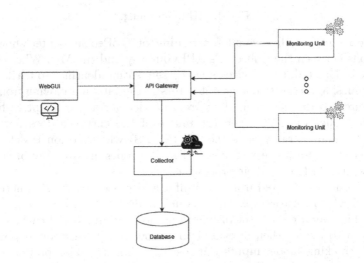

Fig. 2. Bird's-eye view of GióPeopleCounter

System Functioning. MUs continuously run the following tasks by employing pre-trained neural networks deployed to their Neural Compute Stick:

---

[2] Available at: https://docs.openvino.ai/latest/index.html.
[3] Open-sourced at: https://github.com/di-unipi-socc/GPC-PeopleCounterService.

– *Silhouette Detection*. It is performed via the `person-detection-retail-0013`[4], a MobileNetV2 [15] model that features 88.62% average precision, and
– *Silhouette Tracking*. It is performed via the `person-reidentification-retail-0031`[7], based on the RMNet backbone developed for fast inference that features 61.8% average precision.

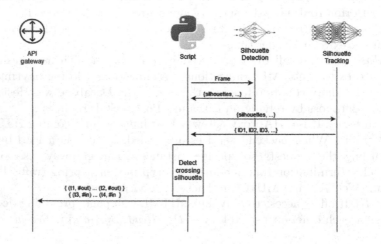

Fig. 3. MU functioning.

Figure 3 sketches the overall functioning of GióPeopleCounter showing the interactions between the Collector's API Gateway and the MU. When a human silhouette is detected, the service assigns a sequential identifier to track it in following frames, and tries to detect if it enters in the building moving from within the gate area to the inside-building area, or vice-versa. An adaptive buffering mechanism collects 8 FPS when the image of the entrance does not change, switching to higher frame rates (i.e. 10–15 FPS) when motion is detected. As the Neural Stick can process around 2–4 FPS, frames are suitably buffered into a queue while waiting for their processing.

Each frame is extracted from the buffer and passed to the silhouette detection model which returns a list of silhouettes detected within the image. The result of this operation is a set of bounding-box coordinates of each silhouette, scaled-down to reduce their sizes and to remove noisy background pixels. The silhouette tracking model inputs the resized silhouettes and produces feature vectors to represent them. A tracking function then assigns an ID to each couple silhouette-vector, by computing the similarity between each current vector and the previously stored ones. Such function assigns a sequential ID if the vector is not similar to any other, otherwise it assigns the same ID of the most similar silhouette previously recognised.

---

[4] Available at: https://github.com/openvinotoolkit/open_model_zoo/.

Silhouettes are organized in two sets named *outsiders* and *insiders*. A silhouette is considered an *outsider* when at the time of its first detection, it overlaps a portion of the gate larger than a threshold. Otherwise, it is considered an *insider*. When the overlapping percentage of an outsider becomes less than the threshold (i.e. 75–80%), we detect an entrance. Exits are detected for insiders the other way around. Anonymised entrance/exit events are finally timestamped and transmitted to the *Collector* (which stores them into the *Database*) via the *API Gateway*. In case transmission fails, to guarantee system accuracy and resiliency to crashes, they are temporarily stored in a local file, waiting for reconnection.

Meanwhile, *Crowd Detection* is performed by comparing the number of identified silhouettes with a threshold (i.e. 8 persons). If too many silhouettes are detected for a time-span longer than 30 s, a crowd alert is sent to the API Gateway and provided through the GUI.

4   Experimental Assessment

Deployment. We tested the prototype of GióPeopleCounter within the Department of Computer Science of our University, deploying four MUs inside the building. Each MU has both power supply and LAN network access, enabling communication with the Collector, without having access to the public Internet. We deployed a dockerised instance of each backend service (i.e. the Database, the API Gateway, and the Collector) in a VM within the University Datacentre.

Experiments Plan. Our experiments with GióPeopleCounter followed 3 main steps:

(A) *System tuning with actors*, consisting in a session with volunteer actors to test the system against non-crowded and crowded situations, which allowed us improving both camera positioning and parameter tuning,

(B) *Live accuracy assessment of tuned prototype*, consisting in manually monitoring MUs' video streaming and comparing such ground truth results with the estimates from GióPeopleCounter, and

(C) *Mismatch-based accuracy assessment*, automatically estimating system accuracy by considering mismatches at reset time along an entire month of deployment of GióPeopleCounter.

Accuracy Metrics. For experiments (A) and (B), we computed the accuracy of people counting as follows. Let IN and OUT be the number of entrance and exit events detected by GióPeopleCounter. Let IN_{gt} and OUT_{gt} be the number of entrances and exits detected by the human observer. We assess accuracy as:

$$1 - \frac{|IN_{gt} - IN| + |OUT_{gt} - OUT|}{IN_{gt} + OUT_{gt}} \tag{1}$$

where the second term in the equation represents the relative error on counts. As an example, consider a human observer that detected 10 entrances and 10 exits ($IN_{gt} = OUT_{gt} = 10$). If GióPeopleCounter detected 9 entrances and 8 exits ($IN = 9$ and $OUT = 8$), then the obtained accuracy is 85%. Analogous formulae have been defined for entrance and exit accuracy separately.

For experiment (C), we estimated the above accuracy metrics as follows. Let IN and OUT be the number of entrance and exit events at 5am (when the Department building is presumably empty). Then we assess accuracy as:

$$1 - \frac{|IN - OUT|}{IN + OUT} \tag{2}$$

The value of |IN - OUT| is considered as the error estimation of the people counting system. As an example, consider that GióPeopleCounter detected 6 entrances and 4 exits ($IN = 6$ and $OUT = 4$), then the estimated accuracy is 80%. Next, we describe experiments (A), (B) and (C) with their results.

(A) System Tuning with Actors. In this experiment, we tested the behaviour of MUs by employing two different positioning of the camera In one case, the MU was placed exactly in front of the entrance (frontal), in the other it was placed with an angle of 45° with respect to the entrance (diagonal).

Then we designed two sets of tests with a different number of actors, i.e. 1 and 6 persons. Each test was repeated three times and results averaged across repetitions. Tests involved the entrance/exit patterns of Fig. 4, where the dashed red line represents the entrance of the building. For single person experiments, we simulate frontal entrances/exits (a)–(b) and left (c)–(d) and right (e)–(f) diagonal entrances/exits. For multiple people we simulate entrances/exits persons aligned each one after the other (a)–(b), all persons trying to enter/exit all together (c)–(d), and couples of persons entering/exiting (e)–(f).

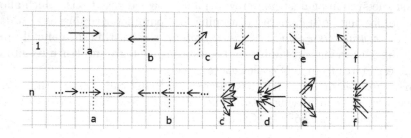

Fig. 4. Set of live tests with 1 and 6 actors

Table 1 and Table 2 list the accuracy achieved for the frontal and diagonal positioning of the camera for situations (a)–(f) (Fig. 4) considering one and six actors, respectively. We use Eq. (1) to compute accuracy.

Results show that the frontal and diagonal alignment perform similarly (i.e. 89% accuracy) in case of single actor. On the other hand, the frontal aligment outperformed the diagonal alignment in more crowded situations with 6 actors (i.e. 76% versus 63%). Across all experiments, the diagonal positioning achieved

76% accuracy and the frontal achieved 82% accuracy. As the frontal positioning showed better accuracy on average, we positioned all cameras accordingly.

During this first set of experiments, it was also possible to tune some parameters to improve GióPeopleCounter perfomance (i.e. increasing the size of the frame buffer to better handle fast movement and crowds, tuning neural networks to perform better assignment of identifiers, reducing entrance/exit area so to exclude from the count people simply passing through the corridor). After the above tuning, we proceeded with experiments (B) and (C).

Table 1. Results with 1 actor

	Accuracy	
	Diagonal	Frontal
a	67%	100%
b	100%	100%
c	67%	100%
d	100%	67%
e	100%	67%
f	100%	100%
Avg	89%	89%

Table 2. Results with 6 actors

	Accuracy	
	Diagonal	Frontal
a	67%	100%
b	100%	100%
c	67%	100%
d	100%	67%
e	100%	67%
f	100%	100%
Avg	63%	76%

(B) Live Accuracy Assessment of Tuned Prototype. Table 3 lists the ground truth of entrances (IN_{gt}) exits (OUT_{gt}) registered by a human observer along 12 h (in different days and time of the day) of live monitoring of GióPeopleCounter, and the corresponding people counts from the service (IN and OUT). We use Eq. (1) to compute accuracy. Table 3 shows the results live test for each monitoring time-range and the overall live-test aggregated results.

Table 3. Live-Test accuracy estimation

#	time-range	IN_{gt}	OUT_{gt}	IN	OUT	Accuracy	Accuracy IN	Accuracy OUT
(i)	16:00–18:00	28	43	27	43	99%	96%	100%
(ii)	8:00–10:30	62	27	54	25	89%	87%	93%
(iii)	10:30–15:00	152	153	143	141	93%	94%	93%
(iv)	17:00–20:00	30	88	28	84	95%	93%	95%
	Avg	272	311	252	294	94%	93%	95%

Live test (*i*) is characterised by more exits than entrances, obtaining 99% average accuracy, 96% for the entrances, and 100% for the exits. Live test (*ii*) was planned to observe morning entrances, characterized by many entrances of many people at the same time. We obtained 89% for the average accuracy,

87% for the entrances, and 93% for the exits. We registered the most crowded situation on live-test in test (*iii*), confirmed by the number of entrances and exits that is the highest in the whole live test-set. GióPeopleCounter maintains an average accuracy of 93%, 94% for entrances, and 93% for exits. The last live test (*iv*) catches a higher number of exits than the first test performed in a similar time-range. We obtained 95% for the average accuracy, 93% for the entrances, and 95% for the exits.

By observing all data collected during the 12 h live testing, our system showed slightly more errors in entrance detection (93% vs 95% accuracy). However, the overall accuracy obtained during live testing settles on average around 94%, which meets the requirement set by US7 in Sect. 2.

(C) Mismatch-Based Accuracy Assessment. Last, we automatically collected the aggregated counts and relative mismatches between entrances and exits for 31 days of deployment of our prototype GióPeopleCounter. We did not consider closing days, as no entrances or exits occurred. On average the daily estimated accuracy of the system (Eq. (2)) settled around 98%, never falling below 94%.

5   Related Work

People counting via cameras exploit two main strategies [12], i.e. detection & tracking (Line of Interest, LOI) and static image analysis (Region of Interest, ROI). As in GióPeopleCounter, LOI considers the number of people crossing a virtual line within consecutive images [6]. To detect the crossing events, the strategy needs to use an object-tracking mechanism, as those developed in [14], that proposes an approach for estimating people and tracking their location in a sequence of video frames. Counting people by tracking can be done in two ways depending on the type of detection used, i.e. detection of the head [9], and detection of the torso area (silhouette) [16], as in GióPeopleCounter, or a combination of the two [11]. Note that tracking people's silhouettes has the support of many pre-trained neural networks in contrast with head detection.

ROI approaches evaluate the number of people within an area in the image(s), at a given time [18]. They try to estimate people counts by detecting them in a single static image to mitigate detection errors. There are 3 main ROI strategies for counting objects in images [13]: by detection, by regression, and by density estimation. Counting by detection (e.g. [10]) is the most intuitive one, and consists of the detection of all objects in the image, despite suffering from objects overlapping and variety in shapes and dimensions. Counting by regression (e.g. [8]) maps image features to the number of objects through supervised machine learning methods (requiring huge labelled datasets). Counting by density estimation (e.g. [1]) provides the estimation of object density function over whole image regions that count objects within that region. ROI strategies are resource demanding and are more suited for density estimation in large areas.

Very recently, [7] described a preliminary proof-of-concept of a service similar to GióPeopleCounter to perform retail analytics by monitoring people presence in physical shops. However, such a service has not been open-sourced, does not account for privacy nor security issues, and has not been quantitatively assessed. To the best of our knowledge, our work is among the first ones designing, prototyping and assessing an open-source EdgeAI-based service to estimate the number of people in a public building with multiple entrances, running over a low-cost Cloud-IoT infrastructure and considering data privacy and security.

6   Concluding Remarks

In this article, we designed, implemented and validated an EdgeAI-based open-source service, GióPeopleCounter, enabling people counting within public building with multiple entrances. GióPeopleCounter can be deployed on a low-cost Cloud-IoT infrastructure, is resilient against network disruptions, and follows privacy-by-design and security-by-design principles. In our experiments, it showed an overall average accuracy around 94%.

Our service can be exploited in *pandemic situations*, to monitor the occupancy of the building, in *emergency situations*, to organise suitable rescue operations, and in *daily situations*, to analyse people flows and enable new smart-ambient applications.

Future work on GióPeopleCounter include: (*i*) improving accuracy in crowded situations by considering alternative neural network models or better tuning them, (*ii*) managing multiple buildings with a single backend instance, e.g. to handle a smart university campus, and (*iii*) enabling further verticals by integrating the people counting functionality with smart-ambient applications.

References

1. Babu Sam, D., Surya, S., Venkatesh Babu, R.: Switching convolutional neural network for crowd counting. In: CVPR (2017)
2. Barnoviciu, E., Ghenescu, V., Carata, S.V., Ghenescu, M., Mihaescu, R., Chindea, M.: GDPR compliance in video surveillance and video processing application. In: SpeD (2019)
3. Bonomi, F., Milito, R., Zhu, J., Addepalli, S.: Fog computing and its role in the internet of things. In: MCC, pp. 13–16 (2012)
4. Cavoukian, A., Dixon, M.: Privacy and security by design: an enterprise architecture approach. Information and Privacy Commissioner of Ontario, Canada (2013)
5. Chen, K.T., Chang, Y.C., Tseng, P.H., Huang, C.Y., Lei, C.L.: Measuring the latency of cloud gaming systems. In: ICM (2011)
6. Iguernaissi, R., Merad, D., Drap, P.: People counting based on kinect depth data. In: ICPRAM (2018)
7. Kanjula, K.R., Reddy, V.V., Abraham, J.S., et al.: People counting system for retail analytics using edge AI. arXiv preprint arXiv:2205.13020 (2022)
8. Kong, D., Gray, D., Tao, H.: A viewpoint invariant approach for crowd counting. In: ICPR, vol. 3, pp. 1187–1190 (2006)
9. Kuplyakov, D., Shalnov, E., Konushin, V., Konushin, A.: A distributed tracking algorithm for counting people in video. Program. Comput. Softw. **45**(4), 163–170 (2019)

10. Lin, Z., Davis, L.S.: Shape-based human detection and segmentation via hierarchical part-template matching. IEEE Trans. Pattern Anal. Mach. Intell. **32**(4), 604–618 (2010)
11. Mamedov, T., Kuplyakov, D., Konushin, A.: Practical people counting algorithm (2021)
12. Monti, L., Mirri, S., Prandi, C., Salomoni, P.: Smart sensing supporting energy-efficient buildings: on comparing prototypes for people counting. In: EAI International Conference on Smart Objects and Technologies for Social Good (2019)
13. Perko, R., Klopschitz, M., Almer, A., Roth, P.M.: Critical aspects of person counting and density estimation. J. Imaging **7**(2), 1–21 (2021)
14. Pervaiz, M., Jalal, A., Kim, K.: Hybrid algorithm for multi people counting and tracking for smart surveillance. In: IBCAST (2021)
15. Sandler, M., Howard, A., Zhu, M., Zhmoginov, A., Chen, L.C.: MobileNetV2: inverted residuals and linear bottlenecks (2019)
16. Shehzed, A., Jalal, A., Kim, K.: Multi-person tracking in smart surveillance system for crowd counting and normal/abnormal events detection. In: ICAEM (2019)
17. Sommerville, I.: Engineering Software Products. Pearson, London (2020)
18. Vazquez, C., et al.: Robust people detection using depth information from an overhead time-of-flight camera. Expert Syst. Appl. **71**, 240–256 (2016)
19. Wang, X., et al.: In-Edge AI: intelligentizing mobile edge computing, caching and communication by federated learning. IEEE Netw. **33**(5), 156–165 (2019)
20. Ye, Q.: A robust method for counting people in complex indoor spaces. In: ICETC, vol. 2 (2010)

A Service-Oriented Middleware Enabling Decentralised Deployment in Mobile Multihop Networks

Luc Hogie[1,2,3]([envelope]) [iD]

[1] CNRS (Centre National de la Recherche Scientifique), Paris, France
luc.hogie@cnrs.fr
[2] I3S Laboratory Université Côte d'Azur, Nice, France
[3] Inria Sophia Antipolis, Biot, France

Abstract. The number of computing devices, mostly smartphones is tremendous. The potential for distributed computing on them is no less huge. But developing applications for such networks is challenging especially as most middleware solutions for distributed computing are tailored to managed grids and clusters, so they lacks the elasticity needed to deal with the difficult conditions brought by multi-hops, mobility, heterogeneity, untrustability, etc. To solve this, several middleware were released, but none of them feature workable deployment solutions. This paper presents the deployment service of the IDAWI middleware, which implements a fully decentralized and automatised deployment strategy into a Open Source middleware tailored to enabling distributed computing in difficult networking conditions like in the IoT/fog/edge.

Keywords: Decentralised systems · Overlay networks · Middleware · Deployment · IoT · Java

Today smartphones are the most common computing devices. Billions of them have been sold all over the world. They all feature network interfaces to communicate through 4G/5G, Wi-Fi and Bluetooth. Broadband 4G/5G networks and Wi-Fi access points enable them to have direct connections to the Internet, while the Wi-Fi ad hoc mode and Bluetooth enable them to have direct P2P connections to *each other*, and to talk to other devices of the IoT. The ubiquity, capabilities, and communication abilities of smartphones make their population a computing platform of a paramount importance. Unfortunately, existing middleware to distributed computing can hardly be used in this context. Indeed, many such middleware dedicated to general distributed computing, like ProActive [8], MPI, JXTA, JMS (Jakarta Messaging API), ActiveMQ [13], 0MQ, JGroups, RMI, and Akka have been proposed through the years. Because they are most often tailored to grid/cloud/cluster environments, they do not accommodate strong heterogeneity, node mobility, etc. that is found in networks involving mobile devices, such as the IoT, the fog, etc. More flexible models and elastic tools were proposed by Researchers, like JavaCà&Là (JCL) [23], GoPrime

J. Troya et al. (Eds.): ICSOC 2022 Workshops, LNCS 13821, pp. 209–220, 2023.
https://doi.org/10.1007/978-3-031-26507-5_17

[7], ParallelTheater [21], ActorEdge [2], and EmbJXTAChord [3], but in spite of their numerous good features, they often are Research tools designed to solve particular scientific problems, which make them hardly usable out-of-the-box in projects involving practical distributed computations. Adapting one of them would be a cumbersome work that has no guarantee of success as source codes, when they are fully available, are always very hard to embrace. Anyway, there is no consensus about which middleware would be the right candidate to start that work from.

Further, we found out that no tool was geared to experimentation, which has specific requirements. In particular, no single tool support the *trial and errors* working process that is usually employed to design and tune an (distributed) algorithm. This consists in doing countless small adjustments in the source code and running many new executions to see their impact. To do that, the middleware needs to be able to deploy and bootstrap distributed applications very quickly, and it needs to provide an easy way to deal at runtime with remote executions.

This article introduces a deployment strategy for Java application, which operates even in the difficult networking conditions of the mobile multihop networks of smartphones, and the IoT. It relies on the IDAWI middleware [17,18], whose the aspects crucial to deployment are first presented here.

Our initial motivation originates from applied Research projects conducted at I3S/Inria, whose goals were to provide effective solutions to practical distributed problems related to graph algorithms [25], networking [10], decentralised protocols [16] for MANETs and more recently the IoT, etc.

1   The IDAWI Middleware

IDAWI is a middleware for distributed computing. It gathers (and improves when possible) the good features of existing tools in a comprehensive fresh one, and it goes beyond by proposing effective solutions to problems not tackled by existing tools. In a few words, on top of its *fully decentralised architecture*, it proposes a SOA-like application model. Its design is mixed: it uses elements of object/message/queue/component/service-based models wherever they proved appropriate. It proposes elastic *collective* and *asynchronous* communication and computation models, augmented with facilities for synchronous calls. IDAWI is Open Source, and can be found at:

　　https://i3s.univ-cotedazur.fr/~hogie/idawi/

We describe in the following the elements of IDAWI that are essential to the development of our deployment solution. A good understanding of them is required to embrace the potential of the deployment strategy.

1.1   An Overlay Network of Components

IDAWI defines a component model. Components represent business entities. They self-organize as a multihop overlay network. In this overlay, two given components are neighbours if they have direct interactions. Any two components can be neighbours unless the underlying network infrastructure prevents it. This may happen in the presence of NATs/firewalls, or because of inherent constraints of wireless technologies such as their limited range, hidden nodes, etc. Two non-neighbours must then rely on intermediary nodes, which then behave as *routers*.

In the usual use case, there will be only one component per device. The role of this component is then to represent the device that hosts it. But in order to facilitate experimentation on large systems, components can deploy other components in their JVM or in another JVM in the same device. Emulation can then be achieved by having more components than devices (then some device host multiple components).

The default routing protocol defines a destination address as a triplet (C, e, d) where C is descriptor matcher (if C is not defined, the address is considered to be a broadcast address); e is the expiration date of the message, and d is the maximum number of hops allowed to travel. This routing protocol is intrinsically multicast/broadcast, which suits the very nature of dynamic multihop networks. *unicast* comes naturally when one single target component is specified in the set of recipient names. In order to address node mobility and scarce connectivity, messages are not dropped after they are forwarded. Instead they are stored into the routing service's internal tables until they expire. Each time a new neighbour component pops up, stored messages are reconsidered for re-emission.

1.2 An Application Model in the Style of SOA

IDAWI proposes a *structuring model* of distributed applications, meaning that applications must conform to a certain organisation defined by the Object-Oriented model (OO). This ensures *consistency* of application source codes, severely reduces the risk of design errors (as most design work is in the middleware), and enables the development of high-level functionalities such as "deployment" which cannot be implemented if applications do not follow a standard pattern.

Component expose their functionality via *services*. A *service* is an object within a host component. It holds data and implements functionality about the specific concern it is about. Also a service has queues which enable them to receive messages. Services are the standard way to incorporate functionality in an IDAWI system. An application is defined by a set of services. System-level functionality is also brought by specific builtin services like the *routing* service internally maintains routing tables and its public API enables other services (hence applications) to obtain topological information like distances between components, paths to reach them, etc.

In turn, services expose functionality via *operations*. An operation is a piece of code that can be triggered remotely from any other one in the system. Just like services, operations are identified by their class. Technically, an operation is described by an inner class of its service class. Its ID (class) then holds the ID of its host service. Operations constitute the *only way* to execute code in an IDAWI system. When the code of an operation is started, it is fed by an input queue of messages. This operation can start/feed new operations, as well as it can send messages to others (already running) operations.

The deployment functionality described in this article comes in the form of a specific service accessible to all other components/services in the component system. It has a particular *deploy* operation that can be triggered from anywhere in the network. As explained in Sect. 2, the deployment service is fully decentralised, meaning that a component does not need any exogenous element to deploy another component. This enables a component to pro-actively deploy new components where it is asked to do so, or it can be asked by another component to perform a deployment. In the latter case, the component requesting the deployment does not need to provide any information other than where the new component has to be deployed to.

1.3   A *many-to-many* Message-Based Communication Model

At the lowest layer, (running) operations communicate by *explicitly* sending/receiving messages of a bounded size. Sending a message is always an *asynchronous* (non-blocking) operation. It provides no guarantee of reception. A message has a probabilistically unique random 64-bit numerical ID. It carries a content (which can be anything), the target service/queue IDs, the route it took so far, and optional routing-specific information. When a message reaches its destination service, it is delivered into its target message queue. Queue are then fetched by operations, in a *synchronous* fashion.

A message queue is a thread-safe container of messages exposing the following primitives: $size()$ gets the number of messages currently in the queue; $get(timeout)$ retrieves and removes the first message in the queue, waiting until the timeout expires if the queue was empty; and $add(timeout)$ adds a message in the queue, waiting until the timeout expires if the queue was full. Using finite timeout ensures that no dead-locks will occur in the system.

IDAWI comes with a default routing protocol which suits the very nature of mobile multihop networks: it defines a destination address as a triplet (C, e, d) where C is set of component names (if C is not defined, the address is considered to be a broadcast address); e is the expiration date of the message, and d is the maximum number of hops allowed to travel. This routing protocol is intrinsically *multicast/broadcast*. *Unicast* comes naturally when one single target component is specified in the set of recipient names. In order to address node mobility and scarce connectivity, messages are not dropped after they are forwarded. Instead they are stored into the routing service's internal tables until they expire. Each time a new neighbour component pops up, stored messages are reconsidered for re-emission.

1.4   A Collective Computation Model

IDAWI defines an innovative computing model, based atop the communication model described hereinbefore, from which it benefits the *collective* approach. It defines a special message called the *exec message*, whose the reception triggers the execution of a particular operation. This enables an operation to be executed in parallel on multiple components.

When it is executed, an operation is provided with a queue that it will use to receive input data. An operation is then able to receive multiple messages at runtime, constituting *unbounded input*. An operation can produce output (intermediary results, final result, warnings, exceptions, progress information, etc.) at any time by sending messages. In most cases, output will be sent to the sender of the exec message. To receive output messages, the caller creates a new local queue, called the *return queue* that aims at storing messages from the running operation. This message queue can play the role of a *future*. Once again, other running operations may obtain the address of the return queue, and send *directly* messages to it. A running operation may execute another one. This enables *composition of services* and *workflows*.

From a programmatic point of view, The *exec*() primitive makes it easy the remote execution of operations. It takes as input the address of the operation to execute, an optional address of the return queue, as well optional initial input data. Just like sending a message (which it does behind the scene), calling *exec*() is asynchronous, but synchronicity can be achieved by invoking synchronous primitives on the return queue. Calling *exec*() then immediately returns a proxy to the remotely running operation. This proxy features the address of the (remote) input queue of the running operation, as well a reference to the aforementioned return queue.

If the operation address describes multiple components, the operation will be executed on all of them. In this case the caller may receive output messages from these multiple executions. To deal with that, the *collect* algorithm can be used to demultiplex messages according to where they come from.

This model allows the parallel execution of the *deploymentoperation* on multiple nodes: multiple nodes get deployed at the same time at different locations in the network.

2 Deployment and Bootstrapping

In many distributed systems, the deployment process involves human work to provide deployment configuration files (which specify the location of binaries, their destination, the mean to deploy them, and how to bootstrap/stop remote elements), and to execute command-line packagers, remote shells, deployment scripts, etc. Generic deployment systems like DeployWare [14,20] target the deployment of any software, along with their complex dependencies, with support to multiple languages. But in fact the number of constraints/requirements/assumptions can be much more that that, which makes deployment hardly automatizable. This problem has motivated several research initiatives like [6,9,11,19]. In practise distributed systems generally come with their own *ad hoc* deployment sub-system, like in ProActive [1], Jade [5,20], OSGi [24], and Frogi [12], an OSGI-based solution to the deployment of Fractal [4] components. Modern solutions often resort to solutions from the Docker ecosystem. These enable deployment in centralized IoT and fog network configurations. But deployment in such scarse networks, as suggested by recent works on deploying applications across unreliable networks foster the use of a decentralized technology like Bit-torrent as a support to deployment [22]. Even closer to IDAWI's considerations, deployment in infrastructure-less mobile heterogeneous networks have been investigated in [15].

Deployment is a generic word that encompasses a wide variety of use cases. There can be deployment of executable code or data, deployment of virtual machines in a grid, deployment of docker images in the cloud, etc. IDAWI deploys Java runtimes: it *clones* the execution environnement (JVM and bytecode) to remote hosts, and it bootstraps a new component in a new JVM on each of them. It is able to do that to any POSIX node providing an access via SSH. In other words, deployment in IDAWI lies in the ability of any component to deploy other components on remote nodes (but also in the same JVM or in a new JVM on the same local node). Deployment in IDAWI can be seen as a zero-configuration process. More precisely, a component does not need any exogenous element to perform a deployment: it has all the functionality to do it. Unlike most tools, IDAWI does not require any pre-installed library to be installed on target nodes, nor it requires any daemon to run. It only requires that an access to SSH is possible and that a few POSIX commands are available (`mkdir`, `rsync`).

Just after deployment of a JVM, a child component is started in it. Bidirectional communication between child and parent is achieved through the SSH connection that was used for the deployment. When this SSH connection breaks, the child component may keep running on its own, or may stop its execution. This is an application-specific policy.

The deployment functionality comes as a specific service available in every components. This service exposes operations that allow any component to request any other component to deploy new ones (Fig. 1).

2.1   The Problem of Shared File Systems

In a context of *trial and errors* workflow, deployment times are crucial for it has a direct impact on the developer quality of Life. Cloning a JVM to a single remote node is a significantly long process. It takes several seconds when best conditions are met (deploying to desktop computers on the LAN). Then performing a sequential deployment on multiple nodes is prohibitive, as deployment durations sum up. Thus, in order to fasten the deployment process, IDAWI resorts to parallelism: it deploys to multiple nodes simultaneously. In practise, deploying to n nodes has roughly the same duration as deploying to a single node. But such parallel deployment is problematic when target nodes share their filesystem. In particular, parallel uncontrolled writes to a file system often produce data inconsistencies. When the computing hardware infrastructure is managed and documented (which is the case usually in grids ands clusters), users know if nodes share or not the file system, and the deployment process can be configured on the basis of this information. But IDAWI is not restricted to these networks.

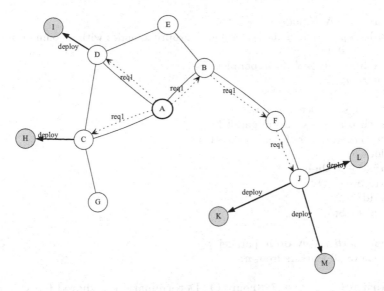

Fig. 1. Component A sends a *same* deployment request to res. nodes C, D and J, asking them to deploy resp. 1, 1 and 3 children components

In the target computing environment it was designed for, it must detect shared file systems.

To do this, IDAWI first executes a distributed algorithm that computes a partition of a set of computers by grouping those which share a same file-system. This algorithm, initiated by a node a uses SSH to create on every node (in parallel) a marker into their file system. This marker takes the shape of a directory, as the *mkdir* system call is the only atomic one (which implies that concurrent calls to mkdir are sequentialized). This mark directory is named against the DNS name of the node that executes mkdir). Mark directories are all created in a parent directory whose the name is the same and known by all. This parent directory is initially empty. This way, at the end of the marking process, every node in N will has in its file-system the marks of other nodes it shares the file-system with. This on-disk information is then retrieved in parallel by node a which computes a partition of the nodes according to file-system shares.

One single node is picked up at random from every set, resulting in a subset of the initial set of nodes. This new set of nodes exhibits the following properties:

- no two nodes share a file-system
- there exists a representative node for every file-system

Deploying code to every node in this set will make it available to all target nodes, avoiding any problem of concurrent access. The process is described in Algorithm 1.

Data: A set N of nodes
Result: a partition of the set of nodes, grouping nodes with a common file
        system
foreach *node* $n \in N$ **do** in parallel
   | mark n;
end
let S be a set of set of nodes
foreach *node* $n \in N$ **do** in parallel
   | retrieves markers from n into set M;
   | lock S;
   | **if** $M \notin S$ **then**
   | | $S \leftarrow S \cup M$;
   | **end**
   | unlock S;
end
foreach *node* $n \in N$ **do** in parallel
   | remove all markers from n;
end

Algorithm 1: sharedFSGroups(): Determination of shared filesystems

2.2   Duplication of the Binaries

Most of the time, deployment tools require the user to provide a configuration specifying the location of binaries and JVM specifications. IDAWI takes benefit of the ability of Java programs to discover them at runtime. Regardless of how the program was started (via the command line on a server, from an IDE, etc.), a Java program knows its classpath, which lists the class directories and jar files constituting it. Thanks to system properties, it also knows the exact version of the JVM that is executing it. An IDAWI component then has a exhaustive view of its binaries, which its deployment service clone when its creates new remote nodes. As a consequence, children nodes end having the exact same binaries as their parent. This eliminates interoperability problems related to incompatible versions.

IDAWI is geared towards experimentation. This implies that IDAWI's users will use it in a particular way: most often in a *trials and errors* mode. This way of working involves many subsequent runs, each one with a slight variation of the source code or of its dependencies. It must be quick in order to have a minimal impact on the user experience.

Many deployment systems consider an image as the deployment unit. Such image can weight up to gigabytes of data and take long times to transfer. IDAWI takes a fine-grained approach. It takes benefit of the Java platform. The deployment unit in IDAWI is the class/resource file. In order to minimize the amount of data transferred, IDAWI resorts to synchronization instead of doing a complete copy: only what is not already there gets transferred. The process of deployment of bytecode and resources is then *incremental*. To do that, IDAWI performs the following steps:

1. in parallel:
   - retrieves a set R of s $(name, size, timestamp)$ for every remote file
   - builds such a set L for local files
2. transfers missing or out-of-date files in $L - R$ (out-of-date files will be over-written)
3. deletes file no longer in use in $R - L$

By doing this, the whole set of files constituting the executable code is transferred only once. This applies to both the byte code and the Java runtime. Subsequent transfers will consider only the differences from previous ones. As these differences are most of the time insignificant, both the amortised time and space complexity is constant.

Thanks to the determination of shared file systems described in Sect. 2.1, IDAWI is able to transfer code to multiple computers *in parallel*. Transferring to one single node or to multiple ones is not much different in time.

2.3 Bootstrapping Remote Components

When the executable code has been deployed and the right JVM has been installed, the remote component is ready to be bootstrapped. To do that, IDAWI uses SSH to execute the previously-verified JVM on the child node. This JVM is bootstrapped with a specific *main* class that uses the SSH input/output to:

1. read information about the child component to be created in the new JVM
2. send an acknowledgement to its parent node to indicate that the child was successfully created and initialised

On the other side, the parent component:

1. sends deployment information for the component to be created in the new JVM
2. waits for an acknowledgement from its child node that was successfully created and initialised

As long as the SSH connection is open, the two components can use it to communicate with each other.

The entire deployment process is described in Algorithm 2.

Data: A set N of target nodes
$S \leftarrow sharedFSGroups(N)$ **foreach** *set of node* $s \in S$ **do** in parallel
   | picks a random component c in s;
   | synchronizes local binaries to c;
end
foreach *node* $n \in N$ **do** in parallel
   | start a JVM on n;
   | bootstrap a new component on n;
end

Algorithm 2: deploy(): Full deployment process

3 Conclusion

The number and variety of computing devices is growing, in particular billions of smartphones have been sold all over the world in the past years, making the potential for distributed computing huge. Unfortunately most middleware for distributed computing is tailored to grids and clusters, so it lack the elasticity needed to accomodate the difficult conditions brought by the dynamics and heterogeneity of mobile networks of smartphones, MANETs, the fog, the IoT. For these purposes, several software solutions were released, but none of them feature workable deployment solutions. This paper presents the deployment service of the IDAWI middleware, which implements a fully decentralised and automatised deployment strategy into an Open Source middleware tailored to enabling distributed computing in mobile heterogeneous networks.

References

1. Aloisio, G., Cafaro, M., Epicoco, I.: A Grid Software Process. In: Cunha, J.C., Rana, O.F. (eds.) Grid Computing: Software Environments and Tools, pp. 75–98. Springer, London (2006). https://doi.org/10.1007/1-84628-339-6_4
2. Aske, A., Zhao, X.: An actor-based framework for edge computing. In: Anjum, A., Sill, A., Fox, G.C., Chen, Y. (eds.) Proceedings of the 10th International Conference on Utility and Cloud Computing, UCC 2017, Austin, TX, USA, 5–8 December 2017, pp. 199–200. ACM (2017). https://doi.org/10.1145/3147213.3149214
3. Battaglia, F., Bello, L.L.: A novel JXTA-based architecture for implementing heterogenous networks of things. Comput. Commun. **116**, 35–62 (2018). https://doi.org/10.1016/j.comcom.2017.11.002
4. Blair, G.S., Coupaye, T., Stefani, J.: Component-based architecture: the fractal initiative. Ann. des Télécommun. **64**(1–2), 1–4 (2009). https://doi.org/10.1007/s12243-009-0086-1
5. Bouchenak, S., Palma, N.D., Hagimont, D., Taton, C.: Autonomic management of clustered applications. In: Proceedings of the 2006 IEEE International Conference on Cluster Computing, 25–28 September 2006, Barcelona, Spain. IEEE Computer Society (2006). https://doi.org/10.1109/CLUSTR.2006.311842
6. Cañete, A., Amor, M., Fuentes, L.: Supporting IoT applications deployment on edge-based infrastructures using multi-layer feature models. J. Syst. Softw. **183**, 111086 (2022). https://doi.org/10.1016/j.jss.2021.111086

7. Caporuscio, M., Grassi, V., Marzolla, M., Mirandola, R.: GoPrime: a fully decentralized middleware for utility-aware service assembly. IEEE Trans. Softw. Eng. **42**(2), 136–152 (2016). https://doi.org/10.1109/TSE.2015.2476797

8. Caromel, D., di Costanzo, A., Mathieu, C.: Peer-to-peer for computational grids: mixing clusters and desktop machines. Parallel Comput. **33**(4–5), 275–288 (2007). https://doi.org/10.1016/j.parco.2007.02.011

9. Chen, Y., Sun, Y., Feng, T., Li, S.: A collaborative service deployment and application assignment method for regional edge computing enabled IoT. IEEE Access **8**, 112659–112673 (2020). https://doi.org/10.1109/ACCESS.2020.3002813

10. Coudert, D., Hogie, L., Lancin, A., Papadimitriou, D., Pérennes, S., Tahiri, I.: Feasibility study on distributed simulations of BGP. CoRR abs/1304.4750 (2013). https://arxiv.org/abs/1304.4750

11. Dautov, R., Song, H., Ferry, N.: Towards a sustainable IoT with last-mile software deployment. In: IEEE Symposium on Computers and Communications, ISCC 2021, Athens, Greece, 5–8 September 2021, pp. 1–6. IEEE (2021). https://doi.org/10.1109/ISCC53001.2021.9631250

12. Desertot, M., Cervantes, H., Donsez, D.: FROGi: fractal components deployment over OSGi. In: Löwe, W., Südholt, M. (eds.) SC 2006. LNCS, vol. 4089, pp. 275–290. Springer, Heidelberg (2006). https://doi.org/10.1007/11821946_18

13. Estrada, N., Astudillo, H.: Comparing scalability of message queue system: ZeroMQ vs RabbitMQ. In: 2015 Latin American Computing Conference, CLEI 2015, Arequipa, Peru, 19–23 October 2015, pp. 1–6. IEEE (2015). https://doi.org/10.1109/CLEI.2015.7360036

14. Flissi, A., Dubus, J., Dolet, N., Merle, P.: Deploying on the grid with Deploy-Ware. In: 8th IEEE International Symposium on Cluster Computing and the Grid (CCGrid 2008), 19–22 May 2008, Lyon, France, pp. 177–184. IEEE Computer Society (2008). https://doi.org/10.1109/CCGRID.2008.59

15. Guidec, F.: Déploiement et support à l'exécution de services communicants dans les environnements d'informatique ambiante. Habilitation à diriger des recherches, Université de Bretagne Sud; Université Européenne de Bretagne, June 2008. http://tel.archives-ouvertes.fr/tel-00340426

16. Hogie, L.: Mobile Ad Hoc Networks: Modelling, Simulation and Broadcast-based Applications. (Réseaux Mobile Ad hoc : modélisation, simulation et applications de diffusion). Ph.D. thesis, University of Luxembourg (2007). http://tel.archives-ouvertes.fr/tel-01589632

17. Hogie, L.: IDAWI: a decentralised middleware for achieving the full potential of the IoT, the fog, and other difficult computing environments. In: Proceedings of MiddleWedge 2022 ACM International workshop on middleware for the Edge. Collocated with ACM/IFIP/USENIX Middleware 2022, Québec, Canada. ACM (2022). to be published

18. Hogie, L.: Idawi: a middleware for distributed applications in the IOT, the fog and other multihop dynamic networks. Research report, CNRS - Centre National de la Recherche Scientifique; Université Côte d'azur, Inria, February 2022. http://hal.archives-ouvertes.fr/hal-03562184

19. Kayal, P.: Kubernetes: towards deployment of distributed IoT applications in fog computing. In: Amaral, J.N., Koziolek, A., Trubiani, C., Iosup, A. (eds.) Companion of the 2020 ACM/SPEC International Conference on Performance Engineering, ICPE 2020, Edmonton, AB, Canada, 20–24 April 2020, pp. 32–33. ACM (2020). https://doi.org/10.1145/3375555.3383585

20. Lacour, S., Pérez, C., Priol, T.: Generic application description model: toward automatic deployment of applications on computational grids. Research Report PI 1757 (2005). http://hal.inria.fr/inria-00000645

21. Nigro, L.: Parallel theatre: an actor framework in java for high performance computing. Simul. Model. Pract. Theory **106**, 102189 (2021). https://doi.org/10.1016/j.simpat.2020.102189

22. Shiau, S.J.H., Huang, Y., Tsai, Y., Sun, C., Yen, C., Huang, C.: A bittorrent mechanism-based solution for massive system deployment. IEEE Access **9**, 21043–21058 (2021). https://doi.org/10.1109/ACCESS.2021.3052525

23. de Souza Cimino, L.,et al.: A middleware solution for integrating and exploring IoT and HPC capabilities. Softw. Pract. Exp. **49**(4), 584–616 (2019). https://doi.org/10.1002/spe.2630

24. The OSGi Alliance: OSGi service platform core specification, release 4.1 (2007). http://www.osgi.org/Specifications

25. Trolliet, T., Cohen, N., Giroire, F., Hogie, L., Pérennes, S.: Interest clustering coefficient: a new metric for directed networks like twitter. J. Complex Netw. **10**(1) (2021). https://doi.org/10.1093/comnet/cnab030

WESOACS: Engineering
Service-Oriented Applications
and Cloud Services

Introduction to the 18th International Workshop on Engineering Service-Oriented Applications and Cloud Services (WESOACS 2022)

The International Workshop on Engineering Service-Oriented Applications and Cloud Services (WESOACS), formerly known as WESOA, was established in 2005 in Amsterdam with the aim of promoting innovative ideas in research and practice of engineering of service-oriented applications. WESOACS 2022 took place on November 29th, 2022, in conjunction with the 20th International Conference on Service-Oriented Computing (ICSOC 2022) in Sevilla, Spain.

Service-oriented applications and cloud computing play an increasingly important role in enterprise computing today. While there is good agreement about the main principles for designing and developing application systems based on the principles of distributed software services, there is still intense interest in this research area. In particular, areas of ongoing research include software service life cycle methodologies, service-oriented enterprise architectures and, more recently, engineering methods for cloud computing environments. The recent shift towards DevOps and microservices and the extensive use of container-based technologies and architectures necessitates the revision of current approaches for developing service-oriented applications.

The WESOACS 2022 technical program included six-high quality research papers that were carefully selected based on at least 3 expert reviews. The contributions focus on microservices-based development, but also deal with Artificial Intelligence (AI) and blockchain applications in the context of service computing:

- "Towards Engineering AI Planning Functionalities as Services" by Ilche Georgievski,
- "BizDevOps Support for Business Process Microservices-Based Applications" by Andrea Delgado, Felix Garcia and Francisco Ruiz,
- "Towards Real-time Monitoring of Blockchain Networks through a Low-Code Tool" by Jesús Rosa-Bilbao and Juan Boubeta-Puig,
- "Data Product Metadata Management: an Industrial Perspective" by Stefan Driessen, Geert Monsieur and Willem-Jan van den Heuvel,
- "FUSPAQ: a Function Selection Platform to Adjust QoS in a FaaS Application" by Pablo Serrano Gutiérrez, Inmaculada Ayala and Lidia Fuentes, and
- "Specification-Driven Code Generation for Inter-parameter Dependencies in REST APIs" by Saman Barakat, Enrique Barba Roque, Ana B. Sánchez and Sergio Segura.

Furthermore, the workshop event included an industry keynote, where Paco Saucedo from Algeciras Port Authority, representing one of the leading European seaports, spoke about practical industry application of distributed service-oriented systems.

Overall, we regard the 18th edition of the workshop as highly successful and wish to thank all authors for their contributions as well as the program committee members whose expert input made this workshop possible. Special thanks to the ICSOC 2022 workshop chairs Raffaela Mirandola and Elena Navarro.

November 2022   WESOACS 2022 Workshop Organizers

Towards Engineering AI Planning Functionalities as Services

Ilche Georgievski[(✉)] [iD]

Department of Service Computing, IAAS, University of Stuttgart,
Stuttgart, Germany
ilche.georgievski@iaas.uni-stuttgart.de

Abstract. As Artificial Intelligence (AI) planning is utilised in industry to address complex real-world problems, the need for the construction of advanced and deployable AI planning systems emerges. This task, however, proves to be difficult due to a general lack of established mechanisms in AI planning for system design, interoperability, and deployment. In this context, we provide an overview of key engineering challenges that one is faced with when developing and using systems that incorporate AI planning functionalities. To help address the challenges, we propose to leverage service-orientation together with architectural patterns. In particular, we identify a set of planning functionalities, and we present an initial concept for engineering the planning functionalities as services. Having planning services would enable not only to quickly compose and deploy service-oriented planning systems but also expand them with more features as required by application domains.

Keywords: Artificial Intelligence planning · Engineering challenges · Software design and development · Service-orientation

1 Introduction

Artificial Intelligence (AI) planning is the process of searching and selecting actions that achieve some user objective. Specifically, it deals with solving a *planning problem*, which consists of an initial state of the world, a goal state, and a set of actions (also called a domain model) [14]. A solution to this problem is a course of action, called a *plan*, whose execution in the initial state leads to the goal one. Due to its powerful modelling and reasoning capabilities, AI planning is increasingly utilised to address real-world problems in a number of domains, such as space missions [2], robotics [20], autonomous driving [3], service composition [22], user activity recognition [10], and smart buildings [13].

After exploring a domain of interest and selecting a planning approach adequate for the problems encountered in that domain, the basic development process of applications that employ AI planning involve *modelling* domain models, developing a mechanism for automatically *generating* problem instances usually from real-time data, developing or selecting existing adequate algorithms

J. Troya et al. (Eds.): ICSOC 2022 Workshops, LNCS 13821, pp. 225–236, 2023.
https://doi.org/10.1007/978-3-031-26507-5_18

for *solving* planning problems, and developing or selecting existing approaches for *validating*, *executing*, and *monitoring* plans [11]. When modelling a planning domain model, one needs to follow a specific syntax and perform experiments to validate and refine the domain model. At the same time, the effectiveness and performance of the solving algorithms can be evaluated. If plans exist, they can be inspected by users and/or executed in the application environment. The plan execution is monitored and mitigation steps can be taken in case contingencies are encountered. In addition, the implementation of any of the previous functionalities is refined as necessary.

In academic settings, engineering and developing AI planning systems is often portrayed as the development of algorithms or engineering of domain models. In practice, however, these ingredients constitute only a part of what is needed to design, develop, and use fully operational planning systems. As a consequence, several challenges are encountered in practice during the construction, deployment, and maintenance of planning systems [7,12,32]. In this context, Gartner reports that only 53% of AI projects go from prototypes to production due to the lack of resources to build and manage production-ready AI systems [8]. To address this problem, a need arises for the consideration of established software-engineering principles and approaches in the development of AI tools [6], including flexible, integrable, and deployable AI planning systems [4,7,12,33].

Our main objective here is to propose leveraging service-oriented computing principles and architectural patterns for building, integrating, and deploying planning systems. We propose to define fine-grained planning functionalities and encapsulate them as interoperable and portable services. Our main contributions are threefold. First, we present and classify the key engineering challenges for developing, deploying, and using planning systems. Second, we present a preliminary set of planning functionalities that represent separate concerns. Third, we present an initial concept and considerations for engineering the planning functionalities as services.

The rest of the paper is organised as follows. We first present and classify the key challenges of engineering AI planning systems. We then present the planning functionalities and the concept for designing these functionalities as services. We close by discussing the related work and conclusions.

2   Engineering Challenges

It can be observed that engineering AI planning systems often consists of two main tasks, the development of (solving) algorithms and engineering of domain models. However, these tasks are only a part of the needed resources to design, develop, and use operational planning systems in actual settings. Motivated by this, we identify and present challenges related to engineering and use of AI planning tools, some of which are extracted from the discussion in [12]. We also provide a structural view of the challenges by classifying them in three areas: architecture, development and deployment, and process. This classification coincides with the classification of engineering challenges in machine learning [6].

2.1 Architecture

The area of architecture is concerned with the definition of planning components and structure of overall tools. We present three main challenges in this area.

A1: Component Complexity. The software of existing planning tools incorporate various data models and algorithms that are complicated and often intertwined, leading to complex functional entanglement. This complexity makes the identification and maintenance of strict functional boundaries of components in existing planning tools difficult.

A2: Interoperability. Groups of planning tools exist that support their input to be specified in a common planning syntax, such as the Planning Domain Definition Language (PDDL) [23], Hierarchical Planning Definition Language (HPDL) [9], and Hierarchical Domain Definition Language (HDDL) [19]. This approach primarily addresses the knowledge-engineering problem in AI planning. However, the software-engineering problem of interoperability remains: a common syntax does not guarantee that planning components or tools are capable of intercommunicating. That is to say, they cannot communicate with each other unless glue code is provided that addresses the lack of interfaces and differences in input and output.

A3: Reuse. Reusing planning components and tools is not trivial mainly due to their complexity and tight coupling, making the separation between generic and specific parts of a component or tool not an easy task. For example, many planners that support PDDL have a component dedicated to parsing the PDDL input, meaning it checks whether the input conforms to the PDDL grammar and then converts that input into programming-level objects. The parsing functionality without conversion is a generic part that is not reused between planning tools. In this context, the International Planning Competition (IPC) community suggested to "encourage and reward" sharing and using existing planner's code (e.g., the parser of the FF planner) [15]. This is also not easy to do so because of A2.

2.2 Development and Deployment

This area is concerned with the development and deployment of AI planning systems. We present three main but highly underestimated challenges.

DD1: Integration. It is often necessary to integrate individual planning components into a single planning system or into some industrial system. Accomplishing integration of planning components or tools is challenging because of at least two reasons. One is the variety of characteristics of underlying data models and algorithms, and domain models. For example, *classical planning* assumes a different plan structure than *probabilistic planning* (cf. a plan as a sequence of actions versus a plan as a policy). The second reason is the lack of mechanism for controlling the interaction of planning components or tools, such as Application Programming Interfaces (APIs).

DD2: Composition. Current planning tools typically offer only a limited spectrum of functionality (e.g., planners *solve* planning problems). In practice, however, significant additional functions may be needed to ensure a full and advanced planning operation. For example, one planning system may need to be composed of functionality for solving planning problems, executing plans, and monitoring their execution, while another may also require support for modelling planning problems. However, neither conditions nor mechanisms have been investigated and developed that enable composing custom planning systems or extending existing ones.

DD3: Deployment. As other software, planning components and tools evolve, which may require their deployment on continuous basis, especially in real-world settings. Their reliable deployment considering versioning, performance measurement, and raising warnings appear challenging since no mechanism has been established or adopted to represent planning software in a portable and machine-readable form.

2.3 Process

Working with or on a single planning functionality or component is relatively easy, however, working with a multitude of planning functionalities or planning tools proves to be challenging. This area is concerned with the process of using planning functionalities and tools. We present three main process challenges that require significant effort for their resolution in an effective way.

P1: Heterogeneity. We identify three aspects of heterogeneity in planning. First is the diversity of planning functionalities; numerous functionalities, some mentioned above, can potentially be distinguished in existing planning tools. Second is the multitude of existing planning tools. There are incomparably more planning tools that provide the numerous functionalities. Though, most are planners, i.e., tools that focus on solving planning problems. For example, one can count 235 planners as participants in IPC from 2006 to 2020.[1] The last aspect covers the classes of planning. Broadly, we have the class of classical planning, which has many restrictions about how the real world looks like, and many other classes that relax one or more of those restrictions, such as temporal planning and probabilistic planning. This multifold heterogeneity makes the identification, selection, and management of planning functionalities and models a non-trivial task.

P2: Set Up. Existing planning tools have many and diverse software requirements that need to be satisfied before the tools can be installed. These requirements are not included in the installation packages of the tools. The typical software requirements for setting up planning tools include the computer's architecture, operating system (e.g., planners typically work on Linux only), libraries

---

[1] More precisely, this number includes a large cut of planners that are improvements of another, smaller cut. Even though they only represent versions with enhanced/new features, the improved planners typically get new names, thus, counted separately.

(e.g., g++, cmake, Common Lisp), and sometimes Web servers. Moreover, external dependencies are generally unmanaged. The restrictive software requirements, the management of dependencies and the lack of instructions on how to set up planning tools require considerable effort to make them initially run.

P3: Monitoring. Once planning tools/components/systems are installed, deployed and used in real-world settings, it is important to monitor their operation and performance, log relevant events and track errors to detect situations where the tools/components/systems do not perform as expected.

3 Service-Orientation

To rise to the challenges of engineering AI planning systems, we suggest to look at Service-Oriented Computing (SOC) and architectural patterns. SOC promises to deliver modular, interoperable, integrable, and reusable software [27], while the latter provides solutions to common issues in software architectures [17]. In particular, we propose planning functionalities to be engineered as services, which would help addressing most of the engineering challenges, that is, a service-oriented AI planning would enable to architect, implement, integrate, deliver, and maintain planning systems.

3.1 Planning Functionalities

We begin with the proposition and encouragement to view and shape planning functionalities as basic and distinct building blocks. This proposition is in line not only with the concept of service within SOC, but also with modularity concepts within AI, such as modular actors [16] and modular intelligences [31]. Getting to the point where planning functionalities are logical modules with separate planning concerns implies following the principles of modularity and abstraction, and requires performing two tasks. First, we need to identify and clearly define the concern of each planning functionality. Second, we need to encapsulate or implement those concerns such that they are loosely coupled. The first task is relatively feasible, while the second one seems complicated mainly due to A1 and P1. As our objective here is the characterisation of planning functionalities, we focus on the first task only.

In the long run, we plan to perform a comprehensive literature review on the topic of planning functionalities. As a first step to identify an initial set of common planning functionalities, we took a bottom-up approach by analysing planning tools known to us and identifying the functionalities they offer. The functional spectrum of the analysed tools goes from modelling and parsing planning problems, through solving them and executing plans, to plan explanation and the like. As some tools offer coarse-grained capabilities, we refined and split them into as basic concerns as possible, thus meeting A1–A3 challenges. In the following, we name and define each *type of planning functionality*. Most names follow the terminology adopted in the AI planning field.

– *Modelling* enables users to manually specify planning problems textually using a given modelling language or using graphical notations.
– *Knowledge Learning* automatically acquires planning domains models, heuristics and other forms of planning control knowledge.
– *Parsing* analyses whether planning problems conform to the rules of the chosen modelling language.
– *Conversion* transforms planning data from one form to another, e.g., planning domain models to programming-level objects.
– *Problem Generation* automatically produces instances of planning problems using real-time data representing the world (e.g., Internet of Things data).
– *Solving* computes plans as solutions to planning problems.
– *Searching* is concerned with a search algorithm used to explore the space of possible solutions to planning problems.
– *Learning* aids the planning process using machine learning techniques.
– *Strategising* employs strategies, such as heuristics and preferences, to quickly find plans, find approximate plans, or improve plan quality.
– *Translation* translates planning problems into other types of problems.
– *Execution* is responsible for executing plan actions.
– *Monitoring* is used to observe the world in which plans are executed and detect potential contingencies during plan execution.
– *Tolerance* is responsible for handling unexpected events or contingencies during execution of plans (e.g., action execution fails due to network issues).
– *Plan Validation* validates the correctness of plans.
– *Explanation* is used to explain planning to users, such as planning steps, the inclusion of actions in some plan, and their plan order.
– *Visualisation* provides the means to display information, such as charts, tables and other statistics relevant to planning.
– *Data* offers a permanent storage of planning domain models and data.
– *System Management* offers routing of messages from one point to another and/or handling systems errors and failures.
– *System Monitoring* enables users to monitor a planning system.

3.2   Service Design

Interoperability is the ability of software components to communicate, work and exchange messages with each other and other systems seamlessly, despite being developed differently and by different parties. Interoperability can be achieved on semantic, syntactic, and connectivity levels. Challenge A2 indicates that standard planning languages provide a certain form of *semantic* and *syntactic* interoperability, meaning that different planning tools could be used for the same functionality, provided the tools can handle the selected planning language (e.g., PDDL). Even more, a standard planning language can be used to identify the semantic compatibility of two or more planning functionalities. However, there are many planning approaches and tools that do not support the same planning specification, and those that support the same language typically provide a limited range of planning functionalities – mostly Modelling, Parsing, and Solving

Table 1. Minimal interfaces of several planning services.

Service	Operation	Input	Output
Parsing	*parseDomain*	Planning language, domain model	Success/failure
	parseProblem	Planning language, problem instance	Success/failure
Solving	*solve*	Algorithm, planning language, domain model, problem instance	ACK
	getResponse	/	Status
Plan validation	*validate*	Domain model, problem instance, plan	Success/failure

functionalities. Most important, using a common planning language does not imply that two or more planning tools can communicate with each other. So, there is a need to support interoperability on a *connectivity* level. While the engineering challenges presented in Sect. 2 complicate things, it is still be possible to make planning components and tools interoperable on a connectivity level.

Interoperability of planning functionalities can be ensured by designing them as services. We require *planning services* to adhere to a communication agreement, meaning they adopt a standardised naming convention, and provide interfaces of what they offer and require. This directly affects the difficulty for designers, developers and other types of users to specify a planning request or to interpret an output as a sequential plan, for example. For the aspect of standardised naming convention, we propose to use the names of planning functionalities presented in the previous section. For the aspect of interfaces, we suggest planning services to have minimal interfaces, where the number of operations is as small as possible. The rationale behind this is to facilitate the use of interfaces and make it easy to implement within existing tools.

To encourage the specification and use of interfaces, we specify a set of interfaces for three planning services as shown in Table 1. The interfaces are not designed to be exhaustive, and include only the minimum necessary operations for the implementation of the services. The Parsing Service requires syntactic models of a planning domain and problem instance. The interface of the Solving Service requires four arguments: a chosen algorithm, chosen planning language, domain model, and problem instance. The interface of the Plan Validation Service requires three arguments: a domain model, problem instance, and a plan.

Challenges A1, A2, DD1 and P1 lead to a situation where a universal solution for communication and integration cannot be easily designed. A proven strategy to address communication and integration issues in such situations is message passing, which provides the basis for designing and developing portable and efficient software components [17]. As a messaging technology, we propose the use of Message-Oriented Middleware (MOM) due its simplicity and heterogeneity hiding, enabling the variety of planning services to work together in a loosely coupled way. In addition, we suggest to design planning services upon the *Hub-and-Spoke* pattern, which enables planning services to asynchronously communicate using the publish-subscribe model [17]. For this, each service needs only one configuration option, which is the address of the MOM, and can have its own incoming and outgoing topics, providing for horizontal scalability. Upon this design choice, planning services can also request other functionality directly without involving another gateway. So, for planning services that require direct communication, we propose to design them upon the RESTful model in the case of synchronous calls and the WebSocket model for asynchronous communication.

Data models used within existing planning tools are dedicated and heavily optimised for performance. To account for all possible required fields of existing planning tools, one would need to specify a massive message interface, which would hardly bring any benefit and would certainly affect the system's usability. Applying inheritance could simplify the structure of the data model, but it would weaken interoperability as not all programming languages allow multiple inheritances. So, we propose messages exchanged between planning services to adopt a structure that consists of three elements, namely a request identifier, callstack, and payload. The *request identifier* is a correlation identifier assigned to an initial user request. The *callstack* represents an object that would adopt the *Routing Slip* pattern [17], whose realisation requires the use of a call stack. The top element of the stack represents the planning service to be called next. Each element below represents a step to be followed next in the system's operation. When a message arrives, the top element will be popped from the stack. The *payload* is specific to the operation taking place and can take any form.

Planning is characterised by a wide variety of techniques even for a single planning service. For example, while PDDL is a commonly used syntax, there are planning tools that are based on other planning languages, such as PDDL+, STRIPS, or HPDL. Consequently, the Parsing Service should support parsing planning problems specified in many planning languages. The choice of language should happen at runtime, depending on the type of planning (see Challenge P1), application requirements, user choice, or other factors. To address this issue in some planning services, we propose to use the *Strategy* pattern, which enables selecting an appropriate strategy at runtime [21]. The pattern suggests that different algorithms or strategies are encapsulated in separate classes and there is one class, called context, that has an argument for storing a reference to one of the strategies. The context is not responsible for the selection of a strategy but rather the chosen strategy is passed to the context. This allows for more flexibility and reusability of planning services (see Challenge A3) because existing strategies can be modified independently from the context and other strategies can be easily added.

As some planning services are computationally intensive, attention should be put on the design decisions related to the processing of the system's state. A system state may consist of a world state and a session state. The world state is the planning state, while the session state includes information about connections established between a planning service and its consuming service(s). If planning services would actively maintain and process the system state, they would constantly consume memory and CPU. It is, therefore, important to achieve statelessness of planning services by separating the system state from planning services whenever possible. As in other advanced systems, our design choice is to defer the management of the system state to a common component which enables planning services to receive or retrieve information from when available or needed (cf. MOM). Planning services for which full statelessness is not possible or desirable can transit to a stateless mode when idle for a long period.

Given Challenges P1 and P2, the manual installation, configuration and deployment of planning software not only require technical expertise but also are time consuming and error prone. To reduce the need to have understanding of technical aspects of planning software, inner workings, installation and deployment and also address in full or partially the DD1-DD3 challenges, we propose to use the concept of containerisation [26]. Each planning service can be packaged and delivered as a container whose installation and that of the full planning system can be automated. Note that this step is also in-line with the recent interest of the planning community to use containerisation, however, only for the purpose of performance comparison of planners within the scope of IPCs.

4 Related Work

Building and integration of planning systems have been of research and development interest both within and outside the AI planning community. Conceptually, our framework is closest to the proposal to servicise planning for the domain of space mission [7]. While interoperability and standardisation are in the focus of that work, the proposal is to standardise only a limited set of planning services for space mission in a way there is a balance between semantics and abstraction. Our treatment is general as it does not focus on a single application domain and goes beyond discussing interoperability and standardisation.

CPEF [25], PELEA [1] and SOA-PE [33] are planning architectures whose components with solving, executing, monitoring, and replanning functionalities are wired to operate in that order. Our treatment investigates and involves a wider spectrum of planning functionalities treated on a more fine-grained level. It also does not assume a predefined workflow but rather planning services are flexible to expresses their interest for communication with other services using the messaging technology.

F4Plan is a framework developed to ease the integration of different solving algorithms into other systems [4]. This framework focuses on the solving functionality only, while our treatment's scope goes beyond this and aims at setting the foundations for designing and integrating fully fledged planning systems.

O-Plan [30], SIPE-2 [34] and PANDA [18] are advanced AI planning systems that share some properties with our work. O-Plan offered a Web service that could have been integrated in any system. SIPE-2 supported integration in the SRI's multiagent system where agents communicated by exchanging messages specified in the Knowledge Query and Manipulation Language. PANDA is supposed to be integrable in other systems, however, the integration approach is unknown. In contrast to these systems, our work proposes an approach that enables integration in any system by using service interfaces, messaging, and modern containersation technology.

EUROPA [5] and LAPKT [29] are frameworks for developing planning techniques. Our work focuses not on building solving techniques but on advanced planning systems, which may incorporate solving techniques. LAPKT is in line with our proposal in that it encourages and supports modularity by separating search algorithms and heuristics from parsing and grounding of planning problems. EUROPA supports integration in other systems by providing C++ and Java interfaces, while LAPKT requires specifying software adapters.

Planning.Domains is an initiative to support researchers and students to develop planning problems [24]. It offers two Web services: one to access planning problems and domain objects, and another to solve and validate planning problems. Our treatment focuses on a wider range of functionalities where solving and validation are decoupled. PDDL4J is a toolkit that focuses on the solving functionality and implementing algorithms of state-of-the-art planners [28]. It also enables parsing, preprocessing, and instantiating planning problems. These functionalities are loosely coupled, allowing developers to separate and integrate them in other systems. Our work goes beyond PDDL4J as it presents challenges, identifies fine-grained planning functionalities, and proposes designing them as services.

In contrast to the aforementioned works, our work presents engineering challenges for developing and using AI planning systems, defines a set of planning functionalities, and proposes an initial concept for their design as services.

5   Conclusions

The prominence of AI is growing exponentially, highlighting the need of building AI systems not only for prototyping and experiments but also for industrial deployments. We showed, though, that engineering and using AI planning systems is challenging. We then identified and defined a preliminary set of planning functionalities with clear boundaries, and proposed an initial concept for designing them as services for interoperability, loose coupling, and automated deployment. The concept suggests to consider planning services only by their interfaces, allowing developers to focus on building and integrating planning solutions. The concept would allow for multiple instances per service, computation at scale, and adding new planning services and features.

The next step in our research is to extend the analysis of existing tools to a systematic literature review that would include a larger corpus of planning tools and potentially lead to a more comprehensive set of fine-grained and well-defined planning functionalities, and, thus, planning services. We are also working on implementing a toolbox of planning services based on our design concept that will enable and accelerate the development and use of advanced planning systems in a stand-alone or integrated mode.

Acknowledgements. I thank Sebastian Graef for the useful input to the design of planning services, and Marco Aiello for the valuable feedback on an earlier version of this paper.

References

1. Alc, V., Prior, D., Onaindia, E., Borrajo, D., Fdez-Olivares, J., Quintero, E.: PELEA: a domain-independent architecture for planning, execution and learning. In: Scheduling and Planning Applications Workshop (2012)
2. Alnazer, E., Georgievski, I., Aiello, M.: On bringing HTN domains closer to reality - the case of satellite and rover domains. In: International Conference on Automated Planning Systems (ICAPS) Workshop on Scheduling and Planning Applications (SPARK) (2022)
3. Alnazer, E., Georgievski, I., Prakash, N., Aiello, M.: A role for HTN planning in increasing trust in autonomous driving. In: IEEE International Smart Cities Conference, pp. 1–7. IEEE (2022)
4. André, F., Daubert, E., Nain, G., Morin, B., Barais, O.: F4Plan: an approach to build efficient adaptation plans. In: Sénac, P., Ott, M., Seneviratne, A. (eds.) MobiQuitous 2010. LNICST, vol. 73, pp. 386–392. Springer, Heidelberg (2012). https://doi.org/10.1007/978-3-642-29154-8_47
5. Barreiro, J., et al.: EUROPA: a platform for AI planning, scheduling, constraint programming, and optimization. In: 4th International Competition on Knowledge Engineering for Planning and Scheduling (2012)
6. Bosch, J., Olsson, H.H., Crnkovic, I.: Engineering AI systems: a research agenda. In: Artificial Intelligence Paradigms for Smart Cyber-Physical Systems, pp. 1–19 (2021)
7. Fratini, S., Policella, N., Donati, A.: A service oriented approach for the interoperability of space mission planning systems. In: Workshop on Knowledge Engineering for Planning and Scheduling, pp. 39–43 (2013)
8. Gartner Inc.: Top strategic technology trends for 2021 (2020). https://www.gartner.com/en/newsroom/press-releases/2020-10-19-gartner-identifies-the-top-strategic-technology-trends-for-2021. Accessed 6 July 2022
9. Georgievski, I.: Hierarchical planning definition language. JBI Preprint JBI, University of Groningen (2013)
10. Georgievski, I.: Office activity recognition using HTN planning. In: IEEE International Conference on Signal Image Technology & Internet-Based Systems (2022)
11. Georgievski, I., Aiello, M.: Automated planning for ubiquitous computing. ACM Comput. Surv. 49(4), 63:1–63:46 (2016)
12. Georgievski, I., Breitenbücher, U.: A vision for composing, integrating, and deploying AI planning functionalities. In: IEEE International Conference on Service-Oriented System Engineering, pp. 166–171 (2021)
13. Georgievski, I., Nguyen, T.A., Nizamic, F., Setz, B., Lazovik, A., Aiello, M.: Planning meets activity recognition: service coordination for intelligent buildings. Pervasive Mob. Comput. 38(1), 110–139 (2017)
14. Ghallab, M., Nau, D.S., Traverso, P.: Automated planning: theory & practice. Morgan Kaufmann Publishers Inc. (2004)
15. Helmert, M., Do, M., Refanidis, I.: IPC 2008: deterministic competition (2008). https://ipc08.icaps-conference.org/deterministic/Results.html
16. Hewitt, C., Bishop, P., Steiger, R.: A universal modular ACTOR formalism for artificial intelligence. In: International Joint Conference on Artificial Intelligence, pp. 235–245 (1973)
17. Hohpe, G., Woolf, B.: Enterprise Integration Patterns: Designing, Building, and Deploying Messaging Solutions. Addison-Wesley Professional (2004)

18. Höller, D., Behnke, G., Bercher, P., Biundo, S.: The PANDA framework for hierarchical planning. In: KI-Künstliche Intelligenz, pp. 1–6 (2021)
19. Höller, D., et al.: HDDL: an extension to PDDL for expressing hierarchical planning problems. In: AAAI Conference on Artificial Intelligence, pp. 9883–9891 (2020)
20. Karpas, E., Magazzeni, D.: Automated planning for robotics. Annu. Rev. Control Robot. Auton. Syst. **3**(1), 417–439 (2020)
21. Lavieri, E.: Hands-On Design Patterns with Java. Packt Publishing Ltd. (2019)
22. Lazovik, A., Aiello, M., Papazoglou, M.: Planning and monitoring the execution of web service requests. In: Orlowska, M.E., Weerawarana, S., Papazoglou, M.P., Yang, J. (eds.) International Conference on Service-Oriented Computing, pp. 335–350 (2003)
23. McDermott, D., et al.: PDDL - the planning domain definition language. Technical Report CVC TR-98-003/DCS TR-1165, Yale Center for Computational Vision and Control (1998)
24. Muise, C.: Planning.domains. In: International Conference on Automated Planning and Scheduling - Demonstrations, pp. 1–3 (2016)
25. Myers, K.L.: CPEF: a continuous planning and execution framework. AI Mag. **20**, 63–69 (1999)
26. Pahl, C., Brogi, A., Soldani, J., Jamshidi, P.: Cloud container technologies: a state-of-the-art review. IEEE Trans. Cloud Comput. **7**(3), 677–692 (2019)
27. Papazoglou, M.P., Georgakopoulos, D.: Introduction: service-oriented computing. Commun. ACM **46**(10), 24–28 (2003)
28. Pellier, D., Fiorino, H.: PDDL4J: a planning domain description library for Java. J. Exp. Theor. Artif. Intell. **30**(1), 143–176 (2018)
29. Ramirez, M., Lipovetzky, N., Muise, C.: Lightweight automated planning toolkit (2015). http://lapkt.org/. Accessed 2 Oct 2022
30. Tate, A., Dalton, J., Levine, J.: O-Plan: a web-based AI planning agent. In: National Conference on Artificial Intelligence/Conference on Innovative Applications of Artificial Intelligence, pp. 1131–1132 (2000)
31. Thorisson, K.R., Benko, H., Abramov, D., Arnold, A., Maskey, S., Vaseekaran, A.: Constructionist design methodology for interactive intelligences. AI Mag. **25**(4), 77 (2004)
32. Vukovic, M., et al.: Towards automated planning for enterprise services: opportunities and challenges. In: International Conference on Service-Oriented Computing, pp. 64–68 (2019)
33. Vulgarakis Feljan, A., Mohalik, S.K., Jayaraman, M.B., Badrinath, R.: SOA-PE: a service-oriented architecture for Planning and Execution in cyber-physical systems. In: International Conference on Smart Sensors and Systems, pp. 1–6 (2015)
34. Wilkins, D.E.: Practical Planning: Extending the Classical AI Planning Paradigm. Morgan Kaufmann Publishers (1988)

Data Product Metadata Management: An Industrial Perspective

Stefan Driessen[1]([⊠])[iD], Geert Monsieur[2][iD], and Willem-Jan van den Heuvel[1][iD]

[1] Tilburg University, JADS, 's-Hertogenbosch 5211DA, The Netherlands
s.w.driessen@jads.nl
[2] Technical University of Eindhoven, JADS, 's-Hertogenbosch 5211DA,
The Netherlands

Abstract. Decentralised data exchanges are promising alternatives to monolithic data lakes and warehouses which are typically emerging around complex service solutions. In theory, this removes some of the bottlenecks of traditional data management solutions. In practice, the road towards achieving such goal is a long way ahead. In this work, we provide an industry perspective on the implications for such work, with a focus on metadata management; the work in question draws from an in-vivo action research approach we enacted at a major German automotive company that is transitioning to an internal decentral data market. Our results provide insight into an industry perspective on the requirements for metadata management. Additionally, we propose and validate a solution design for metadata management in decentralised data exchanges based on semantic web service technology.

Keywords: Data mesh · Data market · Data product · Metadata · Semantic web

1 Introduction

Despite the promises of big data to revolutionise the way companies do business, many organisations still grossly fail to fully capitalise on the data they are generating[1]. For example, several surveys and market analyses show that 60% to 85% of data analytic and data science initiatives never make it to production [18]. Critics have blamed this inability to make full use of data inside an organisation or company on the monolithic approaches typically exploiting such data—e.g., data lakes and warehouses—that are nowadays the standard architecture approach for storing and exchanging data [11,15]. The main downside of these monolithic approaches is that they fail to scale with the number of data sources on the one hand and data science and analytics use cases on the other [15,25].

To address these shortcomings, grey and white literature is showing increasing interest in decentralised data exchanges, such as data markets [6], data

---

[1] https://www.sisense.com/blog/why-businesses-fail-to-capitalize-on-their-data/.

© The Author(s), under exclusive license to Springer Nature Switzerland AG 2023
J. Troya et al. (Eds.): ICSOC 2022 Workshops, LNCS 13821, pp. 237–248, 2023.
https://doi.org/10.1007/978-3-031-26507-5_19

meshes [9], and data spaces [19]. Despite some minor differences in how these platforms approach the sharing and exchange of data, their approaches all focus on offering data as a product/service and are heavily inspired by the microservice paradigm [16,17]. Whereas monolithic approaches rely on a central data office to facilitate data management, in decentralised data exchanges, data providers[2] are responsible for taking (operational) data from their domain and providing it in a manner that is fully optimised for consumption by data consumers from across the organisation.

Despite the theoretical promises of decentralised data exchange platforms, many challenges currently impede their effective implementation and migration. As far as we know, no company or organisation claims to have successfully organised its data exchange in accordance with any proposed theoretical framework. Currently academic studies [9,11,15], and grey literature [23,25] focus on high-level architectural concerns, as well as categorising the challenges and solutions associated with migration and design [3,6]. In this paper we explore one such challenge, namely metadata management in a decentral data exchange. In particular we emphasise the challenge of achieving interoperability (i.e. relating disparate data sources), which has historically always been addressed by adding a central component to the data platform architecture. To supplement existing academic work with practical concerns, we take the industrial perspective of a large German automotive manufacturer who is in the process of transitioning from monolithic architectures towards a decentralised data exchange.

The rest of this paper is organised as follows: In the next section we discuss relevant works on metadata management for decentralised data exchanges and introduce the industrial context provided by the company where our research took place. Section 3 describes how we leveraged design science research to establish goals, problems, requirements and a potential solution. Then, in Sect. 4 we present the results of our research. Finally, in Sect. 5 we discuss the threats to validity in our research approach, the implications of our work and suggestions for follow-up research.

2   Background and Related Literature

We observe that metadata management for internal data exchange platforms is still very much in its infancy. Indeed, Eichler et. al. discuss state-of-the-art metadata management and conclude that there is a research gap in metadata management, especially for internal decentral data exchanges [7]. Some works do exist that focus on the exchange of data *between* companies and organisations. For example, Roman et. al. present an ontology and show how it can be used to harmonise data from different organisations using well-established ontology development methods [20]. Similarly, Spiekermann et. al. present a metadata model for data products in the context of commercial data markets [21].

---

[2] Alternatively called data owners, (data) product providers, or (data) product developers [6].

When it comes to *internal* data exchanges, proposed solutions for metadata management tend to focus on modelling (meta-)data in knowledge graphs using semantic web technology [26]. For example, Hooshmand et. al. emphasise the power of semantic web technology to capture and combine domain knowledge on business objects and technical information on data assets. They propose a transition towards a decentral data mesh for managing data in the product lifecycle management landscape and discuss how different domains can have separate knowledge graphs that can be mapped to achieve interoperability; however, they do not discuss explicitly what metadata management should look like [11]. Other relevant solutions for metadata management have been proposed in the context of centralised architectures. Stach et. al. note the advantages of semantic web technology in terms of ease of use for data consumers who are not experts at data modelling and propose a method for describing desired data products [22]. Similarly, Dibowski and Schmid introduce a full ontology for describing data assets on (internal) data lakes and explain how this improves the discoverability and reusability of data [4].

For our investigation of interoperable data products, we engaged the IT division of a major German automotive manufacturer, which we refer to as the Data Market Implementation Team (DMIT). The company was experiencing challenges in effectively sharing data, and the DMIT was investigating new ways to tackle these challenges with an internal data market. The automotive manufacturer operates with a multi-billion euro revenue in a global market, is organised in several organisational units across multiple continents, employs more than 100.000 employees, and has numerous partner companies in its business ecosystem. Importantly, the operations of this company are not limited to manufacturing but extend to different post-sales services as well. This collaboration allowed us to approach the problem in an industrial setting and get direct input from real-world data providers, data consumers and infrastructure providers.

3   Research Methodology

We employ the design science research approach, which focuses on creating and evaluating artefacts to simultaneously address industry-relevant problems and contribute new knowledge to the scientific community [10]. As shown in Fig. 1, our method consists of three steps in the design cycle: problem evaluation, treatment design, and treatment validation [27]. Below, we describe each of these steps individually, after which Sect. 4 describes the results of each step and how these results informed the consecutive steps.

Problem Evaluation. During the problem evaluation, we started by investigating existing literature on decentral data exchanges in conjunction with repeated interviews with experts from the DMIT, to establish who would be the main stakeholders affected by the implementation of the internal data market. Literature was gathered by snowballing on two existing structured literature reviews (SLRs) for data market- and data mesh design [6,9].

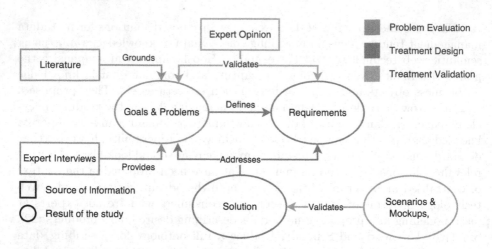

Fig. 1. A figure showing how our methodology relates to the results of the study. The rectangles show external sources of information, and the ellipses show the results presented in this paper. Additionally, the steps of the design cycle [27] are grouped by colour.

These efforts yielded three central stakeholders. 1) The data provider, who is ultimately responsible for the data product. 2) The data consumer, who is the intended user of data products. 3) The platform provider, who is responsible for the IT infrastructure of the decentral data exchange, including the metadata management. Afterwards, we selected several experts from across the company with perspectives for each type of stakeholder, who were then interviewed to establish the different stakeholder goals and problems.

Treatment Design. Based on the goals identified in the interviews and the context provided by the DMIT, we specified the requirements for our treatment and established how satisfying those requirements would contribute to the stakeholder goals. We then considered existing literature on metadata management for effective data sharing and found that an approach based on semantic web technology had the potential to address all the identified requirements.

Treatment Validation. In order to validate our proposed solution, we relied on expert opinion whereby various stakeholders were asked to evaluate a potential solution by coming up with potential problems and benefits [2,14,27]. To help validate that our solution addresses the requirements, we created and described several scenarios for creating, updating, combining and reusing data products and metadata. Furthermore, one or more mock-ups were created for each scenario to illustrate how our solution addressed the corresponding requirements. Afterwards, the scenarios and mock-ups were presented to experts from various domains. This included the interviewees from the problem evaluation step and members of the DMIT, who were asked for feedback. Finally, a workshop was organised where our findings were presented to a large audience of over 50 stake-holders at the company. At this point, feedback was solicited again from these stakeholders.

4   Results

In this section, we discuss the results of our research. As mentioned in Sect. 3, these insights led us to propose a high-level solution and validate it through scenarios and mockups. In order to preserve space, in this paper, we choose to emphasize the results of the interviews, which lead to the formulation of eight goals, eight problems, and five requirements for metadata manage-ment in a decentral data exchange. These problems, goals and requirements can guide practitioners and academics alike in their efforts toward creating metadata management solutions for decentral data exchanges. An overview of our proposed solution, as well as the scenarios and mockups used to val-idate these, can be found online at https://anonymous.4open.science/r/Data-Product-Interoperability-E633.

4.1   Problem Evaluation

In order to accurately identify the requirements for interoperable data product metadata management, we performed interviews with ten expert stakeholders across the company. The experts were selected in consultation with the DMIT to represent the perspectives of the different stakeholders on data exchange. Additionally, as reflected by Table 1, we consciously tried to interview people from various departments with varying levels of expertise and seniority. How-ever, one challenge that arose was that there were no real data providers yet. This seems likely to occur in many organisations looking to transition towards a decentralised data exchange architecture. As mentioned in Sect. 2, in the existing landscape of centralised architectures such as data warehouses and data lakes, onboarding data is the responsibility of a central team of platform providers. Part of moving towards a decentral data exchange entails moving these responsibil-ities to domains' expert data providers who work directly with the operational data [3]. In order to still get the data provider's perspective, we selected inter-viewees that had all been involved in previous initiatives to improve the existing data exchange infrastructure. Consequently, they were platform providers that had explicitly considered the challenge of onboarding new data assets, if not data products.

   Table 1 shows the characteristics of the interviewed experts. On the one hand, the interviewees' experience with the existing data exchange infrastructure and its limitations made them ideal candidates for our investigation because they had already considered the goals and problems for their own initiatives. On the other hand, the emphasis on different perspectives (both domains and roles) ensured that we would not end up with a subset of relevant problems, goals and requirements. The interviews themselves were semi-structured, focusing on existing processes and desired processes for data exchange and the planned internal data exchange. The goals and problems that resulted from these interviews are described in Tables 2 and 3 respectively and are discussed below per stakeholder.

Data Provider. The data provider has three broad goals in the data exchange, the first of which (**G1**) is to decide which data assets would make the most *valuable* data products. However, as captured by **P1**, whenever the data consumer and the data provider come from different domains, it becomes challenging to assess what data products are relevant in the context of the data consumers domain [8,13]. Lack of data engineering expertise and the costs associated with creating and maintaining data products (**P2**) reinforce the need to prioritise when creating data products.

After identifying which data assets to turn into products, the second goal for data providers in an internal data exchange is to create and maintain these data products (**G2**). The literature describing a transition towards a decentralised data exchange platform emphasises that one of the greatest challenges in this transition is the organisational "left shift" whereby domains have to take on the new functional responsibilities of providing data [3]. Our interviews confirm that it is especially challenging to onboard new data providers, particularly if the process of creating and maintaining data products is perceived to be costly (**P2**).

Ensuring that data products are valuable by prioritising is crucial to the success of an internal data exchange. However, this is not enough for the data provider, as they must also convey *why* and *how* the data product is valuable to other actors (**G3**). First among these actors are the data consumers, who might not understand the value, leading to an unused data product. However, many interviewees also explicitly expressed the need to convince colleagues and

Table 1. Overview of the interviewed experts. Providers (P) gave their perspectives on both the platform providing and the data providing. Consumers (C) provided insights for the consumption of data.

Role	Job title	Work experience	Department
P	Enterprise Data Architect	23 years	Enterprise Architecture
P	Manager Enterprise Architecture	7 years	Enterprise Architecture
P	IT-Consultant/IT-Manager	23 years	IT Digital Services
C & P	Data Manager	17 years	Product Digitalisation
C	Manager Data Governance Office	25 years	Finance & Controlling
P	Technical Lead/Methods & Tools	12 years	IT Product Engineering
C	IT Project Manager	10 years	Big Data & AI
P	BI & Analytics Architect	8 years	Technical Architecture Finance Analytics
C & P	Manager Enterprise Business Architecture	29 years	Enterprise Architecture
P	Manager Technology Strategy	15 years	External Consultant

Table 2. The different goals and corresponding problems for each stakeholder. The frequency column shows how many of the interviewed experts (out of nine) mentioned each of the goals.

Stakeholder	Goal	Problems	Freq.
Data provider	**G1** Prioritise data assets to turn into data products	**P1 P2**	7
	G2 Create and maintain data products in a cost-effective manner	**P2**	8
	G3 Convincingly express the value of data products	**P1 P3 P4**	8
Data consumer	**G4** Discover and understand relevant data products	**P1 P3 P4**	7
	G5 Consume & combine data products	**P5**	8
	G6 Incentivise the creation of relevant new data products	**P1 P2 P6**	5
Platform provider	**G7** Create and maintain metadata tools as part of easy-to-use self-serve infrastructure	**(P1–P6) P7**	8
	G8 Extend internal platform to external data exchanges	**P8**	2

Table 3. There are seven problems that the interviewees expect to run into, which describe the obstacles faced by the three main roles. Proper metadata management in an internal data exchange should try to address these problems.

Problem	Description	Freq.
P1	There is a gap between the domain knowledge of data providers and data consumers	7
P2	It is costly to (learn how to) create and maintain data products	8
P3	Similar or identical business objects can lead to significantly different data products	4
P4	It is challenging to understand data product semantics	7
P5	Combining data from different sources is technically challenging	8
P6	Sometimes data is not available but still desired	5
P7	End users lack data engineering expertise	8
P8	External organisations might use different standards	2

management from the provider's domain of the necessity of spending resources on creating and maintaining data products. This is because without the support from these colleagues and managers, providing data is not a sustainable activity. The gap in knowledge between data providers and consumers (**P1**) makes it hard for data providers to convey this value. In contrast, the overall difficulty of understanding the semantics of data products (**P4**) hinders the consumers' efforts to recognise it. Finally, several interviewees reinforced an idea proposed in literature [12] that it is quite difficult to figure out which data is relevant for them whenever multiple data sources are available that describe the same business object from the perspective of different domains (**P3**).

Data Consumer. The data consumer also has three goals: the first one is to find the *right* data for their use case, which requires a *semantic* understanding of the data product (**G4**). This understanding includes the context of the data, the meaning of the different values and attributes, but also the relevant policies and service level agreements. This goal is similar to **G3**, only viewed from the consumer's side. The problems that can be addressed by metadata management are also the same. In particular, the fact that it is challenging to find and understand relevant data products (**P4**) is reinforced by the gap in knowledge between data providers and consumers (**P1**). Additionally, as noted above, differentiating between data products from different domains can be especially challenging (**P3**).

Once the data consumer understands the data product, their next goal is to integrate the data in their use cases, either directly or by combining it with other data (**G5**). Even if the consumer fully understands the data provider's offering, there are still technical challenges associated with consuming and combining data products. In particular, even if it is clear what each attribute in the data product means semantically, this does not automatically lead to a way to connect it to other data (e.g. through schema matching) (**P5**) [8].

Finally, our interviews revealed that data consumers want the ability to discover what data assets exist in operational systems and to incentivise the creation of data products offering data perceived as useful (**G6**). This goal directly tries to address the problem that sometimes data is not available but still desired (**P6**). Additionally, understanding what data exists in operational systems is challenging when these systems exist in domains that are separate from the consumer (**P1**). Furthermore, Incentivisation is hindered by the perceived costs that the data consumer incurs when creating a data product (**P2**).

Platform Providers. The platform providers are charged with creating the internal data exchange on which the data products are exchanged. As such, their main concern is to provide the infrastructure that allows the data providers and data consumers to achieve their goals and overcome their problems (**P1–P6**). However, as data providers and consumers are generally not data engineering experts (**P7**), this infrastructure should come through the creation of an easy-to-use self-serve infrastructure layer [3] (**G7**).

In addition to addressing the goals and problems of the data providers and data consumers, however, the interviewees from the DMIT also expressed the wish to expand their internal data exchange in the long term to work with external platforms such as the Catena-X initiative [1] which connects automotive data platforms (**G8**). The problem that we foresee with this goal is that standards and metadata management initiatives that are developed internally for the automotive company might not extend easily to other platforms (**P8**).

4.2   Treatment Design

Based on the goals and problems described above, we formulate five requirements that *any* approach for metadata management in a decentral data exchange should try to meet (see Table 4).

Table 4. Five requirements were identified to help the actors reach their goals and overcome their respective problems. For each requirement, the goals and problems addressed by that requirement are shown in the final column.

Req.	Description	Addresses
R1.	The metadata management tools should allow data providers to capture domain expertise (i.e. semantic knowledge) as well as technical expertise (i.e. data schemas and statistics) in their models	**G3, G4, G5, P1, P3, P4, P5**
R2.	The resulting models should allow data products to be connected on a data level, even when crossing domain or organisational boundaries	**G5, G8, P5, P8**
R3.	The resulting models should relate data products semantically, even when crossing domain or organisation boundaries	**G3, G4, G5, P1, P3, P4**
R4.	Metadata should be created autonomously by data providers and this should be as easy as possible	**G2, G7, P2, P7**
R5.	The metadata management tools should allow data consumers to express data product requirements	**G1, G6 P1, P6**

The first requirement (**R1**) is a direct consequence of the same goals and problems that motivate a transition towards decentralised data exchanges. Understanding the semantics of the data (e.g. which business processes are involved, how it is collected and for what purpose) is essential for discovering and understanding data (**G4**). Central data offices are not as familiar with these aspects of the data as data providers from the domain, who are better suited to capturing this information in the metadata as the number of sources increases (**G3**). At the same time, technical information, such as the data schema and describing statistics, is still necessary to consume it effectively for a use case (**G5**). Therefore, metadata management in decentral exchanges should allow data providers to explain both types of properties in a human-readable (and possibly machine-readable) manner within the same environment.

The second requirement (**R2**) has always been a main requirement for, and indeed focus of, centralised (meta-)data management. Data warehouses, in particular, address this problem by tightly coupling schemas to a global mediated schema [5]. Meanwhile, for data lakes, interoperability is usually addressed on a use case basis by the members of a central data office. These approaches allow data consumers to easily consume and combine data from different sources (**G5**). However, their reliance on a central bottleneck make them unsuited for decentral data exchanges. Even if data products cannot be tightly coupled to a single cross-domain schema, the metadata management tools should make it easy for data providers and consumers alike to connect (the schemas of) different data products.

The next requirement (**R3** shows that, for the semantic information to be truly effective in helping data consumers find, understand and consume data products (**G4**, **G5**), it needs to relate to their domain knowledge. This helps the data consumer understand the differences, similarities and nuances between business processes that often involve similar business objects (e.g. cars) but generate vastly different data and can greatly reduce the time and efforts required to decide if- and how to use that data. Moreover, if the data provider succeeds in relating their domain knowledge to that of the data consumer, it is more likely that they can convincingly express the value of their data product (**G3**).

The fourth requirement (**R4**) takes into consideration the previously noted organisational "left shift" of responsibilities from the central data office to the data provider that accompanies the transition toward a decentral data exchange (**G2**). Reducing cognitive load for platform users is a problem from cognitive science that has been well-researched for IT artefacts [24]. Therefore tools and standards should be made available that enable data providers to create and manage metadata autonomously, without direct interference from the platform providers (**G7**). In this sense, data products mirror microservices, which are designed to be self-contained.

The final requirement (**R5**) is not as prominent in academic literature. Still, it becomes apparent when realising that innovation in (meta)data management in most industrial settings is driven by data consumers, who feel existing short-comings most acutely. Allowing data consumers to express and incentivise the creation of new data products (**G6**) allows faster data product development and more accurate prioritisation by the data provider (**G1**).

5   Discussion and Conclusion

The requirements discussed in Sect. 4 were mostly consistent with those mentioned in existing literature, but the goals and problems that underlie them had not yet been discussed in detail before. Moreover, we found that an important requirement for practitioners that has been mostly overlooked in academia is the need to assign priorities to data assets that need to be transformed into data products. This prioritisation has two sides: the data providers want to validate their efforts, effectively ensuring that their created data products will be consumed. Similarly, however, data consumers want to express their needs for new data products. Literature on decentral data exchanges seems to have mostly overlooked these goals; only Stach et. al. have investigated this problem in the context of data lakes [22].

Our second finding is that creating proper data providers is a major challenge for organisations trying to transition to decentral data exchanges. Although this may not be a novel insight, the implications this challenge has on metadata management are. Ease of use has already been mentioned in academic literature. However, we find that metadata management tools should also make it easy for data providers to use existing resources (e.g. ontologies or data products) as a template. At the same time, the use of these templates should not be enforced too rigorously, and it should be easy for data providers to deviate from them whenever their ground truth demands it. We believe a metadata management approach based on Semantic Web Technology (SWT) to be a promising way to address these requirements. SWT emphasises the ability of decentral actors to create their own (domain-based) ontologies and standards which can then be related to other domains. These relations can be created either directly between domains as envisioned by Roman et. al. [20], or through a higher-level and more abstract company-wide ontology such as the one proposed by Hooshmand et. al. [11]. Additionally, such an approach can combine semantic and technical metadata into a single entity and present information in a human-readable manner. Moreover, SWT is machine-readable, which opens the door for the development of automatic interoperability tools in the future.

We acknowledge the several threats to the validity of our experiments and conclusions. First, concerning the internal validity, we note that no true data providers existed yet, in the sense that data was provided autonomously by domain teams for one or more external data consumers. We addressed this concern by interviewing extra platform providers and focusing our efforts on those who worked directly with domain teams. A threat to our findings' external validity is that they are founded on investigations inside a single company. To address this concern, we ground the findings in academic literature wherever possible. Additionally, we intend to follow up on our findings with a survey with participants across many organisations. Finally, we note that our research has lead the automotive company to take the first steps towards implementing a semantic-web based approach for metadata management based on our recommendations and validations.

References

1. Catena-X: Automotive Network (2021)
2. Alexander, I.F., Beus-Dukic, L.: Discovering Requirements: How to Specify Products and Services. Wiley, Chichester (2009)
3. Dehghani, Z.: Data Mesh: Delivering Data-Driven Value at Scale, 1st edn. O'Reilly (2022)
4. Dibowski, H., Schmid, S.: Using knowledge graphs to manage a data lake. In: INFORMAITK 2020, Lecture Notes in Informatics (LNI), pp. 41–50 (2021)
5. Doan, A., Halevy, A., Ives, Z.: Principles of Data Integration, 1st edn. Elsevier, Waltham, MA (2012)
6. Driessen, S., Monsieur, G., Van Den Heuvel, W.: Data market design: a systematic literature review. IEEE Access **10**, 33123–33153 (2022). https://doi.org/10.1109/access.2022.3161478
7. Eichler, R., Giebler, C., Gröger, C., Hoos, E., Schwarz, H., Mitschang, B.: Enterprise-wide metadata management: an industry case on the current state and challenges. In: Business Information Systems (July), pp. 269–279 (2021). https://doi.org/10.52825/bis.v1i.47
8. Fernandez, R.C., Subramaniam, P., Franklin, M.J.: Data market platforms: trading data assets to solve data problems. Proc. VLDB Endow. **13**(12), 2150–8097 (2020)
9. Goedgebuure, A.: Data mesh: systematic gray literature study, reference architecture, and cloud-based instantiation at ASML (2022). https://stefan-driessen.github.io/publication/data-mesh-systematic-grey-literature-study/
10. Hevner, A., Chatterjee, S.: Design Research in Information Systems: Theory and Practice, vol. 28. Springer, NY (2010). https://doi.org/10.1007/978-1-4419-5653-8

11. Hooshmand, Y., Resch, J., Wischnewski, P., Patil, P.: From a monolithic PLM landscape to a federated domain and data mesh. Proc. Design Soc. **2**, 713–722 (2022)
12. Koutroumpis, P., Leiponen, A., Thomas, L.: The (unfulfilled) potential of data marketplaces. ETLA Working Papers 2420(53) (2017). http://pub.etla.fi/ETLA-Working-Papers-53.pdf%0Apub.etla.fi/ETLA-Working-Papers-53.pd
13. Koutroumpis, P., Leiponen, A., Thomas, L.D.W.: Markets for data. Ind. Corp. Chang. **29**(3), 645–660 (2020). https://doi.org/10.1093/icc/dtaa002
14. Lauesen, S.: Software Requirements-Styles and Techniques. Pearson Education (2002)
15. Loukiala, A., Joutsenlahti, J.-P., Raatikainen, M., Mikkonen, T., Lehtonen, T.: Migrating from a centralized data warehouse to a decentralized data platform architecture. In: Ardito, L., Jedlitschka, A., Morisio, M., Torchiano, M. (eds.) PROFES 2021. LNCS, vol. 13126, pp. 36–48. Springer, Cham (2021). https://doi.org/10.1007/978-3-030-91452-3_3
16. Narayan, S.: Products over projects (2018). https://martinfowler.com/articles/products-over-projects.html
17. Newman, S.: Monolith to Microservices: Evolutionary Patterns to Transform Your Monolith. O'Reilly (2020). https://www.oreilly.com/library/view/monolith-to-microservices/9781492047834/
18. O'Neil, B.T.: Failure rates for analytics, AI, and big data projects = 85% - yikes! (2019)
19. Otto, B., Steinbuß, S., Teuscher, A., Lohmann, S.: IDSA reference architecture model. International Data Spaces Association (April) (2019). https://internationaldataspaces.org/download/16630/
20. Roman, D., et al.: The euBusinessGraph ontology: a lightweight ontology for harmonizing basic company information. Semantic Web **13**(1), 41–68 (2021). https://doi.org/10.3233/sw-210424
21. Spiekermann, M., Tebernum, D., Wenzel, S., Otto, B.: A metadata model for data goods. In: MKWI 2018 - Multikonferenz Wirtschaftsinformatik 2018-March, pp. 326–337 (2018)
22. Stach, C., Bräcker, J., Eichler, R., Giebler, C., Mitschang, B.: Demand-driven data provisioning in data lakes. In: Association for Computing Machinery, vol. 1 (2021). https://doi.org/10.1145/3487664.3487784
23. Strengholt, P.: ABN AMRO's data and integration mesh (2020). https://www.linkedin.com/pulse/abn-amros-data-integration-mesh-piethein-strengholt/
24. Sweller, J.: Cognitive load during problem solving: effects on learning. Cogn. Sci. **12**(2), 257–285 (1988). https://doi.org/10.1016/0364-0213(88)90023-7
25. Dehghani, Z.: How to move beyond a monothilitic data lake to a distributed data mesh (2019). https://martinfowler.com/articles/data-monolith-to-mesh.html
26. W3C: Semantic web - leading the web to its full potential (2015)
27. Wieringa, R.J.: Design Science Methodology for Information Systems and Software Engineering. Springer, Heidelberg (2014). https://doi.org/10.1007/978-3-662-43839-8

FUSPAQ: A Function Selection Platform to Adjust QoS in a FaaS Application

Pablo Serrano-Gutierrez[1]([envelope]) [ID], Inmaculada Ayala[1,2] [ID], and Lidia Fuentes[1,2] [ID]

[1] Departamento de Lenguajes y Ciencias de la Computación, Universidad de Málaga, Málaga, Spain
{pserrano,ayala,lff}@lcc.uma.es
[2] ITIS Software, Universidad de Málaga, Málaga, Spain

Abstract. Function as a Service (FaaS) development has numerous benefits for application deployment, management, and maintenance. However, the lack of control over the infrastructure and, often, over the FaaS platform itself, makes it necessary to look for external solutions that allow the operation of the application to be adapted to different requirements or changing execution conditions. In a FaaS application, the quality of service (QoS) is determined by the characteristics of the functions executed to perform each workflow operation. Deciding the most suitable functions providing a QoS is a complex process due to the high variability of possible function implementations, each giving different qualities. Leaving this task in the hands of the developer is not a good solution and makes it difficult to program the application. We present FUSPAQ, a framework for working with serverless architectures, which can automatically select the best functions executed at runtime to satisfy specific QoS requirements. With this objective, a Software Product Line approach is used, modeling the application's tasks and operations using Feature Models that specify the variability of functions that can perform the same operation as a family of functions. We use Z3, a cross-platform satisfiability modulo theories (SMT) solver, to generate optimal configurations. As requirements can change over time, the system automatically adapts to these changes to continue maintaining the desired QoS. We test our approach with different QoS parameters, and analyse the value added to serverless frameworks.

Keywords: FaaS · Serverless · QoS · Software product line · Feature model

1 Introduction

Function as a Service (FaaS) promotes decomposing an application into functions ('actions') triggered by events and supported by a platform abstracting the complex resource management task. The FaaS approach is gaining popularity due to its numerous advantages for software developers and application owners. It

J. Troya et al. (Eds.): ICSOC 2022 Workshops, LNCS 13821, pp. 249–260, 2023.
https://doi.org/10.1007/978-3-031-26507-5_20

enables rapid development based on a set of reusable functions. It eases managing tasks like deploying functions to the infrastructure or scaling as a response to increases in resource demand. In addition, the serverless [2] functions used by an application may be provided by third parties and implemented using different programming languages. This heterogeneity offers excellent flexibility to the developer of the application, who can use a high diversity of functions for the same purpose without any integration cost. However, using a fully managed infrastructure has the drawback that it is not possible to control its effect on the quality of service (QoS) of the application. For this reason, it is important to be able to adjust the behaviour related to QoS at the application level.

Considering the diversity of functions that can be used to perform the different operations necessary for the application, and their possible configurations, the application behaviour regarding the QoS could be highly variable. So, selecting one or another function or configuration by the application developer can be decisive in the execution result. Therefore, an optimal choice of functions and execution parameters will allow us to adjust to the desired QoS objectives. Managing this variability and generating the optimal configurations of FaaS applications on the fly is a complex task that should be automated. One of the most accepted approaches to managing variability is Software Product Lines (SPLs) [15], which define a system as a particularisation of a family of software products built using reusable elements. We propose an SPL approach to model the variability of serverless applications by defining families of functions modeled by variability models. The most frequently used variability models are Feature Models [12], which are employed to model the common and variable elements of a family of software products. We will specify the variability of an application through feature modeling in an automated way.

The problem of managing function variability in FaaS architectures is worsened by the lack of adequate tools to manage function reuse, abstractions, and programming models for building non-trivial FaaS applications [13]. The leading platforms provide specific tools [4,11,14] but they focus on the orchestration of functions and do not consider the QoS. Several works tackle optimisation and QoS in the context of FaaS [6,10,16,18], but focusing only in allocating the resources for functions dynamically at runtime. So, they do not consider alternative quality-valued functions nor the overall quality of function configurations.

In this work, we present FUSPAQ, a platform that selects, through an optimisation process, the best functions and configurations to achieve a particular QoS and automatically applies the results to a FaaS environment. The system uses feature modeling at two different levels. Firstly, to model the tasks that make up the application. Secondly, to model the families of functions to carry out each application task. These are the sets of functions that, having a different implementation, can be used to perform the same operation. The result is a feature model whose valid configurations represent the functions to run the application successfully. The main contributions of FUSPAQ are:

1. It provides an environment for running serverless applications in which developers do not need to consider the different alternatives to meet the application

design objectives. It permits them to focus on FaaS application operations solely. FUSPAQ selects the best implementation of these operations and the most adequate parameters at runtime, considering defined QoS. The platform fully integrates with the FaaS framework so its operation is transparent and could be used with existing applications.

2. It supports the change of QoS policies at runtime. So, it can dynamically generate an optimal configuration of the FaaS application that complies with new restrictions.

3. The system adds tuning capabilities to any FaaS framework, its operation does not depend on a specific framework. Also, from the developer's point of view, the application's implementation is done the same way as any serverless application, so no additional training is necessary.

The rest of this paper is structured as follows: Sect. 2 discusses some related work; Sect. 3 presents our case study on a weather widget service; Sect. 4 introduces our approach; Sect. 5 shows the experimental results of the platform in an execution environment; and Sect. 6 presents some conclusions to the paper.

2   Related Work

This section will first discuss the related work that addresses QoS requirements in the FaaS context. Secondly, we discuss SPL approaches dealing with service-oriented applications.

In FaaS, there are many leading platforms that provide tools to assist developers in developing and executing serverless applications. These tools are IBM Cloud Functions [11], Amazon Step Functions [4], and Azure Durable Functions [14]. An interesting evaluation of these tools is presented in the work [9]. These tools' main functionalities are state management of FaaS functions, parallel execution support, software packaging, and repositories, to mention a few. FUSPAQ can complement these approaches with a development process that supports configuring and composing the functions considering QoS.

There are several works that tackle the issue of the QoS in the context of FaaS [6,10,16,18]. The work presented in [10] proposes a closed-loop resource controller, which increases the overall utilisation of the resources while achieving QoS levels enforced by the end-users. Authors use a model predictive controller to predict the events of high workload and allocate more resources for functions considering current and future demands. The paper [16] presents an initial step in realising a fully operational QoS-aware FaaS platform. The platform allocates more resources for functions considering QoS policies as the previous contribution. The experiments show that the QoS-aware FaaS platform provides cost-efficient executions and resource savings. In the context of Fog Computing and for the QoS of security and latency, the work [6] proposes a declarative model, a formal logical definition and a prototype platform named Faas2Fog to address the problem of orchestration in the fog. The approach considers hardware, software and QoS requirements to deploy FaaS functions in the cloud.

For applications deployed in the cloud, FADE [18] is a methodology for application decomposition into fine-grained functions and energy-aware function placement on a cluster of edge devices subject to user-specified QoS guarantees. These works address QoS in the context of FaaS but adapt the application only by considering where to place the function, known as the function placement problem. They do not consider alternative implementations or the internal configuration of the application operations workflow. Also, these approaches need to be able to manipulate the FaaS framework, and in the case of external FaaS providers they are difficult to apply, since they depend on the configuration options offered.

The FUSPAQ approach applies SPL in the context of FaaS applications to optimise deployments. No other work involves SPL in this context, but we can find similar approaches in the web services domain [1,5,8]. MoRE-WS [1] is a model-based reconfiguration engine for web services that use SPL at runtime (also known as Dynamic Software Product Line). The approach uses feature models as adaptation policies to automatically generate and execute a plan to reconfigure service compositions. SPL-TQSSS [8] is an SPL approach that assists users in integrating on the fly the operations of service workflows that meet the transactional property and QoS preferences. In the context of mashups, M. Bashari et al. [5] propose to use concepts of the SPL domain and automated Artificial Intelligence to support the automated composition of service mashups. The approach targets non-expert users that can feel more comfortable dealing with higher-level representations of functionalities, i.e., features, than the underlying specifics of services. All these works show the advantages of using an SPL in the context of services. Unlike these systems that work on the composition of services or microservices, FUSPAQ integrates SPL analysis in a FaaS environment, making it unnecessary to worry about the deployment and orchestration of services. Also, from a development standpoint, there is no need to program the system any differently than for any other application, nor is it required to perform feature modelling.

3   Case Study

To illustrate the operation of our system, we will consider a case study consisting of a weather widget service. This service have two main components, a display for the current weather information and another in which images taken by users are displayed. Weather information can come directly from nearby sensors or be generated by a weather radar. In the first case, the service gets the measured information from different sensor networks registered in this or similar applications. In the other case, it uses any data source related to one of the multiple meteorological radars available in our region. For the second of the components, we will use images that we will assume that users have uploaded through an application and registered in a database, along with their location.

Our application workflow is shown in Fig. 3 in BPMN 2.0 notation. It is composed of the tasks *Show Photos* and *Show Info*, which can be carried out in parallel. The *Show Photos* task is in charge of displaying the images, and there are two exclusive alternatives for the task *Show Info*, that can be *Local Info* or *Sat Info*, which use local or satellite sources to obtain weather info, respectively. As can be observed, some tasks are composed by subtasks. For example, firstly, *Local Info* needs to get data from sensors (*Get Sensor Data*) and then display it correctly formatted (*Show Data*). We will call these subtasks operations and they will be the ones that are implemented through serverless functions.

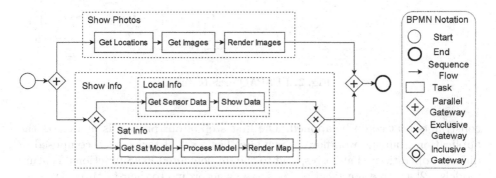

Fig. 1. Application workflow of the case study

4   Overview of FUSPAQ

As we stated, FUSPAQ can tune the behaviour of a FaaS application to meet specific QoS. It processes function requests from an application the same way that a FaaS framework does, but with the difference that it internally applies an optimisation process that decides which functions are executed and with what parameters, to comply with the QoS objective. The system (see Fig. 2), programmed in Python[1], is composed of four components: a model generator that automatically creates the set of feature models that the platform will use, an analysis system that performs the optimisation process based on these models, a requests processor responsible for interacting with the application, and a function manager that communicates with the FaaS framework to execute functions and monitor them.

4.1   Model Generator

To be able to adjust the behaviour of an application, we need to have a complete view of the functional variability of the application. FUSPAQ capture the different variability views with a collection of feature models (Fig. 3), automatically generated from the information provided by the developer. That is, the application's workflow that represents its functional requirements, the set of implemented functions that can perform the operations needed, and the set of

---

[1] Source code available at https://github.com/pserranouma/fuspaq.

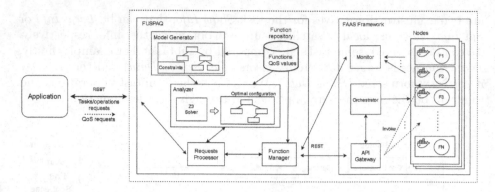

Fig. 2. FUSPAQ architecture

constraints that could be applied. The first step of our process is modelling the application from the workflow, which specifies a set of tasks, each composed of different operations that correspond to the implemented FaaS functions. Feature models [12] are tree specifications of systems according to their features. We generate a feature model from the workflow by doing a mapping process. Each task corresponds to a feature, and the gateways are used to obtain the relationships between them. A parallel gateway is transformed into an AND relationship, that is, a feature compound by a set of mandatory children. Inclusive gateways are transformed into an OR, a feature with alternative children. We will also obtain a feature with exclusive alternative children if the gateway is exclusive.

The second source of information used by the model generator is the set of implemented functions. This information is stored in a function repository. For every function we annotate the operation performed and the QoS information we need to consider, such as execution times, costs and security. We generate a collection of service feature models representing the variability of each executing task. For this, functions are grouped by operation, and every function that can perform the same operation is included in an exclusive group of features that identifies that operation. These groups of features will constitute the leaves of the whole tree considering all the operations performed by a task. This way, in our case study, the *Show Photos* family of services (see Fig. 3) consists of three mandatory operations which are *Get_Locations*, *Get_Images* and *Render_Images*. For simplicity, we will name the available functions for each operation using the same name with different suffixes (letters in alphabetical order). That is, if we have two alternatives, with A and B, if we have 3, with A, B and C, and so. Then, if we assume that we have two possible sensor data sources, the functions will be *Get_Sensor_DataA* and *Get_Sensor_DataB*. Each one has associated different QoS parameters that we store in the *Function Repository*. For example, the entry in this repository related to *Get_Sensor_DataA* could be: *op=Get_Sensor_Data*, *Time(op)=20* and *Energy(op)=1*, being *op* the generic operation that this function implements, and *Time(op)* and *Energy(op)* the time and energy consumed by the operation, respectively.

Also, some functions may have a different behaviour depending on its input parameters, which may affect the QoS. For example, in the case study, the rendering of images can be done with different resolutions. We generate function feature models, considering every parameter marked as tuneable by the developer, resulting in features of that function with other children features according to the possible values of the parameters. In the repository, it is also necessary to store the values or variations that may occur in the QoS parameters based on these entries. For example, we could consider that using a 480p resolution decreases the execution time of *Get_Images* by 50%, and using a 1080p resolution increases it by 50%, compared to using the 720p resolution.

Applying Software Product Lines refactoring techniques [3] to these three sets of feature models, we generate another one with the information from the entire application. FUSPAQ will use it to tune the FaaS application behaviour.

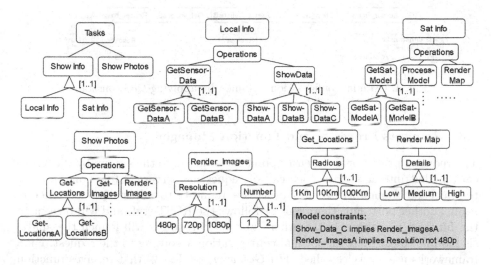

Fig. 3. Feature models generated by the platform

4.2   Analysis System

The next step of our approach is to select the optimal configuration of the system using the generated models. We use a logical and mathematical model built from the Feature Model of the application, adding cross-tree constraints and user-specified restrictions. The conversion of features to this model is done automatically by a recursive process that obtains all the logical relationships between features, assigning to every branch the AND, OR, or XOR logical relationship indicated in the parent node. For example, considering the model of the main tasks of our case study, we get the logical expression *ShowPhotos AND (Local-Info XOR SatInfo)*. We also need to add a set of equations that are different depending on the QoS parameter to be optimised. For example, the total energy consumed by the application will be the sum of the energies consumed by all the selected functions, while the security will be determined by the function executed whose security is lower.

Finally, the Z3 solver uses all this information along with QoS restrictions to generate the system's optimal configuration. This will let us know which functions and parameters will allow us to achieve the desired QoS. In our case study, considering an execution time of less than 100 milliseconds and minimising energy consumption, will result in the configuration shown in Fig. 4.

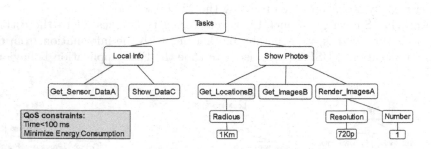

Fig. 4. Optimal configuration obtained by applying QoS constraint

4.3   Requests Processor and Function Manager

The requests processor is the entry point for requests to the system by the application, that interacts with it instead of requesting serverless functions directly to the FaaS framework. It also processes requests to adjust QoS parameters using another port. Function requests follows the REST style and will be sent to the function manager. On the other hand, QoS requests will launch the analysis module to calculate an optimal configuration according to the request. FaaS frameworks use a service called *API Gateway* (see Fig. 2) that receives function requests from the FaaS application. These functions are managed by an orchestrator and will be executed in containers deployed in the cloud. The execution results are returned to the application through this same *Gateway*. As our system uses a communication mechanism through REST requests, similar to the one used with the *API Gateway*, the way of working will be identical to doing it directly with the serverless framework. Function manager directs that calls to a specific implementation deployed by the said framework. After its execution, the returned result is passed through the exact mechanism to the calling application, which will not be aware of this intermediate process.

When programming the application, instead of considering function implementations, the developer will make a call to a generic function being decided at runtime which of the implementations will be executed. So, for example, in our case study, the application call to *GetLocations* results in the execution of *GetLocationsB(Radious=1 Km)*.

Another task of the function manager is to request monitoring information about the execution of a function, so if a function does not respond, a reconfiguration process is launched. This makes the application have the ability to recover from execution failures.

5   Experimental Results

To evaluate the operation of our platform, we have carried out a series of experiments considering different workflows and function implementations. These experiments have been performed using a PC Intel i5-7400, 3.00 GHz, 24 GiB of RAM, and with Python v.3.10.4 and Z3 v.4.8.15. OpenFaaS has been used as the FaaS framework, with Prometheus as the monitoring system. In addition to the case study presented, we have used other workflows with a more significant number of tasks to check the performance and scalability of FUSPAQ.

5.1   Performance

There are mainly three aspects of FUSPAQ that can affect the performance of a serverless application. The first one is the processing time, that is the time elapsed between the QoS request and obtaining the optimal configuration. This time will depend on the complexity of the application, as well as the number of available function implementations. The system is quite fast for the operations and functions considered in the case study, taking 20 milliseconds (ms). Considering that the average number of tasks in a real application is nine [7], a more realistic estimation can be made, obtaining a processing time of only 49 ms.

The second one is the response time, which is the time elapsed between the application calling a function and receiving a response. This time is stable because the system does not have to construct or optimise the models but only needs to transform the function request by applying the selected configuration. The time consumed by the additional REST requests is also involved. To calculate it, we subtract from the measured time the request to the FaaS framework time, obtaining 5 ms over a local machine. This value can vary in each network.

The third aspect that needs to be considered is the reconfiguration time. This is the time that the system requires to reconfigure the application when a change in the behaviour of some function is detected. This time is different from the processing time considered before. Reconfiguration does not require building the models again. It only updates QoS related equations and relaunches the optimisation process. For our case study, the measured value is 15 ms. In a more common scenario with nine tasks, we obtained 26 ms. Considering also the time consumed to get monitoring data, we obtained a total of 32 ms and 43 ms, respectively. This stands for the time between the end of a function call and the completion of a system reconfiguration triggered by it when necessary.

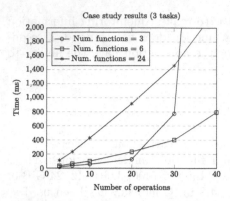
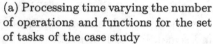
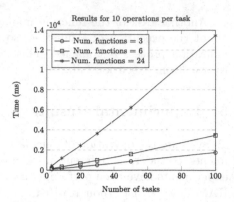

(a) Processing time varying the number of operations and functions for the set of tasks of the case study

(b) Processing time varying the number of tasks of the workflow and functions

Fig. 5. Scalability tests results

5.2 Scalability

To evaluate the system when the problem increases in size we have consider the effect of both tasks and functions. The most affected process is optimisation, since modeling is a linear problem. Response time remains similar, because it depends mainly on requests. The measurements obtained are for the worst case, that is, the one in which there are no defined user restrictions since the restrictions lead to pruning of the feature model and, therefore, to a reduction in complexity. For each set of values tested, 100 executions have been made, noting the average result. Except for the measurements of the unmodified case study, random values have been generated for the tasks, operations, functions and QoS.

Analysing the measurements made on the set of tasks of the case study (Fig. 5a), we find that when the number of operations increases, the system starts to behave exponentially. The most relevant thing is that we observe how the exponential behaviour starts earlier for smaller amounts of functions. Especially noteworthy is the case of the number of functions equal to 3, which with 40 operations far exceeds the other cases of 6 and 24 implementations per operation. This is because having more possibilities to choose from increases the probability of functions that fit the solution. Neither is it convenient to significantly increase the number of implementations per operation since the number of nodes in the tree grows so much that the processing time may be too high for the application.

We have also tested the effect of the number of tasks on performance (Fig. 5b). In this case, we observe that the number of tasks does not have such a decisive effect as the number of operations or functions, and it behaves reasonably linearly for these ranges of tasks. This is because FUSPAQ assigns functions to operations, so these values are the ones that most affect the result since the number of possible combinations is exponential. For example, with ten operations and 24 functions, we have 24^{10} possible combinations. Despite this, the measured times remain within reasonable margins compared to the results of other solvers applied to Feature Models [17]. Considering that the usual number of tasks is much lower than 100, the application's behaviour is reasonably good. Our results are under 2.5 s, assuming 20 tasks, 10 operations per task and 24 functions per operation, that are also high values.

We have measure reconfiguration times too, comparing them with processing times. We have found that they vary proportionally depending on the number of tasks. For example, for 3 tasks, reconfiguration time is approximately the 80% of processing time, while for 10 task it is about the third part. This way, the behaviour is similar to those shown for processing time but scaling them considering these proportions.

6 Conclusions

In this paper, we have presented FUSPAQ, a system that allows exploiting the advantages offered by FaaS programming. FUSPAQ facilitates the development of applications by applying QoS policies in a simple way and out of the development stage. This platform allows the developer not to be conditioned by the choice of the most suitable algorithms or parameters for each function at design time. Likewise, it can improve the performance of an existing FaaS application or provide it with adaptive capabilities.

A key component of our approach is the function repository, which permits adding new functions without rebuilding or re-deploying an existing application. With our system, it is even possible to make this at runtime. It supports the change of QoS requirements on the fly. If a running application requests a change in QoS, FUSPAQ will automatically recalculate a new optimal configuration. Another interesting functionality provided is failure recovery. If any function fails or stops working, our system will detect that it cannot provide the desired QoS so that a reconfiguration will be carried out. In this way, we can ensure the continuous operation of the application using the best possible configuration.

One aspect that can be significant in terms of QoS is the effect the infrastructure can have on the functions that run on it. Several works has reported the importance of this issue [6,10,16,18]. In this sense, as future work, we plan to add resource placement control capabilities to the system.

References

1. Alferez, G.H., Pelechano, V.: Context-aware autonomous web services in software product lines. In: 2011 15th International Software Product Line Conference, pp. 100–109 (2011). https://doi.org/10.1109/SPLC.2011.21
2. Allen, S., Aniszczyk, C., Arimura, C., et al.: CNCF serverless whitepaper (2018)
3. Alves, V., Gheyi, R., Massoni, T., Kulesza, U., Borba, P., Lucena, C.: Refactoring product lines. In: Proceedings of the 5th International Conference on Generative Programming and Component Engineering (GPCE 2006), pp. 201–210. Association for Computing Machinery, New York (2006). https://doi.org/10.1145/1173706.1173737

4. Amazon Web Services: AWS step functions. https://aws.amazon.com/es/step-functions/
5. Bashari, M., Bagheri, E., Du, W.: Automated composition of service mashups through software product line engineering. In: Kapitsaki, G.M., Santana de Almeida, E. (eds.) ICSR 2016. LNCS, vol. 9679, pp. 20–38. Springer, Cham (2016). https://doi.org/10.1007/978-3-319-35122-3_2
6. Bocci, A., Forti, S., Ferrari, G.L., Brogi, A.: Placing FaaS in the fog, securely. In: 5th Italian Conference on Cybersecurity (ITASEC 2021), vol. 2940, pp. 166–179. CEUR-WS (2021)
7. Dietzsch, A.: Ratios to support the exploration of business process models in business process management (2003)
8. Gamez, N., El Haddad, J., Fuentes, L.: SPL-TQSSS: a software product line approach for stateful service selection. In: 2015 IEEE International Conference on Web Services, pp. 73–80 (2015). https://doi.org/10.1109/ICWS.2015.20
9. García López, P., Sánchez-Artigas, M., París, G., Barcelona Pons, D., Ruiz-Ollobarren, A., Arroyo-Pinto, D.: Comparison of FaaS orchestration systems. In: 2018 IEEE/ACM International Conference on Utility and Cloud Computing Companion (UCC Companion), pp. 148–153 (2018). https://doi.org/10.1109/UCC-Companion.2018.00049
10. HoseinyFarahabady, M.R., Lee, Y.C., Zomaya, A.Y., Tari, Z.: A QoS-aware resource allocation controller for function as a service (FaaS) platform. In: Maximilien, M., Vallecillo, A., Wang, J., Oriol, M. (eds.) ICSOC 2017. LNCS, vol. 10601, pp. 241–255. Springer, Cham (2017). https://doi.org/10.1007/978-3-319-69035-3_17
11. IBM: IBM cloud functions. https://www.ibm.com/es-es/cloud/functions
12. Lee, K., Kang, K.C., Lee, J.: Concepts and guidelines of feature modeling for product line software engineering. In: Gacek, C. (ed.) ICSR 2002. LNCS, vol. 2319, pp. 62–77. Springer, Heidelberg (2002). https://doi.org/10.1007/3-540-46020-9_5
13. Leitner, P., Wittern, E., Spillner, J., Hummer, W.: A mixed-method empirical study of function-as-a-service software development in industrial practice. J. Syst. Softw. **149**, 340–359 (2019). https://doi.org/10.1016/j.jss.2018.12.013
14. Microsoft: Azure functions. https://docs.microsoft.com/en-us/azure/azure-functions/functions-overview
15. Pohl, K., Böckle, G., Linden, F.: Software product line engineering: foundations, principles, and techniques. Springer, Heidelberg (2005). https://doi.org/10.1007/3-540-28901-1
16. Sheshadri, K.R., Lakshmi, J.: QoS aware FaaS platform. In: 2021 IEEE/ACM 21st International Symposium on Cluster, Cloud and Internet Computing (CCGrid), pp. 812–819 (2021). https://doi.org/10.1109/CCGrid51090.2021.00099
17. Sundermann, C., Thüm, T., Schaefer, I.: Evaluating SAT solvers on industrial feature models. In: Proceedings of the 14th International Working Conference on Variability Modelling of Software-Intensive Systems, pp. 1–9. Association for Computing Machinery, NY (2020). https://doi.org/10.1145/3377024.3377025
18. Tzenetopoulos, A., Marantos, C., Gavrielides, G., Xydis, S., Soudris, D.: FADE: FaaS-inspired application decomposition and energy-aware function placement on the edge, pp. 7–10. Association for Computing Machinery, New York (2021)

Specification-Driven Code Generation for Inter-parameter Dependencies in Web APIs

Saman Barakat[✉][iD], Enrique Barba Roque[iD], Ana Belén Sánchez[iD], and Sergio Segura[iD]

SCORE Lab, I3US Institute, Universidad de Sevilla, Seville, Spain
saman.barakat@gmail.com

Abstract. The generation of code templates from web API specifications is a common practice in the software industry. However, existing tools neglect the dependencies among input parameters (so called inter-parameter dependencies), extremely common in practice and usually described in natural language. As a result, developers are responsible for implementing the corresponding validation logic manually, a tedious and error-prone process. In this paper, we present an approach for the automated generation of code for inter-parameter dependencies in web APIs. Specifically, we exploit the IDL4OAS extension for specifying inter-parameter dependencies as a part of OpenAPI Specification (OAS) files. To make our approach applicable in practice, we present an extension of the popular OpenAPI Generator tool ecosystem, automating the generation of Java and Python code for the management of inter-parameter dependencies in both servers and clients. Evaluation results show the effectiveness of the approach in accelerating the development of APIs, generating up to 9.4 times more code than current generators, while making APIs potentially more reliable.

Keywords: Web APIs · Scaffolding · Code generation · OpenAPI generator

1 Introduction

Web application programming interfaces (APIs) enable the communication between heterogeneous devices and systems over the Web. They have gained significant interest in the software industry as the *de-facto* standard for software integration. API directories such as ProgrammableWeb [23] and RapidAPI [25] index over 24K and 30K web APIs from different domains such as shopping, finance and social networks. Web APIs can be categorized into various types based on application designs and the communication protocols they use. Hypertext Transfer Protocol (HTTP) APIs, arguably the de-facto standard, use the HTTP protocol to interact—typically through CRUD (Create, Read, Update, and Delete) operations—with resources (e.g., a *video* in the YouTube API [32]

J. Troya et al. (Eds.): ICSOC 2022 Workshops, LNCS 13821, pp. 261–273, 2023.
https://doi.org/10.1007/978-3-031-26507-5_21

or an *invoice* in the PayPal API [22]). HTTP APIs often implement the principles of the REST architectural style for distributed systems, being referred to as RESTful APIs [7]. Henceforth, we will use the term web API to refer to RESTful web APIs or, more generally, to HTTP APIs.

Web APIs are commonly described using the OpenAPI Specification (OAS) format [21]. An OAS document describes a web API in terms of the operations supported, as well as their input parameters and the possible responses. OAS documents are heavily used nowadays for automating certain tasks in the API lifecycle. One of these applications is *scaffolding*: generating code templates for both API servers and clients from the OAS specification of the API. As an example, OpenAPI Generator is a popular code generation tool ecosystem for OAS [20]. It is developed in Java and has over 50 generators for clients and servers in different programming languages.

Web APIs typically include inter-parameter dependencies. These are constraints that restrict the way in which two or more input parameters can be combined to form a valid call to the service. For example, when searching for businesses in the Yelp API[1], the parameter `location` is "required if either `latitude` or `longitude` is not provided", and both parameters are "required if `location` is not provided". A recent study revealed that dependencies are extremely common and pervasive in industrial web APIs: they appear in 4 out of every 5 APIs across all application domains and types of operations [15]. However, OAS provides no support for the formal description of these types of dependencies, despite being a highly demanded feature by practitioners[2]. Instead, users are encouraged to describe them informally using natural language[3]. As a result, current scaffolding tools do not support the generation of validation code for inter-parameter dependencies, as these are not specified in OAS documents. Therefore, the validation code associated to these dependencies must be manually implemented. In the previous example, for instance, developers should write the required assertions to make sure that `latitude` and `longitude` parameters are used together when the `location` parameter is not provided in an API call, both in clients and servers. This is not only tedious, but also error-prone, making validation failures very common in practice [16].

In this paper, we present an approach for the automated generation of code for validating inter-parameter dependencies in web APIs. For this, we leverage IDL4OAS, an OAS extension for specifying *inter-parameter dependencies* as a part of OAS documents using the Inter-parameter Dependency Language (IDL) [11,14]. To make our approach readily applicable in practice, we present an extension of the OpenAPI Generator tool ecosystem enabling the automated generation of Java and Python code for the validation of inter-parameter dependencies in both servers and clients. Evaluation results show that our approach generates up to 940% more lines of code than current generators, 496% on average. More importantly, the automated generation of validation code minimizes

---

[1] https://www.yelp.com/developers/documentation/v3/business_search.

[2] https://github.com/OAI/OpenAPI-Specification/issues/256.

[3] https://swagger.io/docs/specification/describing-parameters.

the possibility of having faults in the validation logic, making APIs significantly more reliable.

A very preliminary version of this work was presented in [3]. This paper represents a major extension including significantly further details and a larger evaluation. Also, we have changed the evaluation setup based on the feedback received, making our results more accurate.

2 Background

This section introduces key concepts to contextualize our proposal, namely, the IDL language, the IDL4OAS extension, and the OpenAPI Generator tool ecosystem.

2.1 Inter-parameter Dependency Language (IDL)

The Inter-parameter Dependency Language (IDL) is a textual domain-specific language used to describe dependencies among input parameters in web APIs [14]. IDL was created based on a study of more than 2.5K operations of 40 real-world APIs. Specifically, IDL supports expressing seven types of inter-parameter dependencies widely used in practice. As an example, Listing 1 shows a fragment of an IDL document describing the inter-parameter dependencies found in the Google Maps Places API [9] (grammar of the language available at [11]). In what follows, we briefly introduce the types of dependencies supported by IDL:

```
 1   // Operation: Search for places within specified area:
 2   ZeroOrOne(radius, rankby=='distance');
 3   IF rankby=='distance' THEN keyword OR name OR type;
 4   maxprice >= minprice;
 5
 6   // Operation: Query information about places:
 7   AllOrNone(location, radius);
 8   Or(query, type);
 9   maxprice >= minprice;
10
11   // Operation: Get photo of place:
12   OnlyOne(maxheight, maxwidth);
13
14   // Operation: Automcomplete place name:
15   IF strictbounds THEN location AND radius;
```

Listing 1. IDL specification of google maps places API.

- **Requires.** This type of dependency emerges when the presence of a parameter *p1* in a request requires the presence of another parameter *p2*. For example, line 3 of Listing 1 indicates that if the parameter *rankby* is set to 'distance', then at least one of the following parameters must be present: *keyword*, *name* or *type*.
- **Or.** Given a set of parameters, one or more of them must be included in the request. As an example, in the Google Maps Places API, when searching for places (Listing 1, line 8), both *query* and *type* parameters are optional, but at least one of them must be used.

- **OnlyOne**. Given a set of parameters, one and only one of them must be included in the request. For example, line 12 in Listing 1 indicates that only one of the parameters *maxheight* and *maxwidth* must be used.
- **AllOrNone**. Given a set of parameters, either all of them must be included in the request, or none of them. For example, as expressed in line 7 from Listing 1, either both *location* and *radius* are used, or none of them.
- **ZeroOrOne**. Given a set of parameters, zero or at most one must be included in the request. For example, line 2 in Listing 1 indicates that if the parameter *radius* is used, then *rankby* cannot be set to 'distance' and vice versa.
- **Arithmetic/Relational**. Relational and arithmetic dependencies relate two or more parameters using standard relational and arithmetic operators. For example, as stated in line 4 in Listing 1, the parameter *maxprice* must be greater than or equal to *minprice*.
- **Complex**. These dependencies are specified as a combination of the previous ones.

2.2 IDL4OAS: An OAS Extension

OAS documents describe web APIs in terms of the elements it comprises, namely, paths, operations, resources, request parameters, and responses. In order to specify inter-parameter dependencies within OAS, Martin-Lopez et al. introduced an extension for OAS called IDL4OAS [14]. IDL4OAS supports specifying inter-parameter dependencies at the operation level.

As an example, Listing 2 shows an excerpt of an OAS document extended with IDL4OAS, corresponding to the get (**/businesses/search**) operation from the Yelp API. As illustrated, the property "x-dependencies" has been added to the "GET /businesses/search" operation. This property is an array of elements, where each element represents a single dependency, therefore they must be preceded by hyphens, following the YAML syntax.

```
1  paths:
2    /businesses/search:
3      get:
4        parameters:
5          - name: location [...]
6          - name: latitude [...]
7          - name: longitude [...]
8          - name: open_now [...]
9          - name: open_at [...]
10         - name: limit [...]
11         - name: offset [...]
12         - [...]
13       [...]
14       x-dependencies:
15         - Or(location, latitude AND longitude);
16         - ZeroOrOne(open_now, open_at);
17         - offset + limit <= 1000;
18         - IF offset AND NOT limit THEN offset <= 980;
```

Listing 2. OAS document of the businesses/search operation from the Yelp API extended with IDL4OAS

2.3   OpenAPI Generator

OpenAPI Generator is a set of tools that automatically generates API clients library, server stubs, configuration, and documentation files based on a given OAS definition of the API [20]. It is developed in Java and has over 50 generators for clients and servers in different programming languages.

OpenAPI Generator has transforming logic as well as templates for each generation of code. Built-in templates are written in Mustache [17], which is a template system with multiple implementations for different languages and technologies. The templates contain common code, independent of the specific API, and have variables that are replaced with the parsed data from the OAS file. As an example, Listing 3 shows the code generated when running OpenAPI Generator on the OAS specification file of the Yelp *businesses/search* operation presented in Listing 2.

```
 1   ...
 2   default ResponseEntity<BusinessesResult> getBusinesses( . . . ) {
 3     getRequest().ifPresent(request -> {
 4       for (MediaType mediaType: MediaType.parseMediaTypes(request.getHeader
           ("Accept"))) {
 5         if(mediaType.isCompatibleWith(MediaType.valueOf("application/json
             "))) {
 6           String exampleString = " . . .";
 7           ApiUtil.setExampleResponse(request, "application/json",
             exampleString);
 8           break;
 9         }
10       }
11     });
12     return new ResponseEntity<>(HttpStatus.NOT_IMPLEMENTED);
13   }
```

Listing 3. Code generated using OpenAPI Generator

3   Approach

We propose to automate the generation of validation code for inter-parameter dependencies described in OAS documents using IDL4OAS. Specifically, we propose to automatically translate IDL dependencies into validation code to check the conformance of API requests with the specification.

To make our approach applicable in practice, we developed an extension of the well-known OpenAPI Generator tool suite, complementing its functionalities to generate Java and Python code to deal with dependencies in both, servers and clients. To this end, we created a fork of the OpenAPI Generator project in GitHub[4] and extended the logic that processes OAS input files. If an operation has dependencies expressed using IDL4OAS [14], they are translated into a conditional block for each assertion, returning a bad request HTTP status code (400) in case the condition is not met as well as descriptive error messages. Figure 1 illustrates this process.

---

[4] https://github.com/enriquebarba97/openapi-generator/tree/java-idl-dependencies.

As an example, Listings 4 and 5 depict the Java server code generated by our OpenAPI Generator extension using the OAS specification of Yelp represented in Listing 2 as an input (including an IDL4OAS block). As illustrated, the tool generates a method for the target operation (Listing 4) including the corresponding conditional blocks to check whether inter-parameter dependencies are met or not. Additionally, a class `DependencyUtil` is created including several support methods for checking complex dependencies, making the code easier to understand and maintain. Listing 5 shows one of these methods, the one used to check *Or* dependencies.

A pull request was opened on August 2021 to gain insight from the community and try to officially integrate our work into OpenAPI Generator. We were encouraged to discuss it with the main developers of the Java and Python brands of the project. This motivated us to conduct this work and the evaluation reported next in an attempt to get empirical evidence of the benefits of our approach.

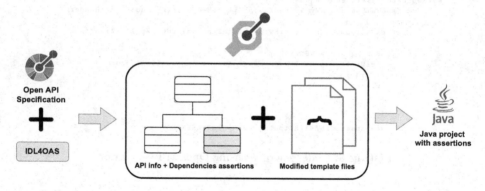

Fig. 1. Process of generating code with OpenAPI Generator + IDL extension.

```
1    ...
2    default ResponseEntity<BusinessesResult> getBusinesses(. . .) {
3      // Check dependency: Or(location, latitude AND longitude);
4      if(DependencyUtil.doNotSatisfyOrDependency(
           (location != null),(latitude != null) && (longitude != null))){
5        return new ResponseEntity("Dependency not satisfied:
           Or(location, latitude AND longitude);", HttpStatus.BAD_REQUEST);
6        }
7      // Check dependency: ZeroOrOne(open_now, open_at);
8      if(DependencyUtil.doNotSatisfyZeroOrOneDependency(
           (openNow != null),(openAt != null))){
9        return new ResponseEntity("Dependency not satisfied:
           ZeroOrOne(open_now, open_at);", HttpStatus.BAD_REQUEST);
10       }
11     // Check dependency: offset + limit <= 1000;
12     if(!(!(offset != null && limit != null) || (offset+limit<=1000.0))){
13       return new ResponseEntity("Dependency not satisfied:
           offset + limit <= 1000;", HttpStatus.BAD_REQUEST);
14       }
15     // Check dependency: IF offset AND NOT limit THEN offset <= 980;
16     if(!(!(offset != null) && !(limit != null) || (offset != null &&
         offset<=980.0))){
```

```
17      return new ResponseEntity("Dependency not satisfied:
            IF offset AND NOT limit THEN offset <= 980;", HttpStatus.BAD_REQUEST);
18      }
19    getRequest().ifPresent(request -> {
20     for (MediaType mediaType: MediaType.parseMediaTypes(request.getHeader
            ("Accept"))) {
21      if (mediaType.isCompatibleWith(MediaType.valueOf("application/json")))
            {
22              String exampleString = ". . .", exampleString);
23              break;
24              }
25          }
26      });
27      return new ResponseEntity<>(HttpStatus.NOT_IMPLEMENTED);
28
29    }
```

Listing 4. Code with inter-parameter dependencies automatically generated

```
1    public static boolean doNotSatisfyOrDependency(boolean... assertions){
2        boolean result = false;
3        for (int i=0;i<assertions.length;i++){
4          result = result || assertions[i];
5
6          if (result)
7            return false;
8        }
9        return true;
10   }
```

Listing 5. Generated supporting code for Or dependency

4   Evaluation

We aim to answer the following research questions:

- **RQ1**: *What are the gains of using our approach in terms of the amount of generated code?* We aim to quantify the gains of our approach in terms of productivity and cost reduction by looking at the number of lines of code automatically generated by our approach in comparison with standard code generators.
- **RQ2**: *Is the generated code able to handle violations of inter-parameter dependencies?* The main goal of our approach is not only reducing manual work by automating the generation of code, but also reducing the possibilities of making mistakes while coding, and therefore minimizing the number of faults in the validation logic. Thus, as a sanity check, we aim to investigate if the generated code is actually effective at detecting dependency violations in API requests.

4.1   Subject APIs

We used a dataset of 13 API operations from 9 real-world APIs previously used by some of the authors in the context of web API testing [26]. These operations represent a diverse set in terms of domains, sizes and dependencies, including all the types of inter-parameter dependencies identified by Martin-Lopez et al. [15] (c.f. Sect. 2.1). Table 1 shows the web API operations used in this study. For each operation, the table shows the name and reference of the API it belongs to, name, number of parameters, number of dependencies, and number (and percentage) of parameters involved in its dependencies (column PD(%)). For each API, we used the OAS specification file provided in [26], which includes the specification of IDL dependencies using IDL4OAS. Since the experiments were run locally, we slightly modified each OAS file changing the server URL and removing security-related configuration details, e.g. OAuth.

Table 1. Subject APIs.

API	Operation	Parameters	Dependencies	PD(%)
Amadeus [1]	Hotel offers	27	8	11 (41%)
DHL [5]	Find by address	10	1	2 (20%)
Foursquare [8]	Venues search	17	3	7 (41%)
Ohsome [18]	Area	11	3	7 (64%)
Ohsome [18]	Area ratio	15	4	9 (60%)
OMDb [19]	Search	9	1	3 (33%)
Travels [26]	Trips user	6	1	2 (33%)
Tumblr [28]	Blog likes	5	1	3 (60%)
Yelp [30]	Businesses search	14	4	7 (50%)
Yelp [30]	Transactions search	3	1	3 (100%)
YouTube [32]	Comments	6	3	4 (67%)
YouTube [32]	Comment threads	11	6	9 (82%)
YouTube [32]	Search	31	15	26 (84%)

4.2   Experiment 1: Code Generation

In this experiment, we aim to answer RQ1 by evaluating the amount of code generated by our approach in comparison to standard specification-driven tools.

Experimental Setup. We used our extension of the OpenAPI Generator tool for generating Java server templates for the subject API operations listed in Table 1. Specifically, for each operation, we generated code using the standard OAS specification files—with no information about inter-parameter dependencies—and the OAS files enriched with IDL4OAS—describing inter-parameter dependencies using IDL. Then, we computed the number of generated lines of code (LoC) on each scenario, with and without dependencies. To make the results more accurate, we restricted the counting of LoC to the method implementing the API operation (and corresponding auxiliary methods), excluding imports and class definitions code, since it is common in both cases. The generated projects are available as part of the supplementary material of the paper [2].

Experimental Results. Table 2 shows the result of our experiment on 13 real-world API operations. On the one hand, the standard OpenAPI Generator tool—with no support for dependencies—generated exactly 10 LoC for each API operation. This is because the code generated is always the same: a method template with some basic media type check (see example in Listing 3). This is an indicator of the lack of support of current generators to deal with API-specific details. On the other hand, our extension of the tool—including support for dependencies—generates between 30% (13 LoC) and 940% (104 LoC) more LoC than the default tool. Unsurprisingly, this improvement seems to be proportional to the number and types of dependencies of the operation. As an example, the largest portion of code (104 LoC) is generated for the API operation with more dependencies, YouTube Search, with 31 parameters and 15 dependencies (c.f. Table 1).

Table 2. #LOC in OpenAPI Generator and IDL extension

API operation	OpenAPI Generator	IDL extension	Increment %
Amadeus-HotelOffers	10	93	830 %
DHL-FindByAddress	10	22	120 %
Foursquare-VenuesSearch	10	53	430 %
Ohsome-Area	10	86	760 %
Ohsome-AreaRatio	10	89	790 %
OMDb-Search	10	47	370 %
Travels-TripsUser	10	13	30 %
Tumblr-BlogLikes	10	37	270 %
Yelp-BusinessesSearch	10	46	360 %
Yelp-TransactionsSearch	10	22	120 %
YouTube-Comments	10	77	670 %
YouTube-CommentThreads	10	86	760 %
YouTube-Search	10	104	940 %

4.3 Experiment 2: Handling IDL Violations

In this experiment, we aim to answer RQ2 by validating the ability of the generated code to detect dependency violations.

Experimental Setup. We used the open-source framework RESTest [16,26] for automatically generating test cases for the API operations under test. Specifically, RESTest supports the generation of both valid and invalid test cases (i.e., API calls satisfying or violating inter-parameter dependencies) starting from an OAS specification file using IDL4OAS. For each subject API operation, we used RESTest to generate 1000 invalid test cases, that is, API calls violating one or more inter-parameter dependencies, as described in their OAS file. Then, we ran the test cases against the validation code generated in Experiment 1 and checked whether it was able to identify the dependency violations. The generated test cases are also available as a part of the supplemental material [2].

Experimental Results. The results confirmed the ability of the generated code to identify all 1000 invalid requests, returning proper 400 HTTP status codes in the responses as well as descriptive error messages. This shows the potential of our work to make APIs potentially more reliable by avoiding developers' mistakes.

5   Related Work

Some work can be found on automated code generation of web APIs. Ed-douibi et al. presented an approach called EMF-REST that takes Eclipse Modeling Framework (EMF) data models as input to generate REST APIs [6]. Gómez et al. introduced the proposal called CRUDyLeaf based on Domain-Specific Languages (DSL). The tool takes an entity with CRUD operations (Create, Read, Update, Delete) to generate Spring Boot REST APIs [10].

Queirós presented Kaang, an automatic generator of REST Web applications. Its goal is to reduce the impact of creating a REST service by automating all its workflow, such as creating file structuring, code generation, dependencies management, etc [24]. This tool is based on Yeoman [31], an open-source, client-side development stack consisting of tools and frameworks intended to help developers build web applications.

Deljouyi et al. introduced MDD4REST, a model-driven methodology that uses Domain-Driven Design (DDD) to produce a rich domain model for web services. Also, it designs REST web services using modeling languages and supports automatic code generation through a transformation of models [4]. The authors in [29] used UML class diagrams to model a set of NoSQL database collections, and then automate the generation of common database access functions and the wrapping of these functions within a set of REST APIs.

Li et al. proposed a Navigation-First Design approach to make a REST API navigable before implementing any service actions [13]. This approach is based on REST Chart [12], which is a model and language to design and describe REST APIs without violating the REST constraints. Rossi [27] proposed a model-driven approach to develop a REST API. First, they used modeling of the API with specific profiles. Then, a model transformation exploited REST API Modeling

Language (RAML) as an intermediate notation that could be used to produce documentation and code for various languages automatically.

In contrast to related papers, and as far as we know, this is the first work addressing the generation of code for inter-parameter dependencies in web APIs. It is worth mentioning that the code generation for testing and documentation is out of the scope of our paper. Evaluation results show that this leads to important gains in terms of productivity and reliability. It is also noteworthy that our work is based on exploiting and enriched version of the OAS specification—de-facto standard in practice—making it easy to integrate our approach in related tools, both in research and industry.

6 Conclusions and Future Work

This paper presents an approach for the automated generation of code for inter-parameter dependencies in web APIs. Specifically, we use IDL4OAS, an OAS extension to specify dependencies that complement the OAS description of an API. To implement this approach, we present an extension of the well-known OpenAPI Generator tool ecosystem to automate the generation of Java and Python code for inter-parameter dependencies in both, servers and clients. Evaluation results show that our approach generates up to 9.4 times more code than standard generators. More importantly, the generated validation code is able to successfully handle dependency violations making API significantly more robust.

Several challenges remain for future work, including a more thorough evaluation and obtaining feedback from the core team of the OpenAPI Generator project for eventually merging our approach into the official tool ecosystem.

Acknowledgements. This work has been partially supported by the European Commission (ERDF) and Junta de Andalucía under project EKIPMENT-PLUS (P18-FR-2895), and by MCIN/AEI/10.13039/501100011033/FEDER, UE under project ATENEA (PID2021-126227NB-C22).

References

1. Amadeus Hotel Search API (2022). https://developers.amadeus.com/self-service/category/hotel/api-doc/hotel-search/api-reference. Accessed July 2022
2. Barakat, S., Barba Roque, E., Sánchez, A.B., Segura, S.: [Supplementary material] Automated code generation for inter-parameter dependencies in REST APIs (2022). https://doi.org/10.5281/zenodo.7105287
3. Barakat, S., Roque, E.B., Sánchez, A.B., Segura, S.: Automated code generation for inter-parameter dependencies in REST APIs. In: Navarro Martínez, E. (ed.) JCIS2022. SISTEDES (2022). http://hdl.handle.net/11705/JCIS/2022/027
4. Deljouyi, A., Ramsin, R.: Mdd4rest: model-driven methodology for developing restful web services. In: MODELSWARD, pp. 93–104. Scitepress (2022)
5. DHL Location Finder API (2022). https://developer.dhl.com/api-reference/location-finder. Accessed Sep 2022

6. Ed-Douibi, H., Izquierdo, J.L.C., Gómez, A., Tisi, M., Cabot, J.: EMF-REST: generation of restful APIs from models. In: Proceedings of the 31st Annual ACM Symposium on Applied Computing, 04–08 April 2016, pp. 1446–1453. Association for Computing Machinery (2016)
7. Fielding, R.T.: Rest: architectural styles and the design of network-based software architectures. Doctoral dissertation, University of California (2000)
8. Foursquare Search for Venues API (2022). https://developer.foursquare.com/reference/v2-venues-search. Accessed Sep 2022
9. Google Maps API (2022). https://developers.google.com/maps/documentation/places/web-service/search. Accessed Sep 2022
10. Gómez, O.S., Rosero, R.H., Cortés-Verdín, K.: CRUDyleaf: A DSL for generating spring boot rest APIs from entity crud operations. Cybern. Inf. Technol. **20**(3), 3–14 (2020)
11. Inter-parameter Dependency Language (IDL) (2022) .https://github.com/isa-group/IDL. Accessed March 2022
12. Li, L., Chou, W.: Design and describe rest API without violating rest: a petri net based approach. In: 2011 IEEE International Conference on Web Services, pp. 508–515 (2011)
13. Li, L., Tang, T., Chou, W.: Automated creation of navigable REST services based on REST chart. J. Adv. Manag. Sci. **4**, 385–392 (2016)
14. Martin-Lopez, A., Segura, S., Muller, C., Ruiz-Cortes, A.: Specification and automated analysis of inter-parameter dependencies in web APIs. IEEE Trans. Serv. Comput. **15**(4), 1–14 (2021)
15. Martin-Lopez, A., Segura, S., Ruiz-Cortés, A.: A catalogue of inter-parameter dependencies in restful web APIs. In: Yangui, S., Bouassida Rodriguez, I., Drira, K., Tari, Z. (eds.) Service-Oriented Computing, pp. 399–414. Springer International Publishing, Cham (2019)
16. Martin-Lopez, A., Segura, S., Ruiz-Cortés, A.: RESTest: black-box constraint-based testing of restful web APIs. In: Kafeza, E., Benatallah, B., Martinelli, F., Hacid, H., Bouguettaya, A., Motahari, H. (eds.) Service-Oriented Computing, pp. 459–475. Springer International Publishing, Cham (2020)
17. Logic-less templates (2022). https://mustache.github.io/. Accessed July 2022
18. Ohsome API (2022). https://docs.ohsome.org/ohsome-api/v1/. Accessed July 2022
19. OMDb API (2022). http://www.omdbapi.com/. Accessed Sep 2022
20. OpenAPI Generator (2022). https://openapi-generator.tech/. Accessed July 2022
21. OpenAPI Specification (2022). https://swagger.io/specification/. Accessed July 2022
22. PayPal Invoicing API (2022). https://developer.paypal.com/docs/api/invoicing/v1/#invoices. Accessed Sep 2022
23. ProgrammableWeb API directory (2022). https://www.programmableweb.com/category/all/apis. Accessed Mar 2022
24. Queirós, R.: Kaang: a restful api generator for the modern web. In: 7th Symposium on Languages, Applications and Technologies SLATE 2018, vol. 62, pp. 1:1–1:15. Schloss Dagstuhl-Leibniz-Zentrum für Informatik (2018)
25. RapidAPI Hub (2022). https://rapidapi.com/hub. Accessed Mar 2022
26. RESTest: Automated Black-Box Testing of RESTful Web APIs (2022). https://github.com/isa-group/RESTest. Accessed Mar 2022
27. Rossi, D.: UML-based model-driven REST API development. In: WEBIST 2016 - Proceedings of the 12th International Conference on Web Information Systems and Technologies, pp. 194–201 (2016)

28. Tumblr API (2022). https://www.tumblr.com/docs/en/api. Accessed July 2022
29. Wang, B., Rosenberg, D., Boehm, B.W.: Rapid realization of executable domain models via automatic code generation. In: 2017 IEEE 28th Annual Software Technology Conference (STC), pp. 1–6 (2017)
30. Yelp API (2022). https://www.yelp.com/developers/documentation/v3. Accessed Sep 2022
31. The web's scaffolding tool for modern webapps (2022). https://yeoman.io/. Accessed Sep 2022
32. YouTube Data API (2022). https://developers.google.com/youtube/v3/docs. Accessed Sep 2022

BizDevOps Support for Business Process Microservices-Based Applications

Andrea Delgado[1(✉)], Félix García[2], and Francisco Ruiz[2]

[1] Instituto de Computación, Facultad de Ingeniería,
Universidad de la República, Montevideo, Uruguay
adelgado@fing.edu.uy
[2] Grupo Alarcos, Escuela Superior de Informática,
Universidad de Castilla - La Mancha, Ciudad Real, Spain
{felix.garcia,francisco.ruizg}@uclm.es

Abstract. The DevOps (Development Operations) approach to software development has been progressively adopted in the last decade, to support the development, testing, continuous integration and deployment of software in an integrated manner. More recently, several extensions have been proposed, one being the BizDevOps (Business DevOps) approach, where business people are also integrated into the development effort, in order to further help in closing what is known as business-systems gap. This gap makes new software developments and changes to existing ones to require important efforts, in general without fulfilling the business area expectations about development and production deployment times. Support for the organization's business processes has been increasingly provided by Business Process Management Systems (BPMS), often integrating internal and/or external services/microservices. Microservices are key allies for the BizDevOps approach realizing business processes providing the application's flexibility and timely results needed. In this paper we present a BizDevOps proposal to support business process microservices-based application. We extended a previous proposal based on services, shifting the focus to microservices development, testing, continuous integration and deployment (DevOps) within the already business-IT alignment (BizDev) view we provided.

Keywords: BizDevOps · Business process · Microservices

1 Introduction

Business Process Management (BPM) [1,14,37] provides support to organizations that want to focus on managing and improving their business processes as basis of their daily operation. The business process (BPs) lifecycle defines phases and activities to guide the modeling, analysis, configuration, implementation, enactment, operation and evaluation of BPs. This lifecycle needs to be supported by adequate platforms and tools that allow carrying out the defined

J. Troya et al. (Eds.): ICSOC 2022 Workshops, LNCS 13821, pp. 274–286, 2023.
https://doi.org/10.1007/978-3-031-26507-5_22

tasks to obtain the expected results. BPM Systems (BPMS) [3] have evolved in the last two decades from previous workflow and other process initiatives [32], to integrate the needed support promoted by the definitions in the OMG standard Business Process Model and Notation (BPMN 2.0) [29] language. BPMN 2.0 includes an XML format for representing BP models that can be enhanced with implementation artifacts, and executed in BPMN 2.0 process engines implementing the standard.

Although BPMS platforms [2,5,7] have been adding in last years more support for integration with: external systems, services/ microservices, Internet of Things (IoT) elements, among others, there is no explicit support for the identification, specification, modeling and design of services/ microservices supporting BPs. Also, there is no explicit guide to help business and development teams into work together for developing BPs services/microservices-based applications. The relationships between BPs and services [17,23] are a key element for organizations to improve in the business and software areas in a coordinated manner, as well as regarding available technologies to improve the way they do business. In particular, from a software perspective the DevOps (Development and Operations) approach has been progressively adopted in the last decade, to support the development, testing, continuous integration and deployment of software in an integrated manner. In parallel, microservices architectures [19,27,30,36] have been also progressively adopted within DevOps, evolving both monolithic and service-oriented systems to fine grained, self contained, independent services that are easier to develop, integrate, test and deploy by different teams. The synergy between devops and microservices has been highlighted as a success factor, underlining the need to tailor the devops strategy for this purpose [15].

On the business view, support for the organization's business processes has been increasingly provided by BPMS platforms often integrating internal and/or external services/microservices. The importance of the business perspective is also evidenced with one of the most-known extensions of DevOps which have been proposed, namely BizDevOps (Business DevOps) [31] approach, where business people are also integrated into the development effort, in order to further help in closing what is known as business-systems gap [17,23]. This gap makes new software developments and changes to existing ones to require important efforts, in general without fulfilling the business area expectations about development and production deployment times. To help in closing this gap, in the last decades we have been working in an integrated framework to support business-IT alignment based on providing integrated support for BPs implemented by services with a model-driven approach [4–6,9–12].

In previous works [13] we have extended the BPs lifecycle from [37] by adding specific activities for measuring and continuously improving BPs and the services supporting them, and with a service lifecycle [6] to serve as a guide on how to integrate services with business processes, to support any existing methodology used in organizations. We have also proposed a specific Business Process Service Oriented Methodology (BPSOM) [12] which can be added on top on the software development process already in use in the organization. BPSOM proposes activities with focus on deriving services from BPs, guiding the identification, categorization, design, modeling, implementation and testing of services. The complete proposal integrates a model-driven approach [9] to automatically derived services from service tasks in business processes, from BPMN 2.0 models to SoaML models [4,11] and to Java Web services implementation including quality attributes specification and implementation [5].

In this paper we present a BizDevOps proposal to support business process microservices-based applications development. We extended the previous proposal BPSOM based on services [12] which is available as a process[1] modeled with OMG Software & Systems Process Engineering Metamodel (SPEM) [28], shifting the focus to microservices development, testing, continuous integration and deployment (DevOps) within the already business-IT alignment (BizDev) view we provided. The contributions of this paper are threefold: i) we define specific activities to guide microservices identification, specification and modeling from business process to support the BizDev integration; ii) we also define specific activities for microservices development, testing, continuous integration and deployment to support the DevOps integration, iii) we propose automated support for carrying out the activities.

The rest of the document is organized as follows: in Sect. 2 we present our BizDevOps approach to support business process microservices-based applications. In Sect. 3 we present an example of application. In Sect. 4 we discuss related work and finally in Sect. 5 we present conclusions and future work.

2   BizDevOps BPSOM Extension Proposal

The BizDevOps proposal for business process microservices-based applications is based on our previous work on a Business Process Service Oriented Methodology (BPSOM) [12] where we already proposed a business-IT alignment (BizDev) approach to help in closing the business-system gap. We reviewed our previous proposal changing the focus to microservices to support BPs, including support for microservices development, testing, continuous integration and deployment (DevOps) to complete the approach. In Fig. 1 the BizDevOps process is presented modeled using BPMN 2.0.

Figure 1 shows in the upper rectangle (dark gray with first two lanes) the business-IT alignment (BizDev) proposal, and in the bottom side rectangle (dark gray with three last lanes) the development, testing, continuous integration and deployment (DevOps) proposal. We believe that the business-IT alignment should be at the business analysis and design phases in order to provide already agreed definitions to the development phase.

2.1   BizDev for BPs and Microservices Analysis and Design

Involving business people in the definition of key elements to support the BPs in the organization is not straightforward. Several challenges arise when dealing

---

[1] https://alarcos.esi.uclm.es/minerva/BPSOM/Published/.

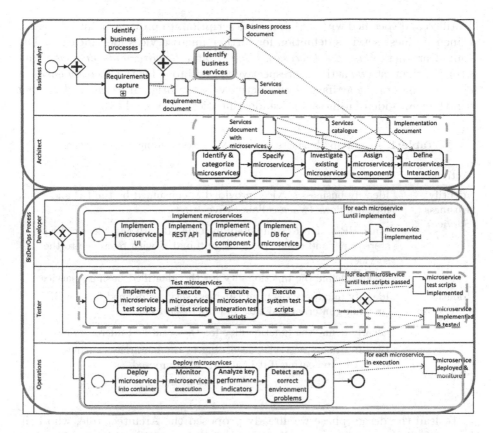

Fig. 1. BizDevOps process for business process microservices-based applications

with different views of the technological support that is needed to implement those processes. A key element in bringing this different views together is the BPs modeling language that is used to specify and model processes, where a common understanding of the notation constructions allows to find agreements on the definitions. We use BPMN 2.0 which can be easily understood and used by business people with a little training, also integrating newest languages e.g. Decision Model Notation (DMN) and Case Management Model Notation (CMMN) for flexible BPs modeling [8].

We already proposed a Business Analyst role to lead the activities of *"Identify business processes"* and *"Requirements capture"*, which are not modified in this extension. This role can be performed by both business people (BPs responsibles, managers, business domain experts) and software analysts, keeping a mixed view in the business analysis team which help into reaching the needed agreements.

To further strengthen the participation and integration of business people in the microservice-based application, we define a new activity for this role, the *Identify business services*, marked with a light gray rectangle indicating it is new for the extension. In this activity, business services associated to BPs can be identified and specified with a high-level description, to provide an initial coarse-grained business services definition for further microservices identification. The original artifacts *Business Process document* and *Requirements document* are output of the first two activities respectively, and input for the *Identify business services*. The output artifact of this activity is the original *Services document* with the new added business service identification section added.

Table 1. Identifying business services & corresponding Microservices

Activity	Detailed steps
Identify Business Services	Identify business services provided & consumed by the BP and its message flows (when collaborative)
	Mark BP activities completely automated with the "ServiceTask" stereotype, and others partially automated with reference to the service
	Clearly define the functionality for the identified business service
Identify & categorize microservices	Identify microservices from Business services defined for the BP (including internal and external microservices)
	Clearly define the functionality for the identified microservice
	Classify the microservice according to the hierarchy (business, technical) indicating if it is atomic or composed

To lead the design phase we already proposed the Architect role, who is in charge of all the activities regarding microservices identification, specification, catalogue, componentization and interactions definition. We already proposed these activities with focus on services, which in the extension we changed to microservices, marking the complete sequence of activities with a yellow rectangle to show that there is a change in the extension. The changed activities are now named as: *"Identify & categorize microservices"*, *"Specify microservices"*, *"Investigate existing microservices"*, *"Assign microservices to components"* and *"Define microservices interaction"*. The Services document artifact is input of all activities and also output with the changes or additions that each one does over the document data.

In particular in the *"Identify & categorize microservices"*, microservices are defined based on the coarse-grained business services initially identified. Finer-grained microservices are identified from business services, which means that they can be split in two or more microservices, or defined as the same if the granularity is already fine enough. For example, in a Loan request business process, a business service can be identified as Credit service, which involves a Credit check of the client loan request. The Credit service can be then divided into an internal Credit microservice to support the BP service task and register information regarding the credit check of the client, and a another Credit entity check microservice, which is provided by an external organization and is invoked from the internal Credit microservice. Also, the categorization of microservices helps in identified microservices that are specific to support the BP (Business microservices derived from Business services), and microservices that have a more technical use and can be transversal and used by several other microservices (Technical microservices). In all design activities microservices patterns [30] are used as basis for the definition of the needed elements regarding the BPs implementation context and available infrastructure.

Other artifacts involved in the microservices design activities are the Services catalog document and the Implementation document. The first one is used to reuse existing microservices already defined and implemented by another development effort, and the second one to state the implementation elements for the microservice, that will be used as key input for the next phase.

2.2 DevOps for Microservices-Based BP Construction

Key elements of the DevOps approach are the continuous integration and continuous deployment (CI/CD) automated pipelines, that allow faster and quality code (as it includes automated testing) development and delivery. We propose microservice-based teams to be in charge of each microservice defined, which are integrated by the Developer, Tester and Operations roles, that can be carried out interchangeably by each member of the team.

For the implementation of microservices, the Developer role is in charge of activities *Implement microservice UI, Implement REST API, Implement microservice component* and *Implement DB for microservice*, that are carried out over each microservice that the team is responsible for. The input for these activities is the *Implementation document*, which includes the definitions made in the microservices design activities and the key microservices patterns applied. These activities are marked with a light gray rectangle indicating they are new for the extension, although there was an *Implement services* activity already defined in BPSOM, it is now tailored specifically to microservices. The output of these activities is the *microservice implemented and build* in the code repository. The structure of the repository that we recommend is one project by microservice, where automated builds can be performed and followed by test scripts execution in the CI pipeline, in one repository for each microservice-based application.

The Tester role is in charge of implementing and executing test scripts for the defined microservices, for unit testing and integration testing (considering microservices interactions as defined in the *Implementation document*), and system testing. These scripts test are then executed for the implemented microservice, and if any test fail the microservice goes back to the implementation activities, in order to fix the errors detected. The defined activities are *Implement microservice test scripts, Execute microservice unit test scripts, Execute microservice integration tests scripts* and *Execute system test scripts* marked with a light gray rectangle with dotted lines indicating they are adapted in the extension. Script tests are included in the CI pipeline to support the automated microservices build and testing, and the output is the *microservice implemented and tested*.

The Operations role is in charge of the activities for deploying and monitoring microservices into selected environments. The defined activities are *Deploy microservices into container, Monitor microservice execution, Analyze key performance indicators* and *Detect & correct environment problems*, marked with a light gray rectangle indicating they are new for the extension. We applied the design pattern Service instance per container, but also the Service instance per VM can be applied, since both are specializations of the Single Service Instance per Host which is the key element to be considered for microservices execution independence. In this way, each microservice execution can be monitored in isolation, key performance indicators can be analyzed for each service instance, and problems can be detected and corrected in each environment. An automated CD pipeline can deploy micoservices to different environments such as testing, staging and production. Also, the delivery to production can be defined as manual, if an approval is needed. The output is the *microservice deployed and monitored*.

A key element to support the automation of the CI/CD pipelines is supporting the development and operations activities performed by the microservice-based teams with existing tools for automation already from the repository code, such as the ones provided by GitLab[2] with kubernetes, GitHub[3] or Jenkins[4].

3   Example of Application

For the example of application we used a simplified "Birth certificate application" BP, which allow citizens to request Birth certificates in the Municipality Decentralized offices of a city. We modeled and implemented it in Activiti BPM v6.0[5] with Java, a Tomcat web server v9.0[6] and a PostgreSQL database v14[7]. The focus is on the implementation of the microservice-based application to support the BP following our approach.

The BP comprises three participants: the Municipality Decentralized Office (MDO) which is the owner of the BP, the Citizen who is the initiator of the BP and the target of the BP results value, and the Civil Registry Office (CRO) to which citizens requesting non digitized birth certificates are deferred. The BP starts when a citizen goes to the MDO and makes an application for a birth certificate to the Citizen support area. The clerk registers the application and after that it is checked whether the birth certificate is digitized or not.

If not, a request for appointment is made to the CRO for the citizen to go and get the certificate from the original book, and the assigned date is received, for which a certificate for the appointment is given. If the birth certificate is digitized, a payment document is provided to the citizen to pay the fees, and when paid, the certificate is issued. It has to be validated and signed by the Office

---

[2] https://about.gitlab.com/features/continuous-integration/.
[3] https://resources.github.com/devops/tools/.
[4] https://www.jenkins.io/doc/book/pipeline/.
[5] https://www.activiti.org/.
[6] https://tomcat.apache.org/.
[7] https://www.postgresql.org/.

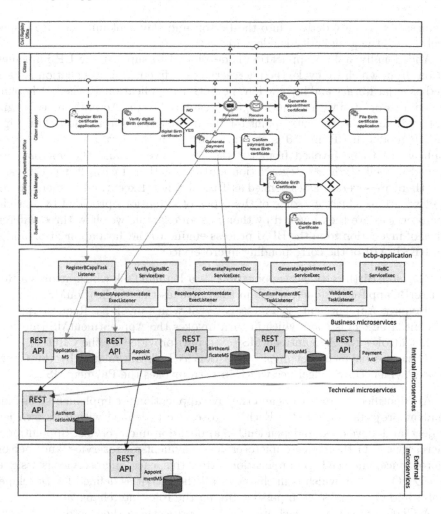

Fig. 2. BP example with java application and microservices in Activiti BPMS

Manager, but if after 10 min it is still waiting, it is escalated to the Supervisor. No mater if the birth certificate is digitized or not, the last task in the process is to file it.

Once the BP is modeled with BPMN 2.0, the associated business services can be identified. In this BP, business services are: BCApplication (for Birth Certificate), Person, Payment and Appointment (from message flows interactions). From these, microservices are derived, as presented in 1, which can be of the same granularity if it is adequate, or can be split into more than one. In this case the business service Application is further refined into Application and Birthcertificate microservices, and Appointment is also divided into an internal Appointment microservice and an external Appointment microservice to be invoked from the Civil Registry Office organization. The Person and Payment business services are derived into the Person and Payment microservice respectively, since the granularity is adequate.

Additionally, a Java application is developed to support the BP implementation, from which to invoke the microservices defined. This application is packaged as a .jar library and included in the Activiti application for the BP, hooking behavior associated with the user-logic for each BP to the Activiti process engine runtime[8], acting as the entry point for the microservices from the BP. In Fig. 2 the BP model in BPMN 2.0 is shown, along with the Java application (bcbp-application) to be invoked from BP tasks and events, and the microservices defined as well as their categorization and interaction. In Fig. 2 it can be seen that there are several classes defined as TaskListener, ExecutionListener and ServiceExecution, which are some of the types of extensions provided by Activiti. Microservices are then invoked by them; as an example we show three different types of invocation from the BPM process engine to the Java application and to the REST API of the corresponding microservice:

- "Register Birth certificate application" is a HumanTask which invokes a RegisterBCappTaskListener, which in turn invokes the ApplicationMS.
- "Request Appointment" is a message event which invokes a RequestAppointmentdateExecListener, which in turn invokes the AppointmentMS (internal) that invokes the AppointmentMS (external) provided by the CRO
- "Generate payment document" is a ServiceTask automated by the GeneratePaymentDocServiceExec which in turn invokes the PaymentMS

All identified microservices and the java application are implemented as independent projects of the BP [9]. Each microservice is defined within its own java project and developed independently: application-microservice, appointment-microservice, birthcertificate-microservice, payment-microservice and person-microservice, and the bcbp-application. After this, each microservice is assigned to a DevOps team, which is in charge of all the activities defined for Developer, Tester and Operations, with persons taking the roles interchangeably.

A CI/CD pipeline for each microservice project can then be defined within each project in GitLab using its support, for building the project, testing it with the automated scripts in junit for unit tests and integration tests involving the bcbp-application and the microservices developed to support the BP execution. Then, the automated deployment is made to a container (e.g. kubernetes), which can be staged and then manually sent to production, or can be directly sent to production. Each microservice execution is monitored gathering basic metrics to evaluate it and be aware and solve execution problems. We will not delve into this since the automated support for DevOps provided by GitLab is well-known and it is used as other similar tools.

---

[8] https://www.activiti.org/userguide/#eventDispatcherConfigurationProcessDefinition.

[9] https://gitlab.fing.edu.uy/open-coal/bcbp-application/.

4   Related Work

Research has been conducted into various aspects of DevOps, such as its benefits [20], challenges [24], principles and practices [21], and how DevOps might be related to other paradigms such as the microservices approach [15,19,34]. Due to space restrictions we can only present key related work. In particular, [34] focus in the DevOps part of the microservices development and operation similarly to our proposal, but not integrating BPs modeling or microservices support for BPs, as we do. Other studies were carried out on the need of also integrating the business needs into the development efforts, such as [38] to help fulfill the business area expectations. The BizDevOps extension to DevOps aims at this. Despite the importance of BizDevOps implementation in companies [18,25,38] there are still no defined standard methods and processes to describe how to implement BizDevOps [16] or established standard practices to implement BizDevOps [26].

Regarding the focus on business processes in organizations and modeling languages, since our first BPSOM proposal, we integrated the BPMN 2.0 standard for modeling and implementing BPs with business people as key ally with services design [17,23]. Also, several studies show that BPMN 2.0 is seen as de facto standard and user-friendly for all stakeholders in the organization (e.g. [22,35]. Although other languages are being proposed with focus on business people such as [18], its benefits over BPMN are not yet studied. Although for the development of systems to support BPs execution several methodologies and approaches have been proposed [14,37], few are specifically focused on services development with a model-driven approach as ours [12,13], and to the best of our knowledge, there is no proposal that integrates a BizDevOps microservices-based approach to support BP systems complete lifecyle, as we proposed here.

5   Conclusions

In this paper we have presented an extension of a previous work the BPSOM methodology, that we have defined for implementing BPs with services and a model-driven approach, to include a BizDevOps approach and a microservices-based support for their implementation. We strengthen the integration of business people already defined in BPSOM in the analysis and design activities for BPs and business services, since the identification and specification of these elements are key for an aligned view on the results. We provided guides to derive microservices from business services, categorize them, define their interaction and, also identified the need for using external microservices. We also extended the development, testing and deployment original activities, with a DevOps view on a microservices architecture based on microservices patterns, and each assigned to a DevOps team, that deals with each one independently. We showed how to identified business services from BPs and derive microservices as independent projects within a code repository in which CI/CD pipelines are defined to automate tasks from building to test to deploy each microservice. We provided an example of application of the BizDevOps BPSOM extension we presented.

We are working on evaluating the approach with final users to get feedback and improve it accordingly, and with case studies in organizations that are incorporating these approaches to their operation. We are also working on extending the tools support for the complete cycle from modeling BPs, business services and microservices to their development, e.g. with automated transformations between artifacts, supporting the code repository creation from the microservice specification, and modeling tool support. We also plan to strengthen the integration and participation of business people in the BPs development effort, by adding an Archimate [33] global view of the elements in the organization, in which all layers and components can be aligned and maintained.

Acknowledgement. This work has been partially supported by OASSIS project (PID2021-122554OB-C31, funded by MCIN/ AEI / 10.13039/501100011033 / FEDER, EU) and Programa de Desarrollo de las Ciencias Básicas (PEDECIBA) Informática, Uruguay.

References

1. van der Aalst, W.M.P., ter Hofstede, A.H.M., Weske, M.: Business process management: a survey. In: van der Aalst, W.M.P., Weske, M. (eds.) BPM 2003. LNCS, vol. 2678, pp. 1–12. Springer, Heidelberg (2003). https://doi.org/10.1007/3-540-44895-0_1
2. Calegari, D., Delgado, A.: Systematic evaluation of business process management systems. CLEI Electr. J. **21** (2018)
3. Chang, J.: BPM Systems: Strategy and Implementation. CRC Press, Boca Raton (2016)
4. Delgado, A.: Towards pattern-based generation of services to support business process execution. In: International Conference on Services Computing, pp. 171–178. IEEE (2014)
5. Delgado, A.: QoS modeling and automatic generation from SoaML service models for BP execution. In: International Conference on Services Computing, pp. 522–529. IEEE (2015)
6. Delgado, A.: A services lifecycle to support bps lifecycle: from modeling to execution and beyond. In: International Conference on Services Computing (SCC), pp. 831–835. IEEE (2016)
7. Delgado, A., Calegari, D.: Evaluating non-functional aspects of bpm systems. In: XLIII Latin American Computer Conference (CLEI), pp. 1–10. IEEE (2017)
8. Delgado, A., Calegari, D.: Towards integrating BPMN 2.0 with CMMN and DMN standards for flexible business process modeling. In: XXII Iberoamerican Conference on Software Engineering, (CIbSE), pp. 697–704. Curran Associates (2019)
9. Delgado, A., Ruiz, F., García-Rodríguez de Guzmán, I.: A reference model-driven architecture linking business processes and services. In: Proceedings of 51st Hawaii International Conference on System Sciences (HICSS), pp. 4651–4660. Scholarspace (2018)
10. Delgado, A., Ruiz, F., García-Rodríguez de Guzmán, I., Piattini, M.: MINERVA: model drIveN and sErvice oRiented framework for the continuous business process improVement and relAted tools. In: Dan, A., Gittler, F., Toumani, F. (eds.) ICSOC/ServiceWave -2009. LNCS, vol. 6275, pp. 456–466. Springer, Heidelberg (2010). https://doi.org/10.1007/978-3-642-16132-2_43

11. Delgado, A., Ruiz, F., de Guzmán, I.G.R., Piattini, M.: Model transformations for business-IT alignment: from collaborative business process to SoaML service model. In: Proceedings of the 27th Symposium on Applied Computing (SAC), pp. 1720–1722. ACM (2012)

12. Delgado, A., Ruiz, F., de Guzmán, I.G.-R., Piattini, M.: Business process service oriented methodology (BPSOM) with service generation in SoaML. In: Mouratidis, H., Rolland, C. (eds.) CAiSE 2011. LNCS, vol. 6741, pp. 672–680. Springer, Heidelberg (2011). https://doi.org/10.1007/978-3-642-21640-4_49

13. Delgado, A., Weber, B., Ruiz, F., de Guzmán, I.G.R., Piattini, M.: An integrated approach based on execution measures for the continuous improvement of business processes realized by services. Inf. Softw. Tech. **56**(2), 134–162 (2014)

14. Dumas, M., Rosa, M.L., Mendling, J., Reijers, H.: Fundamentals of Business Process Management, 2nd edn. Springer, Cham (2018)

15. Ebert, C., Gallardo, G., Hernantes, J., Serrano, N.: Devops. IEEE Softw. **33**(3), 94–100 (2016)

16. Erich, F., Amrit, C., Daneva, M.: A mapping study on cooperation between information system development and operations. In: Jedlitschka, A., Kuvaja, P., Kuhrmann, M., Männistö, T., Münch, J., Raatikainen, M. (eds.) PROFES 2014. LNCS, vol. 8892, pp. 277–280. Springer, Cham (2014). https://doi.org/10.1007/978-3-319-13835-0_21

17. Erl, T.: SOA: Concepts, Technology, and Design. Prentice Hall, Hoboken (2005)

18. Forbrig, P.: BizDevOps and the role of S-BPM. In: Proceedings 10th International Conference on Subject-Oriented Business Process Management (S-BPM One). ACM (2018)

19. Fowler, M., Lewis, J.: Microservices (2014). http://martinfowler.com/articles/microservices.html. Accessed 2 Oct 2022

20. Jabbari, R., bin Ali, N., Petersen, K., Tanvee, B.: Towards a benefits dependency network for devops based on a systematic literature review. J. Softw. Evol. Process **30** (2018)

21. Jabbari, R., bin Ali, N., Petersen, K., Tanveer, B.: What is DevOps? a systematic mapping study on definitions and practices. In: Proceedings of the Scientific Workshop XP2016 (XP Workshops), pp. 1–6. ACM (2016)

22. Kocbek, M., Jošt, G., Heričko, M., Polančič, G.: Business process model and notation: the current state of affairs. Comp. Sci. Inf. Syst. **12**, 509–539 (2015)

23. Krafzig, D., Banke, K., Slama, D.: Enterprise SOA. Prentice Hall, Best Pracs (2004)

24. Leite, L., Rocha, C., Kon, F., Milojicic, D., Meirelle, P.: A survey of DevOps concepts and challenges. ACM Comput. Surv. **52**, 1–35 (2018)

25. Lohrasbinasab, I., Acharya, P.B., Colomo-Palacios, R.: BizDevOps: a multivocal literature review. In: Gervasi, O., et al. (eds.) ICCSA 2020. LNCS, vol. 12254, pp. 698–713. Springer, Cham (2020). https://doi.org/10.1007/978-3-030-58817-5_50

26. Lwakatare, L.E., Kuvaja, P., Oivo, M.: An exploratory study of DevOps extending the dimensions of DevOps with practices. In: 11th International Conference on Software Engineering Advances (ICSEA), vol. 104 (2016)

27. Newman, S.: Building Microservices: Designing Fine-Grained Systems, 1st edn. O'Reilly, Sebastopol (2015)

28. OMG: Software systems process engineering metamodel (spem). Technical report, OMG (2008). https://www.omg.org/spec/SPEM/

29. OMG: Business Process Model and Notation(BPMN)v.2.0. Technical report, OMG (2011). https://www.omg.org/spec/BPMN/2.0/

30. Richardson, C.: Microservices Patterns. Manning, Shelter Island (2018)

31. Sanjurjo, E., Pedreira, O., García, F., Piattini, M.: Measuring the maturity of BizDevOps. In: Shepperd, M., Brito e Abreu, F., Rodrigues da Silva, A., Pérez-Castillo, R. (eds.) QUATIC 2020. CCIS, vol. 1266, pp. 199–210. Springer, Cham (2020). https://doi.org/10.1007/978-3-030-58793-2_16
32. Smith, H., Fingar, P.: BPM: The Third Wave. Meghan Kiffer, Seattle (2003)
33. The Open Group: Archimate enterprise architecture modeling language version 3.1. Technical report, The Open Group (2019)
34. Throner, S., et al.: An advanced DevOps environment for microservice-based applications. In: International Conference on Service-Oriented System Engineering (SOSE), pp. 134–143 (2021)
35. Vega-Márquez, O.L., Chavarriaga, J., Linares-Vásquez, M., Sánchez, M.: Requirements comprehension using BPMN: an empirical study. In: Empirical Studies on the Development of Executable Business Processes, pp. 85–111. Springer, Cham (2019). https://doi.org/10.1007/978-3-030-17666-2_5
36. Waseem, M., Liang, P., Shahin, M.: A systematic mapping study on microservices architecture in DevOps. J. Syst. Softw. **170**, 110798 (2020)
37. Weske, M.: Business Process Management - Concepts, Languages, Architectures, 3rd edn. Springer, Cham (2019)
38. Wiedemann, A., Wiesche, M., Gewald, H., Krcmar, H.: Implementing the planning process within devops teams to achieve continuous innovation. In: Proceedings of the 52nd Hawaii International Conference on System Science (HICSS), pp. 7017–7026. Scholarspace (2019)

Towards Real-Time Monitoring of Blockchain Networks Through a Low-Code Tool

Jesús Rosa-Bilbao[✉][iD] and Juan Boubeta-Puig[iD]

UCASE Software Engineering Research Group, Department of Computer Science
and Engineering, University of Cadiz, Avda. de la Universidad de Cádiz 10,
11519 Puerto Real, Cádiz, Spain
jesus.rosabilbao@alum.uca.es, juan.boubeta@uca.es

Abstract. Blockchain is a secure and distributed technology which is growing in popularity since it enables the traceability, immutability and transparency of data. However, monitoring blockchain networks requires experts who have vast experience in this technology. To address this challenge, in this paper we present a low-code tool, which allows inexperienced blockchain developers to define graphical flows that specify inputs, outputs and the logic necessary to monitor in real time the elements of a blockchain network. This tool has been successfully applied to a vaccine delivery scenario, facilitating the monitoring of a smart contract that stores temperature measurements of a certain vaccine. As a result, when a new transaction is mined in the blockchain network, it will be promptly notified and sent to the different data sinks specified in the flow modeled by a non-expert in blockchain.

Keywords: Blockchain · Smart contract · Low-code · Monitoring · Vaccine

1 Introduction

Blockchain [24] is a new and growing technology that allows the exchange of assets without the need for intermediaries. Some studies estimate that, within a few years, blockchain will be used worldwide and will reach a volume of approximately 2 trillion per year of goods and services [12].

Blockchain is a distributed ledger database where cryptography is used to sign transactions. These transactions are grouped into blocks, and each block is

---

This work was supported by the Spanish Ministry of Science and Innovation and the European Regional Development Fund (ERDF) under projects FAME [RTI2018-093608-B-C33] and AwESOMe [PID2021-122215NB-C33], the Andalusian Plan for Research, Development and Innovation and ERDF under project DECISION [P20_00865], and the Research Plan from the University of Cadiz and Grupo Energético de Puerto Real S.A. under project GANGES [IRTP03_UCA].

J. Troya et al. (Eds.): ICSOC 2022 Workshops, LNCS 13821, pp. 287–298, 2023.
https://doi.org/10.1007/978-3-031-26507-5_23

cryptographically linked to the previous block once it has been validated [25]. When a new block is mined, it is replicated across all participating nodes belonging to the network. In addition, the distribution of all transactions throughout the network allows for high traceability and security.

However, blockchain requires a vast knowledge and wide experience in this technology, not being accessible for everyone. For example, a person who is an expert in other technologies, but not in blockchain, will have difficulty to monitor and manage a blockchain network.

Currently, there are not many solutions capable of monitoring blockchain networks. Etherscan [9] is a block explorer and analyzer for the Ethereum platform. It allows for the monitoring of all network transactions of user accounts and smart contracts. Among other things, it allows for the monitoring of the gas costs of transactions, miner rewards received for mining blocks, and the number of transactions per block. In addition, Etherscan provides an Application Programming Interface (API) that can be used by users to integrate it with other applications. However, Etherscan does not allow for the monitoring of different Ethereum blockchain networks at the same time nor the use of other input and output elements that allow it to be integrated into other more complex systems.

Therefore, the aim of this paper is to propose a low-code tool that hides all implementation details of blockchain from non-expert developers in this technology. In particular, this tool allows end users to intuitively define graphical flows that specify inputs, outputs and the logic necessary to monitor in real time the elements of a given blockchain network, such as blocks, transactions, public addresses, as well as all details of each of these elements monitored. Moreover, our proposal allows for the monitoring of different Ethereum blockchain networks in the same flow as well the integration with more complex systems thanks to the other nodes available in the low-code tool.

The rest of the paper is organized as follows. Section 2 describes the background. Section 3 presents the proposed low-code tool. Section 4 shows an application scenario of the tool. Section 5 describes the work related to this proposal. Finally, Sect. 6 draws conclusions and lines of future work.

2   Background

2.1   Blockchain

Blockchain is a distributed database in which transactions are recorded and confirmed. These transactions must be verified, recorded and combined with others to produce new blocks that will be replicated in all nodes belonging to the network, thus creating the distributed network [3].

A blockchain network involves a series of phases to create and secure blocks. These tasks deal with collecting and computing data into blocks, securely unifying the blocks, validating the blocks, and maintaining consensus among the various nodes in the network.

When a transaction is mined, the information is recorded and shared by users belonging to the network. The blocks that are formed from these transactions are time-stamped, which allows them to be organized in a sequential order, thus avoiding duplication or errors since these blocks are immutable. Any participant who wants to see the history of the blockchain network will obtain the same result and in the same order [7].

Blockchain technology has several elements, one of which is the hash function [2]. This function is a cryptographic algorithm, which makes the link that takes place between the blocks of the network impossible to break, since the information of each block is used to create a unique sequence of characters that uniquely identifies a block.

Therefore, each of the blocks that form the network has a hash that is added to the data of the next block. That is, when a new block is mined, it contains information from the previous block. Thereby, if any person tries to manipulate a block, it will cause the whole chain to change. This process is repeated for all the blocks that are in a blockchain network, making it possible the detection of a manipulated network [25].

Currently, there are several platforms that are based on blockchain technology [24]. In our work, we use the Ethereum [8] blockchain network, as it is a platform especially used to create open source decentralized applications [20]. These applications allow us to control the digital value and run a program from anywhere in the world. In addition, the Ethereum blockchain network allows for high traceability, integrity and transparency of data.

The blockchain technology pursues the use of an egalitarian approach, i.e. promoting collaboration. Ethereum allows to write business logic and agreements as smart contracts. A smart contract is an agreement that describes how a transaction is to be carried out between various agents belonging to the network. These agreements can be executed to deal with information that is transmitted over the network or that has been extracted from other interconnected systems. More specifically, a smart contract will be automatically executed when its conditions are satisfied by all parties involved. Moreover, thanks to smart contracts, it is possible to automate some processes in a secure way [21].

Smart contracts can be implemented with the use of high-level programming languages. There are several languages for the development of smart contracts, but the most widespread within the Ethereum network is Solidity [23].

2.2 Low Code

The **low-code paradigm** [19] allows for the development of products without requiring a vast knowledge of programming languages, based on graphical user interfaces and visual elements. Additionally, it saves time since it is not necessary to manually program each of the elements. More specifically, low-code paradigm is an innovative and increasingly present in the software industry to develop products by using little technological knowledge [5].

Although "low-code" is a cutting-edge terminology, its foundations are not new. Low-code has derived from the Model-Driven Development (MDD) paradigm [4], considering low-code as a more restrictive version of MDD [6].

Low-code programming or low-code development is an approach that allows domain experts to abstract and automate the different steps of the software lifecycle. It allows them to streamline product delivery and meet business needs. It is a new way to develop software that is scalable and achieves value in a short period of time [15].

Low-code platform provides a graphical user interface development environment used to produce functional applications; requiring some additional coding in certain situations. This type of platform reduces the amount of manual coding, thus enabling faster application delivery. People with little programming knowledge have the possibility to intervene in the development of a larger application. In addition, it reduces the cost of configuration, training, deployment and maintenance [14].

Several low-code platforms have been developed over the last years. Node-RED [17] is one of the most popular low-code platforms. This platform allows connecting hardware, APIs and services through a graphical tool. This tool provides an editor that assists end users with creating flows by dragging and dropping the nodes available in its palette. A flow is a directed graph of processing nodes [26]. Each node performs part of the computation of a data-driven application when the node receives data, while edges establish flow dependencies between nodes. In Node-RED, nodes are functions (pieces of code) implemented in JavaScript [16]. These nodes can be easily deployed with a single click. The Node-RED palette can be extended with new nodes, as we do in this work.

3   Our Proposal

This section describes our low-code proposal for monitoring blockchain in real time. Figure 1 gives an overview of our proposed architecture, which is composed of two main layers, as detailed below.

3.1   On-Chain Runtime

The on-chain runtime layer is composed of some of the elements that can be found in a blockchain network. These elements are mainly blocks, accounts and smart contracts. Smart contracts can be deployed, resulting in the creation of transactions. The created transactions are grouped together to create blocks. Concretely, this proposal is based on the Ethereum blockchain network.

As illustrated in Fig. 1, the blockchain network contains information about blocks, smart contracts and accounts. This information provides details of the elements such as block number, transaction number, transactions that form a block, or gas cost. These data can be automatically consumed by several nodes.

All the information, received from the blockchain network, can be used to monitor specific accounts, contracts or events. Our proposal allows us to subscribe to the public addresses of the accounts or smart contracts in order to listen in real time to the transactions that have origin or destination to the address to which we have subscribed to.

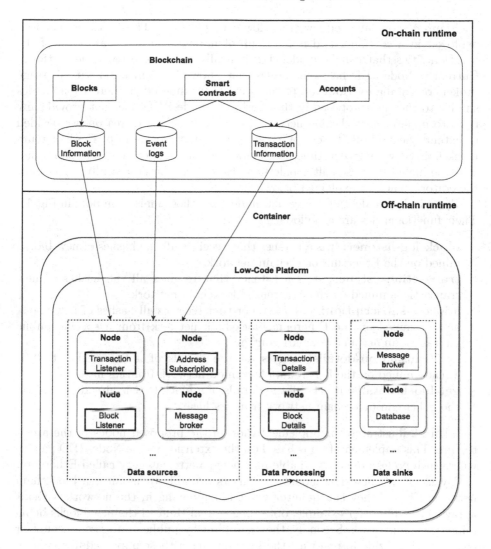

Fig. 1. Overview of the proposed approach.

3.2 Off-Chain Runtime

The off-chain runtime layer is the main contribution of our proposal. The presented architecture uses software containers with the aim of achieving a lighter and portable solution, since it could be used in any machine, without the need of knowledge about aspects of configuration or operating systems. This will allow anyone, even with little knowledge in blockchain, to be able to deploy our proposal with minimal effort.

Figure 1 shows an overview of the low-code platform. This platform has been deployed in a container and is made up of nodes. The nodes are each of the functionalities that can be modeled graphically within the low-code platform. Currently, Node-RED has some nodes that allow the connection with message brokers or databases. However, to the best of our knowledge, there are no nodes similar to the ones proposed in this work, i.e. Node-RED does not provide any node to monitor a blockchain network in real time. For this reason, we decided to extend the Node-RED tool by creating new nodes to monitor the Ethereum blockchain network in real time. Each new node has a specific functionality and must be included in the editor palette so that it can be graphically modeled in the editor's flows, as explained below.

Specifically, we developed five new nodes (see those marked in bold in Fig. 1). Their functionalities are as follows:

- **block_log-listener:** it is a listener that receives all the hashes of new blocks mined on the Ethereum blockchain network.
- **transaction-listener:** it is a listener that receives all the hashes of new transactions mined on the Ethereum blockchain network.
- **address-subscription:** it is a listener that receives all hashes of new transactions mined on the Ethereum blockchain network from a specific public address of an account or smart contract.
- **get-transaction-details:** it gets all the details of a transaction that is already mined on the Ethereum blockchain network from its hash.
- **get-block-details:** it gets all the details of a block that is already mined on the Ethereum blockchain network from its hash.

Figure 2 illustrates our implementation of the proposed nodes in the architecture. This implementation is based on the extension of the Node-RED palette where such nodes are now available in a new palette category called Ethereum.

By using all these new nodes, end users are able to monitor a blockchain network. Firstly, they can monitor what is happening in the network without applying any filter; for example, obtaining in real time all the new blocks being mined on the network. Secondly, they can filter by public address of account or contract, visualizing in real time the interactions of these public addresses with the blockchain network. Thanks to the transparency of some networks, it is not necessary to have any additional permissions so that any person or contract can visualize all transactions in real time.

Fig. 2. Node-RED palette extended with nodes for monitoring Ethereum in real time.

4   An Application Scenario

This section presents an application scenario based on AstraZeneca's COVID-19 vaccine [10] whose main purpose is to monitor in real time when a new temperature, to which vaccines are exposed, has been registered in a transparent and traceable way in a blockchain network. For this, we propose the application of our low-code tool presented in Sect. 3.

Please note that all data used for this application scenario have been collected from a temperature sensor placed in a refrigerator to simulate a real vaccine monitoring situation.

4.1   Smart Contract

A smart contract was implemented in Solidity to register in a blockchain the temperatures to which vaccines are exposed. The proposed smart contract, whose code is available in [1], has two main functions. The first one is "TemperatureReading" where the temperatures, sent by a sensor to the blockchain network, are received. The second one is "TemperatureWarning" which registers in the blockchain when the received temperature is lower than $2\,°C$ or higher than $8\,°C$ [10]. These temperature thresholds are the appropriate ones for the correct vaccine conservation according to the pharmaceutical supplier. Therefore, when a registered temperature is outside this range, an incident will be registered with the information on how many times that vaccine has been exposed to anomalous temperatures.

Basically, the information received by the smart contract for its correct operation is as follows:

- **sensorId:** an id that uniquely identifies a device that is in charge of taking and sending temperatures.
- **temperature:** a temperature value taken at a specific time and sent by the sensor.
- **timestamp:** the timestamp value at which the temperature was measured by the sensor.

When all this information is sent by the sensor, it will be registered in the Ethereum blockchain network in a transparent and immutable way.

This smart contract has been deployed on the Ropsten Ethereum private network. Ropsten is the oldest Ethereum testnet. It allows developers to test their contributions before releasing them on the mainnet. Ropsten is similar to the main Ethereum network and identical to other test networks. In these test networks there is no real money at risk in case of technical failures. Since its launch, the Ropsten network has thousands of daily transactions, i.e. it is a network currently used by many developers. Specifically, the smart contract can be queried by anyone through the assigned public address "0x4B4bf83C0a-46D22146428be5EEAcd8CcD35B1b17".

4.2   Flow Modeling

Once such a contract was successfully implemented in Solidity and deployed on the Ethereum blockchain network, we defined a Node-RED flow by using our palette extension presented in Sect. 3.2. This flow is in charge of monitoring all transactions in real time and displaying them in a graphical and user-friendly way through a dashboard.

Figure 3 shows the flow graphically designed for monitoring the blockchain in real time. This flow is composed of a node for subscribing to the public address of the deployed contract, a processing node for obtaining all details of transactions to be received from the previous node, and several data sink nodes in which all transaction details of the contract will be published simultaneously. In this case, the data received by the previous node will be displayed in a user friendly way through a dashboard, where each of the monitored transactions can be seen in real time.

The "Public Address Subscription" node is in charge of listening for new transactions mined with respect to a public address (the one we have specified). Secondly, the "getTransactionHash" node obtains the hash of the new mined transaction in order to obtain all its details later on. Next, the "Get Transaction Details" node queries the corresponding blockchain network to obtain from the transaction hash all the details of the transaction. The following orange nodes in Fig. 3, such as "getGasPrice", are nodes that are responsible for splitting each of the different details that we get from the transaction from the blockchain network. Finally, the blue nodes, such as "Block Hash", show the data received from the blockchain in the dashboard generated automatically by the tool. Please note that all information obtained in real time from the blockchain network does not imply any action on the blockchain network. In other words, there are no security issues derived from listening blockchain data in real time.

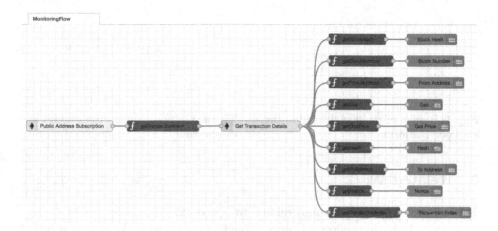

Fig. 3. Flow defined in the low-code platform.

4.3   Results

Once the flow was defined and executed in the Ethereum blockchain, the low-code platform was ready to wait for new transactions to be mined in the blockchain network, and then sending the details of the produced transactions to the defined data sink nodes.

Figure 4 shows the dashboard generated from the graphical flow previously defined in the low-code platform. This dashboard illustrates the details of every of the transactions produced in the blockchain. Specifically, this dashboard contains a lot of information about the block, such as the hash of the block, the account that made the transaction, the block number or the transaction cost in gas.

Thanks to the use of our proposed graphical tool, all implementation necessary for receiving all this information as messages in the low-code platform is hidden from end users.

In order to test the robustness of our proposal, it was executed uninterruptedly during 4 days with the aim of searching for possible errors in its operation. Figure 5 shows the number of transactions monitored in real time for each of the 4 days on the smart contract deployed on the Ethereum blockchain network. This contract is the one proposed at the beginning of this section based on AstraZeneca's COVID-19 vaccine.

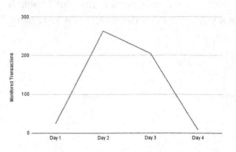

Fig. 4. Results of the flow defined in the low-code platform.

Fig. 5. Graph of transactions monitored in real time.

5   Related Work

This section discusses proposals related to our work.

Gorski et al. [13] propose a Unified Modeling Language (UML) approach that assists end users with the modeling and deploying of distributed ledger network configurations. It is similar to our proposal in the sense that a person with little experience in blockchain can use it. However, unlike our proposal, it is not able to monitor the blockchain network or to listen to its elements.

Firouzi et al. [11] propose an exhaustive analysis on the new technologies which are most powerful for dealing with relevant or critical situations, such as the COVID-19 pandemic. This makes blockchain a strong candidate, as we considers it in our proposal. However, no low-code solution or real-time monitoring of the blockchain network is provided by Firouzi et al.'s work.

Paramasivam et al. [18] propose an approach for off-chain monitoring of situations of interest against COVID-19 and then storing sensor data in a blockchain network. Therefore, the proposal does not allow for the on-chain monitoring of what happens in the blockchain network. In addition, the approach is not based on a low-code solution, so it cannot be used by non-experts in the technology.

Singh et al. [22] propose a blockchain solution for real-time monitoring of the COVID-19 vaccine supply chain. The monitoring is performed by sensors and data are stored in the blockchain network because of its transparency features. However, this is not a low-code solution, so the difficulty to be used by non-expert in blockchain is higher than in our work.

6   Conclusions and Future Work

In this work, we proposed a low-code container-based solution that allows developers, who are inexpert in blockchain, to monitor a blockchain network in real time. To this end, our solution assists these users with the graphical definition of the flows necessary for collecting in real time information about blocks, transactions, people's accounts or smart contracts deployed in a blockchain network, as well as sending all this information to several data sinks.

Thanks to the use of containers, this proposal can be executed in most of the lightweight devices. Moreover, through our solution, the immutability, transparency and traceability of information are conducted in a user-friendly way.

Our proposal was tested with a scenario applied to AstraZeneca's COVID-19 vaccine. This consists of the reception of temperatures from a sensor and their registration in the Ethereum blockchain network. By using our proposal, users without knowledge on blockchain can monitor in real time when a new temperature is issued to the Ethereum blockchain network or when there is a temperature outside the recommended thresholds ($2\,°C$–$8\,°C$).

As future work, we plan to extend the editor's palette of our low-code solution. This will allow end users to calculate real-time statistics of the blockchain network. In particular, this will allow them to detect any situation of interest, and check which hours are more active or when mining a block is more expensive. Additionally, we will apply our low-code container-based solution to other application scenarios such as the smart management of water supply networks. Furthermore, we plan to carry out additional usability tests of our tool through independent users with different expertise.

References

1. Rosa Bilbao, J., Boubeta-Puig, J.: Dataset for Towards Real-time Monitoring of Blockchain Networks through a Low-code Tool. Mendeley Data, v1 (2022). https://doi.org/10.17632/fktyhdgf23.1
2. Bitpanda: What is a hash function in a blockchain transaction? (2021). https://bit.ly/3BZ3mMO. Accessed 29 June 2022
3. Boubeta-Puig, J., Rosa-Bilbao, J., Mendling, J.: CEPchain: a graphical model-driven solution for integrating complex event processing and blockchain. Exp. Syst. Appl. **184**, 115578 (2021). https://doi.org/10.1016/j.eswa.2021.115578
4. Brambilla, M., Cabot, J., Wimmer, M.: Model-Driven Software Engineering in Practice, 2nd edn. Morgan & Claypool Publishers, San Rafael (2017)
5. Brunschwig, L., Campos-López, R., Guerra, E., de Lara, J.: Towards domain-specific modelling environments based on augmented reality. In: 2021 IEEE/ACM 43rd International Conference on Software Engineering: New Ideas and Emerging Results, pp. 56–60 (2021). https://doi.org/10.1109/ICSE-NIER52604.2021.00020
6. Cabot, J.: Low-code vs model-driven: are they the same? (2022). https://modcling-languages.com/low-code-vs-model-driven/. Accessed 29 June 2022
7. Drescher, D.: Blockchain Basics: A Non-Technical Introduction in 25 Steps, 1st edn. Apress, New York (2017)
8. Ethereum Foundation: Ethereum (2022). https://ethereum.org. Accessed 29 June 2022
9. Etherscan: Etherscan (2022). https://etherscan.io. Accessed 29 June 2022
10. European Medicines Agency: COVID-19 Vaccine AstraZeneca - Product Information (2021). https://bit.ly/3orjQVC. Accessed 29 June 2022
11. Firouzi, F., Farahani, B., et al.: Harnessing the power of smart and connected health to tackle COVID-19: IoT, AI, robotics, and blockchain for a better world.

IEEE Internet Things J. **8**(16), 12826–12846 (2021). https://doi.org/10.1109/JIOT.2021.3073904

12. Gartner: Blockchain Technology & How it Helps Business Growth (2020). https://www.gartner.com/en/information-technology/insights/blockchain. Accessed 29 June 2022

13. GÓrski, T., Bednarski, J.: Transformation of the UML deployment model into a distributed ledger network configuration. In: 2020 IEEE 15th International Conference of System of Systems Engineering (SoSE), pp. 255–260 (2020). https://doi.org/10.1109/SoSE50414.2020.9130492

14. Kenneweg, B., Kasam, I., McMullen, M.: Building Low-Code Applications with Mendix: Discover Best Practices and Expert Techniques to Simplify Enterprise Web Development. Packt Publishing, Birmingham (2021)

15. Mendix: The low-code guide (2022). https://www.mendix.com/low-code-guide/. Accessed 29 June 2022

16. Mozilla: JavaScript (2022). https://developer.mozilla.org/es/docs/Web/JavaScript. Accessed 29 June 2022

17. OpenJS Foundation: Node-RED (2022). https://nodered.org/. Accessed 29 June 2022

18. Paramasivam, S., Shen, C.H., Zourmand, A., Ibrahim, A.K., Alhassan, A.M., Eltirifl, A.F.: Design and modeling of IoT IR thermal temperature screening and UV disinfection sterilization system for commercial application using blockchain technology. In: 2020 IEEE 10th International Conference on System Engineering and Technology, pp. 250–255 (2020). https://doi.org/10.1109/ICSET51301.2020.9265363

19. Ploder, C., Bernsteiner, R., Schlögl, S., Gschliesser, C.: The future use of low-code/nocode platforms by knowledge workers – an acceptance study. In: Uden, L., Ting, I.-H., Corchado, J.M. (eds.) KMO 2019. CCIS, vol. 1027, pp. 445–454. Springer, Cham (2019). https://doi.org/10.1007/978-3-030-21451-7_38

20. Rosa-Bilbao, J., Boubeta-Puig, J.: RectorDApp: decentralized application for managing university rector elections. In: 2021 IEEE International Conference on Service-Oriented System Engineering (SOSE), pp. 161–165. IEEE, Oxford, United Kingdom (2021). https://doi.org/10.1109/SOSE52839.2021.00024

21. Rosa-Bilbao, J., Boubeta-Puig, J., Rutle, A.: EDALoCo: enhancing the accessibility of blockchains through a low-code approach to the development of event-driven applications for smart contract management. Comput. Stand. Interfaces **84**, 103676 (2023). https://doi.org/10.1016/j.csi.2022.103676

22. Singh, R., Dwivedi, A.D., Srivastava, G.: Internet of things based blockchain for temperature monitoring and counterfeit pharmaceutical prevention. Sensors (Switzerland) **20**(14), 1–23 (2020)

23. Solidity: Solidity documentation (2022). https://docs.soliditylang.org/en/v0.8.4/. Accessed 29 June 2022

24. Xu, X., Weber, I., Staples, M.: Architecture for Blockchain Applications. Springer, Cham (2019). https://doi.org/10.1007/978-3-030-03035-3

25. Yaga, D.J., Mell, P.M., Roby, N., Scarfone, K.: Blockchain Technology Overview. NIST Pubs 8202, NIST, Gaithersburg, MD (2018). https://doi.org/10.6028/NIST.IR.8202

26. Zarrin, B., Baumeister, H.: Towards separation of concerns in flow-based programming. In: Companion Proceedings of the 14th International Conference on Modularity, pp. 58–63. ACM, New York, NY, USA (2015). https://doi.org/10.1145/2735386.2736752

Ph.D. Symposium

Introduction to the Ph.D. Symposium

The ICSOC Ph.D. Symposium is an international forum for Ph.D. students working in all areas related to service-oriented computing. The event is intended to bring together Ph.D. students and provide them an opportunity to present and discuss their research with an audience of peers and senior faculty in a supportive environment, as well as to participate in a number of plenary sessions with service-oriented computing academics. The International Ph.D. Symposium on Service Computing was held in conjunction with the 20th International Conference on Service-Oriented Computing (ICSOC 2022) on November 29th - December 2nd, 2022, in Sevilla, Spain, following a series of successful editions held in conjunction with the ICSOC conferences from 2005.

In the 2022 edition, the Ph.D. Symposium received 9 valid submissions. Each submission was reviewed by three members of the program committee and after a thorough review process 6 submissions were accepted to constitute the program of the Ph.D. symposium. Authors of accepted papers were invited to present their work in front of a panel of experts, giving Ph.D. students an opportunity to showcase their research and providing them with feedback from both senior researchers and fellow Ph.D. students.

In addition to the presentations of participants, the students had the opportunity to attend two coaching sessions on Ph.D. Journey mastery and Academic Career mastery by Prof. Schahram Dustdar (TU Wien, Austria) and Prof. Martin Gaedke (Chemnitz University of Technology, Germany), with presentations and Q&A sessions, where participants could work and exchange ideas and experiences.

We would like to thank very much all the program committee members, coaching sessions professors S. Dustdar and M. Gaedke, and the members of the expert panels for their willingness and commitment to participate in the ICSOC 2022 Ph.D. Symposium. It has been a pleasure to work with such a brilliant team and coordinate this important ICSOC 2022 event. Also, we want to express our gratitude to the ICSOC organization committee for their support in the organization of the symposium. Finally, we wish good luck to all the students, and we hope they made the most of this enriching experience at ICSOC 2022.

November 2022   Ph.D. Symposium Organizers

Data-Aware Application Placement and Management in the Cloud-IoT Continuum

Jacopo Massa(✉)

Department of Computer Science, University of Pisa, Pisa, Italy
jacopo.massa@phd.unipi.it

Abstract. With the widespread adoption of the Internet of Things (IoT), billions of devices are now connected to the Internet and can reach computing facilities along the Cloud-IoT continuum to process the data they produce. This has led to a dramatic increase in the amount of deployed IoT-based applications as well as the data they need to crunch. Those applications often have Quality of Service (QoS) requirements to be met by determining suitable placements for all services they are made of and all data they manage, as well as software-defined routings across the IoT and all different application components. In this context, we aim at supporting the QoS- and *data*-aware placement as well as management of multi-service applications onto Cloud-IoT resources. We describe our main objectives and discuss some preliminary results of our research.

Keywords: Data-awareness · Application management · Cloud-IoT

1 Introduction

The Internet of Things (IoT) has been giving rise to the so-called *data deluge*, with more than 30 billion connected devices [5], producing a huge amount of data, which cannot suitably be transmitted, stored, and/or processed by employing traditional Cloud architectures. Cloud-IoT paradigms – e.g. Fog, Edge, Mist, Osmotic computing – were proposed to tame this problem. Such paradigms exploit heterogeneous computing capabilities along the Cloud-IoT continuum to process data as close as possible to their sources. This allows: *(i)* achieving context- and location-awareness of data insights, *(ii)* avoiding unnecessary data transfers, and *(iii)* obtaining lower latencies to cyber-physical stimuli.

A considerable research effort focused on where to deploy applications and services along the Cloud-IoT continuum to meet a plethora of application requirements, from hardware/software capabilities to suitable latency and bandwidth between interacting components, operational costs, or security policies.

Supervised by Antonio Brogi, Stefano Forti, and Patrizio Dazzi

J. Troya et al. (Eds.): ICSOC 2022 Workshops, LNCS 13821, pp. 301–307, 2023.
https://doi.org/10.1007/978-3-031-26507-5_24

Guaranteeing such requirements implies deciding where to (temporarily or permanently) store the data along the Cloud-IoT continuum. Optimal placement and management of such application services and data can reduce *data gravity* issues and operational costs (i.e., avoiding the need to move or replicate data among services that use them), improve data security and reduce data access latencies, thus improving the overall application performance. Additionally, software-defined networking (SDN) can further improve on this through the possibility of instructing optimal *ad-hoc* routing paths for different applications to guarantee suitable bandwidth and latency for data to be moved at run-time.

2   Considered Problem

The research problem we aim to study can be stated as follows [2]:

> *Let A be a multi-service application with a set of requirements R, and let I be a distributed Cloud-IoT infrastructure. Solutions to the application placement problem are mappings from each component of A to some computational node in I, meeting all requirements set by R and optimising a set of objective metrics O used to evaluate their quality. Solution mappings can be many to many, i.e. a component can be placed onto one or more nodes, and a node can host more than one component.*

At large, the challenging problem related to the *data-aware placement and management of multi-service application onto multi-level Cloud-IoT infrastructures has been only marginally investigated* [23]. Moreover, requirements R can persist even after the deployment and vary due to the dynamicity and churn of the Cloud-IoT infrastructure or for the users' demand. Hence, our research focuses also on *dynamic (re)configuration* and *management* of applications to keep assured QoS constraints whilst minimising the likelihood of service disruption.

In this context, one of the main ingredients for the considered problem is represented by (micro)service-based applications that are a good fit for heterogeneous Cloud-IoT infrastructures, as they can fully exploit Cloud-IoT functionalities [15]. For instance, the workload can be better distributed among the most suitable nodes, and data can be moved as little as possible to help those latency-sensitive and bandwidth-hungry applications.

As already mentioned, we must deal with billions of heterogeneous nodes when considering the Cloud-IoT continuum. Starting from Cloud datacenters, with (virtually) unbounded resources but with unbound latencies and costs to be reached out by data, we go through Edge/Fog nodes that collect and produce data from end devices, moving computation closer to where data is created. Finally, we consider IoT devices as the smallest objects in the continuum, which are the generators and final users of most of the data.

Since we aim at enhancing and devising *data-aware* application placement and management methodologies, data represent another key ingredient in our research targets. Many data aspects exist, known as *V-properties* [14]. Among those properties, we will focus on *volume* (the whole amount of data), *velocity* (how rapidly data are generated, distributed and collected), *variety* (diversity in data representation), *veracity* (quality and trustworthiness of data), and *value* (the usefulness of gathered data for the application). Placing application services by considering the above "V-properties" can reduce access latencies and data gravity issues. Besides, data movement is also an aspect that cannot be ignored as it uses a tremendous amount of energy and significantly impacts network usage [27]. Thus, reducing data movement can benefit Cloud providers in terms of energy costs, which are expensive, if we also consider other impacting factors like energy demands by power distribution or cooling system [17].

3   Related Work

Managing applications over the Cloud-IoT continuum introduces new challenges, mainly due to infrastructure scale and heterogeneity, the need for QoS-awareness, dynamicity and support for interactions with the IoT, which are rarely considered in Cloud-only scenarios. Next, we briefly summarise the state of the art in the Cloud-IoT multi-service application placement and management field, referring to recent surveys [2, 19, 25] for further details.

Among the first proposals investigating the peculiarities of Cloud-IoT application placement, [12] proposed a simple search algorithm to determine an eligible deployment of (multi-service) applications to tree-like Cloud-IoT infrastructures, open-sourced in the iFogSim Java prototype. Building on top of iFogSim, various works tried to optimise different metrics, e.g. service delivery deadlines [18], load-balancing [26], or client-server distances [11].

Brogi and Forti [1] proved the NP-hardness of the placement problem. They devised a backtracking strategy to determine context-, QoS- and cost-aware placements of multi-service applications to Cloud-IoT infrastructures, employing continuous reasoning [7] They have also exploited logic programming to assess the security and trust levels of application placements [8] and to determine the placement and network routing of Virtual Network Function chains in Cloud-IoT scenarios [10]. Still, with a declarative approach, [4] and [22] devised a strategy for service coordination based on *aggregate computing*, aiming at managing opportunistic resources via a hybrid centralised/decentralised solution by relying on a self-organising peer-to-peer architecture to handle churn and mobility. Similarly, they proposed a declarative, fully decentralised solution to write and enforce QoS-aware application and infrastructure management policies [9]. To tame the complexity of the problem, also (meta)heuristic and bio-inspired solutions have been proposed, such as genetic algorithms [3], ant colony [6] or particle swarm [13]. None of the works surveyed above considers data characteristics to determine eligible application placements and traffic routing. Indeed, as stated by Salaht *et al.* [23], most existing works in application placement in Cloud-IoT settings do not consider data awareness.

To the best of our knowledge, only Naas et al. [20, 21] propose some modelling of data storage services, IoT sources and destinations to determine *data flows* across the infrastructure. They model the placement problem as a *Generalised Assignment Problem* (GAP)using a *divide and conquer* approach to tame the exp-time complexity of the problem, i.e. partitioning the infrastructure to solve sub-problems. Similarly [16] exploits centrality indices to determine the closest and most balanced distance to data sources to obtain a target bandwidth distribution and better network usage. However, none of the research mentioned above considers security, data rates and run-time data binding, nor exploits continuous reasoning to speed-up decision-making.

4   Research Objectives

The ultimate objective of this work can be stated as follows:

> *This thesis aims at contributing with models, strategies and methodologies to support the data- and QoS-aware placement and management of multi-service applications onto Cloud-IoT resources. Particularly, we aim at considering the following important aspects that were never holistically considered by recent work: scalability and load-balancing, fault-awareness, and security- and energy-awareness.*

In what follows, we better detail the aspects mentioned above that we intend to jointly pursue, with a data-aware approach, to extend state of the art:

Scalability and Load Balancing. A major objective is to devise systems that scale services and data elastically, handling a massive amount of heterogeneous devices and satisfying application QoS requirements. This will inevitably lead to *data duplication*, thus to the consequent need of *eventual consistency mechanisms*. In this context, we plan to devise new programming models that should provide modules to support scalability, i.e. elasticity engines that allocate resources according to the requirements of user applications. Furthermore, another purpose for replicas placement and management is to balance the workload of a system to a certain extent, thereby enhancing the efficiency and availability of the system, especially in the case of distributed architectures.

Fault-awareness. Cloud-IoT continuum is subject to continuous changes, including link and node failures, or service outages. In terms of *fault-tolerance*, our model aims at considering the requirements stemming from the need for immediate responses for real-time application services and guaranteed continuous connectivity among services so that each of them can complete its task and successfully exchange data. To allow application services to be run continuously and always respecting user constraints, we will study and devise methodologies for automatically (i.e. reactively) migrating services and data, or even identify in advance (i.e. proactively) suitable backup nodes that are close enough and have the required capabilities to perform the same services.

Security- and Energy- awareness. We already devised approaches that suitably consider *QoS* and *operational costs*, as described in Sect. 5, but we want to add a broader set of aspects that have only been partially considered so far, specifically we point to energy and security. Regarding *energy consumption*, one of the major concerns is data movement, so another objective will be to find a way to soften data workflows to the bare minimum, e.g. reducing the portion of involved infrastructure in the placement process (i.e., bin packing techniques, nodes ranking, infrastructure partitioning). Also, *security* preservation and risk assessment are essential to guarantee continuity in the deployment of services, hence also security requirements will be considered, both in terms of placing services on infrastructure nodes and ensuring privacy and security in the data movement between services.

5   First Results and Next Steps

We already obtained preliminary results that pursue the objectives of this research and were successfully published in the proceedings of an international conference [24]. We devised a *declarative* solution to determine, in a data-aware manner, application service placements and data routing over Cloud-IoT infrastructures while meeting functional (software, hardware, IoT) and non-functional (security, latency, bandwidth) application requirements. The novelty of this work is in that it follows a *data-aware* approach as it considers QoS requirements (e.g. latency, bandwidth, security) dictated by different data types handled by an application, within their characteristics (viz. security, volume and velocity) instead of set requirements. Besides, by employing *continuous reasoning* [7], our solution can locally and continuously handle changes in the application requirements (e.g., increased data frequency or volume, new security need) and infrastructure conditions. Continuous reasoning speeds up the reconfiguration of application placements and routing decisions at run-time, mainly focusing on decision-making on the replacement of services in need of attention (i.e. that do not currently meet their requirements). The designed model and placement strategy are implemented into an open-source[1] Prolog prototype, DAPlacer, has been assessed over a scenario based on lifelike data.

In our immediate future work, we intend to define a cost model that combines energy consumption and financial costs to assess the optimality of different management strategies, extend decision-making capabilities to handle scalability and load-balancing, and assess our proposals on real use cases.

References

1. Brogi, A., Forti, S.: QoS-aware deployment of IoT applications through the fog. IEEE Internet Things J. **4**(5), 1185–1192 (2017)
2. Brogi, A., Forti, S., Guerrero, C., Lera, I.: How to place your apps in the fog: state of the art and open challenges. Softw. Pract. Experience **50**(5), 719–740 (2020)
3. Canali, C., Lancellotti, R.: GASP: genetic algorithms for service placement in fog computing systems. Algorithms **12**(10), 201 (2019)

---

[1] Available at: https://github.com/di-unipi-socc/daplacer.

4. Casadei, R., Viroli, M.: Coordinating computation at the edge: a decentralized, self-organizing, spatial approach. In: FMEC 2019 (2019)
5. Cisco: Cisco Annual Internet Report (2018–2023). White Paper, Cisco (2020)
6. Farshin, A., Sharifian, S.: A modified knowledge-based ant colony algorithm for virtual machine placement and simultaneous routing of NFV in distributed cloud architecture. J. Supercomput. **75**(8), 5520–5550 (2019)
7. Forti, S., Bisicchia, G., Brogi, A.: Declarative continuous reasoning in the cloud-IoT continuum. J. Logic Comput. **32**(2), 206–232 (2022)
8. Forti, S., Ferrari, G.L., Brogi, A.: Secure cloud-edge deployments, with trust. Future Gener. Comput. Syst. **102**, 775–788 (2020)
9. Forti, S., Lera, I., Guerrero, C., Brogi, A.: Osmotic management of distributed complex systems: a declarative decentralised approach. J. Softw. Evol. Process **34**(10), e2405 (2021)
10. Forti, S., Paganelli, F., Brogi, A.: Probabilistic QoS-aware placement of VNF chains at the edge. Theor. Pract. Logic Prog. **22**(1), 1–36 (2021)
11. Guerrero, C., Lera, I., Juiz, C.: A lightweight decentralized service placement policy for performance optimization in fog computing. J. Ambient. Intell. Humaniz. Comput. **10**, 2435–2452 (2019)
12. Gupta, H., Vahid Dastjerdi, A., Ghosh, S.K., Buyya, R.: iFogSim: a toolkit for modeling and simulation of resource management techniques in the internet of things, edge and fog computing environments. Soft. Pract. Exp. **47**(9), 1275–1296 (2017)
13. Hajji, M.A., Mezni, H.: A composite particle swarm optimization approach for the composite SaaS placement in cloud environment. Soft. Comput. **22**(12), 4025–4045 (2018). https://doi.org/10.1007/s00500-017-2613-8
14. Khan, N., et al.: The 51 v's of big data: survey, technologies, characteristics, opportunities, issues and challenges. In: Proceedings of International Conference on Omni-layer Intelligent Systems, pp. 19–24 (2019)
15. Lan, D., Taherkordi, A., Eliassen, F., Horn, G.: A survey on fog programming: concepts, state-of-the-art, and research challenges. In: Proceedings of 2nd International Workshop on Distributed Fog Services Design (2019)
16. Lera, I., Guerrero, C., Juiz, C.: Comparing centrality indices for network usage optimization of data placement policies in fog devices. In: 2018 Third International Conference on Fog and Mobile Edge Computing (FMEC) (2018)
17. Liao, Q., Wang, Z.: Energy consumption optimization scheme of cloud data center based on SDN. Procedia Comput. Sci. **131**, 1318–1327 (2018)
18. Mahmud, R., Ramamohanarao, K., Buyya, R.: Latency-aware application module management for fog computing environments. ACM TOIT **19**(1), 1–21 (2018)
19. Mahmud, R., Ramamohanarao, K., Buyya, R.: Application management in fog computing environments: a taxonomy, review and future directions. ACM Comput. Surv. **53**(4), 1–43 (2020)
20. Naas, M.I., Lemarchand, L., Boukhobza, J., Raipin, P.: A graph partitioning-based heuristic for runtime IoT data placement strategies in a fog infrastructure. In: Proceedings of 33rd Annual ACM Symposium on Applied Computing (2018)
21. Naas, M.I., Parvedy, P.R., Boukhobza, J., Lemarchand, L.: iFogStor: an IoT data placement strategy for fog infrastructure. In: 2017 IEEE 1st International Conference on Fog and Edge Computing (ICFEC) (2017)
22. Pianini, D., Casadei, R., Viroli, M., Natali, A.: Partitioned integration and coordination via the self-organising coordination regions pattern. Future Gener. Comput. Syst. **114**, 44–68 (2021)

23. Salaht, F.A., Desprez, F., Lebre, A.: An overview of service placement problem in fog and edge computing. ACM Comput. Surv. **53**(3), 1–35 (2020)
24. SummerSOC: 16th Symposium and Summer School On Service-Oriented Computing. https://www.summersoc.eu. Accessed 10 Oct 2022
25. Vaquero, L.M., Cuadrado, F., Elkhatib, Y., Bernal-Bernabe, J., Srirama, S.N., Zhani, M.F.: Research challenges in nextgen service orchestration. Future Gener. Comput. Syst. **90**, 20–38 (2019)
26. Wang, S., Zafer, M., Leung, K.K.: Online placement of multi-component applications in edge computing environments. IEEE Access **5**, 2514–2533 (2017)
27. Wangsom, P., Lavangnananda, K., Bouvry, P.: Multi-objective scientific-workflow scheduling with data movement awareness in cloud. IEEE Access **7**, 177063–177081 (2019)

Towards a Context-Aware Framework for Internet of Things and Smart Everything

Adrian Bazan-Muñoz^(✉) (iD)

Department of Computer Science, University of Cádiz, Cádiz, Spain
adrian.bazan@uca.es

Abstract. New applications and new needs to be dealt with arise every day in nowadays society of the Internet of Things (IoT) and smart everything. Even though there are many applications for these domains, most of them do not facilitate context integration in their data processing. There are applications that present solutions to this problem, however, they are either too domain-specific or too general, and therefore cannot be easily reused in other software products. To fill this gap, we propose a context-aware framework that makes use of an ontology reusable for multiple IoT and smart domains. The framework will also provide an integration mechanism and an event pre-processing system, which will facilitate the work of developers. The latter will make use of the ontology by facilitating the definition of contextual events and their integration into decision-making systems. All this, together with our complex-event processing decision-making system will finally make possible to offer intelligent context-aware services and applications.

Keywords: Context awareness · Ontology · Smart everything · Complex-event processing

1 Motivation and Problem Statement

In recent years a large number of applications and services for Smart Everything [1] in general, and Smart Cities in particular, have emerged thanks to the growing im-portance of the IoT, cheaper communications and the increased capabilities of mobile devices. These applications and services improve the quality of life of citizens, the productivity of companies, the management of administrations and the sustainability of the environment around us. With the aim of achieving greater knowledge of the environment, better decision-making and, therefore, offering ser-vices that are more in line with existing needs, it is essential for these services and applications to be context-aware.

Over the years, research related to context awareness has highlighted the need to reach an agreement on the definition of specific contexts applicable to various application domains [2, 3], and there have been several proposals, especially focused on the definition of ontologies, in order to fill this gap. However, technologies have advanced significantly

Supervised by Guadalupe Ortiz [0000-0002-5121-6341], Department of Computer Science, University of Cádiz, Cádiz, Spain, guadalupe.ortiz@uca.es and very fast, and although there are recent proposals [4], they are not adapted to current needs. Firstly, although they contemplate sensorics and in some cases mobile devices, they are not designed for intelligent environments; and secondly, they do not provide effective mechanisms for the integration of the ontology and the implemented system for decision making. In particular, we have seen how software architectures based on Complex Event Processing (CEP) are an efficient solution for real-time decision making in intelligent environments [5, 6] and, therefore, we deem it advisable that this is one of the types of systems to be easily integrated with context ontologies.

These are the two gaps that we seek to solve in this doctoral thesis: firstly, the definition of a context ontology generic enough to be applied to various application domains of smart everything and, at the same time, with the appropriate mechanisms to tailor its elements to the needs of each of these domains. Secondly, an integration mechanism that facilitates the work of the developer to make use of the context ontology and easily define contextual events that can be automatically integrated into decision-making systems for their processing to provide intelligent services and applications.

The rest of the paper is organized as follows. Research challenges are given in Sect. 2. In Sect. 3 we describe our proposal. We expose the research plan in Sect. 4, followed by related work in Sect. 5. Finally in Sect. 6 we end with conclusions.

2 Research Challenges

In this PhD, we will face the following research challenges:

1. First of all, defining an ontology generic enough to be useful in multiple smart every-thing application domains, but at the same time providing the appropriate mechanisms to tailor the ontology elements to be useful to every particular domain: as previously said nowadays, despite of the huge number of existent ontologies, they are not easily adaptable to various application domains.
2. Secondly, designing a data preprocessing structure that facilitates the integration of the contexts defined through the ontology within the software architectures that process the context data, since current ontologies do not provide mechanisms for this purpose. This will provide a mechanism to transform contextual events to the adequate format required by the processing system.
3. Thirdly, approaching the definition in the ontology of the actions to be taken in a context aware situation, which is not provided by current ontologies and would imply a significant reduction in processing times and workloads for the implemented decision-making system.
4. Finally, creating a mechanism that allow developers to define contextualized events with a Domain-Specific Language (DSL) which would facilitate a wider adoption of the ontology.

3 Proposed Solution

As mentioned in the introduction we aim to define an ontology for context-awareness and to facilitate the integration of contexts with CEP-bases software architectures. When talking about context, we refer to any information that can be related to a person, a place or an application, and that can be helpful to improve the interaction between the user and the application or system in question [7]. A Context-aware system, is therefore a system in which context information is used to provide useful information or services to the user, fitting the behavior of the system to specific necessities of a specific user [8]. ON the other hand, CEP [9] is a technology that allow us to receive real time data, namely simple events, and analyzing and processing them using a series of event patterns. Such even patterns consist of conditions previously stablished which permit the detection of useful information for our system that are called complex events. Now that we have introduced the main concepts lets explain the proposed solution: we propose an ontology which facilitates the creation of context-aware systems for multiple different domains, as well as a mechanism to integrate the contextual events in a CEP-based smart system. The proposed framework, shown in Fig. 1, has the following functioning:

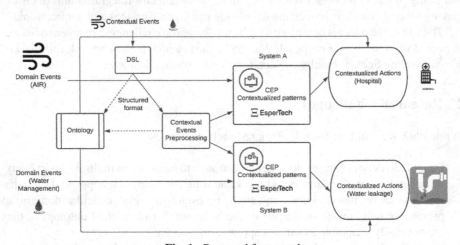

Fig. 1. Proposed framework

- Firstly, we have an ontology that will be generic enough to be useful in several domains and with the appropriate mechanisms to tailor its elements to provide sufficient details for every domain. This ontology will be consulted by our DSL and by our preprocessing system, in order to obtain information about the structure of the events format as well as the actions to be taken.
- Secondly, we have one or more domains which send domain-specific data to the system. For illustration purposes we have represented two domains in the figure, one for air quality and another for water management. These two domains are independent and will produce a series of domain events to be processed in their particular processing system. Please note that the fact of representing more than one domain is to illustrate that the ontology, the DSL and the preprocessing modules can be reused in different domains.
- Thirdly, the system will also receive contextual events from the environment. These events should reach the system already following the structure defined by the ontology,

a DSL might be used for this purpose, so that they can be easily integrated to the processing systems.

- Fourthly, there will be a preprocessing module that will automatically transform the ontology-based contextual events in the format required by the processing system; that is, the systems will receive contextual events properly structured, and this module will provide the adequate format for being processed (for instance formatting to JSON).
- Fifthly, both, contextual events preprocessed, and domain events, will be sent to one of our processing systems. The system will have a CEP engine with a series of event patterns that will deal with both domain and contextual events.
- Finally, the system will produce a contextualized action, which might also be defined through the context ontology.

4 Research Plan

In this section we schedule the tasks to be performed during the thirty-six months expected for the development of the PhD, which we roughly identify between November 2022 and November 2025 (see Fig. 2).

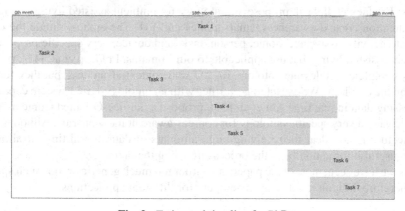

Fig. 2. Estimated timeline for PhD

1. Conducting an extensive state of the art study related to the stated problem and proposed solution.
2. Studying technologies and tools that might support an efficient solution.
3. Developing the ontology for smart everything and the preprocessing system.
4. Integrating all the components in the framework and software architecture.
5. Developing a DSL to facilitate contextual events definition by developers, as well as transformation rules and mechanisms required to automatically generate the code necessary for their integration with the software architecture.
6. Evaluating the developed framework through several case studies in relevant domains.
7. Writing and defending the PhD.

Preliminary results are currently not available, because we are in the first year of the PhD and actually, we are in the early stages of the development of the PhD.

5 Related Work

Concerning context-aware applications for IoT and smart everything, there are several proposals in which ontologies are used. However, most of them are not adaptable to different domains. Elkady et al. [4], proposed an architecture with an ontology focused in the relation between the final user and the application. The main limitation is that they proposed an ontology which is applicable to several applications due to its simplicity, but it is not applicable to more specific domains because it is too generic.

Two relevant works deserve mentioning: Chen et al. [3], made a first a approach on the subject with COBRA, a context-based ontology. Its main constraint is modelling of people, agents, places, and presentation events is too simple, which makes it unspecific. The work was extended as a new system called SOUPA [2], with an architecture for ubiquitous and pervasive applications, with a very extensive ontology, but focused on agents modelling and Belief-Desire-Intention concepts, which makes it too limited in question of the final implementation system. We can also mention some more recent works: Kenfack et al. [10], propose an ontology for ambient assisted living taking into consideration context-awareness, smart homes and IoT. The authors divide the ontology into activity, assistance, home, person, task, and device; very specific proposal for ambient assisted living, but not applicable to our domains. Pradeep et al. [11], propose a very complete and flexible ontology for IoT and context-awareness, but they focused only on the ontology. We expect to go further with an ontology-based system capable of processing data in real time. Gu et al. [12], propose a Service-Oriented Context-Aware Middleware, a very specific ontology for context-aware home scenarios. Although their architecture is not ideal for receiving large amounts of data in real time, it allows to obtain useful information from the processing using the ontology.

As we have seen, most of the papers are either too much generic or too much specific and therefore difficult to reuse by developers for different applications.

6 Conclusion

We have outlined a PhD focused on providing a real time context-aware system for IoT and smart everything. We envision a solution based on a context-aware framework and software architecture, which by means of the appropriate mechanisms, it can tailor the context ontology to the specificity of the particular domain, but at the same time being generic enough to allow its use for different domains. In addition, we envision the creation of an integration mechanism and a preprocessing system to facilitate the work of developers in defining the contextual events of the system. With this proposal we manage to provide systems that are more context-aware and therefore more adapted to the end user. And finally, we manage to make possible to offer intelligent services and applications.

Acknowledgments. This work has been funded through the grant programme for R&D&i projects, for universities and public research entities qualified as agents of the Andalusian Knowledge System, within the scope of the Andalusian Plan for Research, Development and Innovation (PAIDI 2020). Project 80% co-financed by the European Union, within the framework of the Andalusia ERDF Operational Programme 2014–2020 "Smart growth: an economy based on knowledge and innovation". Project funded by the Ministry of Economic Transformation, Industry, Knowledge and Universities of the Andalusian Regional Government. DECISION project with reference P20_00865.

References

1. Streitz, N.: Beyond 'smart-only' cities: redefining the 'smart-everything' paradigm. J. Ambient. Intell. Humaniz. Comput. **10**(2), 791–812 (2018). https://doi.org/10.1007/s12652-018-0824-1

2. Chen, H., Perich, F., Finin, T., Joshi, A.: SOUPA: standard ontology for ubiquitous and pervasive applications. Presented at the September 22 (2004). https://doi.org/10.1109/MOBIQ.2004.1331732

3. Chen, H., Finin, T., Joshi, A.: An ontology for context-aware pervasive computing environments. Knowl. Eng. Rev. **18**, 197–207 (2003). https://doi.org/10.1017/S026988890400025

4. Elkady, M., Elkorany, A., Allam, A.: ACAIOT: a framework for adaptable context-aware IoT applications. Int. J. Intell. Eng. Syst. **13**, 271–282 (2020). https://doi.org/10.22266/ijies2020.0831.24

5. Garcia-de-Prado, A., Ortiz, G., Boubeta-Puig, J.: COLLECT: collaborative context-aware service oriented architecture for intelligent decision-making in the internet of things. Expert Syst. Appl. **85**, 231–248 (2017). https://doi.org/10.1016/j.eswa.2017.05.034

6. Ortiz, G., Caravaca, J.A., Garcia-de-Prado, A., Chavez de la O, F., Boubeta-Puig, J.: Real-time context-aware microservice architecture for predictive analytics and smart decision making. IEEE Access **7**, 183177–183194 (2019). https://doi.org/10.1109/ACCESS.2019.2960516

7. Dey, A.K.: Understanding and using context. Pers. Ubiquitous Comput. **5**, 4–7 (2001). https://doi.org/10.1007/s007790170019

8. Abowd, G.D., Dey, A.K., Brown, P.J., Davies, N., Smith, M., Steggles, P.: Towards a better understanding of context and context-awareness. In: Gellersen, H.-W. (ed.) HUC 1999. LNCS, vol. 1707, pp. 304–307. Springer, Heidelberg (1999). https://doi.org/10.1007/3-540-48157-5_29

9. Luckham, D.C.: Event Processing for Business: Organizing the Real-Time Enterprise. John Wiley & Sons, Hoboken, N.J., USA (2012)

10. Ngankam, H.K., Pigot, H., Giroux, S.: OntoDomus: a semantic model for ambient assisted living system based on smart homes. Electronics **11**, 1143 (2022). https://doi.org/10.3390/electronics11071143

11. Pradeep, P., Krishnamoorthy, S., Pathinarupothi, R.K., Vasilakos, A.V.: Leveraging context-awareness for internet of things ecosystem: representation, organization, and management of context. Comput. Commun. **177**, 33–50 (2021). https://doi.org/10.1016/j.comcom.2021.06.004

12. Gu, T., Wang, X.H., Pung, H.K., Zhang, D.Q.: An ontology-based context model in intelligent environments (2020). http://arxiv.org/abs/2003.05055, https://doi.org/10.48550/arXiv.2003.05055

Simulating IoT Systems from High-Level Abstraction Models for Quality of Service Assessment

José A. Barriga(✉) (iD)

Quercus Software Engineering Group, Department of Computer and Telematic Systems Engineering, University of Extremadura, Av. Universidad s/n, 10003 Cáceres, Spain
{jose,pjclemente}@unex.es
http://quercusseg.unex.es

Abstract. In the context of IoT systems, the use of services is a key element in managing system complexity. Concepts such as service-oriented computing/architecture or quality of service (QoS) are present in many IoT systems and are the aim of several studies. However, the analysis and assessment of the behaviour of these concepts requires the deployment of the IoT system, implying high investments in hardware and software. Thus, in order to decrease these costs, the system can be simulated. In this regard, IoT simulations have been tackled focusing on low level aspects such as networks, motes, etc. rather than on high-level concepts, such as services or computing layers. In this proposal, a model-driven development approach named SimulateIoT is proposed to model, generate code and deploy IoT systems simulations from a high abstraction level (from models). Besides of modeling the IoT environment call generation, the IoT system could be simulated. From these simulations it is possible to assess QoS-related aspects such as the delay or jitter between two nodes, the variation of delay or jitter over time, the use of bandwidth, the packet loss, the variation of these parameters as the system changes (e.g. increase of sensors), check whether Service level agreements (SLA) are met, etc. In order to show the proposal, a case study, focused on an Internet of Vehicles (IoV) system is presented.

Keywords: IoT systems · IoT simulation · Model-driven development · Quality of service · Service-oriented computing

This work was funded by the Government of Extremadura, Council for Economy, Science and Digital Agenda under the grant GR21133 and the project IB20058 and by the European Regional Development Fund (ERDF); and Cátedra Telefónica de la Universidad de Extremadura (Red de Cátedras Telefónica).
Supervised by Pedro J. Clemente [0000-0001-5795-6343], Quercus Software Engineering Group, Department of Computer and Telematic Systems Engineering, University of Extremadura, Av. Universidad s/n, 10003, Cáceres, Spain, pjclemente@unex.es

J. Troya et al. (Eds.): ICSOC 2022 Workshops, LNCS 13821, pp. 314–319, 2023.
https://doi.org/10.1007/978-3-031-26507-5_26

1   Introduction

An IoT system involves different devices and services belonging to the Mist, Edge, Fog or Cloud layers. Handling the technological heterogeneity underlying IoT systems requires overcoming a learning curve and investing time and money in system development and hardware acquisition.

For this reason, in the literature, around 90% of studies that need to corroborate or test their proposals in an IoT system use simulators [4]. However, although there are several simulators in the literature (Contiki-Cooja [11], OMNeT++ [14], CupCarbon [7] or IoTSim-Edge [5]), they generally focus on modeling the system at a low level of abstraction rather than focusing on the high level IoT domain concepts and their relationships.

Model-Driven Development (MDD) [12] is an emerging software engineering research area that aims to develop software guided by models based on Meta-modeling technique. In MDD, a MetaModel defines the domain concepts and relationships in a specific domain in order to model partial reality. A Model defines a concrete system conform to a Metamodel. Then, from these models it is possible to generate totally or partially the application code by model-to-text transformations [13]. Thus, high level definition (models) can be mapped by model-to-text transformations to specific technologies (target technology). Consequently, the software code can be generated for a specific technological platform, improving the technological independence and decreasing error proneness.

So, MDD is proposed to tackle the technological heterogeneity underlying IoT systems by increasing the *abstraction level* where the software is implemented, focusing on the domain concepts and their relationships.

The main contributions of this paper include:

- Evidence that Model-Driven Development techniques are suitable to develop tools and languages to tackle successfully the complexity of heterogeneous technologies in the context of IoT simulation environments.
- A Model-Driven solution for researchers and practitioners that allows them to design and simulate IoT systems from a high abstraction level.
- A simulator from which gain knowledge about the IoT system and its services, such as QoS-related parameters (delay, packet loss, jitter variation, SLAs compliance, etc.).
- The application of *SimulateIoT* to one case study focused on the Internet of Vehicles (IoV).

The rest of the paper is structured as follows. In Sect. 2, we present *SimulateIoT*, including the *SimulateIoT* metamodel, the graphical editor and the model-to-text transformation developed. In Sect. 3 an IoV case study is presented. Section 4 outlines the future works. Finally, Sect. 5 concludes the paper.

2   SimulateIoT Overview

SimulateIoT [1,2] is a model-driven approach to design, generate code and execute IoT simulations. The main components of SimulateIoT are: a) The Abstract

Syntax or Metamodel; b) The Concrete Syntax or Graphical editor; and c) The Model-to-Text Transformations.

A) **SimulateIoT Metamodel:** In the context of Model-Driven Development, a MetaModel defines the concepts and relationships in a specific domain in order to model partially reality [12]. Later, Models conform to the Meta-Model could be defined and they could be used to generate total or partially the application code. The software code could be generated for a specific technological platform, improving its technological independence and decreasing the error proneness.

The SimulateIoT metamodel (available in [3]) includes concepts related to sensors, actuators, databases, fog and cloud nodes, synthetic data generation, communication protocols, stream processing, and deploying strategies (such as deployment on Fiware platform), among others.

B) **SimulateIoT Graphical Concrete Syntax and Validator:** In order to facilitate modeling IoT environments, a Graphical Concrete Syntax (Graphical editor) has been generated using the Eugenia tool [6]. The Graphical Concrete Syntax generated from SimulateIoT metamodel is based on Eclipse GMF (Graphical Modeling Framework) and EMF (Eclipse Modeling Tools). Consequently, models (EMF and OCL (Object Constraint Language) [10] based) can be validated against the defined metamodel (EMF and OCL based). Figure 1B shows an example of model defined by using the Graphical Concrete Syntax generated.

C) **SimulateIoT Model to Text Transformations:** Once the models have been defined and validated conforming to the *SimulateIoT metamodel*, a model-to-text transformation defined using Acceleo [9] can generate several artefacts. Thus, the generated software includes, MQTT messaging broker (based on MQTT protocol [8]), device infrastructure, databases, a graphical analysis platform, a stream processor engine, docker container specification, configuration files for each component, a deploy script, etc.

Figure 1A shows the deployment of the architecture of a generic IoT environment where the above mentioned artefacts and their interactions can be observed. Note that the deployment of the architecture is carried out by running the deployment script that is generated by the model-to-text transformations (script that includes all the configurations defined in the previous system modeling).

3   Case Study. Internet of Vehicles

IoV is an emerging area where delay plays a key role [15]. This is because some critical services, such as those focused on passenger safety, are delay-sensitive services that require specific QoS and SLAs [15]. With the aim of verifying whether the services comply with the specified QoS and SLAs before being deployed in

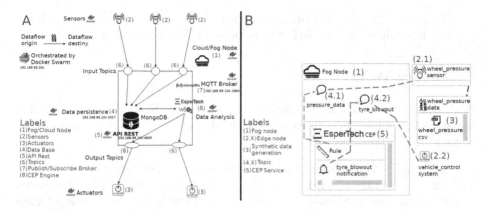

Fig. 1. A) Example of deploy diagram. B) Case study. A delay-sensitive IoV model. Note that Figure B has been developed with SimulateIoT's concrete syntax, however, the size of the name of each element has been increased to provide a better readability.

production, the system can be simulated. Thus, in this section, an Internet of Vehicles delay-sensitive system is modeled and simulated by using SimulateIoT tools.

3.1 Case Study. Model Definition

This model defines an IoV system in which several IoT devices are integrated into a vehicle and cooperate to assist the driver in the event of a tyre blowout. In this sense, a wheel pressure sensor (Fig. 1B, label 2.1) is integrated in each vehicle's wheel, which monitors the pressure of the wheels in real time. These sensors publish the wheel pressure data (Fig. 1B, label 3) in a Topic (Fig. 1B, label 4.1) deployed by a Fog node (Fig. 1B, label 1). A Complex event processing (CEP) (Fig. 1B, label 5) service deployed on this Fog node analyses the data and, in case of a tyre blowout detection, notifies the event (Fig. 1B, label 4.2) to the Actuator (Fig. 1B, label 2.2) in charge of assisting the driver.

3.2 Case Study. Code Generation and Deployment

Once the model has been defined, the model-to-text transformation is applied with the following goals: i) to generate code (Java, Python, Node, etc.) which wraps each device behaviour; ii) to generate configuration code to deploy the message brokers necessary, including the *topic* configurations defined; iii) to generate the configuration files and scripts necessary to deploy the databases and stream processors defined; and finally, to generate the code necessary to query the databases where the data will be stored; Later on, the systems can be deployed using specific scripts generated ad-hoc to improve the user productivity. iv) to generate for each `ProcessNode` and `EdgeNode` a *Docker* container which can be deployed throughout a network of nodes using *Docker Swarm*;

Thus, executing the simulation modelled and later on deploying it, makes it possible to analyse the final IoT system before it is implemented and deployed.

4   Future Work

With the aim of increasing the scope and usability of SimulateIoT, some additional concepts have been identified in the literature and will be included to SimulateIoT in future works:

- Mobile nodes. Node mobility is one of the key concepts in many IoT systems. Therefore, giving SimulateIoT the ability to simulate node movement would allow many users to observe, analyse and optimise the behaviour of their mobile nodes by simulating them. This future work is particularly interesting for service-oriented computing as mobility directly affects the specified QoS and SLAs, since, for instance, a gateway switch could be a critical event where the specified QoS and SLAs may not be met.
- Task scheduling. Task scheduling is a concept that has gained relevance in the IoT area due to its potential to increase the QoS of IoT systems. Including this concept in SimulateIoT is interesting as users could test their task scheduling architectures or algorithms. Thus, being able to test if they are effective, in which situations they are more or less effective, how much they improve QoS with respect to other proposals, etc. Note that this future work is of special interest for service-oriented computing, as task scheduling techniques are aimed at optimising the QoS of the services deployed in an IoT system.

5   Conclusions

The Model-driven development (MDD) approach proposed in this paper, SimulateIoT, shows that MDD techniques are a suitable way to tackle the complexity of domains where heterogeneous technologies are integrated. Besides, SimulateIoT helps users to design, generate, deploy, analyse, and optimise their IoT systems, streamlining the process of IoT systems development and saving costs. Especially, in those IoT systems involving critical services that cannot be deployed in production until it has been verified that they comply with the specified QoS and SLAs.

Acknowledgment. This work was funded by the Government of Extremadura, Council for Economy, Science and Digital Agenda under the grant GR21133 and the project IB20058 and by the European Regional Development Fund (ERDF); and Cátedra Telefónica de la Universidad de Extremadura (Red de Cátedras Telefónica).

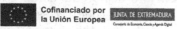

References

1. Barriga, J.A., Clemente, P.J., Hernández, J., Pérez-Toledano, M.A.: SimulateIoT-FIWARE: domain specific language to design, code generation and execute IoT simulation environments on FIWARE. IEEE Access **10**, 7800–7822 (2022). https://doi.org/10.1109/ACCESS.2022.3142894
2. Barriga, J.A., Clemente, P.J., Sosa-Sánchez, E., Prieto, E.: SimulateIoT: domain specific language to design, code generation and execute IoT simulation environments. IEEE Access **9**, 92531–92552 (2021)
3. Corchero, J.A.B., Clemente, P.J.: SimulateIoT metamodel. Mendeley Data, v1 (2022). https://doi.org/10.17632/4mmgv82k2c.1
4. Hosseinioun, P., Kheirabadi, M., Kamel Tabbakh, S.R., Ghaemi, R.: aTask scheduling approaches in fog computing: a survey. Trans. Emerg. Telecommun. Technol. **33**(3), e3792 (2022). https://doi.org/10.1002/ett.3792, https://onlinelibrary.wiley.com/doi/abs/10.1002/ett.3792. e3792 ETT-19-0285.R1
5. Jha, D.N., et al.: IoTSim-edge: a simulation framework for modeling the behavior of internet of things and edge computing environments. Softw. Pract. Experience **50**(6), 844–867 (2020)
6. Kolovos, D.S., García-Domínguez, A., Rose, L.M., Paige, R.F.: Eugenia: towards disciplined and automated development of GMF-based graphical model editors. Softw. Syst. Model. **16**(1), 229–255 (2015). https://doi.org/10.1007/s10270-015-0455-3
7. Mehdi, K., Lounis, M., Bounceur, A., Kechadi, T.: Cupcarbon: a multi-agent and discrete event wireless sensor network design and simulation tool. In: 7th International ICST Conference on Simulation Tools and Techniques. Lisbon, Portugal, 17–19 March 2014, Institute for Computer Science, Social Informatics and Telecommunications Engineering (ICST), pp. 126–131 (2014)
8. Oasis: Message queuing telemetry transport (MQTT) v5.0 Oasis Standard (2019). https://docs.oasis-open.org/mqtt/mqtt/v5.0/mqtt-v5.0.html. Accessed 13 June 2022
9. Obeo: Acceleo project (2012). http://www.acceleo.org. Accessed 13 June 2022
10. OMG: OMG Object Constraint Language (OCL), Version 2.3.1 (2012). http://www.omg.org/spec/OCL/2.3.1/. Accessed 13 June 2022
11. Sehgal, A.: Using the Contiki Cooja simulator. Jacobs University Bremen Campus Ring, Technical report, Computer Science (2013)
12. Selic, B.: The pragmatics of model-driven development. IEEE Softw. **20**(5), 19–25 (2003)
13. Sendall, S., Kozaczynski, W.: Model transformation: the heart and soul of model-driven software development. IEEE Softw. **20**(5), 42–45 (2003)
14. Varga, A., Hornig, R.: An overview of the OMNeT++ simulation environment. In: Proceedings of the 1st International Conference on Simulation Tools and Techniques for Communications, Networks And Systems & Workshops, ICST (Institute for Computer Sciences, Social-Informatics and Telecommunications Engineering), p. 60. (2008)
15. Xu, W., et al.: Internet of vehicles in big data era. IEEE/CAA J. Autom. Sinica **5**(1), 19–35 (2018). https://doi.org/10.1109/JAS.2017.7510736

Internet of Things Semantic-Based Monitoring of Infrastructures Using a Microservices Architecture

Marc Vila[1,2]([⊠]) [iD]

[1] Universitat Politècnica de Catalunya, Barcelona, Spain
marc.vila.gomez@upc.edu
[2] Worldsensing, Barcelona, Spain

Abstract. We live in an Internet-connected world, where tens of billions of *smart* entities are constantly sending information, the Internet of Things (IoT). In some cases, the communication of data messages is straightforward. Devices are connected in the same ecosystem, where it is pretty easy to agree on the communication data format. However, when devices have to communicate information to outside environments, each manufacturer defines its own data communication format. In the IoT domain, these cases are not covered extensively, and information homogenization must be done. In this thesis, we propose an ontology, an abstract interpretation of domain concepts and data, aiming to provide a solution for data heterogeneity in the domain. For this regard, we also propose a working environment where operators can manipulate all the system's information, developed using a microservices architecture.

Keywords: Internet of things · Interoperability · Sensor networks · Ontologies · Semantics · Context-awareness · Industrial PhD

1 Problem Statement and Challenges

In IoT, a *Thing* is an entity that aims to exchange information with other entities over the Internet, such as devices, sensors, or actuators. Nowadays, there are more than 14 billion *Things*, communicating data periodically, heterogeneously, and globally [5]. Mainly used as human consumables (e.g., wearables or health trackers) and in industrial applications (e.g., Industry 4.0 or Smart Cities).

When IoT devices from different manufacturers have to communicate with each other, efforts have to be made to ensure they are interoperable and work well together. One of the biggest challenges is to provide generic solutions in data semantics that apply to different IoT environments, such as ontologies. The main concern in this domain is that *Things* have their own properties, data

Supervised by: Maria-Ribera Sancho (Universitat Politècnica de Catalunya and Barcelona Supercomputing Center, Barcelona, Spain) and Ernest Teniente (Universitat Politècnica de Catalunya).

J. Troya et al. (Eds.): ICSOC 2022 Workshops, LNCS 13821, pp. 320–326, 2023.
https://doi.org/10.1007/978-3-031-26507-5_27

formats, and communication technologies, resulting in almost all companies or ecosystems creating its own mechanisms of data communication. Ontologies can be understood as an abstraction of particular syntaxes and data formats of *Things* and its systems . They provide common vocabularies for all managed information and improve the interoperability of devices. Another challenge is to handle the vast amount of data being generated and transmitted by IoT devices. Hence, it is not realistic to think that a human operator will be able to process that information in real-time, thus having clear conclusions about what is happening in the environment being monitored to act accordingly.

This PhD research is carried out within the "Industrial Doctorates Plan - Generalitat de Catalunya" and has a four year schedule. The academic component is carried out at the Universitat Politècnica de Catalunya, and it also has an industrial component, carried out in an industrial environment at Worldsensing.

2   Research Methodology

In our research, we apply the *Design-Science Research* methodology [4]: "A research paradigm in which a designer answers questions relevant to human problems via the creation of innovative artifacts [...]. The designed artifacts are useful and fundamental to understanding that problem." The authors define several guidelines to help implement this methodology: "Design as an Artifact", the result must be a viable artifact; "Problem Relevance"; "Design Evaluation", demonstrated utility, quality, and efficacy; "Research Contributions"; "Research Rigor", in construction and evaluation; "Design as a Search Process"; "Communication of Research". These concepts, placed in three cycles, are shown in Fig. 1. The "Relevance Cycle", the initial design research that considers environmental requirements, such as problems and opportunities. The "Design Cycle", the artifact is meant to be built and evaluated as a product and as a process. And then the "Rigor Cycle", once the artifact is evaluated, the scientific context can be extracted from it and based on it as a knowledge base.

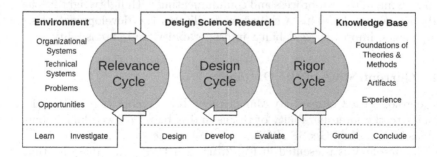

Fig. 1. Design science research cycles

Within the framework of the thesis, for each part to investigate, we review the domain's state-of-the-art research. We then evaluate the viability of the proposal.

After that, we propose and implement the solution. Finally, we evaluate the results. If these are the expected results, then it is accepted and concluded.

To research, design, and implement our ontologies, we follow Noy and McGuiness [8] recommendation: the *Knowledge-Engineering Methodology*. As they suggest, there is no single way to develop semantics, as the modeling of a domain depends to some extent on several factors, including the purpose of the system it will support. The process of modeling an ontology is iterative and summarized as follows: Determine the domain and scope of the ontology; sketch a list of competency questions that should be answered; consider reuse of existing ontologies; enumerate important terms in the ontology; develop the ontology (classes, class hierarchy, properties, ...); And, finally, validate the list of competency questions.

3   Internet of Things Semantic-Based Monitoring of Infrastructures Using a Microservices Architecture

The goal of our thesis, which is twofold, is to overcome heterogeneity in the communication of IoT devices and to improve the effectiveness of providing tools to develop new applications and use cases.

We propose an ontology as a step forward toward a feasible solution to the problem of IoT interoperability. Our proposal is aimed at allowing tools for monitoring assets employing IoT devices, from the sensing part to the actuation part. Allowing end-users to obtain information, access it, monitor it, and perform actions if necessary. Our proposal is general enough to be used by software systems that can handle the components specified herein. Users benefit from having an ontology to use as a basis and an example.

Furthermore, we propose a Cloud software platform where users can onboard IoT devices to and monitor entities, including awareness capabilities through predefined context-aware rules, which allows one to set warning or alarm thresholds. Our solution's architecture is based on Microservices. An almost new architectural style that considers developing an application "as a suite of small services, each running in its own process and communicating with lightweight mechanisms with the others" [3]. This architecture facilitates the development of software components, improving scalability, interoperability, and extensibility.

3.1   Current State of the Ontology

Our ontology, the Connectivity Management Tool Semantics (CMTS) [11], contributes to the interoperability of things and is based on well-known ontologies such as SSN/SOSA, GeoSPARQL, and OWL-Time.

The ontology is presented in Fig. 2, using a UML class diagram that specifies the structure of a system that shows its classes, attributes, methods, and relationships between objects. The ontology builds from two key concepts: *Site*, which are the physical areas to be monitored, and the *Devices*, which are installed in the *Sites* to allow data communication. We divide *Devices* into three types of common IoT devices: *Gateways*, physical entities that act as routers, receiving data from other entities, mainly *Nodes*, and sending it to the Cloud server; *Nodes*, a small physical entity with limited processing capabilities, reads information from *Sensors* and communicate it to the *Gateways*; and *Sensors*, the entities that are capable of making observations or measurements of a given feature. We also describe *ObservableProperty*: the entities, features, or properties observed by *Sensors*. In addition to *Observations*, the measurement from an *ObservableProperty* using a *Sensor*, at a given moment of time, using *OWL-Time*. *Devices* and *Sites* can be located using the *GeoSPARQL Location* entity.

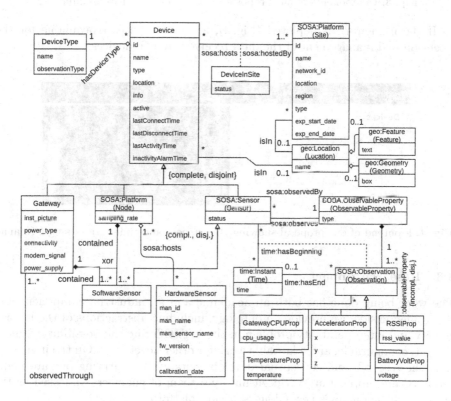

Fig. 2. Conceptual overview of the current state of our Ontology

3.2   Current State of the Framework

We also propose a framework that makes use of the ontology mentioned above. The prototype, shown in Fig. 3, is designed using a Microservices architecture. Each functional module (box in the figure) is an isolated component and communicates with each other via HTTP interfaces. This initial version of the framework was published in Vila et al. [10].

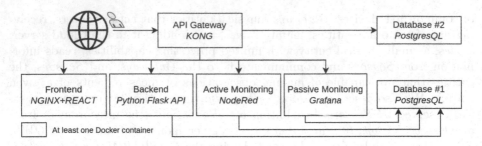

Fig. 3. Components of our proposal using a Microservices architecture

If the framework is deployed (Fig. 4), a set of services is available for the reception and management of the data received by IoT devices.

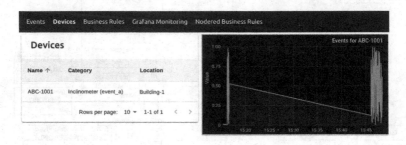

Fig. 4. Frontend of our proposal showing the Devices and time-series using Grafana

3.3   Research Impact

The work being done has both an academic and an industrial component. On the academic side, we provide an ontology, including abstractions of the heterogeneity and interoperability problem in the IoT. Offering the possibility of more elegant, configurable, and adaptable work for other developers. On the industrial side, the research and conceptual developments we are carrying out are being proposed and applied at Worldsensing by a team of engineers and used as the basis for the company's new Cloud software platform.

3.4   Research Plan

This thesis was started at the end of 2019. At present, we have presented a first proposal for the software architecture that includes observation capabilities. We also have presented an ontology that covers the definition of data management for devices and their sensors. We are now focused on the concepts and mechanisms to letting systems understand the measurements sent by the devices and providing means of answering certain pre-defined criteria, the Context-Aware mechanisms and *Response Plans*, allowing users to receive information, warns, or alerts from received measurements. Afterward, we will merge all the knowledge acquired during the thesis to make the final architecture version that supports all the components studied. Then plan and execute the end-to-end tests. For these, we plan to use generic IoT devices available on the market, although we would like to use Worldsensing production devices, so we have set the latter as a nice-to-have.

4   Progress Beyond the State of the Art

Our proposed ontology extends SSN/SOSA [6], an ontology to semantically enable applications interoperability, aiming to answer the need for a domain-independent and end-to-end model for sensing applications. In our proposal, we want to go one step further than SSN/SOSA in that, although they allow modeling the sensing part, we find that the actuation part has some work to do in terms of the conceptual definition of the tasks to perform when a certain event occurs, the Context-Aware mechanisms, and the responses to perform as reactions. In addition, other ontologies empower the Interoperability of Things. The NGSI-LD ontology [9], an ETSI standard that adds contextual information to the schema information sharing but does not support actuation environments. SAREF [2], an ETSI-standardized ontology for IoT Smart Appliances, focused on the monitoring and control of entities. However, it is not general enough and has a specific domain. Kiljander et al. [7] propose interoperability of semantic information brokers that supports the sensor and actuator parts. However, they do not consider the modeling of context-awareness rules. In Alirezaie et al. [1], authors propose a context-aware housing system using semantics, but it applies only to a specific domain and, therefore, is not general enough.

Our contribution to the research is to go one step further. We observe that in state-of-the-art research, either the observing or the actuating side is taken into account. However, it is not easy to find both together to support interoperability on different domains in what we believe is the end-to-end IoT loop: from data collection to data knowledge, which allows taking into account the obtained information and react accordingly.

Acknowledgments. This work is partially funded by Industrial Doctorates from Generalitat de Catalunya (2019 DI 001). SUDOQU project, PID2021-126436OB-C21 from MCIN/AEI, 10.13039/ 501100011033, FEDER, UE. With the support of in Lab FIB UPC and Worldsensing.

References

1. Alirezaie, M., Renoux, J., et al.: An ontology-based context-aware system for smart homes: E-care@home. Sensors **17**(7), 1586 (2017)
2. Daniele, L., Garcia-Castro, R., et al.: SAREF: the Smart Applications REFerence ontology (2020). https://saref.etsi.org/core/v3.1.1/. Accessed 27 Aug 2022
3. Fowler, M., Lewis, J.: Microservices, a definition (2014). https://martinfowler.com/articles/microservices.html. Accessed 16 Aug 2022

4. Hevner, A., Chatterjee, S.: Design Research in Information Systems: Theory and Practice. Springer Publishing, New York (2010). https://doi.org/10.1007/978-1-4419-5653-8
5. IoT Analytics: Number of connected IoT devices growing 18% to 14.4 billion globally (2022). https://iot-analytics.com/number-connected-iot-devices. Accessed 24 Sep 2022
6. Janowicz, K., Haller, A., et al.: SOSA: a lightweight ontology for sensors, observations, samples, and actuators. J. Web Semant. **56**, 1–10 (2019)
7. Kiljander, J., D'elia, A., et al.: Semantic interoperability architecture for pervasive computing and internet of things. IEEE Access **2**, 856–873 (2014)
8. Noy, N.F., McGuinness, D.L.: Ontology development 101: a guide to creating your first ontology. Technical report. Knowledge Systems - Stanford University (2001)
9. Privat, G.: Guidelines for Modelling with NGSI-LD. Technical report, ETSI (2021)
10. Vila, M., Sancho, M.R., Teniente, E.: XYZ monitor: IoT monitoring of infrastructures using microservices. In: Service-Oriented Computing - ICSOC 2020 Workshops, pp. 472–484 (2021)
11. Vila, M., Sancho, M.-R., Teniente, E., Vilajosana, X.: Semantics for connectivity management in IoT sensing. In: Ghose, A., Horkoff, J., Silva Souza, V.E., Parsons, J., Evermann, J. (eds.) ER 2021. LNCS, vol. 13011, pp. 297–311. Springer, Cham (2021). https://doi.org/10.1007/978-3-030-89022-3_24

On Balancing Flexibility and Compliance of Business Processes: Functional Constraints Modeling and Verification

Jingwei Zhu[1,2(✉)]

[1] School of Computer Science, Fudan University, Shanghai, China
jwzhu20@fudan.edu.cn
[2] Shanghai Key Laboratory of Data Science, Shanghai Institute of Intelligent
Electronics and Systems, Shanghai, China

Abstract. When handling long-tailed changes (LTC) in business processes, there is a tension between flexibility and compliance. The tension has been addressed in our previous work, while compliance needs further discussion. Compliance is often expressed in terms of functional and nonfunctional constraints. This paper studies the modeling and verification of functional constraints.

Keywords: Business process · Long-tailed change · Flexibility · Compliance · Functional constraint

1 Introduction

A business process is a set of activities performed in coordination to realize a business goal [8]. Business processes are dynamic in nature and prone to changes [6]. Among many kinds of changes, a special kind named long-tailed changes (LTC) brings new challenges to change management [9]. LTC is induced by sporadic, wide-spectrum, but significant business events, named long-tailed business events (LBE), which affect the execution of business processes.

LTC needs to be tackled timely, requiring business processes to be flexible. At the same time, business goals must be realized, requiring business processes to comply with business regulations. Thus, there is a tension between flexibility and compliance, which is unique in LTC scenarios such as emergency response.

Harmon [3] provides concepts and methods of process change, and emphasizes the compliance during process change. Song and Jacobsen [7] provide a comprehensive survey of process change. Awad et. al. [2] propose a compliance checking framework based on BPMN-Q. They study process change and compliance a lot, but do not address LTC and the tension.

Our previous work [9] proposes a low-code adaptation framework to handle LTC and resolve the tension between flexibility and compliance. With the

---

Supervised by Prof. Liang Zhang at Fudan University (lzhang@fudan.edu.cn).

J. Troya et al. (Eds.): ICSOC 2022 Workshops, LNCS 13821, pp. 327–333, 2023.
https://doi.org/10.1007/978-3-031-26507-5_28

framework, front-line persons (on-site staff) flexibly adjust process behavior by annotating the process model with a domain-specific language (DSL). The annotation affects process behavior by modifying the values of process variables. Back-end persons (headquarters, authorities) ensure the compliance during LTC by imposing functional and non-functional constraints. Functional constraints are constraints on the execution order between activities, while non-functional constraints are constraints to ensure business quality, performance, security, etc.

Our previous work is unable to fully address compliance. This paper discusses functional constraints in detail and makes two technical contributions: (1) A method for modeling functional constraints on annotated process models. (2) A method for verifying annotated process models against functional constraints.

2   Running Example

BoYuan, an imaginary liquefied natural gas (LNG) logistics company, operates LNG tankers at sea. Yantai-Dalian route, one of the company's operating routes, is accident-prone because it crosses other waterways. LNG is a kind of danger-ous goods. If an accident happens to an LNG tanker, causing LNG to leak, it will be a disaster. To plan for LNG leakage, BoYuan developed an emergency response process, as shown in Fig. 1. The process includes three parallel threads, separately controlling the movement of the tanker, the rescue of the injured, and leak plugging. The execution of emergency response depends on many factors, as shown in Table 1. Although the number of factors is limited, the number of factor combinations is very large. Due to cost constraints, it is impossible to make plans for all these combinations in advance. When a particular accident (LBE) happens, its response requires an LTC in the emergency response process.

According to a related work about LNG bunkering [4], the safeguard has three layers, i.e., normal operation, prevention, and mitigation, as shown in Fig. 2. Many situations are covered by emergency plans, but accidents will happen. LBE is the accident. LTC is to handle the accident and mitigate the risk.

3   Modeling Functional Constraints on Process Models

The functional perspective of a business process consists of activities [6,8]. Func-tional constraints are constraints on activities. To handle LTC, annotations can change the execution order between activities. To ensure compliance, some key orders cannot be changed. We employ the graphical language ConDec [5] for back-end persons to model functional constraints. ConDec can be used to model business processes in a declarative approach that declares *what to do* but does not prescribe *how to do*. We employ ConDec to model *what must be done*, ensur-ing business goals are always realized. ConDec notations can be mapped into Linear-time Temporal Logic (LTL) formulas, as shown in Table 2. Besides propo-sitional atoms and logical connectives, LTL formulas support temporal connec-tives, which are useful for expressing the execution order between activities. Instead of constructing ConDec models separately, we add ConDec as custom

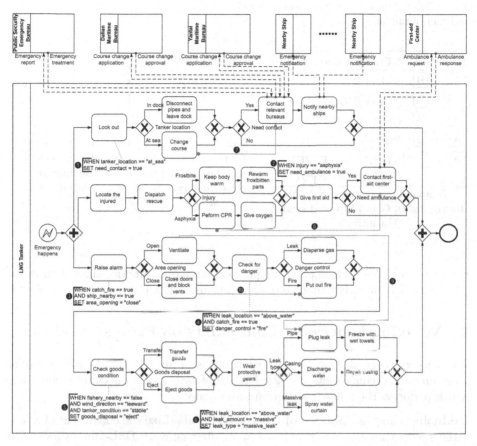

Fig. 1. LNG tanker emergency response process. The annotations in green are to adjust process behavior. The functional constraints in yellow are to ensure compliance with regulations. The annotations and the constraints will be discussed in detail in the following sections. (Color figure online)

Table 1. Factors determining the execution of emergency response

Factor	Value range
Tanker_location	in_dock, at_sea
injury	frostbite, asphyxia
leak_location	above_water, under_water
leak_amount	little, medium, massive
catch_fire	true, false
tanker_condition	stable, unstable
ship_nearby	true, false
fishery_nearby	true, false
wind_direction	windward, leeward

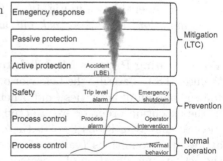

Fig. 2. LNG bunkering safeguard layers [4]. LBE is the accident. LTC is to handle the accident and mitigate the risk.

Table 2. Functional constraint notations
and LTL formulas

Notation	LTL formula
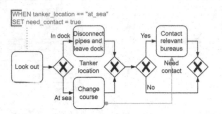 A ● ─ B	$F\,A \to F\,B$
A ● ─● B	$F\,A \leftrightarrow F\,B$
A ● ─● B	$G\,(A \to F\,B)$
A ● ─● B	$F\,B \to (\neg B\;U\;A)$
A ● ─● B	$(G\,(A \to F\,B)) \land$ $(F\,B \to (\neg B\;U\;A))$

* Temporal connectives: F (some future state), G (all future states), U (until).

Fig. 3. A process fragment extracted from Fig. 1. The annotation decides whether contact is needed. The functional constraint requires that contact is necessary after a change of course.

notations to BPMN. Thus, back-end persons can model functional constraints on BPMN models directly using ConDec notations. An example is shown in Fig. 3.

4   Verifying Functional Constraints on Process Models

To verify whether all possible execution paths of an annotated process model meet functional constraints, we develop a tool with model checking techniques, which performs the following steps automatically.

Reducing the Complexity of Process Models. Like the enactment of annotated process models described in [9], we first convert DSL-annotations into tasks. Thus, annotations can be treated as activities. To mitigate the state space explosion in model checking, we employ the reduction rules in [1] to remove activities and gateways that are irrelevant to annotations and functional constraints. For example, the process fragment shown in Fig. 3 is reduced to the process fragment shown in Fig. 4 (a). The annotation is converted into an activity *Annotation*; activities *Look out* and *Disconnect pipes and leave dock* are removed.

Transforming Process Models into Labeled Transition Systems (LTS). We use LTS to describe the behavior of process models. We use states to express the completion of activities (and other flow objects), because we are interested in the execution order between activities. We use transitions to express activities, so that transitions lead to the completion of activities. We use labels to express the conditions (values of process variables) to trigger transitions and the actions (modification of process variables) during transitions. The treatment of gateways is the key to transformation. For exclusive gateways, we use labels to express the branch-selecting conditions. For example, the process fragment shown in Fig. 4 (a) is transformed into the LTS shown in Fig. 4 (b). For parallel

gateways, we have to generate all possible states based on interleaving semantics. For example, the process shown in Fig. 4 (c) is transformed into the LTS
shown in Fig. 4 (d). Other kinds of gateways can be reduced to the combination
of exclusive and parallel gateways.

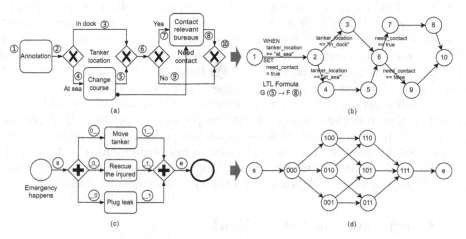

Fig. 4. (a) A process fragment containing exclusive gateways. (b) The LTS and the
LTL formula transformed from (a). (c) A process containing parallel gateways. (d) The
LTS transformed from (c). Circles represent states.

Model Checking with NuSMV. We use NuSMV[1] to verify an LTS against
LTL formulas. To this end, we need to encode the LTS and the LTL formulas in a
NuSMV input file. We encode states with a variable *state* and encode transitions
with the value changes of *state*. We encode process variables with variables in
the input file and encode the transitions' modification of process variables with
the value changes of variables.

Explaining Verification Results. The verification result is either *true* or
false. In case of a *false* result, the front-line person who adds the annotation
should get an explanation about the conflict. At that time, we will analyze the
counterexample provided by NuSMV and mark the conflict on the process model.

5 Case Study

BoYuan employs our framework [9] to handle LTC. Suppose an LNG tanker
is sailing at sea and one of its valves suddenly breaks. LNG leaks, catches fire,
and asphyxiates nearby people. The emergency response process starts. To adjust
process behavior, front-line persons (the crew of the tanker) annotate the process
model, as shown in green in Fig. 1: ❶ As the tanker is at sea and changes its

---

[1] https://nusmv.fbk.eu/.

course, front-line persons decide to contact relevant bureaus and notify nearby ships. ❷ As some people are asphyxiated, front-line persons decide to call an ambulance. ❸- ❻ According to relevant factors, front-line persons decide to close the area, put out fire, eject goods, and spray water curtain.

To make adjustments comply with regulations, back-end persons (the headquarters of BoYuan) impose functional constraints on the process model, as shown in yellow in Fig. 1: ❼ After changing the course, the tanker must contact maritime bureaus. ❽ After rescuing the seriously injured, people must contact first-aid center for an ambulance. ❾ Before plugging leak, people must ventilate the area to reduce the gas concentration. ❿ Before putting out fire, people must close doors and block vents to cut off oxygen and control the fire area.

Front-line persons are the first to perceive LTC and are best suited for LTC reaction. Our framework enables front-line persons to flexibly adjust process behavior in reaction to LTC. However, front-line persons are not process professionals, so the resulting process may violate some regulations. Our framework enables back-end persons to impose functional constraints in pursuit of compliance. Thus, our framework balances flexibility and compliance during LTC.

6   Conclusion and Future Work

To ensure compliance of business processes during LTC, this paper studies functional constraints modeling and verification. The prototype of our framework can be accessed at the repository[2]. In the future, we will enhance the framework to support more process change operations, e.g., inserting and skipping activities.

Acknowledgements. This work is supported by Projects of International Cooperation and Exchanges NSFC-DFG (Grant No. 62061136006).

References

1. Awad, A., Decker, G., Weske, M.: Efficient compliance checking using BPMN-Q and temporal logic. In: Dumas, M., Reichert, M., Shan, M.-C. (eds.) BPM 2008. LNCS, vol. 5240, pp. 326–341. Springer, Heidelberg (2008). https://doi.org/10.1007/978-3-540-85758-7_24
2. Awad, A., Weidlich, M., Weske, M.: Visually specifying compliance rules and explaining their violations for business processes. J. Visual Lang. Comput. **22**(1), 30–55 (2011)
3. Harmon, P.: Business Process Change: A Business Process Management Guide for Managers and Process Professionals. Morgan Kaufmann, Burlington (2019)
4. MISPINAS, I.: Guidance on LNG bunkering - to port authorities and administrations. EMSA: European Maritime Safety Agency (2018)
5. Pesic, M., van der Aalst, W.M.P.: A declarative approach for flexible business processes management. In: Eder, J., Dustdar, S. (eds.) BPM 2006. LNCS, vol. 4103, pp. 169–180. Springer, Heidelberg (2006). https://doi.org/10.1007/11837862_18

---

[2] https://github.com/SOARingLab/RESILIENCE.

6. Reichert, M., Weber, B.: Enabling Flexibility in Process-Aware Information Systems - Challenges, Methods, Technologies. Springer, Cham (2012)
7. Song, W., Jacobsen, H.A.: Static and dynamic process change. IEEE Trans. Serv. Comput. **11**(1), 215–231 (2016)
8. Weske, M.: Business Process Management: Concepts, Languages. Architectures. Springer-Verlag, Berlin Heidelberg (2019)
9. Zhu, J., Peng, J., Zhang, L., Truong, H.L.: Improving business process resilience to long-tailed business events via low-code. In: 2022 IEEE International Conference on Web Services, ICWS 2022, pp. 343–348 (2022)

Change Recommendation in Business Processes

Arash Yadegari Ghahderijani[✉][ID]

University of Groningen, Groningen, The Netherlands
a.yadegari.ghahderijani@rug.nl

Abstract. Process-aware information systems are valuable for automating business tasks leading to cost reduction and efficiency. This research aims to advance the state of the art in process management towards autonomic process performance improvement by contributing control-flow change recommendations for process instances that is supporting automatic change enactment as a response to predicted KPI violations. Towards that goal, the related literature has been investigated in two literature review studies and research gaps have been identified. The proposed generic architecture provides a feedback loop that enables evaluation of the resulting recommendations for future process instances. We also present the current state of the research and future plans.

Keywords: Autonomic process performance improvement ·
Recommender systems · Process monitoring · Process
change/adaptation · Key Performance Indicators (KPIs) ·
Process-aware information systems · (Business) process management

1 Introduction

Business process management research focuses on all phases of process life cycle and process-aware information systems (PAIS) have been developed to enable all available concepts and techniques in these phases. The most recent advances in predictive monitoring of processes [1,4,5] enable a number of performance indicator predictions, such as process instance remaining time, cost, or process instance outcome. Currently, such estimations are used by business owners and other stakeholders to recommend process improvements, however, we observe that there is still a disconnect between the tools for predictive monitoring and the process execution environments, which makes the automated recommendation and enactment of changes for running process cases/instances impossible. This in turn prohibits the advancement toward autonomic process performance improvement [6] and is the main objective of our research.

Supervised by Dimka Karastoyanova [0000-0002-8827-2590], University of Groningen, Groningen, The Netherlands, d.karastoyanova@rug.nl

The initial benefit of using process-aware information systems for business processes is to allow for monitoring key performance indicators (KPIs) to different stakeholders (via e.g. a dashboard) to provide a general overview of the current state of running process instances and thus support decision making. In addition, current developments in research allow for logs to be used for further assistance in decision-making by predictions and recommending actions based on them. Therefore, the long-term research objective is to contribute to this assistance by recommending changes in business processes based on the learned impact of changes/adaptations on process KPIs. In this research specifically, our goal is to focus on KPI violation prevention by recommending process control-flow changes using a learned model on historical data.

The general idea is to utilize advances of the artificial intelligence research and extend the flexibility of processes in run time using the prediction capabilities of the literature in the predictive monitoring area to take change actions. This idea has been identified in our previous study [6]. In addition, [2] proposes a research manifesto on augmented business process management systems, where artificial intelligence techniques aid in making processes in a PAIS more adaptable, proactive, explainable, and context-sensitive.

Towards that goal, we performed 2 literature review studies considering the guidelines for conducting a systematic literature review [3] and identified the limitations of the current research. In an attempt to address some of these limitations, we will focus on providing a recommender system for change recommendation and how it will be integrated into PAIS. We will work towards this contribution along the following three steps: i) synthetic event log generation, ii) correlation identification between process log attributes, need for change and type of change action/pattern, and iii) control-flow change recommendation.

We will present the approach, preliminary results and future steps as follows: Sect. 2 investigates the related work by representing our reviews of literature. Section 3 illustrates a big picture of the approach and our research road map. Current research on the change recommendation and preliminary results have been explained in Sect. 4. In the end, Sect. 5 concludes the paper.

2   Related Work

We have carried out two literature reviews to capture the current state of the art.

Our *Literature review on prediction and change of business processes* looked into the available works that report concepts and solutions to combine "prediction" and "change" on a process, service composition, or service choreography [6].

The studies we identified in this review[1] apply various change approaches such as control-flow change, service replacement, service/fragment substitution, and data manipulation. The type of systems considered is service composition in most of the studies and service choreography in only one study. Although

---

[1] https://docs.google.com/spreadsheets/d/1Vb56k0xxGHvqPaEdbdONVg7lqaRI CDf5.

some studies facilitate KPI prediction, the prediction approaches considered in the literature do not thoroughly study the three main dimensions of KPIs – time, cost, and quality. Furthermore, we concluded that there are no process-aware solutions available that enable the combination of process adaptation and predictive process monitoring natively in generic manner and automatically, so that they can enable an autonomic feedback loop. The research limitations are in terms of reference architectures and in term of detailed concepts and realizations relevant to the autonomic PAIS.

In our *literature review on learning from the changes in business processes*, we consider works that focus on recording or mining of changes in a business process, workflow, service composition, service orchestration, or PAIS in general.

Among the identified studies that consider learning from changes[2] , only one study mentions change recommendation in a proposed framework. The proposed approach, however, is different from our approach as it considers process variants, whereas, we are interested in the changes for KPI improvements. Overall the sparse literature shows that this area has the potential to be further explored and is relevant to the findings in our literature review on autonomic process change based on predictions.

3   Approach Overview and Research Road Map

Aligned with the general goal of autonomic process performance improvement, we proposed a generic architecture shown in Fig. 1 in a previous study [6], where we reconstructed the architecture based on existing realizations identified in our first literature review. This architecture shows 5 logical component groups shown in dotted lines. On the left side of the architecture, there is a process execution environment (PAIS). This system sends monitoring data to the monitoring component that stores process execution data as logs. These logs will then be used by the analysis component for further analysis and by the prediction component. The prediction component is where the works on predictive monitoring of business processes could be applied. In addition, this component consumes processed data from the analysis component. As a result of predictions on process instances, violations may arise and then could indicate a trigger for change. The adaptation component handles changes on process instances and feeds back the need for change enactment into the PAIS, thus closing the feedback loop. On the basis of this architecture, the ultimate goal of this research is to enable control-flow change recommendations based on the predictions produced by the prediction component. The proposed recommender system extends the part of the architecture dealing with adaptation identification and enactment. Significant part of the approach is related to measuring and recording the impact of the recommended changes onto processes and learning from that information for continuous learning of the adaptations.

Following the presented generic architecture in [6], we proposed a research road map. In this road map, a research direction has been noted to identify the

---

[2] https://docs.google.com/spreadsheets/d/1VZ1R43SakuVCG25ZqXcIiFzyIkaF7W2i.

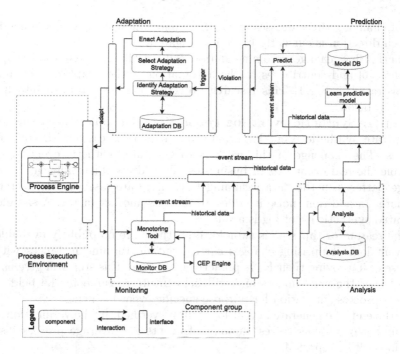

Fig. 1. Generic architecture of a system enabling autonomic process performance improvement [6]

best type of change upon detection of a certain type of violation and the way this change is selected and its effects will be measured. Following this research road map, the research on the control-flow change recommendation has been investigated. In the scope of this research, the research challenges/questions for the control-flow change recommendation we identified are:

- How can we learn from the process instances that exhibit control-flow changes?
- How can we map what is learned from the process instances to control-flow changes?
- How a learned model from the process instances with control-flow changes could be used for change recommendation?

In the next section we will present the preliminary results towards addressing these open research questions.

4   Change Recommendation - Preliminary Results

As mentioned above, overall, two literature review studies have been conducted to identify available literature and gaps in the research area. Following the identified gaps, a generic architecture for autonomic process performance improvement has been proposed. To complete the autonomic loop and make the manual part of changing the processes assisted, a control-flow change recommendation research direction is currently being investigated.

Control-flow change recommendation follows the research road map presented in [6] and contributes to the automation of the adaptation component demonstrated in Fig. 1. This research objective has been broken into 3 steps explained below.

Step 1: Synthetic event log generation. The objective of this step is to generate synthetic event logs that contain process cases with control-flow changes. The challenge of this work is to generate synthetic event logs that resemble the real event logs of businesses. To address this challenge, we inject change patterns in the data assuming that there are discoverable patterns in real data. In addition, noise is added to data as another factor. A sample of a generated synthetic event log is available[3].

The reason for this step is twofold, first, there are no publicly available real life event logs comprising changes carried out on running instances with the purpose of improving their KPIs proactively. Second, this step will give us more control over the experiments and will help future research in the field to use business process simulation for purpose-specific event log generation.

In the end, the generated event logs will be verified. In the verification stage, the number of process traces, number of events and average process instance duration will be reported.

Step 2: Correlation identification in the event logs. This step aims to identify the correlations between process log attributes, need for change (with focus on the time KPI) and type of change action/pattern and show them in a model in order to be used for categorizing process cases and label them for the change action/pattern. The challenge of this step is to identify a method that can extract these correlations and show them in an interpretable model. To address this challenge, decision tree machine learning methods have been chosen due to their interpretablity. A sample of the resulting decision tree trained on the encoded event logs is demonstrated in Listing 1.

```
1 trace_duration <= 249.81615: False (587.0)
2 trace_duration > 249.81615: True (413.0)
```

Listing 1: Learned decision tree on synthetic event logs for a sample process model

The model in Listing 1 explains that the traces with a total duration above 249.8 min are considered to be the cases with a control-flow change (i.e. the change label is True for these cases) and without change otherwise. Note that this model is very simplistic as the generated synthetic data was used to examine

---

[3] https://docs.google.com/spreadsheets/d/1gifw6Zt9Ie_vSxbiHZlW57d2iw_nd3-b2iQnqp0BSmw.

the learning ability of the decision tree learning method. An experiment on real data would demonstrate a more realistic model.

To evaluate the learned model, machine learning metrics (such as F-measure) will be considered. To prevent over-fitting, experiments consider cross-validation of the data. In addition, a comparative experiment on the different supervised machine learning methods will be beneficial to compare the effectiveness.

Step 3: Control-flow change recommendation. This is the final step towards the goal of recommending control-flow changes for process cases, which consumes the learned model in the previous step. In this step, the data of a process case in the event logs will be labeled for the type of control-flow change required based on the learned model (specifically, a decision tree similar to the sample shown in Listing 1). This label will give a recommendation for control-flow change.

The control-flow change recommender will be evaluated by comparing the recommended change and the change label of the process cases in the synthetic event logs. If the real label and the recommended change are equal, it is considered a successful recommendation and an unsuccessful recommendation otherwise.

Overall, we plan to design a simple basic experiment for each step and move towards more complicated experiments with multiple control-flow change possibilities and consider more aspects of a real-world setting.

5   Conclusion

This paper aims towards autonomic process performance improvement by referring to the identified gaps in the state of the art, which are captured in literature review studies. A control-flow change recommendation on business process cases is under study, which has been explained in this paper using a three steps approach of synthetic event log generation, correlation identification in the event logs, and control-flow change recommendation. In future, we plan to continue the research on process change recommendation considering the generic architecture and the research road map. This research will provide insights for academia on purpose-oriented process data generation and contribute in applying machine learning methods in process-aware information systems. It will also benefit industry by providing change recommendations in processes and assisting in KPI-oriented decision making.

References

1. Di Francescomarino, C., et al.: Predictive process monitoring methods: which one suits me best? In: BPM Conference (2018)
2. Dumas, M., et al.: Augmented business process management systems: a research manifesto. CoRR abs/2201.12855 (2022). https://arxiv.org/abs/2201.12855
3. Kitchenham, B., Charters, S.: Guidelines for performing systematic literature reviews in software engineering. Technical report (2007)

4. Marquez-Chamorro, A.E., Resinas, M., Ruiz-Cortes, A.: Predictive monitoring of business processes: a survey. IEEE Trans. Serv. Comput. **11**(6), 962–977 (2018)
5. Verenich, I., Dumas, M., Rosa, M.L., Maggi, F.M., Teinemaa, I.: Survey and cross-benchmark comparison of remaining time prediction methods in business process monitoring. ACM Trans. Intell. Syst. Technol. **10**(4), 1–34 (2019)
6. Ghahderijani, A.Y., Karastoyanova, D.: Autonomic process performance improvement. In: IEEE EDOC Workshop (2021)

Demonstrations Track

Introduction to the Demonstrations Track

Service-Oriented Computing (SOC) has rapidly evolved in the last years over various areas such as Cloud/Edge Computing, Internet of Things, Augmented Reality, Artificial Intelligence and many others. This has promoted the development of innovative products and services, while facing new challenges in the scope of SOC.

The goal of the ICSOC Demo Track was to provide opportunities for participants from academia and industry to present their latest practical developments in Service-Oriented Computing. It has been held as part of the 20th International Conference on Service-Oriented Computing (ICSOC) in Sevilla, Spain, from November 29 to December 2, 2022.

Every demo paper has been reviewed double-blind by at least 3 members of the international program committee. Finally, only 60% of the submissions have been accepted for publication and presentation at the conference. This has resulted in an attractive selection of different service technologies, research areas and application domains. In particular, the Demo Track included the following topical sessions and demo papers:

Service-Based Mining and Analytics

- Bravo, Alfonso; Cabanillas, Cristina; Peña, Joaquín; Resinas, Manuel "Board Miner: A Tool to Analyze the Use of Board-Based Collaborative Work Management Tools"
- Pourbafrani, Mahsa; Gharbi, Firas; van der Aalst, Wil M.P. "A Tool for Business Processes Diagnostics"

Service-Oriented Architecture and Engineering

- Rosa-Bilbao, Jesús; Boubeta-Puig, Juan "Node4Chain: Extending Node-RED Low-code Tool for Monitoring Blockchain Networks"
- Pesl, Robin Dominic; Breitenbeucher, Uwe; Georgievski, Ilche; Aiello, Marco "Service-Oriented Integration of SuperTuxKart"

Service-Based Quantum Computing

- Romero-Álvarez, Javier; Alvarado-Valiente, Jaime; Moguel, Enrique; Garcia-Alonso, Jose; Murillo, Juan M. "Using Open API for the development of Hybrid Classical-Quantum Services"
- Beisel, Martin; Barzen, Johanna; Garhofer, Simon; Leymann, Frank; Truger, Felix; Weder, Benjamin; Yussupov, Vladimir "Quokka: A Service Ecosystem for Workflow-Based Execution of Variational Quantum Algorithms"

RESTful Services for Big Data

- De Pascale, Daniel; Cascavilla, Giuseppe; Tamburri, Damian; Van Den Heuvel, Willem-Jan "SENSEI: Scraper for ENhanced analySis to Evaluate Illicit trends"

- Razgkelis, Konstantinos; Karakasidis, Alexandros "PRES3: Private Record Linkage using Services, Spark and Soundex"

Services for IoT Platforms and Applications

- Yang, Pengwei; Abusafia, Amani; Lakhdari, Abdallah; Bouguettaya, Athman "Towards peer-to-peer sharing of wireless energy services"
- Laso, Sergio; Flores-Martin, Daniel; Cortés-Pérez, Juan Pedro; Soriano Barroso, Miguel; Cortés-Pérez, Alfonso; Berrocal, Javier; Murillo, Juan M. "IoT System for Occupational Risks Prevention at a WWTP"
- Fu, Qianlong; Chen, Dezhi; Sun, Haifeng; Qi, Qi; Wang, Jingyu; Liao, Jianxin "AlsoDTN: An Air Logistics Service-Oriented Digital Twin Network based on Collaborative Decision Model"

We acknowledge the support of the contributors to this Demo Track and express our gratitude to the program committee members for the time and effort they have put into reviewing papers. We also like to thank the conference organizers for their most helpful support.

November 2022   Demonstrations Track Organizers

BOARD MINER: A Tool to Analyze the Use of Board-Based Collaborative Work Management Tools

Alfonso Bravo[1]([✉])[ID], Cristina Cabanillas[1,2][ID], Joaquín Peña[1][ID], and Manuel Resinas[1,2][ID]

[1] I3US Institute, Universidad de Sevilla, Seville, Spain
{abllanos,cristinacabanillas,joaquinp,resinas}@us.es
[2] SCORE Lab, Universidad de Sevilla, Seville, Spain

Abstract. Board-Based Collaborative Work Management Tools (BBTs) like Trello and Microsoft Planner are commonly used as low-code tools to manage the data and processes that support the services an organization provides. Their main advantage over other process execution platforms like traditional business process management systems is that they can be adapted by the users themselves. This is particularly useful in agile and changing environments. However, this flexibility carries some risks, such as badly designed boards, or inefficient or improper board uses (even with quality board designs). BOARD MINER is a library that leverages board event logs, which capture all the activity that has taken place within the boards, to analyze how boards are used and evolve over time. Therefore, the user will be able to understand the behavior that is hidden behind the structure of the board, which facilitates the detection of inefficient uses or errors that reduce the quality of the board.

Keywords: Board-based tools · Board mining · Collaborative Work Management Tools · Design patterns

1 Introduction

Board-Based Collaborative Work Management Tools (BBTs for short) like Trello, Planner, and Asana are widespread and massively used. They are built of three main elements: boards, lists and cards. A board contains a set of lists that can be created, updated or closed by the user. Each of these lists contains a set of cards that can also be created, updated and removed or closed. In addition, cards can be moved from one list to another. These three elements will represent different concepts of the real world depending on the context of the problem.

This work has been funded by grants RTI2018-100763-J-I00 and RTI2018-101204-B-C22 funded by MCIN/ AEI/ 10.13039/501100011033/ and ERDF A way of making Europe; grant P18-FR-2895 funded by Junta de Andalucía/FEDER, UE; and grant US-1381595 (US/JUNTA/FEDER, UE).

J. Troya et al. (Eds.): ICSOC 2022 Workshops, LNCS 13821, pp. 345–349, 2023.
https://doi.org/10.1007/978-3-031-26507-5_30

One common use of BBTs is as low-code tools to manage the processes that support the services an organization provides [1]. Unlike more traditional business process management systems, BBTs do not require a technical team to customize them, but the process execution platform is adapted by their own users by creating, moving, deleting, or updating boards, lists, or cards.

This flexibility brings significant advantages in agile and changing environments because the process execution platform can be configured by the process participants themselves. However, it makes it more prone to errors introduced by the users during the (re-)design and use of the boards, especially caused by the lack of restrictions that these tools impose. For instance, we cannot restrict the movement of cards to follow a specific path, so users could potentially move cards without following a predetermined flow.

The goal of BOARD MINER is to let the user analyze how a board is being used and how it has been used in the past. The input of the tool is a board event log produced by a BBT. These logs capture all the activity that has taken place within the boards during their design and use. Its output is a set of graphical representations and metrics that let the user understand, among others, which is the board design in terms of the lists created and how cards flow through them, which are the structural changes performed in the board over time, and which are the patterns of card creation, update and removal. Knowing the boards' history might be helpful when performing audits as well as to detect why the boards have stopped to be used at some point in time. The user can hence find out whether a board has been used properly and for the purpose for which it was designed. Thus, with the use of this tool one can assess the quality of design and use of the boards, and warn of possible inefficient or improper uses.

Next, we describe BOARD MINER and detail its main characteristics. We conclude by discussing the main innovations of the tool.

2   Description of the Tool

BOARD MINER is an open source library developed in Python that uses the Pandas library to implement board analysis operations[1]. As a library, it can be used as part of a bigger application, or it can be directly used to analyze a board in a Jupyter notebook. The advantage of this approach is that, since it uses the Pandas library, all additional features to analyze data in Python can be used to augment the functionality of BOARD MINER.

The library can directly import a Trello board by means of its public URL using the Trello API. At this moment, only Trello is supported, although support for other BBTs can be easily added by implementing a connector. The main types of analyses that can be performed in BOARD MINER are the following ones.

Board Discovery. As a result of executing the board discovery algorithms included in BOARD MINER, the user can reconstruct the board and understand how it has been used during a selected period of time. The characteristics that

---

[1] The link to the tool is not included on purpose to ensure anonymization.

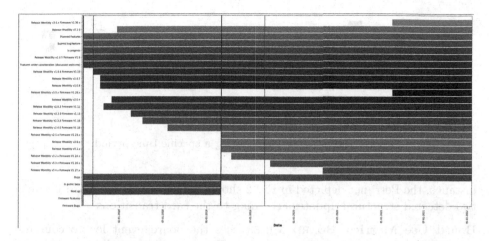

Fig. 1. Evolution of the lists of a board over time (x-axis). Each row represents a list. The vertical lines represent the structural updates (red when it starts and blue when it finishes).(Color figure online)

can be inferred include the *card flow* and the *semantic precedence*. The former relates to whether the cards stay in the same list during their lifetime (no card flow) or, on the contrary, they are moved through board lists. The latter identifies order relationships between lists that cannot be observed in the visual representation of the board. For example, if the lists represent steps of a process, the cards should be moved following specific sequences or rules. Eight board design patterns have been defined in the literature that determine different ways of using a board [2].

Board Evolution Analysis. The user can visually analyze the evolution of the board over time. The actions carried out on the board lists (creating, updating or deleting lists) can reveal whether the use of the board has been consistent or it has changed over time. Structural changes identified in the use of a board may be related to a board redesign. An example of this can be seen in Fig. 1. The vertical lines highlight four moments in which numerous changes in the board lists can be observed (e.g. some lists stop to be used and some start to be used). Looking into this along with the use of cards over time (e.g. whether and how they are moved between lists), changes in the way the board is used can be identified. For instance, the board may not have card flow during a period of time and include card flow afterwards. This may indicate that a different design pattern is being used [2].

Process-Oriented Board Model. BOARD MINER is provided with a log transformation framework that automatically transforms a board event log into a process event log. This is especially useful for boards that follow design patterns that are used to execute processes like the Information Lifecycle and the Process Tasks patterns [2], as the application of process mining algorithms over the resulting event logs allows the discovery of the underlying processes. For

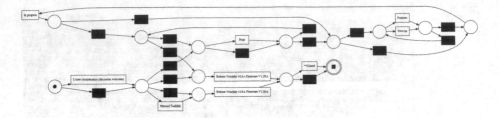

Fig. 2. Petri net of a board during a specific time period.

instance, the Petri net depicted in Fig. 2 shows the behavior of a board between two detected structural updates according to the card transitions.

Board Use Metrics. BOARD MINER uses the board event log to compute metrics that help to characterize its use. These metrics can be grouped into three categories, namely: basic statistics like the number of cards or number of lists; metrics related to card movements like the number of lists with card movement, the percentage of cards with movement, or the average number of movements per card; and metrics related to other actions over cards like the percentage of cards closed, or the average number of updates per card. These metrics help analysts to identify the design pattern that is behind each board.

3   Innovation of the Tool

In this demo, we introduce BOARD MINER, an open-source library to analyze how a board is being used and how it has been used in order to detect problems or to design improvements. Board log data has also been used to analyze how people interact with the boards. Some examples of these approaches are Pisoni et al. [3], which identifies collaboration patterns in surgical research, Shamshurin et al. [4], which assesses participants' performance within educational settings, and Screenful[2], which generates dashboards and reports for software projects.

However, all of these tools have been designed for a specific domain and assume a specific board design. Instead, BOARD MINER can be applied to any domain and does not make any assumption about the board design. Furthermore, unlike these tools, BOARD MINER gives insights about the evolution of the board structure and about how cards are moved through the board lists.

References

1. Khoury, A., Bucknor, A., King, I., Kerstein, R., Nduka, C.: Use of Trello as a project management tool for collaborative surgical research and audit. Br. J. Surg. **109** (2022)

---

[2] https://screenful.com/trello/dashboards-for-trello.

2. Peña, J., Bravo, A., del-Río-Ortega, A., Resinas, M., Ruiz-Cortés, A.: Design patterns for board-based collaborative work management tools. In: La Rosa, M., Sadiq, S., Teniente, E. (eds.) CAiSE 2021. LNCS, vol. 12751, pp. 177–192. Springer, Cham (2021). https://doi.org/10.1007/978-3-030-79382-1_11
3. Pisoni, G., Gijlers, H., Chen, H., Nguyen, T.H.: Collaboration patterns in students' teams working on business cases. In: WSDM Workshops (L2D), vol. 2876, pp. 14–27 (2021)
4. Shamshurin, I., Saltz, J.: A predictive model to identify Kanban teams at risk. Model. Assist. Stat. Appl. **14**, 321–335 (2019)

A Tool for Business Processes Diagnostics

Mahsa Pourbafrani[✉], Firas Gharbi, and Wil M. P. van der Aalst

Chair of Process and Data Science, RWTH Aachen University, Aachen, Germany
{mahsa.bafrani,firas.gharbi,wvdaalst}@pads.rwth-aachen.de

Abstract. Recorded event data of processes inside organizations is a
valuable source for providing insights and information using process mining. Most techniques analyze process executions at detailed levels, e.g.,
process instances, which may result in missing insights. Techniques at
detailed levels using detailed event data should be complemented by techniques at aggregated levels. We designed and developed a standalone tool
for diagnostics in event data of business processes based on both detailed
and aggregated data and techniques. The data-driven framework first
analyzes the event data of processes for possible compliance and performance problems, e.g., bottlenecks in processes. The results are used for
aggregating the event data per window of time, i.e., extracting features
in the time series format. The tool is able to uncover hidden insights
in an explainable manner using time series analysis. The focus of the
tool is to provide a data-driven business process analysis at different levels while reducing the dependencies on the user's domain knowledge for
interpretation and feature engineering steps. The tool is applied to both
real-world and synthetic event data.

Keywords: Process mining · Change point · Event logs · Time series

1 Introduction

A specific activity being performed for a process instance (case) at a specific
point in time is an event. These stored events inside processes form event logs,
i.e., the data source of data-driven process analysis. Tools and techniques to find
such problems, find recurrent patterns, concept drifts, and anomalies, as well as
predict the future state of processes, are of high interest. These diagnostics affect
process performance and understanding of the processes for future improvement.
Techniques such as Dotted Charts [8], visualize the detailed event data of processes and patterns such as the arrival rate of cases and potential concept drifts.
Current tools and techniques mostly rely on the user for interpretation. Moreover, the patterns and insights at higher levels are ignored. In [1], it is discussed
that the drift in the execution of processes can be captured while features are

Funded by the Deutsche Forschungsgemeinschaft (DFG, German Research Foundation)
under Germany's Excellence Strategy-EXC-2023 Internet of Production-390621612. We
also thank the Alexander von Humboldt (AvH) Stiftung for supporting our research.

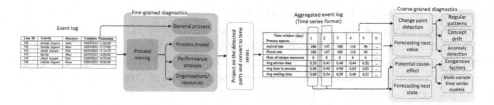

Fig. 1. The framework of the designed tool for data-driven process diagnostics.

defined and the data are transformed into different levels, e.g., calculating the daily arrival rate shows that the order of execution of activities in the process has changed (a concept drift occurred). However, such techniques are limited in feature extraction, dependent on specific diagnostics, and highly subject to the user for both forming features and interpreting the results.

In this paper, we focus on using the idea of systematic transformation of event data to time series data regardless of the process context in [5]. The authors use that for aggregated simulation. Time series and data science techniques can be applied to the aggregated event data. Automatic feature extraction per window of time out of event data and implemented techniques in a user-friendly interface enable the extended analysis of business processes. The data analysis techniques enable the revealing of the hidden patterns inside business processes, e.g., concept drifts, and anomalies. Furthermore, it enables prediction models based on time series models. The tool can be applied to any generic form of event data. The detailed techniques for the application of the time series data of processes' event data have been proposed in [6]. Our tool includes three modules, diagnostics insights at detailed levels, single perspective analysis (process variables), and multiple perspective analysis. The two last modules are based on the generated time series data from the detailed event data at a higher level, e.g., daily, or weekly. Figure 1 shows the framework of the developed tool, including the techniques and modules. A process variable, e.g., arrival rate per window of time, is a process aspect, and multiple process aspects form a process state at a point in time, e.g., the state of the process in a day.

2 Coarse-Grained Diagnostics Architecture and Features

Interesting parts based on process mining techniques, such as an activity with a bottleneck, are pointed out to the user, and the user is redirected to the time series generator modules. Then the generated aggregated event logs are fed into the single aspect analysis, and by selecting each of the aspects, the change points, patterns, and potential anomalies inside a process variable are detected. Change point detection [4], i.e., the discovery of points in a time when the values of the process variables are not consistent with the previous values, represents the behavior of the process w.r.t. that process aspect, e.g., an increase in daily arrival rate every Monday. Moreover, the relationship of each process variable with other variables is assessed. For instance, the increase in the number of cases waiting in the process per week causes an increase in the number of assigned resources. The last module enables uploading different generated time series data sets of processes to assess their relations with each other and the possibility of training time series models based on other process variables. The three main modules of the tool are as follows:

- *Diagnostics Insights* is for detailed performance analysis of activities, resources, and organization.
- *Single Perspective Analysis* is for detecting the change points in a single process aspect, i.e., patterns, concept drifts, and anomalies. The implemented techniques are PELT [3], Binary Segmentation, and Kolmogorov Smirnov [4]. The differences are in the search of the subsequences for the change points [6]. For relation detection, the Granger Causality test is implemented [2].
- *Multiple Perspective Analysis* is for the relations among different process aspects and whether they have causal effect relations are assessed in this module. This module employs multivariate time series analysis [7].

Technical Implementation. The tool is implemented in Python and uses the Flask library and is available as a web application. Each module is available for separate usage and integration with different platforms.

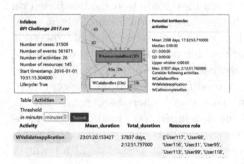

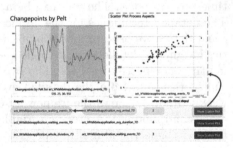

Fig. 2. A Screenshot of coarse-grained diagnostics tool using BPIC'17. (Color figure online)

Fig. 3. A Screenshot of the aspect analysis results for the process aspect analysis using BPIC'17.

3   Application Domain and Scenarios in Practice

The source code and the event logs are publicly available.[1] We show the presented tabs and modules using screenshots of their output in practice. Figure 2 shows the diagnostic insights tab for the real-world event log, BPIC'17 [9]. The performance

---

[1] https://github.com/mbafrani/Coarse-grained-Process-Diagnostics.

analysis reveals a bottleneck in activity *W Validate Application* shown in red in Fig. 2. The process model, deviation, and performance information are provided as the results of the first step. The results are also provided for resources and organizations.

Fig. 4. A Screenshot of coarse-grained diagnostics tool for the process aspect analysis.

Fig. 5. A screenshot of the analyzing multiple aspects module in the coarse-grained analysis tool.

Using these detailed insights, we transform the event log into time series data sets for the detected activity over the steps of time to look for undiscovered insights. The parameters and different implemented techniques in single aspect analysis are presented in Fig. 4. The seasonality, linear and nonlinear Granger Causality, and different introduced change point detection techniques, can be assessed on the transformed data. For forecasting and training time series models for a single variable, the number of periods to predict is input. For instance, the cause and effect relation between the number of waiting cases and the average arrival rate in the detected activities in BPIC'17 has been detected with lag 2. The scatter plot of the relation, and the change points can be seen in Fig. 3. The same can be investigated for all the variables and their relations, among other variables. In Fig. 5, a screenshot for multiple perspective analysis is shown. This module performs the analysis among different aspects and process logs, such as using multivariate time series analysis [7]. Our tool is designed to support users in analyzing their processes with less dependency. The aim is to fill the gap by transforming event logs into a higher level of time granularity where the hidden insights at the detailed level are discovered.

References

1. Bose, R.P.J.C., van der Aalst, W.M.P., Žliobaitė, I., Pechenizkiy, M.: Handling concept drift in process mining. In: Mouratidis, H., Rolland, C. (eds.) Advanced Information Systems Engineering, pp. 391–405 (2011)
2. Granger, C.: Some recent development in a concept of causality. J. Econometrics **39**(1), 199–211 (1988)

3. Killick, R., Fearnhead, P., Eckley, I.A.: Optimal detection of changepoints with a linear computational cost. J. Am. Stat. Assoc. **107**(500), 1590–1598 (2012)
4. Martjushev, J., Bose, R.P.J.C., van der Aalst, W.M.P.: Change point detection and dealing with gradual and multi-order dynamics in process mining. In: Matulevičius, R., Dumas, M. (eds.) BIR 2015. LNBIP, vol. 229, pp. 161–178. Springer, Cham (2015). https://doi.org/10.1007/978-3-319-21915-8_11
5. Pourbafrani, M., van der Aalst, W.M.P.: PMSD: data-driven simulation using system dynamics and process mining. In: Proceedings of Demonstration & Resources Track at BPM 2020, vol. 2673, pp. 77–81. CEUR-WS.org (2020)
6. Pourbafrani, M., Gharbi, F., van der Aalst, W.M.P.: Process diagnostics at coarse-grained levels. In: Proceedings of the 24th International Conference on Enterprise Information Systems, ICEIS 2022, vol. 1, pp. 484–491 (2022)
7. Reinsel, G.C.: Elements of multivariate time series analysis. In: Elements of Multivariate Time Series Analysis (1995)
8. Song, M., van der Aalst, W.M.P.: Supporting process mining by showing events at a glance. In: WITS, pp. 139–145 (2007)
9. van Dongen, B.F.: BPIC 2017. Eindhoven University of Technology (2017)

Node4Chain: Extending Node-RED Low-Code Tool for Monitoring Blockchain Networks

Jesús Rosa-Bilbao(✉)🆔 and Juan Boubeta-Puig🆔

UCASE Software Engineering Research Group, Department of Computer Science and Engineering, University of Cadiz, Avda. de la Universidad de Cádiz 10, 11519 Puerto Real, Cádiz, Spain
jesus.rosabilbao@alum.uca.es, juan.boubeta@uca.es

Abstract. Blockchain is a distributed, secure and leading technology that enables the immutability, traceability and transparency of data. Nevertheless, integrating blockchain network monitoring with other systems is a difficult task that requires a vast knowledge of the technology. To deal with this challenge, in this demo we present Node4Chain, a novel extension of the Node-RED low-code tool that allows for defining graphical flows that specify data inputs, outputs and processing logic needed to monitor in real time blockchain networks, such as Ethereum, Binance or Polygon, as well as integrating it with other systems and technologies.

Keywords: Blockchain · Low-code · Monitoring · Tool

1 Introduction

Blockchain is a cutting-edge technology that enables the exchange of assets without the need for intermediaries [2]. Mainly, it is a distributed ledger database in which cryptography is used to sign transactions. Once mined, transactions are grouped into blocks. These blocks are cryptographically linked to the previous block once it has been validated. Moreover, the distribution of all transactions in the network allows for high traceability and security [5].

Nevertheless, the use of blockchain technology requires vast knowledge and experience, so it is not accessible to everyone. For this reason, being able to integrate blockchain-based solutions with other systems is a cumbersome task. For example, a person who is an expert in other technologies, but not in blockchain,

This work was supported by the Spanish Ministry of Science and Innovation and the European Regional Development Fund (ERDF) under projects FAME [RTI2018-093608-B-C33] and AwESOMe [PID2021-122215NB-C33], the Andalusian Plan for Research, Development and Innovation and ERDF under project DECISION [P20_00865], and the Research Plan from the University of Cadiz and Grupo Energético de Puerto Real S.A. under project GANGES [IRTP03_UCA].

J. Troya et al. (Eds.): ICSOC 2022 Workshops, LNCS 13821, pp. 355–358, 2023.
https://doi.org/10.1007/978-3-031-26507-5_32

will find it difficult to monitor and manage a blockchain network [4]. We consider monitoring as the ability of a system to obtain real-time blockchain data.

Currently, there are some solutions capable of monitoring blockchain networks. As an example, Blockchair [1] is a block explorer and analyzer for monitoring all blockchain network transactions of user accounts and smart contracts. It allows us to monitor when a block has been mined, the number of transactions per block and the rewards miners receive for mining blocks, among others. However, as other state-of-the-art tools, Blockchair does not allow the monitoring of different blockchain networks at the same time, nor does it allow the graphical definition of data flows that facilitate their integration with other external systems.

To address these challenges, in this demonstration we propose Node4Chain, a new extension of the well-known Node-RED [3] low-code tool that allows users to monitor different blockchain networks, such as Ethereum, Binance or Polygon, in real time and at the same time. Specifically, this tool allows users to intuitively define graphical data flows where they specify inputs, outputs and the processing logic needed to integrate real-time monitoring of the elements of a given blockchain network together with other systems and technologies.

2 Our Proposal: Node4Chain

Figure 1 provides an overview of our proposed Node4Chain architecture for supporting the extension of the Node-RED low-code tool for real-time blockchain monitoring. This architecture is composed of two main layers, as detailed below.

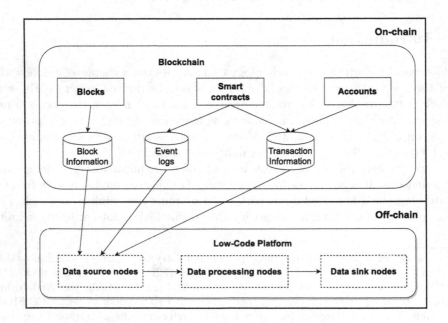

Fig. 1. Overview of the proposed Node4Chain architecture.

2.1 On-Chain Layer

The on-chain layer is composed of several elements that can be found in a blockchain network. These elements are mainly accounts, smart contracts and blocks. Smart contracts can be deployed in a blockchain network, resulting in the creation of transactions. These transactions are grouped into blocks.

As illustrated in Fig. 1, a blockchain network contains information about blocks, smart contracts and accounts, among others. This information provides details of items such as block number, transactions that form a block, transaction number or the cost of gas. All these data can be consumed automatically and in real time by various data nodes.

All monitored information from the blockchain network can be used to control accounts, contracts or specific events. Among other advantages, our proposal allows listening in real time to the transactions whose origin or destination is a public address of an account or smart contract to which we have subscribed.

2.2 Off-Chain Layer

The off-chain layer provides the low-code platform. This platform is made up of nodes. Nodes are each of the functionalities that can be graphically modeled within the low-code platform in the form of graphical flows. Currently, Node-RED has some nodes that allow connection to external systems. For example, through databases or message brokers. However, to the best of our knowledge, there are no nodes similar to the ones proposed in this demo, i.e., Node-RED does not provide any element (node) to monitor a blockchain network in real time. For this reason, we propose the extension of the Node-RED tool through the creation of new nodes to monitor a blockchain network in real time. Each of the new nodes has a specific functionality. These nodes have to be included in the editor palette so that they can be graphically modeled in the editor flows, as explained below.

Specifically, in this demo we present the development of five new nodes. Their functionalities are as follows:

- **Block Listener**: it is a listener that receives all the hashes of new blocks mined on a blockchain network.
- **Transaction Listener**: it is a listener that receives all the hashes of new transactions mined on a blockchain network.
- **Address Subscription**: it is a listener that receives all hashes of new transactions mined on a blockchain network from a specific public address of an account or smart contract.
- **Transaction Details**: it gets all the details of a transaction that is already mined on a blockchain network from its hash.
- **Block Details**: it gets all the details of a block that is already mined on a blockchain network from its hash.

Through all these new nodes, end users will be able to monitor a blockchain network. One of the advantages is that they can monitor what is happening in the network without applying any filter, for example, obtaining in real time all the new blocks being mined on the network. Another advantage is being able to visualize in real time the interactions of public addresses with a blockchain network. These public addresses can be filtered. Thanks to the data transparency of some blockchain networks, such as Ethereum, Binance or Polygon, no additional permissions are required for blockchain data to be visualized in real time by any person or contract.

A practical demonstration of Node4Chain is available at https://youtu.be/8PgxGez9qBA. This video shows how this tool works and highlights the functionalities and some of the advantages mentioned in this paper.

3   Conclusions

In this demo, we propose Node4Chain, a novel extension of the well-known Node-RED low-code tool. This extension allows for real-time monitoring of a blockchain network through the real-time gathering of information on blocks, transactions, user accounts and/or smart contracts deployed in a blockchain network.

By using this extension, end users can, among other things, to obtain in real time all the new blocks that are mined in a network or to visualize in real time the interactions of public addresses with a blockchain network. In addition, users can use filters to obtain information only from the desired public addresses. Moreover, due to the transparency of Ethereum Virtual Machine (EVM)-based blockchain networks, no permissions are required to obtain data from such networks.

As future work, we plan to extend the tool to support other non-EVM based blockchain networks, such as Cardano, Solana or Polkadot.

References

1. Blockchair: https://blockchair.com/es (2022). Accessed 29 Sept 2022
2. Boubeta-Puig, J., Rosa-Bilbao, J., Mendling, J.: CEPchain: a graphical model-driven solution for integrating complex event processing and blockchain. Expert Syst. Appl. **184**, 115578 (2021). https://doi.org/10.1016/j.eswa.2021.115578
3. OpenJS Foundation: Node-RED. https://nodered.org/ (2022). Accessed 4 Oct 2022
4. Rosa-Bilbao, J., Boubeta-Puig, J., Rutle, A.: EDALoCo: enhancing the accessibility of blockchains through a low-code approach to the development of event-driven applications for smart contract management. Comput. Stan. Interfaces **84**, 103676 (2023). https://doi.org/10.1016/j.csi.2022.103676
5. Yaga, D.J., Mell, P.M., Roby, N., Scarfone, K.: Blockchain technology overview. NIST Pubs 8202, NIST, Gaithersburg, MD (2018). https://doi.org/10.6028/NIST.IR.8202

Service-Oriented Integration
of SuperTuxKart

Robin D. Pesl[✉][iD], Uwe Breitenbücher[iD], Ilche Georgievski[iD],
and Marco Aiello[iD]

Institute of Architecture of Application Systems, University of Stuttgart,
Stuttgart, Germany
{robin.pesl,uwe.breitenbuecher,ilche.georgievski,
marco.aiello}@iaas.uni-stuttgart.de

Abstract. Recent developments in the automotive industry show a rising demand for in-car gaming and entertainment. Series-produced vehicles offer high-performance hardware, displays, sensors, and actors, which can be used for gaming. This trend was recently confirmed in particular by the Mercedes-Benz Group AG, which integrated the racing game SuperTuxKart in its series-produced Mercedes-Benz CLA Coupé. However, integrating and interacting with C++ games, such as SuperTuxKart, is cumbersome as developers need deep technical knowledge about the internal structure of the game and its APIs. This makes development processes time consuming, knowledge-intensive, and error-prone. To overcome this issue, we developed (i) a domain model for SuperTuxKart and (ii) a REST API supporting this model. The developed API serves as an abstraction layer that enables developers as well as researchers to integrate SuperTuxKart in a service-oriented manner into other applications.

Keywords: SuperTuxKart · REST API · Integration · In-car gaming

1 Introduction

SuperTuxKart[1] is a 3D open-source kart racing game, which is a natural candidate for *in-car gaming* as well as for creating automotive demonstrators and case studies in this rising field. One impressive use as a demonstrator was shown at the Mobile World Congress 2019 where the Mercedes-Benz Group AG showed the integration of SuperTuxKart into the Mercedes-Benz CLA Coupé line, which they refer to as *"a game console on wheels"* [3]. The game was executed on the CLA's internal entertainment system using the screen in the center console as well as the car's audio system for in-game sounds. The gas pedal, brake, and steering wheel were used as input devices. To make the in-car gaming even more immersive, the airstream of the air conditioning was adjusted to match

---

[1] https://supertuxkart.net/.

J. Troya et al. (Eds.): ICSOC 2022 Workshops, LNCS 13821, pp. 359–363, 2023.
https://doi.org/10.1007/978-3-031-26507-5_33

the velocity and the airflow in-game. Moreover, the ambient light was used to mirror the ambient in-game and the driver's seat reacted to the movements of the kart, e.g., by fastening the seat belt. The main objective of this showcase was to demonstrate the abilities of the in-car user-experience system as well as to adapt to the rising gamification trend and interest in video games [3]. SuperTuxKart was also used in other automotive demonstrators, which shows its practical relevance [2,4].

Besides integrating games such as SuperTuxKart into cars there are many more use cases in which an integration of such games into other applications is desirable. For example, to integrate smart home systems with the gaming experience of game consoles. As a result, to take advantage of these possibilities, *there is a need for easy integration of games into other applications*. However, currently, such integration requires a deep technical understanding of the internals of the games. For example, SuperTuxKart is written in C++ and exposes no API that could be directly used by external applications. Thus, this makes integration a complex and time-consuming task, which results from the lack of a means to efficiently integrate and externally control the game and to enable bidirectional data exchange between the game and other IT systems.

In this paper, we tackle these issues by demonstrating how service-orientation can be used to ease such kinds of integration based on the example of Super-TuxKart. The contributions are twofold: We (i) introduce a *domain model for SuperTuxKart*, which provides the foundation (ii) for a new open-source *REST API* that enables accessing and controlling the game based on HTTP requests. Thus, developers need no knowledge about the internal structure and implementation of SuperTuxKart but can use an HTTP-based service interface as it is common today in modern software architectures. Please note that the API supports changing the resources in the running game, e.g., the weather, the music, or the karts themselves, but provides no functionalities for real-time driving.

2   Domain Model for SuperTuxKart

A domain model lists the most relevant resources and sets them into relation. It is therefore useful to get an overview of the involved resources and how they interconnect. The presented domain model is extracted from the SuperTuxKart class hierarchy and represents the subset of all SuperTuxKart resources that are appropriate for external access and control. The resulting class hierarchy is shown in Fig. 1. Attributes are omitted for the sake of brevity, but details can be found online[2]. Gray-hued resources are only accessible while a race is running.

3   REST API for SuperTuxKart

We mapped the domain model directly to a REST API. Each class of the domain model corresponds to an endpoint of the API managing that resource. Multiplicity is realized as resource collections, where individual instances can be obtained

---

[2] https://github.com/rpesl/stk-code/blob/main/doc/Domain-Model.svg.

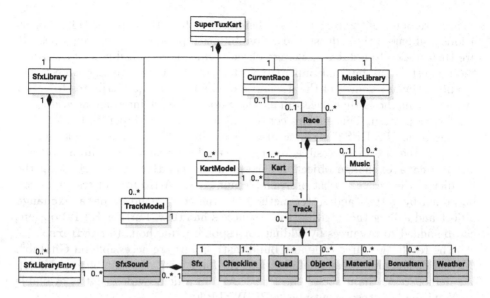

Fig. 1. SuperTuxKart domain model as UML class diagram.

by appending the resource identifier to the URI of the collection. The root level resource is *SuperTuxKart* and corresponds therefore to /. The addressing scheme is thereby derived from the name of the resources, e.g., the *TrackModels* are accessible under /*tracks*. Subresources are addressable via their parent, e.g., the objects within a race are available at /*races*/{*raceId*}/*objects*. The complete OpenAPI specification of the API is available online[3].

The REST API is implemented by extending the SuperTuxKart C++ code base with the proposed REST functionality over HTTP. Its usage is eased by facilitating the standards JSON, for resource exchange, and ZIP, for multi-file input. The handling of the HTTP requests is done in parallel to the game logic to not interrupt the gameplay. The synchronization between HTTP requests and the game is performed in the time between the computation of two frames. Errors are transformed into HTTP messages with corresponding status codes.

The request processing in the API internally works as follows. The REST API is realized using an HTTP library[4], which listens to a specific port and parses the HTTP requests. The interaction with this library is realized via a callback mechanism, which is encapsulated in the API's `Server` class. When a request arrives, a callback is invoked. The callback parses the request's path and path parameters and forwards it to a `handler` based on the request's path. The mapping between paths and handlers is done by a list maintained within the server, which contains pairs of a handler and a regular expression representing a certain path. Each `handler` is responsible for handling the HTTP operations of

---

[3] https://github.com/rpesl/stk-code/blob/main/doc/REST-API-OpenAPI.yaml.
[4] https://github.com/yhirose/cpp-httplib.

a single resource of the REST API. Therefore, it offers the exposed HTTP operations and parses the request body. Possible path parameters and request body are then passed to a `data exchange` object, which is responsible for forwarding the request to the internal SuperTuxKart logic. A `data exchange` object represents a single resource of the domain model and maps its attributes to getter and setter methods that encapsulate the SuperTuxKart internals according to the facade pattern. This enables convenient access to the SuperTuxKart code.

Based on the REST architectural style, this realization is extensible, for example, the list of accessible resources can be extended by simply adding another `data exchange` object, a corresponding `handler`, and registering the handler in the `server's` list of available `handlers`. Attributes of resources can be added by getter- and setter-methods to the corresponding `data exchange` object and calling them within the resource's `handler`. Further HTTP options can be added to resources by adding corresponding methods to `handlers`.

The resulting source code and build instructions are accessible on GitHub[5]. Further documentation and details about the implementation can be found in [1]. We demonstrate the usage of the REST API in a demo video that is available on YouTube at https://youtu.be/2zBBiWXkR30.

4   Concluding Remarks

To ease the integration of games such as SuperTuxKart, we propose the usage of a REST API as an abstraction layer to the game's source code and internals. This enables accessing and controlling of in-game resources during the game based on service-orientation, which reduces the complexity of integrating such games. A major limitation of our approach is the lacking support for real-time stream input, e.g., for input devices and multi-player features. This may be mitigated by extending the API with WebSocket capabilities. Another goal for future research is to develop an abstraction framework that generally supports and guides developers in making game internals accessible via REST APIs as we demonstrated in this paper for SuperTuxKart and also for other games.

Acknowledgements. This work was partially funded by the German Federal Ministry for Economic Affairs and Climate Action (BMWK) project Software-Defined Car (SofDCar) (19S21002).

References

1. Pesl, R.D.: Concepts for Advanced Integration of SuperTuxKart into Connected Cars. Master's thesis, University of Stuttgart (2021). https://doi.org/10.18419/opus-11884. Accessed 04 Nov 2022
2. Raviglione, F., Malinverno, M., Casetti, C.: Demo: open source platform for IEEE 802.11p NICs evaluation. In: 2019 IEEE 20th International Symposium on "A World of Wireless, Mobile and Multimedia Networks" (WoWMoM), pp. 1–3 (2019). https://doi.org/10.1109/WoWMoM.2019.8793023. Accessed 04 Nov 2022

---

[5] https://github.com/rpesl/stk-code.

3. Sattler, S.: In-car Gaming at Mercedes-Benz | Mercedes-Benz Group (2019). https://
group.mercedes-benz.com/magazine/technology-innovation/in-car-gaming.html.
Accessed 04 Nov 2022
4. Vetter, A., Obergfell, P., Guissouma, H., Grimm, D., Rumez, M., Sax, E.: Development processes in automotive service-oriented architectures. In: 2020 9th Mediter-
ranean Conference on Embedded Computing (MECO), pp. 1–7 (2020). https://doi.
org/10.1109/MECO49872.2020.9134175. Accessed 04 Nov 2022

Using Open API for the Development of Hybrid Classical-Quantum Services

Javier Romero-Álvarez[1] , Jaime Alvarado-Valiente[1]([✉]) , Enrique Moguel[1] ,
José García-Alonso[1] , and Juan M. Murillo[2]

[1] University of Extremadura, Badajoz, Spain
{jromero,jaimeav,enrique,jgaralo}@unex.es
[2] Computing and Advanced Technologies Foundation of Extremadura,
Badajoz, Spain
juan.murillo@cenits.es

Abstract. Quantum Computing has started to demonstrate its first practical applications. As the technology develops to a point of maturity that allows quantum computers to expand commercially, large companies such as Google, Microsoft, IBM and Amazon are making a considerably effort to make them accessible through the cloud so that research and industry initiatives can test their capabilities. The characteristics of this paradigm and the lack of mature tools still make the process of defining, implementing, and running quantum, or hybrid classical-quantum software systems difficult compared with the procedures used for pure classical ones. To address this lack, we present a demonstration of a method for defining quantum services and the automatic generation of the corresponding source code through an extension of the Open API Specification. In this demo we present an extension that enables developers to define quantum services with a high abstraction level, link them with quantum circuits, and generate the source code of the service to be deployed in a quantum computer in the same way they do for classical services.

Keywords: Service engineering · Quantum software · Hybrid classical-quantum services · Open API

1 Introduction and Motivation

Quantum computing is a young topic attracting increased interest among researchers and industry [1]. However the technology is still immature and, as Gartner identifies [2], it will take at least 10 more years of technology hype before it starts to deliver value. The same firm also encourages companies to break through now by setting up working groups, select high-impact use cases and prioritize quantum skills development. All the above with the aim of paving the way for their future incorporation into the productive sectors.

To make advances in quantum computing accessible to companies and research teams, leading manufacturers are already investing considerable efforts in making their technologies accessible through the cloud [3,4]. Companies like Amazon have even begun to play a leading role in the market as brokers for access to quantum computers [5]. This effort is also justified by the fact that it is now commonly accepted that future computing systems will be hybrids (classical/quantum) with both parties interacting following the principles of service-oriented computing [6].

Thus, the technology now being developed for the purpose of enabling the access to quantum computers will form the basis for making it possible to have complex software systems with classical and quantum interacting components. In these systems, quantum components and algorithms will coexist with classical pieces of software, and one of the best known ways for heterogeneous components to coexist is through service oriented computing [7]. Significant efforts are already being devoted in this path for both, the industry that is focusing on providing access to quantum computers following the traditional PaaS scheme and the research community that is focusing on the use of Service Oriented Computing for the development of hybrid software systems [8,9].

Nevertheless, the development and operation of quantum service oriented software is still a complex task very different to the development of classical services to which professional are used to [10].

To address this, in this demo we present and adaptation of the Open API tools to support quantum services. Open API is one of the most widely used standards for API description and, for this purpose, defines a vendor-independent description format for REST-compliant services [11].

By allowing the creation of quantum services through the use of Open API, we not only simplify the process of creating this services but also facilitate the transition from classical services developers by providing them with the same set of tools and support mechanism they are used to.

2 Open API Specification for Quantum Services

To implement a classic service using Open API, a developer needs to combine two main aspects. The business logic of the service, which is specific to each service, and the endpoint of the service. To this end, using the specification provided by Open API and a standard interface, that is language-independent for RESTful APIs, the service endpoint is defined.

Based on this specification and by using a source code generator, the code structure is generated, in a programming language chosen by the developer, where the business logic of the service is also added to have a fully operative web service.

The code generator called Open API Generator[1] will be modified to support the process of defining and creating quantum web services. To achieve this, an extension of the Open API specification, including custom properties, and an

---

[1] https://openapi-generator.tech/.

extension of the Open API Generator, to allow defining and generating code for quantum applications, have been developed.[2]

In this way, starting from an Open API specification, enriched with custom quantum properties, and a quantum circuit it is possible to automatically generate the source code of the quantum service. For this work, we will use the Python programming language for the generated services, as it is one of the most widely used languages in quantum software development [12]. Anyway, the programming language for the generation of quantum services can also be changed to any other language supported by the Open API Generator with the appropriate modifications to support quantum services.

In order to carry out the generation of hybrid classical-quantum services, the following process is proposed, which is depicted in the Fig. 1.

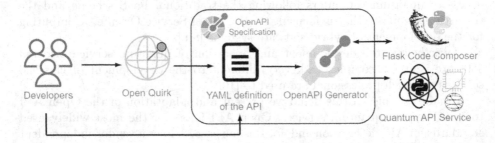

Fig. 1. Quantum services definition process with Open API

The first step is to define the business logic of the service as a quantum circuit using the Open Quirk Composer[3]. At the same time, the endpoints of the desired services have to be defined using the Open API Specification (using a YAML definition of the API).

Later, the defined circuit has to be linked with the specific endpoint that is going to be used to access that business logic. In order to do that, the Quirk URL of the circuit has to be included in the YAML specification of the API.

After that, the proposed extension of the Open API code generator is used to generate the source code of the quantum services. The generated source code uses Flask[4], a widely used and lightweight Python web application framework, to compose the code from the provided quantum circuit and API specification.

Finally, developers can deploy the generated quantum API services and make RESTful calls to the endpoints of the API, which encapsulate the code of the quantum algorithm. Currently, two quantum hardware providers are supported by the extension of the Open API Generator, Amazon Braket and IBM Quantum. Therefore, the generated quantum services have to be executed through one of those providers.

---

[2] https://github.com/JaimeAlvaradoValiente/QuantumOpenAPI.git.

[3] https://algassert.com/quirk.

[4] https://flask.palletsprojects.com/.

3 Conclusion

In this demo, we have proposed a method to standarize the definition process of quantum services using the Open API Specification and provided an extension to the Open API Generator able to generate the source code of quantum services from an API specification and a quantum circuit. This way, service developers that are familiar with high-level abstraction tools that simplify the development and deployment process of classical services can have an easier transition to quantum service development. To validate the proposal, we have used Flask classical services that encapsulates quantum circuits. Therefore, it is feasible to automatically generate REST APIs that include quantum services starting from an Open API Specification. The generated services can be invoked using classical Service-Oriented Computing tools and, therefore, the creation and use of Quantum APIs can be integrated in a more traditional Service-oriented development process.

Acknowledgments. This work was supported by the projects PID2021-124054OB-C31 funded by the Spanish Ministry of Science and Innovation; QSalud Project; GR21133 and GR21183 funded by the Department of Economy, Science and Digital Agenda of the Government of Extremadura and the European Regional Development Fund (ERDF); and by the Ministry of Economic Affairs and Digital Transformation of the Spanish Government through the Quantum ENIA project call - Quantum Spain project, and by the European Union through the Recovery, Transformation and Resilience Plan - NextGenerationEU within the framework of the Digital Spain 2025 Agenda.

References

1. Zhao, J.: Quantum software engineering: landscapes and horizons (2020). https://arxiv.org/abs/2007.07047
2. G. Research: Hype cycle for compute infrastructure (2021). https://www.gartner.com/en/documents/4003921
3. Devitt, S.J.: Performing quantum computing experiments in the cloud. Phys. Rev. A **94**(3), 032329 (2016)
4. Soeparno, H., Perbangsa, A.S.: Cloud quantum computing concept and development: a systematic literature review. Procedia Comput. Sci. **179**, 944–954 (2021)
5. Gonzalez, C.: Cloud based QC with Amazon Braket. Digit. Welt **5**(2), 14–17 (2021)
6. Karalekas, P.J., Tezak, N.A., Peterson, E.C., Ryan, C.A., da Silva, M.P., Smith, R.S.: A quantum-classical cloud platform optimized for variational hybrid algorithms. Quantum Sci. Technol. **5**(2), 024003 (2020)
7. Moguel, E., Rojo, J., Valencia, D., Berrocal, J., Garcia-Alonso, J., Murillo, J.M.: Quantum service-oriented computing: current landscape and challenges. Softw. Qual. J. 1–20 (2022). https://link.springer.com/article/10.1007/s11219-022-09589-y
8. Junior, P.E.Z., de Camargo, V.V.: A systematic mapping on quantum software development in the context of software engineering, arXiv e-prints, pp. arXiv-2106 (2021)

9. Kumara, I., Van Den Heuvel, W.-J., Tamburri, D.A.: QSOC: quantum service-oriented computing. In: Barzen, J. (ed.) SummerSOC 2021. CCIS, vol. 1429, pp. 52–63. Springer, Cham (2021). https://doi.org/10.1007/978-3-030-87568-8_3

10. Rojo, J., Valencia, D., Berrocal, J., Moguel, E., Garcia-Alonso, J., Rodriguez, J.M.M.: Trials and tribulations of developing hybrid quantum-classical microservices systems. In: Pérez-Castillo, R., Serrano, M.A., Piattini, M. (eds.), Short Papers Proceedings of the 2nd International Workshop on Software Engineering & Technology (Q-SET 2021) co-located with IEEE International Conference on Quantum Computing and Engineering (IEEE Quantum Week 2021), Virtual Conference, 19 October 2021, ser. CEUR Workshop Proceedings, vol. 3008, pp. 38–53. CEUR-WS.org (2021)

11. Schwichtenberg, S., Gerth, C., Engels,G.: From open API to semantic specifications and code adapters. In: 2017 IEEE International Conference on Web Services (ICWS), pp. 484–491. IEEE (2017)

12. Silva, V.: Practical Quantum Computing for Developers: Programming Quantum Rigs in the Cloud using Python, Quantum Assembly Language and IBM QExperience. Apress, Berkeley, CA (2018). https://doi.org/10.1007/978-1-4842-4218-6

Quokka: A Service Ecosystem for Workflow-Based Execution of Variational Quantum Algorithms

Martin Beisel[1]([✉])[iD], Johanna Barzen[1][iD], Simon Garhofer[2][iD],
Frank Leymann[1][iD], Felix Truger[1][iD], Benjamin Weder[1][iD],
and Vladimir Yussupov[1][iD]

[1] University of Stuttgart, Universitätsstr. 38, 70569 Stuttgart, Germany
`{beisel,barzen,leymann,truger,weder,yussupov}@iaas.uni-stuttgart.de`
[2] University of Tübingen, Sand 13, 72076 Tübingen, Germany
`simon.garhofer@uni-tuebingen.de`

Abstract. Hybrid quantum-classical applications are often implemented as monolithic applications that comprise various tightly-coupled classical and quantum tasks. However, the lifecycle of such applications can benefit from using service-oriented architectures, as they simplify scalable and resilient deployments and improve development processes by decoupling complex processes into more comprehensible work packages. In this demonstration, we (i) introduce Quokka, a service ecosystem that facilitates workflow-based development and execution of quantum applications by providing dedicated services for implementing each task in variational quantum algorithms. Further, (ii) we show how it can be used to orchestrate an example quantum application using workflows.

Keywords: Quantum computing · Microservices · Workflows · SoC

1 Motivation: Quantum Applications as Workflows

Quantum computing enables solving various problems with improved precision and in a more time- and energy-efficient manner by leveraging quantum mechanical phenomena, such as superposition and entanglement. However, quantum algorithms depend on multiple pre- and post-processing tasks that often need to be executed on classical hardware, e.g., data preparation, result analysis, and parameter optimization. As currently available *Noisy Intermediate-Scale Quantum (NISQ)* devices are error-prone, the majority of today's quantum algorithms are designed as so-called *Variational Quantum Algorithms (VQAs)* [2]. VQAs alternate between executing parameterized quantum circuits on a quantum device and classically optimizing the quantum circuit parameters by evaluating the quality of execution results. Moreover, quantum devices are not suitable for many traditional tasks, such as data persistence or visualization, which makes them rather special co-processors that complement classical computers.

J. Troya et al. (Eds.): ICSOC 2022 Workshops, LNCS 13821, pp. 369–373, 2023.
https://doi.org/10.1007/978-3-031-26507-5_35

Quantum applications are, hence, inherently hybrid and must be designed with classical and quantum perspectives as well as their integration in mind [4].

While software engineering research is well-established for classical software, the topic of quantum software engineering is still in its early stage, with several works investigating the applicability of classical software engineering paradigms to quantum software [4]. In particular, workflow-based execution of quantum applications has multiple advantages brought by workflow technology, such as robustness, scalability, and reusability of created models [3]. To facilitate the modeling of quantum workflows, a quantum-specific BPMN extension has been developed, introducing a set of custom-tailored quantum-related tasks. Figure 1 shows an example workflow model for solving the *Travelling Salesman Problem (TSP)* using the *Quantum Approximate Optimization Algorithm (QAOA)*. As a prerequisite, users need to specify the TSP problem instance as an adjacency matrix and decide on hyperparameter for the workflow execution, which are passed to the workflow engine on workflow instantiation. After instantiation, the circuit for the given TSP problem instance is *(i) generated* and *(ii) executed*. Subsequently, occurred readout errors need to be *(iii) mitigated* and the execution result's quality is *(iv) evaluated*. Finally, the circuit parameters are *(v) optimized until convergence*. The result of the algorithm's last iteration is the final solution, which could be analyzed, e.g., by a following user task.

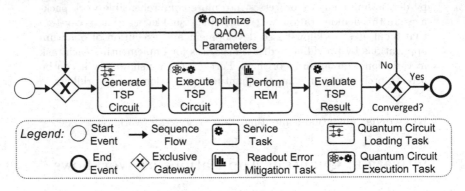

Fig. 1. Overview of a typical quantum workflow implementing a VQA.

The currently predominant way to implement such integrations of classical and quantum tasks is to use monoliths instead of workflows. However, hybrid quantum-classical applications can benefit from architectural styles such as microservice-based architectures that promote distribution, loose coupling, and better modularization. Employing these concepts leads to various advantages, such as reusability, maintainability, robustness, or scalability that improve the development and operations process. In particular, the reuse of existing and well-tested components leads to a cheaper, less repetitive and less error-prone development process with increased time-to-market. To tackle this problem, we (i) introduce QUOKKA, a service ecosystem that simplifies executing different tasks in VQAs, such as generation and execution of quantum circuits as well as readout error mitigation, and (ii) demonstrate how QUOKKA facilitates workflow-based execution of a VQA based on the scenario described in Fig. 1.

2   The Quokka Ecosystem

The workflow model shown in Fig. 1 describes the required steps to determine a suitable route for a given TSP problem instance. However, it does not provide an implementation of these steps, leaving the complex and time-consuming task of implementing them to the developer. By providing a set of microservices for each specific task type, the QUOKKA service ecosystem simplifies implementing these tasks. QUOKKA's system architecture is depicted in Fig. 2, comprising the QUOKKA Gateway and five quantum task-specific microservices. All QUOKKA microservices are implemented in Python, enabling easy integration of the currently predominant Python-based quantum SDKs, including Qiskit and Braket. Furthermore, they follow a modular design, enabling developers to easily extend them and integrate code for specific use cases into the microservices.

QUOKKA Gateway: This Java-based API Gateway facilitates the request routing for clients, by uniting all QUOKKA microservices in a single REST API. It is built upon the *Spring Cloud Gateway* and intercepts and forwards incoming client requests to the respective microservices. Further, features brought by the Spring Cloud Gateway, e.g., monitoring or security, can be taken advantage of.

Circuit Generation Service: Composing quantum circuits is a complex task that is typically performed using quantum SDKs, which provide functions to generate complete quantum circuits but also allow the creation of scripts to assemble custom circuits. The circuit generation service provides on-demand

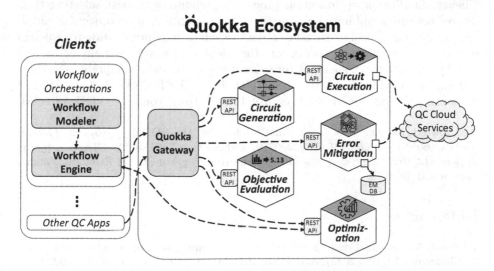

Fig. 2. Overview of the overall system architecture.

circuit implementations for a set of quantum algorithms that users can extend by integrating their custom circuit generation scripts. API requests must include the required parameters for the generation process of the respective quantum algorithm and receive a circuit in the de facto standard language *OpenQASM*.

Circuit Execution Service: This service enables the execution of quantum circuits on various cloud-based quantum devices and simulators. In addition to error-free simulators, the service offers access to noisy simulators capable of simulating device errors, such that an algorithm's performance can be simulated without the common, long queuing times of current quantum devices.

Error Mitigation Service: To improve the quality of noisy execution results, various error mitigation methods, e.g., matrix inversion-based readout error mitigation, can be used via the error mitigation service [1]. These methods typically require up-to-date information about the used quantum device's error rates, which is obtained by executing additional circuits on the device. Since VQAs repeatedly execute similar circuits on the same device, error rates can be saved and reused, significantly improving the efficiency of the error mitigation process.

Objective Evaluation Service: This service enables a quality assessment of the execution result, which, for example, can be used for optimization or benchmarking. To assess an execution result's quality, first, a problem-specific cost function determines the cost of each measured bit string, e.g., traveled distances for a TSP. Subsequently, an objective function is used to compute a single value on the basis of the measurements' frequencies and costs, e.g., the expectation value, describing the overall quality of the result. Furthermore, a graphical representation of the result is provided, e.g., a graph highlighting the best route.

Optimization Service: This service provides a selection of optimizer implementations available for Python, including SciPy and Qiskit Terra optimizers. Clients initialize an optimization process by sending a request selecting their desired optimizer and initial parameters. Once an optimization process is initialized, messaging is used to exchange objective values and optimization parameters between the optimization service and the client, e.g., a workflow engine.

The QUOKKA source code repository, documentation, and a comprehensive tutorial can be found on GitHub: https://github.com/UST-QuAntiL/Quokka. The demonstration video is available on YouTube: https://youtu.be/VQUz9Sj1r4M.

Acknowledgments. This work was funded by the BMWK projects *PlanQK* (01MK20005N), *EniQmA* (01MQ22007B), and *SeQuenC* (01MQ22009B), and by the project *SEQUOIA* funded by the Baden-Wuerttemberg Ministry of Economic Affairs, Labour and Tourism.

References

1. Beisel, M., et al.: Configurable readout error mitigation in quantum workflows. Electronics **11**(19) (2022). Article no. 2983 https://www.mdpi.com/2079-9292/11/19/2983

2. Cerezo, M., et al.: Variational quantum algorithms. Nat. Rev. Phys. **3**(9), 1–20 (2021)
3. Weder, B., et al.: Integrating quantum computing into workflow modeling and execution. In: Proceedings of the 13th IEEE/ACM International Conference on Utility and Cloud Computing (UCC 2020), pp. 279–291. IEEE (2020)
4. Weder, B., et al.: Quantum software development lifecycle. In: Serrano, M.A., Perez-Castillo, R., Piattini, M. (eds.) Quantum Software Engineering, pp. 61–83. Springer, Cham (2022). https://doi.org/10.1007/978-3-031-05324-5_4

SENSEI: Scraper for ENhanced AnalySis to Evaluate Illicit Trends

Daniel De Pascale[1]([✉]), Giuseppe Cascavilla[2], Damian A. Tamburri[2],
and Willem-Jan Van Den Heuvel[1]

[1] Tilburg University - Jheronimus Academy of Data Science,
's-Hertogenbosch, The Netherlands
d.de.pascale@tue.nl
[2] TU/e - Eindhoven University of Technology, Eindhoven, The Netherlands

Abstract. Over the last years, we faced an exponential growth of illegal online market services in the Dark Web, making it easier than ever before of acquiring illicit goods online via a simple service interaction. To study and understand this emerging illegal services economy, we developed a trend analysis and (dark-)web services monitoring tool: SENSEI, which stands for 'Scraper for ENhanced analySis to Evaluate Illicit trends'. SENSEI extracts specific service transaction trends and analyses the human behaviours behind, to produce symmetric insights on specific service transaction habits from both customers and vendors on the Dark Web. Moreover, a trend analysis tool is provided to discover and typify relationships among different criminal activities and hence provide evidence and support investigation activities and Law Enforcement Agencies (LEAs) detecting criminal operations.

Keywords: Dark Web · Trend analysis · LEAs · Illicit goods

1 Introduction

Nowadays, the number of illegal drugs market services is rapidly increasing [3] in the unaccessible area of services and internet computing, also known as, the *Dark Web*. The Dark Web [2] plays a key role in this exponential growth due to its concealed nature, part of the web not indexed by search engines and hence chosen by criminals to build illegal service transactions.

The goal of this work is to build a service transaction investigation platform called SENSEI to help Law Enforcement Agencies (LEAs) analyze big data coming from Dark Web services (e.g., monitoring of drugs movements accross the world). The framework provides a collection of tools for big data analysis to extract valuable insights for cybercrime investigations. The framework's features include but are not limited to trend analysis of specific temporal snapshots, network analysis of vendors, and comparison of trends between different countries to evaluate the movement of illicit goods across the world. Moreover, the platform allows narrowing the field, acting on a specific time range to provide more specific information. To the best of our knowledge, SENSEI is the

© The Author(s), under exclusive license to Springer Nature Switzerland AG 2023
J. Troya et al. (Eds.): ICSOC 2022 Workshops, LNCS 13821, pp. 374–383, 2023.
https://doi.org/10.1007/978-3-031-26507-5_36

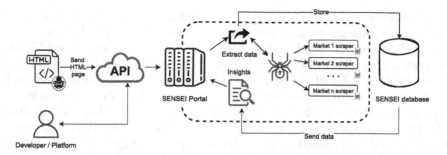

Fig. 1. Overview of the SENSEI SOA architecture, following the classical storing/retrieving cycle.

first open-source proof of concept platform for big data analysis on crime and user behavior activities from the Dark Web. Major big data analysis platforms like those offered by technologies such as Palantir[1] which result in expensive licensing and are often limited in their analytic and architectural extensibility capacity. Conversely, SENSEI relays solely on open-source technologies to provide an accessible analysis platform.

2   SENSEI Solution Architecture

SENSEI platform relies on a Service-Oriented Architecture (SOA) to store and retrieve insights from Dark Web pages and on a web platform to show them, instrumenting each analysis with explanatory narratives that explain the results.

SENSEI SOA allows interaction with the end-user by implementing a RESTful API architecture. The architecture enacts endpoints clustered into two main categories: *Load services*, to load new HTML files (or a zip HTML file) and store the information into a database (DB) and *Get services*, to collect and group the information stored from the database to visualize the analysis through the GUI (Sect. A in the online appendix [1] for further details). The input source of the architecture are HTML pages retrieved using a Dark Web crawler designed by us, working on the TOR darknet. Currently, the tool supports three Dark Web markets: Agartha, Cannazon, and Dark Market. Nevertheless, the platform eases the integration of new marketplaces by adding a python script with the scraping rules without changing the architecture. Each scraper is based on the HTML tag structure in order to extract the information. Hence, if the HTML structure of a Dark Web page changes, the scraper set of rules must be updated accordingly.

Lastly, the SOA architecture relies on a MySQL database to store the scraped data. The database is structured into three tables: *vendor*, *product* and *review*. We adopt a MySQL database system to increase the platform's performances by considerably speeding up all the writing and loading queries. Unlike

---

[1] https://www.palantir.com/.

other databases, such as NoSQL or Graph databases, MySQL optimizes high-performance joins across multiple indexes tables [5] (e.g., join between vendor and review to retrieve vendor's info given a review). Introducing a solid DBMS, the system reduces the server's workload while searching all the requested features for our final Trend Analysis tool in a fast, tractable and secure manner [4].

On top of the architecture, we built a web platform to show the insights provided by SENSEI API. The API receives the information needed, converts it into a JSON format, and sends it to the back-end platform, ready to be visualized in the web-based GUI. Based on the different types of analysis available, to visualize them in the front-end, the back-end platform provides 25 services grouped into 6 categories: *country, drug, market, vendor, trend analysis* and *general*.

3   Trend Analysis Services

The trend analysis platform provides multiple views divided into six different pages. Each page provides a specific type of analysis and insight (major details of each service are available in Sect. B in the online appendix [1]).

The home page shows an overview of the information retrieved after scraping the HTML pages loaded in the SENSEI SOA platform. It contains five general analysis tabs. *General analysis overview* shows the total markets available for analysis, the number of vendors, the number of products, and reviews collected through all the scraped markets. *Number of sales for each country* tab includes analysis displayed as a geo-map. It is possible to highlight a country to receive specific information related to vendors and the number of sales. *Top 4 countries* is a home page section that highlights countries based on the number of sales. The home page provides an overview of the seven most active vendors using the number of products sold in the *top vendors* tab. For a more general analysis, we provide raw data for all the countries in the *countries insights* tab. It does not organize the data to show any insight. Conversely, they are displayed in a table to be examined and reviewed. Lastly, the *trend analysis snapshot* tab shows the analysis regarding the products on sale in a specified period and time. The value of each day is the sum of all the products on sale in all countries involved.

The trend analysis page provides a line chart for three categories: drugs, markets, and countries. The platform performs the trend analysis by price, the number of products, or the number of vendors. In addition, the platform allows picking a specific date, showing the trend analysis by year (trend analysis of 2021) or month (trend analysis of January 2021). Along with the trend analysis page, showing the trend of a specific category, the platform provides an additional page, namely *Trend Analysis Comparison* page, where the end user can see the trend analysis of two different categories and compare them. The comparative analysis provides information on users' behavior and the type of drugs consumed. Moreover, the analysis is not only related to products. Conversely, it also gives an overview of the money involved in comparing the total revenue of products and vendors between the two countries. The platform allows the comparison of two categories: drugs, filtering by markets, or markets, filtering by drugs.

The tree-map page provides detailed information regarding vendors and the number of items sold. The tree-map visualization helps to have a glance an overall idea about the most active vendors with higher profits. The financial information about vendors plays a vital role during an investigation to better understand the investigation subject. Moreover, by clicking on a specific vendor, it is possible to know the number of items on sale per drug category.

The vendor's search page enables finding specific vendors and all the related information organized on the same page. The tool then provides two views: general vendor's and specific vendor's information. The general vendor's information provides the vendor's id, the name, the market or the markets where is active, the origin country specified in the marketplace and the delivery available places. When the user selects a vendor, the tool provides a side panel with the vendor's details, such as the vendor's score, email, phone number, Wickr's username [6], the country delivery place, and the number of snapshots done. For example, if the tool receives five dumps with the same vendor, the snapshot value is five.

The last page provides an interactive network map to build relationships among vendors and markets. The graph eases the identification of vendors in different markets providing all the interconnection. The analysis provides a graphical visualization of the available network among vendors and markets and contributes to understanding the marketplace size based on the number of vendors and the extent of a vendor's business among different markets. Moreover, the network map is interactive, meaning the investigator can have more information on a specific vendor by simply clicking on a vendor node. An investigator can retrieve information from the interactive network map, like the number of markets where the vendor is active and the number of products sold in each market.

4 Conclusions and Future Work

Our Trend Analysis tool aims to support LEAs during cybercrime investigations. The overall framework encompasses two main platform with their respective architectures, the SENSEI SOA platform, used to feed it with data from different investigations and the SENSEI platform, with a web-based GUI to show insights and trends in real-time. We outlined the framework architecture and platform components, from the trend analysis to the interactive market-vendor graph, describing the key design decisions and assumptions. The Trend Analysis platform has been built on top of RESTful API architecture, continuously fed with data.

Currently, SENSEI lacks of an exhaustive experimentation because we do not have enough data to feed the tool. Our priority is to gather data from several Dark Web marketplaces to validate our work. We provide a tutorial of SENSEI at the following link: https://youtu.be/aaT4J0Yd9lQ.

Requirement

In the following, we provide installation information and the interaction process between the SENSEI platform and the SENSEI SOA architecture.

Installation

The SENSEI architecture lays on Docker to build and run its components. Docker-compose is used to create an interconnected infrastructure, where the database can communicate with the SENSEI SOA tool and then with the SENSEI platform. The usage of a docker-compose eases the configuration settings, the building process, and the execution process. Indeed, to build and execute the entire framework, it is sufficient to run, the first time, from the main project folder, the following commands:

```
sudo docker network create anita-network
```

to create the network where the SENSEI framework operates and this command:

```
sudo docker-compose up --build
```

to build and execute the framework. The platform is available in the GitHub repository: https://github.com/danieldp92/SENSEI.

A   Services

A.1   Load Services

Table 1. Original dataset. The attribute name is an identifier. Instead age, gender and postcode are quasi-identifiers.

Service name	Description
Delete dumps	Delete all market's dumps for each market passed as input from the local folder
Upload dump	Upload into local folder and scrape data to store into the DB
Delete market dumps	Delete all market's dumps (local folder and DB)

Load services manage the loading of datasets and the extraction of data from HTML pages passed as input. Table 1 shows the endpoint list of all LOAD services developed.

The *upload dump* endpoint reads the HTML page received and extract information to store into the database. As shown in Fig. 1, the tool has as many scrapers as the number of dark markets taken into account. This work takes into account three dark markets: Agartha, Cannazon and Dark Market.

The *delete dumps* is used to delete one or more markets scraped in the past. It is possible to set parameters as 'timestamp' and 'market name'.

A.2   Get Services

Get services allow the end-user to effectively retrieve information stored during the loading process. The information retrieved by the GET services includes

Table 2. Get services.

Service name	Description
Market services	
Get markets	This module provides different services for the integration and the editing of new marketplaces
Get dumps	Get all dumps stored for each market
Get market's dumps	Get all market's dumps
Vendor services	
Get vendors	Get the list of all vendors stored in the system (only the name of the vendor and the marketplace to which it refers)
Get vendor	Get the vendor in a specific marketplace. This service provides detail information of a vendor
Get vendor's products	Get the products of a vendor in a specific marketplace (only the name of each product sold by a vendor)
Get vendor's product	Get the product of a vendor in a specific marketplace. This service provides detail information of the product
Product services	
Get products	Get the list of all products stored in the system (only the name of the product and the marketplace to which it refers)
Get product	Get the product in a specific marketplace. This service provides detail information of a product
Graph analysis by vendor's name	Provides the graph analysis of a vendor, showing the relation with all marketplaces available
Graph analysis services	
Graph analysis by vendor's pgp key	Provides the graph analysis of a vendor, showing the relation with all marketplaces available, based on its pgp key

information like vendors and the product list and data selection to build the graph analysis by vendor's name or PGP key. The services provided in this macro category can be grouped into four main categories:

- Market services: services used to get information regarding marketplaces, such as details of a specific marketplace stored, timestamp, size of the dump, and the number of pages.
- Vendor services: services used to retrieve information about vendors.
- Product services: services used to retrieve information about products.
- Graph analysis services: services used to show the connections of a vendor among marketplaces, leveraging the vendor's username and the vendor's PGP key.

In Table 2 we provided a detailed list of all the services under the GET category. In addition, we listed all the service names and a short description for each of them to explain their purpose.

B   Trend Analysis Platform

B.1   Home Page

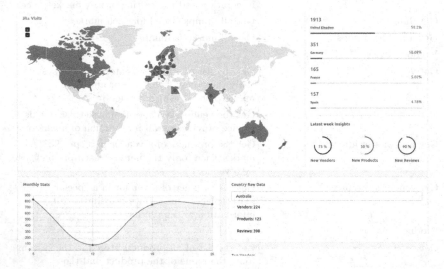

Fig. 2. SENSEI platform screen: home. It contains general info about the top vendors, a trend analysis of the last month recorder, general info for each country and a map containing the number of products sold in every country.

Table 3. Platform home services.

Service name	Description
GET /insights/	Retrieve the following insights: number of markets, number of vendors, number of products, number of reviews
GET /country/sales/	For each country, get the number of products on sale in the last month
GET /country/top-sales/	Get the top 4 countries with the highest number of products on sale
GET /top-vendors/	Retrieve the top vendors of the last month
GET /country/list/	Return all the countries recorded by the platform
GET /country/rawdata/	Return the raw data for each country. Raw data: "number of products", "number of vendors", "number of reviews"
GET /ta/sales/last-month/	Retrieve the sales of the last month

B.2 Trend Analysis Page

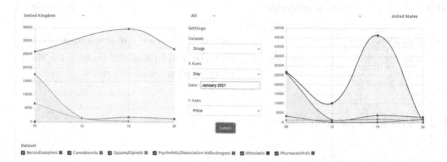

Fig. 3. SENSEI platform screen: trend analysis. Comparison between two countries based on the amount of drug, counted as the total price, in all the markets.

Table 4. Platform trend analysis services.

Service name	Description
GET /ta/drugs/	Get the trend analysis of all drugs in the marketplace
GET /ta/markets/	Get the trend analysis of all markets in the marketplace
GET /ta/countries/	Get the trend analysis of all countries in the marketplace

Table 5. Platform trend analysis comparison services.

Service name	Description
GET /ta/drugs/	Get the trend analysis of all drugs in the marketplace
GET /ta/markets/	Get the trend analysis of all markets in the marketplace
GET /ta/countries/	Get the trend analysis of all countries in the marketplace
GET /country/list/	Get the list of all the countries stored
GET /market/list/	Get the list of all the markets stored
GET /drug/list/	Get the list of all the drugs stored

B.3 Vendor's Tree-Map Page

In Table 6 we provide the list of services used to build the tree-map analysis. In the first row of the table, we have GET /vendor/treemap/n-products, the service is in charge of retrieving the number of products on sale per each vendor. Next, the service GET /market/list/ is used to show the market list as a treemap's filtering option. The last service, GET /vendor/treemap/vendor-name extracts further details about the number of products on sale per each drug of a specific vendor.

Table 6. Platform treemap services.

Service name	Description
GET /vendor/treemap/n-products/	Get the total products on sale for each vendor
GET /market/list/	Get the list of all the markets stored
GET /vendor/treemap/{vendor-name}	Get the total products on sale for each drug's category of a vendor

B.4   Vendor's Search Page

Fig. 4. SENSEI platform screen: vendors general info with detailed information regarding a specific vendor.

In Table 7 are shown the two services used in the vendor search page. The first service is in charge of retrieving the general data of all the vendors. While, the second one GET /vendor/info/vendor-name retrieves the information of a specific vendor.

Table 7. Platform search vendor services.

Service name	Description
GET /vendor/search/	Get the general insights (name, market, country) of all the vendors
GET /vendor/info/{vendor-name}	Get the vendor's info

B.5   Vendor-Market Graph Analysis

Table 8 shows the services used to build the interactive graph. First, GET /market/n-products/ is used to estimate the impact of the vendor in a market, retrieving the number of products sold. Next, GET /market/graph/ service provides the list of all the vendors from a specific market. Last, the service `GET` `/market/graph/vendor/` provides additional information, like the number of markets connected to a vendor and the number of products for each market.

Table 8. Platform interactive graph services.

Service name	Description
GET /market/n-products/	Get the number of products for each market
GET /market/graph/	Graph info. Tt contains the mapping between vendors and markets
GET /market/graph/vendor/	Retrieve the number of markets where the vendor is active and the number of products on sale for each market

References

1. Appendix: Sensei (2022). https://doi.org/10.6084/m9.figshare.21131557.v2
2. Chen, H.: Dark web: exploring and mining the dark side of the web. In: 2011 European Intelligence and Security Informatics Conference, pp. 1–2. IEEE (2011)
3. EMCDDA: European drug report (2021). https://doi.org/10.2810/18539
4. Foster, E.C., Godbole, S.: Overview of MySQL. In: Database Systems. Apress, Berkeley, CA (2016). https://doi.org/10.1007/978-1-4842-1191-5_24
5. Győrödi, C., et al.: A comparative study: MongoDB vs. MySQL. In: 2015 13th International Conference on Engineering of Modern Electric Systems (EMES), pp. 1–6. IEEE (2015)
6. Mehrotra, T., Mehtre, B.M.: Forensic analysis of Wickr application on android devices. In: 2013 IEEE International Conference on Computational Intelligence and Computing Research, pp. 1–6. IEEE (2013)

PRES³: Private Record Linkage Using Services, Spark and Soundex

Konstantinos Razgkelis[✉] and Alexandros Karakasidis[iD]

Department of Applied Informatics, University of Macedonia, Thessaloniki, Greece
{dai16250,a.karakasidis}@uom.edu.gr

Abstract. One of the most challenging tasks that emerged in the last few years is linking records from distinct organizations, while maintaining privacy. Private Record Linkage is by definition a resource demanding task. Considering the continuously increasing volumes of data that have to be linked is a fact leading us to develop solutions that will conclude the process in a timely manner. To this end, we demonstrate PRES³, a system for performing private record linkage based on a service-oriented architecture, harvesting the power of Apache Spark.

Keywords: Record Linkage · Privacy · Services · Spark · Big data

1 Introduction

Data integration is usually not a trivial task, as data held by distinct organizations may not necessarily have common unique identifiers, thus requiring the use of combinations of attributes, usually strings [1], called quasi-identifiers, to form a composite key. These data, involving personal information, usually suffer from low quality due to manual input errors, e.g. in web forms, requiring approximate string matching operators. Furthermore, as the volume of online transactions increases, makes this identification of corresponding entries a particularly resource-intensive task.

The situation we have just described is known as the Record Linkage problem. Nevertheless, the fact that these data usually contain personal information may prevent their integration, since recent legislation, as GDPR and HIPAA, imposes strict rules. To this end, the privacy of described individuals has to be safeguarded, leading us to perform Private Record Linkage, where dataholders gain no knew knowledge apart from identifying their common entities.

With this demonstration, we exhibit PRES³, a system for Private REcord linkage, based on Services, Spark and Soundex, which we are certain that it offers a solid solution to the aforementioned problem. Our system is designed for privately linking large volumes of records using alphanumeric quasi-identifiers, leveraging a service-oriented architecture to facilitate easy upgrades and seamless deployment and the use of Apache Spark for scalability. Soundex has been employed as a well-known string matching operator [1] available in many commercial RDBMS's, in the context, however, of private matching [4].

© The Author(s), under exclusive license to Springer Nature Switzerland AG 2023
J. Troya et al. (Eds.): ICSOC 2022 Workshops, LNCS 13821, pp. 384–387, 2023.
https://doi.org/10.1007/978-3-031-26507-5_37

While Private Record Linkage systems as MAINSEL [5] and SOEMPI [6] exist, to the best of our knowledge, this is the first effort employing a service-oriented architecture and Apache Spark. The service-oriented architecture offers extendability and loosely coupling so as to incorporate future developments, e.g. fairness aware matching [2], without altering the entire system, and location and platform independence, to facilitate seamless deployment. Apache Spark has been employed as a solution that will efficiently process large volumes of data offering scalability.

2 PRES[3]

In this section, we describe the architecture of our system[1]. First, we present its architectural components and then we proceed by describing their operation.

2.1 Architectural Components

Our system is based on the privacy-preserving protocol presented in [4] assuming two types of entities, dataholders and a join party in an Honest but Curious setup without collusion. Dataholders are organizations willing to privately link their data. The join party performs the linkage operation. In our demonstration. We assume two dataholders named Alice and Bob and a join party called Carol, whose role is to refrain Alice and Bob from accessing each other's data, while measures taken by Alice and Bob do not allow Carol to infer any information [3]. Third parties are not uncommon in modern security setups, considering, for instance, certificate issuing authorities.

Each of these three participants have their data privately stored in a HDFS file system within its own cluster. Our system comprises of a collection of services, each executing within its own Docker container. For the purposes of this demonstration, all these services have been implemented in Python 3, utilizing Flask to expose their REST APIs.

Let us begin the description of the architectural components with the case of dataholders. Both of the dataholders operate under the same business logic, but with different configurations and with their own data. At each dataholder, there are two services: the *Front-End Service* and the *Back-End Service* (Fig. 1).

Dataholder Front-End Service. The dataholder Front-End service is responsible for user interaction. It is built on React and allows the user to perform a series of operations necessary for the protocol operation. First, the user selects from the file system the dataset she wishes to link. Then she selects the matching fields, i.e. the quasi-identifiers that are going to be used for matching. Then, the user selects the amount of noise to inject within the dataset by adding fake rows, as a measure for privacy preservation [3]. Finally, when all these are set, there is a button for the user to launch the matching process.

---

[1] Implementation available at: https://github.com/kostasrazgkelis/PRES3.

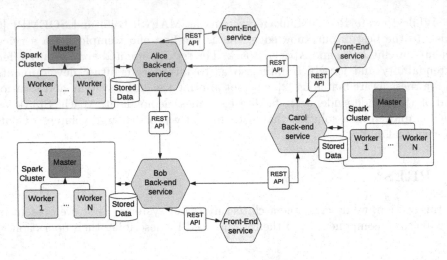

Fig. 1. PRES[3] system architecture.

Dataholder Back-End Service. The Back-End service is responsible for transforming the dataholder's data based on the choices received by the Front-End Service, as illustrated in Fig. 1. Beyond this transformation, it communicates with Carol's back end service and the other dataholder's service as part of the private record linkage protocol. It has direct access to the dataholder's HDFS filesystem where data are stored before and after their transformation.

The transformation operations, implemented through Apache Spark, are the following. First, there is a *Map* operation transforming each field into a Soundex code and then to a secure hash function. Then, a *Parallelize(RandomSoundex())* operation is launched, which creates records with fake Soundex codes hashed with the same secure hash function. Then a *Union* operation takes place so as to merge real and noise data. Afterward, an *orderBy(rand())* operation is performed so as to shuffle real and fake records.

Matching Party Front-End Service. The Matching Party (aka Carol) Front-End service is used to notify the corresponding user that the dataholders have delivered their data so as to initiate the matching process. For this purpose, The Matching Party user may monitor the encrypted data received by Alice and Bob and launch the matching process.

Matching Party Back-End Service. The Matching Party Back-End Service is responsible for data communication with Alice and Bob's services. It is connected to the Matching Party's Spark cluster and as such, it launches the respective join operation. To do so, it also has direct access to Carol's HDFS file system.

2.2   Operation

Let us now describe the operation of our system. First, users at Alice and Bob select the data to be merged through their Front-End services. These communicate through a REST API with the respective Back-End services which initiate the transformations described earlier at the local Spark clusters. When these transformations conclude, each party independently delivers her output to Carol's Back-End service, using REST again, through a secured transmission channel.

Carol's Back-End service who expects for incoming data, accepts them and stores them within her local HDFS fie system. Then, the Back-End service notifies, using REST, her Front-End service that data have been received by Alice and Bob. Carol's operator launches the join operation through her Front-End service. This results in her Back-End service to command her local Spark cluster to start joining the data using all available matching fields. When this operation concludes, the Back-End service notifies the operator through a message to the Front-End service. Then, it identifies the matching records of each of Alice and Bob and respectively delivers them back to their Back-End services. Upon reception, these services phase out records identified to be fake and directly exchange them with the corresponding matching party.

3   Conclusions and Future Work

We have demonstrated PRES³, a system for performing Private Record Linkage. This system relies on Services, Spark and Soundex. Our next steps include adding matching operators for other data types (e.g. numbers), perform an extensive empirical evaluation on the performance of our system so as to fine-tune it and, finally, develop and incorporate methods for fair-aware record linkage.

References

1. Christen, P.: Data Matching - Concepts and Techniques for Record Linkage, Entity Resolution, and Duplicate Detection. Springer, Data-Centric Systems and Applications (2012)
2. Efthymiou, V., Stefanidis, K., Pitoura, E., Christophides, V.: FairER: entity resolution with fairness constraints. In: Proceedings of the 30th ACM International Conference on Information & Knowledge Management, pp. 3004–3008 (2021)
3. Heng, Y., Armknecht, F., Chen, Y., Schnell, R.: On the effectiveness of graph matching attacks against privacy-preserving record linkage. PLoS ONE **17**(9), e0267893 (2022)
4. Karakasidis, Alexandros, Koloniari, Georgia: Phonetics-based parallel privacy preserving record linkage. In: Xhafa, Fatos, Caballé, Santi, Barolli, Leonard (eds.) 3PGCIC 2017. LNDECT, vol. 13, pp. 179–190. Springer, Cham (2018). https://doi.org/10.1007/978-3-319-69835-9_16
5. Stammler, S., et al.: Mainzelliste secureepilinker (MainSEL): privacy-preserving record linkage using secure multi-party computation. Bioinformatics **38**(6), 1657–1668 (2022)
6. Tóth, C., Durham, E.A., Kantarcioglu, M., Xue, Y., Malin, B.A.: SOEMPI: a secure open enterprise master patient index software toolkit for private record linkage. In: AMIA Annual Symposium Proceedings, pp. 1105–1114 (2014)

Towards Peer-to-Peer Sharing of Wireless Energy Services

Pengwei Yang, Amani Abusafia[✉], Abdallah Lakhdari,
and Athman Bouguettaya

The University of Sydney, Sydney, NSW 2000, Australia
pyan8871@uni.sydney.edu.au,
{amani.abusafia,abdallah.lakhdari,athman.bouguettaya}@sydney.edu.au

Abstract. Crowdsourcing wireless energy services is a novel convenient alternative to charge IoT devices. We demonstrate *peer-to-peer wireless energy services sharing between smartphones* over a *distance*. Our demo leverages (1) a service-based technique to share energy services, (2) state-of-the-art power transfer technology over a distance, and (3) a mobile application to enable communication between energy providers and consumers. In addition, our application monitors the charging process between IoT devices to collect a dataset for further analysis. Moreover, in this demo, we compare *the peer-to-peer energy transfer between two smartphones using different charging technologies*, i.e., cable charging, reverse charging, and wireless charging over a distance. A set of preliminary experiments have been conducted on a real collected dataset to analyze and demonstrate the behavior of the current wireless and traditional charging technologies.

Keywords: Energy services · IoT services · Wireless charging · IoT · Crowdsourcing · Energy sharing · Wireless power transfer

1 Introduction

Wireless power transfer (WPT), also known as wireless charging, has been widely adopted as a flexible and ubiquitous solution to charge IoT devices [1,2]. Several studies leveraged the service paradigm to propose the concept of crowdsourcing wireless energy as *energy services* to charge nearby IoT devices [3–5]. Energy Service is defined as the abstraction of the wireless energy transfer from one IoT device (i.e., *provider*) to another device (i.e., *consumer*) [6]. Energy services may be shared wirelessly with the development of new technologies known as "Over-the-Air" wireless charging [2,4].

Recent studies have made substantial progress in addressing several challenges in crowdsourcing energy services, including service composition, fairness and quality of experience [3–5,7]. However, existing works rely on simulation analysis of the proposed techniques using synthetic datasets. In other words, there is no demonstration of the existing literature on *real devices using wireless*

© The Author(s), under exclusive license to Springer Nature Switzerland AG 2023
J. Troya et al. (Eds.): ICSOC 2022 Workshops, LNCS 13821, pp. 388–392, 2023.
https://doi.org/10.1007/978-3-031-26507-5_38

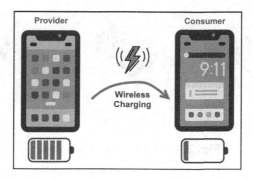

Fig. 1. Wireless energy charging scenario

power transfer over a distance. Hence, in this paper, we demonstrate peer-to-peer sharing of wireless energy services among smartphones over a distance. Our demo leverages a service-based technique to share energy services, the state-of-the-art power transfer technology over a distance, and an extension of the proposed app by [8]. Similar to the previously mentioned app, our app enables consumers and providers to share energy conveniently and to monitor the sharing process for further analysis. In addition, unlike the previous app, our demo allows users to (1) share energy by requesting an amount of energy or requesting to be charged for a certain time period and (2) transfer energy wirelessly over a distance. Moreover, in this demo, we conduct preliminary experiments to verify the feasibility and stability of the platform with wireless charging over a distance. We also compare and analyze the performance of the wireless charging technology with reverse and cable charging technologies.

2   System Overview

We consider a scenario where people congregate in confined areas (e.g., restaurants, coffee shops, and movie theaters). In the confined areas, we assume that IoT users will share their spare energy or request energy with nearby devices (See Fig. 1). IoT users will use our mobile application to request energy as *energy consumers* or to accept energy requests as *energy providers*. In our app, IoT users send and receive requests directly using Bluetooth. Moreover, our mobile application extends the app proposed by [8] because of its limitations in terms of synchronization, variety of request types, and using built-in reverse charging. In contrast, our application expends the previous application with the following features: (1) our app allows users to send and receive energy based on size. For instance, a consumer may ask a provider to charge 1000 mAh. (2) our app also offers the option of requesting energy based on a time period. For instance, a consumer may ask a provider to charge them for the next 10 min. Finally, (3) our application records the battery status of providers and consumers every time interval t, e.g., every 10 s, with the actual time of each record. This enables us

(A) Wireless charging   (B) Reverse charging   (C) Cable charging

Fig. 2. Used charging technologies

to synchronize the monitoring process by ensuring that the data is recorded at the exact time, e.g., second. The recorded data may be used for further analysis, e.g., studying the charging rate or optimizing the energy loss.

3   Demo Scenario

Our application runs in the following scenario. Once a consumer has submitted a request. Our platform will automatically submit a request to the closest provider and wait for the provider's response. If the provider accepts, the energy sharing and monitoring process will start. Then the process will end once the consumer receives their request (e.g., an amount of energy or being charged for a specific period). Simultaneously, the platform synchronizes the monitoring process between the provider and consumer and captures the data of the entire energy transfer process. Once the sharing process ends, the app uploads the collected data to the edge service management system (e.g., a router associated with the confined area). The current version of our energy-sharing platform supports a one-to-one energy transfer mode and has demonstrated reliable performance in monitoring and demonstrating the wireless energy-sharing process over a distance.

4   Demo Setup

Our demo will exhibit our platform through a real case of wireless charging over a distance between two smartphones. In this case, we use near-field wireless charging (i.e., inductive coupling wireless technique). The inductive coupling device consists of two coils, and the electrical energy is delivered based on the magnetic field (See Fig. 2(A)). We use a Google Pixel 5 smartphone as the provider and a Google Pixel 3 as the consumer. We connect both the consumer and provider to the wireless charging coils, and then we run a case similar to the previously mentioned scenario in Sect. 3. Additionally, we will display a video of the entire process of using the devices and app to request, receive and monitor the energy-sharing process in real time. The video is published at this link: youtu.be/d-bdFGk6z4A. We will also bring other charging technologies for the visitors to our booth to try with our app (See Fig. 2(B) and (C)).

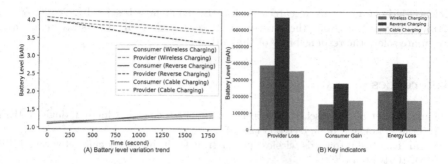

Fig. 3. Comparison among different charging technologies

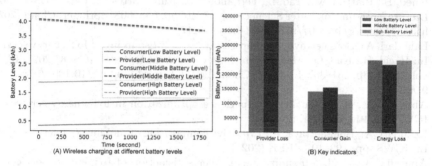

Fig. 4. Comparison of wireless charging with different battery levels for consumer

5   Preliminary Experiments

We conducted preliminary experiments to demonstrate our platform's feasibility and monitor different charging processes. We used the same setup mentioned in Sect. 4. We ran two experiments on the collected dataset from the charging process to analyze and demonstrate the behavior of each charging technology, i.e., wireless charging, reverse charging, and cable charging (See Fig. 2). In wireless charging, the distance between the two coils is set to 2 cm. The first set of experiments aims to compare differences between charging technologies in terms of battery level variation trend, provider loss, consumer gain, and energy loss. The start battery of the consumer was 40%; the provider battery was 100%. We ran the experiment using a time-based request to receive energy. The requested time was 30 min. Additionally, we set the recording interval to 1 s. The experiment shows that all approaches have similar behavior (See Fig. 3). However, the provider with reverse charging had the highest energy loss. It is worth noting that energy loss involves the energy consumed to share energy and to run the device, e.g., run the operating system, system applications, etc.

The second set of experiments aims to test wireless charging with different battery levels for the consumer at each experiment. The consumer's start battery level was tested on 10%, 40%, and 70% and labeled as low, middle, and high battery levels. The experiment shows that varying battery levels have less impact on the charging process (See Fig. 4).

Acknowledgment. This research was partly made possible by LE220100078 and LE180100158 grants from the Australian Research Council. The statements made herein are solely the responsibility of the authors.

References

1. Fang, W., et al.: Fair scheduling in resonant beam charging for IoT devices. IEEE Internet Things J. **6**(1), 641–653 (2018)
2. Sakai, K., et al.: Towards wireless power transfer in mobile social networks. TNSE **9**(3), 1091–1103 (2021)
3. Abusafia, A., et al.: Service-based wireless energy crowdsourcing. In: Troya, J., Medjahed, B., Piattini, M., Yao, L., Fernández, P., Ruiz-Cortés, A. (eds.) ICSOC 2022. Lecture Notes in Computer Science, vol. 13740, pp. 653–668. Springer, Cham (2022). https://doi.org/10.1007/978-3-031-20984-0_47
4. Lakhdari, A., Bouguettaya, A.: Fairness-aware crowdsourcing of IoT energy services. In: Hacid, H., Kao, O., Mecella, M., Moha, N., Paik, H. (eds.) ICSOC 2021. LNCS, vol. 13121, pp. 351–367. Springer, Cham (2021). https://doi.org/10.1007/978-3-030-91431-8_22
5. Abusafia, A., et al.: Quality of experience optimization in IoT energy services. In: ICWS, pp. 91–96. IEEE (2022)
6. Lakhdari, A., Bouguettaya, A.: Proactive composition of mobile IoT energy services. In: ICWS, pp. 192–197. IEEE (2021)
7. Abusafia, A., et al.: Maximizing consumer satisfaction of IoT energy services. In: Troya, J., Medjahed, B., Piattini, M., Yao, L., Fernandez, P., Ruiz-Cortés, A. (eds.) Service-Oriented Computing ICSOC 2022. Lecture Notes in Computer Science, vol. 13740, pp. 395–412. Springer, Cham (2022). https://doi.org/10.1007/978-3-031-20984-0_28
8. Yao, J., et al.: Wireless IoT energy sharing platform. In: PerCom Workshops, pp. 118–120. IEEE (2022)

IoT System for Occupational Risks Prevention at a WWTP

Sergio Laso[1](✉), Daniel Flores-Martin[2], Juan Pedro Cortés-Pérez[2],
Miguel Soriano Barroso[3], Alfonso Cortés-Pérez[4], Javier Berrocal[2],
and Juan M. Murillo[2]

[1] Global Process and Product Improvement S.L., Cáceres, Spain
slasom@unex.es
[2] University of Extremadura, Badajoz, Spain
{dfloresm,jpcortes,jberolm,juanmamu}@unex.es
[3] INYGES CONSULTORES S.L., Plasencia, Spain
msoriano@inyges.es
[4] AC2 INNOVACIÓN S.L., Torremocha, Spain
info@ac2sc.es

Abstract. Biohazards and noise risks in wastewater treatment plants
are a real concern. These stations generate risks of gas inhalation due
to contaminants carried by the wastewater and exposure to dangerous
high noise generated by the work equipment. The stations are equipped
with sensors that are capable of monitoring ambient gas levels and noise
levels. This is not sufficient and geolocation of the operators is necessary. However, indoor geolocation is still a problem due to limited GPS
accuracy. There are alternatives such as Bluetooth, which allow more
accurate geolocation to be obtained. In this work, we present a IoT system that allows to geolocate the operators indoor through Bluetooth
beacons and cross-reference it with the information from gas and noise
sensors to prevent occupational risks.

Keywords: IoT · Indoor geolocation · Prevention of occupational
risks · WWTP

1 Introduction

Wastewater treatment plants (WWTP) are infrastructures that ensure the
proper conservation of the environment. These stations are responsible for filtering waste from water used by humans.

WWTPs involve different hazards for the people who work there, due to the
amount of existing biological load and toxic gases carried by the wastewater,
or the noise of the equipment [3]. These hazards are mitigated and monitored
by expert occupational risk prevention teams. In addition to traditional safety
measures such as the use of helmets, gloves, etc., there are also different types of
water pressure, or CO_2 sensors to monitor for dangerously high levels. Exposure

J. Troya et al. (Eds.): ICSOC 2022 Workshops, LNCS 13821, pp. 393–397, 2023.
https://doi.org/10.1007/978-3-031-26507-5_39

to these elements is only harmful when certain levels and times are exceeded [2]. Therefore, to prevent risks to people, it is necessary to know the location to check if they have been in the area where a sensor acts and for how long.

These exposures tend to be more dangerous indoors in the plant where a higher concentration of gases or noise can occur. Indoor location is a problem due to the low accuracy provided by GPS-based technologies. As an alternative, other technologies allow this indoor localisation in a more precise way, such as WiFi, RFID, LoRa or Bluetooth [5]. However, Bluetooth geolocation [1] is the most appropriate for this work due to its low energy consumption, environmental conditions and because it is an easily deployable and affordable solution.

In this demonstration, we develop an IoT system that helps automate occupational risk prevention. This system has been deployed at the Coria WWTP (Extremadura, Spain)[1] where tests are being carried out with workers.

On the one hand, existing indoor geolocation techniques are used via Bluetooth based on electronic Bluetooth beacons strategically placed in the wastewater treatment plant and, on the other hand, the levels of toxic gases and noise are monitored in the areas where the operators move around. This is achieved through a mobile application developed to monitor the activity of the operators automatically to alert them to possible levels of biological hazards. In this way, certain risks can be prevented automatically.

The rest of the document is structured as follows: Sect. 2 details the architecture of the IoT system and Section 3 explains how it has been implemented at the Coria WWTP. Finally, Sect. 4 presents the conclusions of this work.

2   DSIndoorLocation Architecture

The DSIndoorLocation monitors the operators geolocation along with monitoring sensors to avoid possible risks that may occur in the plant. Figure 1 shows a diagram of the system architecture. Each of its components are detailed below:

- **IoT Devices:** IoT devices are made up of two types. Sensors (in this case gases and noise) are responsible for detecting the levels of toxic gases and noise. These devices are connected to the Internet and are monitored in real-time sending the values obtained to the Cloud. The Beacons are deployed in the indoor area that is intended to improve geolocation and communicate with the mobile application via Bluetooth. These beacons must be strategically placed to cover the entire coverage range.
- **Cloud:** The Cloud is composed of different services used by the other components. On the one hand, it has services to capture sensor values and another one to expose those values to be consumed by the mobile application. On the other hand, it also has another service deployed to store the generated activities (work routes) of the operators.

---

[1] https://goo.gl/maps/cCJyoGCWz6ikjc8W6.

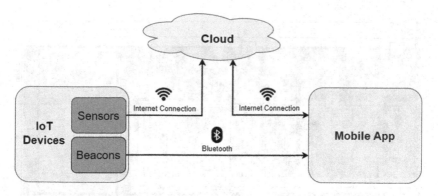

Fig. 1. DSIndoorLocation architecture.

– **Mobile App:** The mobile application is the most important component of the architecture. The application is responsible for calculating the geolocation through the neXenio library [4], which uses the Multilateration algorithm to triangulate the location based on the relatives' distance (received Bluetooth signal strength) of the beacons and their location. To obtain the sensor values, it consumes the Cloud services. In turn, it contrasts the information from both parts (geolocation and sensors) to alert the operators about any dangerous exposure in the area where they are at that moment. In addition, all operator activities are stored locally and sent to the Cloud.

3 Use Case: Coria WWTP

This section details how DSIndoorLocation was deployed at the Coria WWTP.

First, an analysis of the coverage of the beacons was performed, which was then analyzed on the floor map to place them strategically to cover the entire area of the plant. Figure 2 shows the placement of the beacons with a distance between them of no more than 10 m after coverage analysis. Secondly, gas and noise sensors have been placed in specific areas of the plant recommended by expert sensor installers. Finally, the beacons must be configured in the mobile application. The beacons (id) and their location in the WWTP must be indicated so that the app can correctly calculate the operator's geolocation.

The application interface is simple. Figure 3a shows the main interface consisting of the plant map, the location of the beacons (squares), and the operator's location (circle) in real-time. At the bottom are two buttons, "Start/End" and "Exit". The "Start/End" button is used for the operator to press when starting or finishing work. The "Exit" button stops all services running in the background and terminates the application.

The application works as follows. When the operator starts working and presses the "Start" button, the application starts monitoring its location, as well as the sensor values. This process is done in the background so the operator does not have to interact with the device until he finishes his work. When the

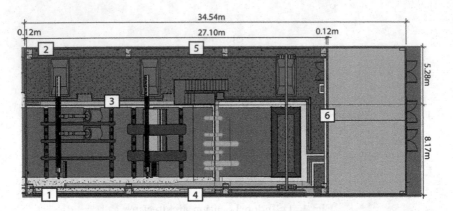

Fig. 2. Location of the beacons at the WWTP.

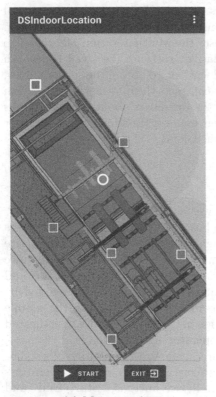
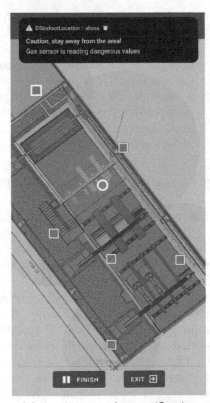

(a) Main interface   (b) **Application alert notification**

Fig. 3. DSIndoorLocation application.

operator approaches a sensor with elevated levels, the application will alert with sound and vibration, and display a notification informing the operator of this situation as shown in Fig. 3b.

4   Conclusions

Occupational risk prevention is a very important issue in WWTPs. There are multiple risks for the people working there, e.g. exposure to biological hazards due to contaminants carried by the wastewater. In this demonstration, we present an IoT system that allows the automation and control of occupational risk prevention deployed at the Coria WWTP. This system allows monitoring the operators of the plant through indoor geolocation while monitoring the level of different toxic gas sensors where they work, alerting them in cases of possible danger levels. We are currently working on finalizing the deployment in the plant and starting the study to obtain the first results. In future work, we are working on the extension of this system by extending the monitoring of the operators also in the external parts of the plant, in order to be able to monitor any danger in the whole area occupied by the WWTP.

Acknowledgements. This work has been partially funded by grant DIN2020-011586, funded by MCIN/AEI/10.13039/501100011033 and by the European Union "Next GenerationEU/PRTR", by the Ministry of Science, Innovation and Universities (project RTI20 18-094591-B-I00 and by grant FPU17/02251), by the 4IE+ project (0499-4IE-PLUS-4-E) funded by the Interreg V-A Spain-Portugal (POCTEP) 2014–2020 programme, by the Regional Ministry of Economy, Science and Digital Agenda of the Government of Extremadura (GR21183, GR21133, IB18030) and the European Regional Development Fund (ERDF).

References

1. Bai, L., Ciravegna, F., Bond, R., Mulvenna, M.: A low cost indoor positioning system using bluetooth low energy. IEEE Access **8**, 136858–136871 (2020)
2. Carducci, A., Donzelli, G., Cioni, L., Federigi, I., Lombardi, R., Verani, M.: Quantitative microbial risk assessment for workers exposed to bioaerosol in wastewater treatment plants aimed at the choice and setup of safety measures. Int. J. Environ. Res. Public Health **15**(7), 1490 (2018)
3. Granados, I.C.G.: Generación, caracterización y tratamiento de lodos de EDAR. Ph.D. thesis, Universidad de Córdoba (2015)
4. neXenio: BLE Indoor Positioning. https://github.com/neXenio/BLE-Indoor-Positioning. Accessed on 27 Oct 2022
5. Zafari, F., Gkelias, A., Leung, K.K.: A survey of indoor localization systems and technologies. IEEE Commun. Surv. Tutor. **21**(3), 2568–2599 (2019)

AlsoDTN: An Air Logistics Service-Oriented Digital Twin Network Based on Collaborative Decision Model

Qianlong Fu, Dezhi Chen, Haifeng Sun, Qi Qi[✉], Jingyu Wang,
and Jianxin Liao

State Key Laboratory of Networking and Switching Technology,
Beijing University of Posts and Telecommunications, Beijing, China
{fql2018,chendezhi,hfsun,qiqi8266,wangjingyu,liaojx}@bupt.edu.cn

Abstract. As cities expand and the pace of life accelerates, modern logistics services need to explore new air routes. While air logistics is fast and convenient, it also faces many problems, such as time-sensitive dynamic order requirements, the limited battery power of unmanned aerial vehicle (UAV) and so on. Besides, UAVs need to cooperate and make decisions in real time to meet city-wide logistics needs. However, limited by the computing power, it is difficult to process massive logistics demands in real time. In this paper, we propose an Air Logistics Service-Oriented Digital Twin Network based on collaborative decision model, called AlsoDTN. Firstly, in order allocation task, we establish an information fusion mechanism based on Transformer architecture to obtain the optimal order. Secondly, to adapt to the long-term route planning task, we use multi-agent deep reinforcement learning technology to make UAVs cooperate with each other. Experimental results show that our algorithm has an improvement of 18% relative to baseline algorithm.

Keywords: Service-oriented architecture · Digital twin network · Logistics transport · Multi-agent deep reinforcement learning

1 Introduction

With the future development of cities, modern logistics services need to explore new air routes. Compared to traditional logistics [1], unmanned aerial vehicles (UAVs) are used to improve the scheduling efficiency and reduce the labor cost. But firstly, the computation and communication capabilities of UAVs are limited, which cannot meet the real time and accuracy of order acquisition. Secondly, if we use distributed UAV-level devices to train deep reinforcement learning (DRL) models, the training speed may be unacceptable due to inefficient data acquisition. Thirdly, using UAVs to collect data directly in the real environment is prone to risk [2]. The above problems limit the application of DRL to the UAVs field. Fortunately, digital twin (DT), a key technology for digitizing physical entities, offers a promising solution. In DT applications, experts built high-fidelity digital

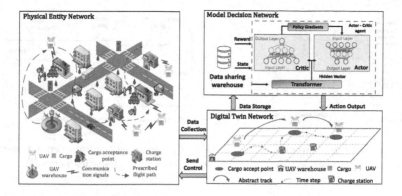

Fig. 1. The system model of air logistics network based on digital twin network

models based on real world data in cyberspace [3]. Therefore, we can build a DT model of an air logistics network, reflect the UAVs with high-fidelity and realize UAVs cooperation through the DRL method, which solves the problem of limited computing power and avoids the danger in UAVs training data collection.

However, how to apply DT in DRL architecture is still a problem to be solved [4]. We considered the following two questions: the real time problem of order allocation and long-term route planning task of UAVs. Firstly, in order allocation problem, UAVs usually need frequent communication to achieve real-time order, which is limited by the computing power. Therefore, we propose an order-driven decision model. An information fusion mechanism based on Transformer architecture is established, it can obtain the optimal order in the low-frequency communication situation between UAVs. Secondly, UAV cargo transport is a time-step and continuous mission, so we design a hierarchical reinforcement learning (HRL) model to learn the route planning task.

2   System Model

To support intelligent cooperation of the UAVs, we propose an air logistics service-oriented digital twin network based on collaborative decision model as illustrated in Fig. 1. The network consists of three parts: the physical entity of air logistics network; the digital twin network that monitors the physical space; the decision model that makes intelligent cooperation decisions. These three parts collaborate with each other and provide optimal decisions in real time. In the following, we introduce each part in detail.

2.1   Physical Entity

We designed a square area as a simulation site for logistics transmission. The acceptance point of cargoes and charging stations are randomly generated. Firstly, the UAV has to make decisions to select the cargoes to be transported.

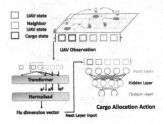

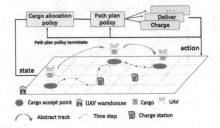

Fig. 2. Transformer architecture of air logistics network.

Fig. 3. Hierarchical reinforcement learning framework of air logistics network.

When the cargo is fully loaded, the UAV makes the route planning decision to go to the cargo acceptance point. During the flight, UAV can choose to fly to a charging station to ensure sufficient energy. In each time slot of the route planning task, the UAV flies a certain distance and consumes a certain amount of energy.

2.2 Digital Twin Network

Digital twins are virtual models of physical elements and digital representations of physical systems. Different from virtual prototype, digital twin can not only reflect the characteristics of physical system, but also predict and simulate the system, which plays an important role in optimizing resources. In our DTN, we can utilize digital twin to build the physical air logistics network, monitor the network parameters and models, and optimize the policy network.

2.3 Model Decision Network

The decision model integrates artificial intelligence and data analytics to explore global optimal strategies and controls the physical entity through a virtual-physical interface. The model decision network provides optimal decisions for various tasks, such as order allocation and route planning for multiple UAVs.

3 Algorithm

In this section, we describe the key algorithm of air logistics service-oriented digital twin network. The cargo allocation decision is set as the upper-level task, and the route planning of the UAV is set as the lower-level task. We expound the solution of order allocation problem in Sect. 3.1. Then we discuss the solution to route route planning problem in Sect. 3.2.

3.1 The Solution of Order Allocation

In the upper-level order allocation task, due to the variability of UAV and cargo quantity, it is difficult to be modeled by standard DNN model which is based on

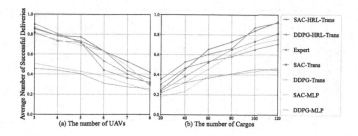

Fig. 4. The impact on average number of successful deliveries

fixed dimension, so we designed Transformer architecture, which is invariant to the arrangement of input vectors as shown in Fig. 2. Based on Transformer architecture, UAVs can process variable cargo and neighbor messages during flight and pay attention to important parts of complex and heterogeneous information.

3.2 The Solution of Route Planning

UAV cargo transport is a continuous task involving a large exploration space. Therefore, we designed a HRL model, which divides the cargo delivery task into sub-task to effectively reduce the exploration space. In each time step of the cargo delivery task, the UAV can choose to charge or fly towards the cargo acceptance point. When a cargo transport task is completed, the UAV will re-make the cargo allocation decision and assign new cargo orders, as shown in Fig. 3.

4   Result

We use the average waiting time of all cargoes to represent the fairness of air logistics network and use the average number of successful deliveries per UAV to represent the efficiency. In this demo, we obtain an air logistics transportation solution based on soft actor critic (SAC) [5] algorithm and deep deterministic policy gradient (DDPG) algorithm and compare our model with the following baseline algorithms to perform ablation experiments:

- **Expert:** In the selection of cargoes, UAVs select the nearest unselected cargoes; In UAV route planning, the UAV will go to charge when the energy is below a certain value.
- **AlsoDTN:** Taking SAC algorithm as an example, we divided the AlsoDTN model into SAC-HRL and SAC-MLP according to whether it used HRL architecture and we divided the model into SAC-Trans and SAC-MLP according to whether it used Transformer architecture.

4.1   Network Fairness Performance

As shown in Fig. 4, the comparison between SAC-MLP and SAC-Trans shows that with the increase of cargoes, our Transformer architecture can further focus

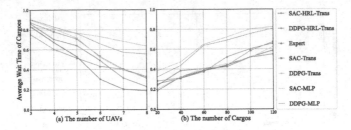

Fig. 5. The impact on average waiting time of cargoes.

on the important information, which makes the UAV policy network more is more inclined to choose cargoes with long waiting time, thus improving the fairness of air logistics network.

4.2 Network Efficiency Performance

As shown in Fig. 5, with the increase of cargoes, the model based on HRL can enable UAV policy network to select tasks more intelligently, which improves the sustainability of UAV tasks. The experimental results show that SAC-HRL-Trans has an efficiency improvement of 18%.

5   Conclusion

In this demo, we present AlsoDTN, an air logistics service-oriented digital twin network, which focuses on solving the order allocation and route planning of UAVs. We believe air logistics through digital twin network will attract more researchers in the near future.

Acknowledgements. This work was supported by the National Natural Science Foundation of China under Grants (62071067, 62171057, 62101064, 62001054), in part by the Beijing University of Posts and Telecommunications-China Mobile Research Institute Joint Innovation Center.

References

1. Kang, L., Shen, H.: A Reinforcement learning based decision-making system with aggressive driving behavior consideration for autonomous vehicles. In: IEEE SECON, pp. 1–9 (2021)
2. Janszen, J., Shahzaad, B., Alkouz, B., Bouguettaya, A.: Constraint-aware trajectory for drone delivery services. In: Hacid, H., et al. (eds.) ICSOC 2021. LNCS, vol. 13236, pp. 306–310. Springer, Cham (2022). https://doi.org/10.1007/978-3-031-14135-5_26
3. Lv, Z., Chen, D., Feng, H. (eds.): Digital twins in unmanned aerial vehicles for rapid medical resource delivery in epidemics. IEEE Trans. Intell. Transp. **23**, 25106–25114 (2021)
4. Wang, Y. C., Zhang, N., Li, H. (eds.): Research on digital twin framework of military large-scale UAV based on cloud computing. In: Journal of Physics: Conference Series, vol. 1738, p. 012052. IOP Publishing (2021)
5. Haarnoja, T. (eds.): Soft actor-critic: off-policy maximum entropy deep reinforcement learning with a stochastic actor. In: ICML, pp. 1861–1870. PMLR (2018)

Tutorials

Distributed Computing Continuum Systems – Opportunities and Research Challenges

Victor Casamayor Pujol[(✉)] [iD], Praveen Kumar Donta[iD], Andrea Morichetta[iD],
Ilir Murturi[iD], and Schahram Dustdar[iD]

Distributed Systems Group, TU Wien, Vienna, Austria
{casamayor,donta,morichetta,murturi,dustdar}@dsg.tuwien.ac.at

Keywords: Distributed Computing Continuum Systems · Human
body · SLO · Self-adaptation · AI · Monitoring · Knowledge · Security

1 Vision

Internet distributed systems are subjected to a new transformation thanks to the
success of Cloud Computing. The scientific community is looking beyond Cloud
Computing and tackling its limitations with new paradigms such as Edge Computing [11]. In this tutorial, we aim at showing that we need to look towards
a Distributed Computing Continuum Systems (DCCS) paradigm; further, we
discuss that the complexity of such a paradigm requires new methods and techniques [2]. Some of these can be inspired by other complex systems that we have
in our surroundings. In this regard, we aim at showing that the human body
can be a useful analogy for the DCCS, hence, we aim to use it to encourage the
general audience and the scientific community in this research.

A key aspect of complex systems, such as the human body, is that they are
homeostatic, keeping their vital signs within their expected range, such as the
body temperature. In Cloud systems, Service Level Indicators (SLIs) are metrics
of the infrastructure, such as CPU usage, that are monitored to be within the
ranges specified by the Service Level Objectives (SLOs). Hence, if the SLI is not
in the range, an elastic strategy is triggered, and the SLI returns within its range.
DCCS need this homeostatic behavior, however, the heterogeneity, distribution,
scale, and interconnection of the infrastructure challenge the current approach.
Further, the seamless integration between the infrastructure and the application
on DDCS demands focus on the infrastructure.

Interestingly, when the human body has an issue, we feel first a general
malaise, and then we can trace it down to the specific part that is not right.
Following this idea, we assume that DCCS also need a hierarchical structure
for its definition, from abstract and general metrics such as cost, quality, and
performance [3], to the aforementioned CPU usage of a component. Last, each
of these defining metrics would be an ontological Markov Blanket [5], having
the capacity to sense and act on its environment, further, this would allow us to

J. Troya et al. (Eds.): ICSOC 2022 Workshops, LNCS 13821, pp. 405–407, 2023.
https://doi.org/10.1007/978-3-031-26507-5_41

actually define Markov Blankets at the needed granularity [9] enabling a scale-free methodology. Our road map for this vision works on four parallel tracks.

2   Research Lines

Self-adaptation. We propose an artifact called DeepSLO, which is a hierarchically structured set of SLOs that relate causally and purposefully. Hence, we could capture in a single artifact both the state of the infrastructure and the application running on top. This would instantiate our vision of the homeostatic DCCS including elastic strategies associated with each SLO. Nonetheless, the development of DeepSLOs is still in progress as many challenges arise once you scratch their surface, in this regard, we are currently investigating how to model them and their relations, or how to analyze it.

Inter-relations. A captivating idea derived from biology [6] and neural science [4] is to have an architecture composed of independent, autonomous models. These models represent mechanisms that - in the causality sense [8] - perform specific functions and *cause* the accomplishment of an action, e.g., clicking on the switch to turn on the light. These modules learn from the data to specialize in distinct tasks. These mechanisms adapt to various environments through reciprocal interaction, guaranteeing better generalization and adjusting to various applications and SLOs [7].

Monitoring & Knowledge. A healthy body and mind result in a happy life; similarly, healthy computing devices and efficient processing improve the quality of service. The context of the DCCS's health monitoring includes continuous diagnosis, prediction, and cure of problems to maintain the system healthy. Representation learning is a solution to monitor the system and give notifications and predictions timely to the administrators. We discuss possible solutions using recent technologies as future research directions [1].

Security. In the human body, the immune system distinguishes pathogens from the organism's healthy tissues via protein markers in each cell. The immune system is a safelist; through protein distinguishment, it will eliminate any organic entity that fails to present that specific body protein marker. In the context of DCCS, threats and malicious activities should be identified and eliminated like in the human body. Protecting resources and identifying malicious activities are among the core challenges that should be addressed. Therefore, we investigate the current trend toward protecting distributed resources with Zero Trust [10] concepts, its particular characteristics, and challenges to implement and execute on DCCS.

3   Conclusion

In this tutorial, we have conveyed key ideas for the future generation of Internet distributed systems. Leveraging the human body as an analogy for DCCS allows a clearer definition of the requirements for the systems, as well as inspiration for the research. Moreover, it helps convey the challenges to a broader audience increasing the impact of the research and, hopefully, involving a larger community in the future. We have presented our main research lines with their current objectives and challenges to spark discussion among the scientific community and boost this topic.

References

1. Donta, P.K., Dustdar, S.: The promising role of representation learning for distributed computing continuum systems. In: 2022 IEEE International Conference on Service-Oriented System Engineering (SOSE), pp. 126–132. IEEE (2022)
2. Dustdar, S., Casamajor Pujol, V., Donta, P.K.: On distributed computing continuum systems. IEEE Trans. Knowl. Data Eng. IEEE Computer Society (2022). https://doi.org/10.1109/TKDE.2022.3142856
3. Dustdar, S., Guo, Y., Satzger, B., Truong, H.L.: Principles of elastic processes. IEEE Internet Comput. **15**(5), 66–71 (2011). https://doi.org/10.1109/MIC.2011.121
4. Goyal, A., et al.: Coordination among neural modules through a shared global workspace. ArXiv abs/2103.01197 (2022)
5. Kirchhoff, M., Parr, T., Palacios, E., Friston, K., Kiverstein, J.: The Markov blankets of life: autonomy, active inference and the free energy principle. J. Royal Soc. Interface **15**(138), 20170792. The Royal Society (2018) https://doi.org/10.1098/RSIF.2017.0792, http://royalsocietypublishing.org/doi/abs/10.1098/rsif.2017.0792
6. Kozachkov, L., Ennis, M., Slotine, J.J.E.: RNNs of RNNs: recursive construction of stable assemblies of recurrent neural networks (2021)
7. Morichetta, A., Pujol, V.C., Dustdar, S.: A roadmap on learning and reasoning for distributed computing continuum ecosystems. In: 2021 IEEE International Conference on Edge Computing (EDGE), pp. 25–31 (2021). https://doi.org/10.1109/EDGE53862.2021.00021
8. Parascandolo, G., Rojas-Carulla, M., Kilbertus, N., Schölkopf, B.: Learning independent causal mechanisms. In: ICML (2018)
9. Pujol, V.C., Raith, P., Dustdar, S.: Towards a new paradigm for managing computing continuum applications. In: IEEE 3rd International Conference on Cognitive Machine Intelligence, CogMI 2021, pp. 180–188. Institute of Electrical and Electronics Engineers Inc. (2021). https://doi.org/10.1109/COGMI52975.2021.00032
10. Rose, S., Borchert, O., Mitchell, S., Connelly, S.: Zero trust architecture. Technical report. National Institute of Standards and Technology (2020)
11. Shi, W., Dustdar, S.: The promise of edge computing. Computer **49**(5), 78–81. IEEE Computer Society (2016). https://doi.org/10.1109/MC.2016.145

Location-Aware Cloud Service Brokering in Multi-cloud Environment

Tao Shi[1]([✉]), Sven Hartmann[2], Gang Chen[3], and Hui Ma[3]

[1] Qingdao Agricultural University, Qingdao, China
shitao@qau.edu.cn
[2] Clausthal University of Technology, Clausthal-Zellerfeld, Germany
sven.hartmann@tu-clausthal.de
[3] Victoria University of Wellington, Wellington, New Zealand
{aaron.chen,hui.ma}@ecs.vuw.ac.nz

More and more enterprises are increasingly gaining technical and economic benefits from the global cloud marketplace. A multi-cloud environment makes it possible to orchestrate the access and management of multiple cloud resources at the global scale [7]. Cloud service brokers can be regarded as the intermediate to discover, integrate, aggregate, customize, and optimize cloud services, e.g. Infrastructure as a Service (IaaS), from different cloud providers [17,18]. However, there are still not effective approaches to properly choose resources in cost efficient way. This tutorial provides the fundamentals of multi-cloud brokering, covering their computational development, technical capabilities, and the roles of services, cloud, and edge computing in a cyber-physical space from a social-technical perspective. The tutorial also presents some research works on cloud service brokering, which demonstrate that cost-efficient cloud service brokering play a critical role in supporting software application and service deployment, interdisciplinary research in cloud computing, artificial intelligence, and information systems. Finally, this tutorial investigates new practices and directions.

We cover the fundamental concepts of multi-cloud brokering, discuss variations of the problem that have been investigated in research and practice, and present related multi-cloud frameworks with illustrative examples. Note that network latency between end-users and cloud services in different locations significantly affects the performance of cloud services [3,5,6,10,16], Besides, the prices of cloud resources in different regions often vary substantially. That is, the *location* of cloud services significantly impacts both the *cost* and *performance* of cloud services [9,11]. This gives rise to the problem of *location-aware cloud service brokering in multi-cloud* [2,8]. This problem aims to select suitable cloud services from widely distributed multi-cloud data centers to balance the cost and performance. Existing research works did not pay full attention to the key impact of the location of cloud services for application deployment [4]. Therefore, it is essential to study the problem both theoretically and in practice.

In this tutorial, we discuss the composite application deployment problem that jointly considers both the performance optimization and budget control in multi-cloud at the global scale [13]. To tackle this, we explore the development of

J. Troya et al. (Eds.): ICSOC 2022 Workshops, LNCS 13821, pp. 408–410, 2023.
https://doi.org/10.1007/978-3-031-26507-5_42

evolutionary computation approaches such as a hybrid genetic algorithm (GA) techniques, featuring new design of domain-tailored service clustering, repair algorithm, solution representation, population initialization, and genetic operators. Experiments show that the proposed approach can outperform significantly state-of-the-art approaches, achieving up to about 8% performance improvement in terms of response time, and 100% budget satisfaction in the meantime.

We then address the global-wide cloud application replication and deployment problem that consider the application average response time, including particularly application execution time and network latency, subject to the budgetary control [12]. We present a genetic algorithm based approach with domain-tailored solution representation, fitness measurement, and population initialization. Experiments show that the proposed approach outperforms common application replication and placement strategies in industry.

The tutorial will further address the application replication and deployment problem with the goal to minimize the total deployment cost of all application replicas subject to a stringent requirement on average response time [14]. We develop an approach under a two-stage optimization framework that can optimize both replica deployment and request dispatching by combining mixed-integer linear programming with domain-tailored large neighborhood search. Experiments show that the proposed approach can achieve up to 25% reduction in total deployment cost compared with several recently developed approaches.

In order to dynamically select and lease virtual machines to process online requests at the global scale, we introduce the development of machine-learning methods such as deep reinforcement learning (DRL) techniques [15]. We will study the usefulness of deep Q-networks to minimize the average network latency. We will also investigate the use of penalty-based reward function for effective budget control. The experiments based on the real world datasets show the trained brokering policies significantly outperform several heuristic-based algorithms in terms of both average network latency and budget satisfaction.

We conclude the tutorial and give some research directions related to deployment scenarios, such as data sovereignty and edge computing. Also, for algorithmic design, multi-objective approaches [1,9] and multi-agent reinforcement learning are promising to satisfy some practical requirements of multi-cloud application deployment.

References

1. Chen, Y., Shi, T., Ma, H., Chen, G.: Automatically design heuristics for multi-objective location-aware service brokering in multi-cloud. In IEEE SCC, pp. 206–214 (2022)
2. Heilig, L., Buyya, R., Voß, S.: Location-aware brokering for consumers in multi-cloud computing environments. ACM JNCA **95**, 79–93 (2017)
3. Poaka, V., Hartmann, S., Bochinski, M., Seggelke, N.: New architectural design of the runtime server for remote vehicle communication services. SAE Int. J. Connected Autom. Veh. **3**, 19–26 (2020)

4. Qu, C., Calheiros, R.N., Buyya, R.: Auto-scaling web applications in clouds: a taxonomy and survey. ACM CSUR **51**, 1–33 (2018)
5. Sadeghiram, S., Ma, H., Chen, G.: A novel repair-based multi-objective algorithm for QoS-constrained distributed data-intensive web service composition. In: Huang, Z., Beek, W., Wang, H., Zhou, R., Zhang, Y. (eds.) WISE 2020. LNCS, vol. 12342. Springer, Cham (2020). https://doi.org/10.1007/978-3-030-62005-9_35
6. Sadeghiram, S., Ma, H., Chen, G.: Priority-based selection of individuals in memetic algorithms for distributed data-intensive web service compositions. IEEE TSC **15**(5), 2939–2953 (2022)
7. Shi, T.: Location-aware application deployment in multi-cloud. PhD thesis, Victoria University of Wellington (2022)
8. Shi, T., Ma, H., Chen, G.: A genetic-based approach to location-aware cloud service brokering in multi-cloud environment. In IEEE SCC, pp. 146–153 (2019)
9. Shi, T., Ma, H., Chen, G.: A seeding-based GA for location-aware workflow deployment in multi-cloud environment. In IEEE CEC, pp. 3364–3371 (2019)
10. Shi, T., Ma, H., Chen, G.: Divide and conquer: seeding strategies for multi-objective multi-cloud composite applications deployment. In ACM GECCO Companion, pp. 317–318 (2020)
11. Shi, T., Ma, H., Chen, G.: Seeding-based multi-objective evolutionary algorithms for multi-cloud composite applications deployment. In: IEEE SCC, pp. 240–247. IEEE (2020)
12. Shi, T., Ma, H., Chen, G., Hartmann, S.: Location-aware and budget-constrained application replication and deployment in multi-cloud environment. In: IEEE ICWS, pp. 110–117 (2020)
13. Shi, T., Ma, H., Chen, G., Hartmann, S.: Location-aware and budget-constrained service deployment for composite applications in multi-cloud environment. IEEE TPDS **31**, 1954–1969 (2020)
14. Shi, T., Ma, H., Chen, G., Hartmann, S.: Cost-effective web application replication and deployment in multi-cloud environment. IEEE TPDS **33**, 1982–1995 (2021)
15. Shi, T., Ma, H., Chen, G., Hartmann, S.: Location-aware and budget-constrained service brokering in multi-cloud via deep reinforcement learning. In: Hacid, H., Kao, O., Mecella, M., Moha, N., Paik, H. (eds.) ICSOC 2021. LNCS, vol. 13121, pp. 756–764. Springer, Cham (2021). https://doi.org/10.1007/978-3-030-91431-8_52
16. Tan, B., Ma, H., Mei, Y., Zhang, M.: Evolutionary multi-objective optimization for web service location allocation problem. IEEE TSC **14**, 458–471 (2021)
17. Ma, H., Schewe, K., Thalheim, B., Wang, Q.: A formal model for the interoperability of service clouds. SOCA **6**, 1–17 (2012)
18. Ma, H., Schewe, K., Wang, Q.: An abstract model for service provision, search and composition. In IEEE APCSC, pp. 95–102 (2009)

Testing of RESTful Web APIs

Alberto Martin-Lopez[1,2](✉) and Juan C. Alonso[3]

[1] Schaffhausen Institute of Technology, Schaffhausen, Switzerland
alberto.martin@sit.org
[2] Università della Svizzera Italiana, Lugano, Switzerland
[3] Smart Computer Systems Research and Engineering Lab (SCORE),
Research Institute of Computer Engineering (I3US), Universidad de Sevilla,
Seville, Spain
javalenzuela@us.es

Abstract. RESTful web APIs nowadays may be considered the de facto standard for web integration, since they enable interoperability between heterogeneous software systems in a standard way, and their usage is widespread in industry. Testing these systems thoroughly is therefore of utmost importance: a single bug in an API could compromise hundreds of services using it, potentially affecting millions of end users. In recent years, there has been an explosion in the number of tools and approaches to test RESTful web APIs, making it difficult for researchers and practitioners to select the right solution for the problem at hand.

In this tutorial, we overview some of the main industrial and research tools for testing RESTful APIs, with a primarily practical approach. We analyze different testing tools and frameworks from three different perspectives: a) manual vs automated testing; b) black-box vs white-box testing; and c) online vs offline testing. First, we show the capabilities of industrial tools and libraries for manual testing of web APIs, including REST Assured [3] and Postman [1]. Then, we delve into some of the main research tools for automatically generating test cases for RESTful APIs such as RESTler [6], EvoMaster [5], and RESTest [7]. Finally, we overview existing industrial Testing as a Service (TaaS) platforms such as RapidAPI [2] and Sauce Labs [4], and we show the latest research advances on the provision of continuous online testing of RESTful APIs (including automated test generation and execution) with the RESTest testing ecosystem [8]. We finish the tutorial outlining some of the most pressing research challenges in the domain of web API testing automation, which will hopefully open a range of opportunities for future researchers working on the topic.

Keywords: RESTful APIs · Web APIs · OpenAPI specification · Black-box testing · White-box testing

Biographies

Alberto Martín López is a postdoctoral fellow at the Schaffhausen Institute of Technology (SIT) and the Universitá della Svizzera Italiana (USI), in Switzerland. He belongs to the Software Testing and Analysis Research (STAR) group,

J. Troya et al. (Eds.): ICSOC 2022 Workshops, LNCS 13821, pp. 411–413, 2023.
https://doi.org/10.1007/978-3-031-26507-5_43

led by Professor Mauro Pezzè. Before that, he did a PhD in Software Engineering at the SCORE Unit of Excellence of the University of Seville, from where he also obtained a Bachelor degree in Telecommunications Engineering and a Master's degree in Software Engineering and Technology. He was also a Fulbright fellow at the University of California, Berkeley (USA) and an external lecturer at the Kristiania University College (Oslo, Norway). The main research interests of Alberto span varied topics within the areas of software testing and service-oriented systems, including field testing, web API testing, test oracle generation, and AI4SE, among others. He is the author and main developer of the registered tool RESTest, a comprehensive framework for automated black-box testing of RESTful web APIs, thanks to which he and his team have found numerous bugs in commercial APIs such as YouTube, Yelp, GitHub, and more. He has published in some of the main conferences and journals related to his field such as ESEC/FSE, ICSOC, TSE and TSC. To know more about Alberto, visit his personal website: https://personal.us.es/amarlop.

Juan Carlos Alonso Valenzuela is a PhD student and a teaching assistant at the University of Seville, in Spain. He is part of the Applied Software Engineering (ISA) group and the SCORE Unit of Excellence of the University of Seville. His current research interests lie in the areas of software testing, Artificial Intelligence and Natural Language Processing. He obtained a Bachelor degree in Software Engineering and a Master's degree in Data Science, both of them in the University of Seville. He is one of the core developers of RESTest and the main contributor of ARTE, an approach for the generation of realistic test inputs for web APIs thanks to which he and his team have found domain-specific bugs in the APIs of DHL and Amadeus. To know more about Juan Carlos, visit his personal website at www.javalenzuela.com.

Acknowledgments. This work has been supported by the European Commission (FEDER) and Junta de Andalucía under projects MEMENTO (US-1381595), APOLO (US-1264651) and EKIPMENT-PLUS (P18-FR-2895), by the Spanish Government (FEDER/Ministerio de Ciencia e Innovación - Agencia Estatal de Investigación) under project HORATIO (RTI2018-101204-B-C21), by MCIN/AEI/10.13039/501100011033/FEDER, UE under project BUBO (PID2021-126227NB-C22), and by the Excellence Network SEBASENet 2.0 (RED2018-102472-T).

References

1. Postman. https://www.postman.com. Accessed Nov 2022
2. RapidAPI. https://rapidapi.com. Accessed Nov 2022
3. REST Assured. https://rest-assured.io. Accessed Nov 2022
4. Sauce Labs. https://saucelabs.com. Accessed Nov 2022
5. Arcuri, A.: RESTful API automated test case generation with EvoMaster. ACM Trans. Softw. Eng. Methodol. **28**(1), 1–37 (2019)
6. Atlidakis, V., Godefroid, P., Polishchuk, M.: RESTler: stateful REST API fuzzing. In: IEEE/ACM 41st International Conference on Software Engineering, pp. 748–758 (2019)

7. Martin-Lopez, A., Segura, S., Ruiz-Cortés, A.: RESTest: automated black-box testing of RESTful web APIs. In: Proceedings of the 30th ACM SIGSOFT International Symposium on Software Testing and Analysis, pp. 682–685 (2021)
8. Martin-Lopez, A., Segura, S., Ruiz-Cortés, A.: Online testing of RESTful APIs: promises and challenges. In: Proceedings of the 30th ACM Joint European Software Engineering Conference and Symposium on the Foundations of Software Engineering, pp. 408–420 (2022)

Author Index

© The Editor(s) (if applicable) and The Author(s), under exclusive license
to Springer Nature Switzerland AG 2023
J. Troya et al. (Eds.): ICSOC 2022 Workshops, LNCS 13821, pp. 415–416, 2023.
https://doi.org/10.1007/978-3-031-26507-5

Printed in the United States
by Baker & Taylor Publisher Services